Epistemology and Science Education

How is epistemology related to the issue of teaching science and evolution in the schools? Addressing a flashpoint issue in our schools today, this book explores core epistemological differences between proponents of intelligent design and evolutionary scientists, as well as the critical role of epistemological beliefs in learning science. Pre-eminent scholars in these areas report empirical research and/or make a theoretical contribution, with a particular emphasis on the controversy over whether intelligent design deserves to be considered a science alongside Darwinian evolution. This pioneering book coordinates and provides a complete picture of the intersections in the study of evolution, epistemology, and science education, in order to allow a deeper understanding of the intelligent design vs. evolution controversy.

- Part I, Epistemology, deals with general issues of evolutionary science and the evolution of science, focusing in particular on its implications for science education.
- Part II, Intelligent Design and Evolution, explores the relations between creationism, intelligent design, and Darwinian evolution, and what they show about the nature of science and science education.
- Part III, Teaching Science, looks at authentic inquiry through model creation and refinement as a way of making more accessible to students some of the core assumptions about science and the power of natural selection as an explanatory framework.

This is a very timely book for teachers and policy makers who are wrestling with issues of how to teach biology and evolution within a cultural context in which intelligent design has been, and is likely to remain, a challenge for the foreseeable future.

Roger S. Taylor is Assistant Professor in the Psychology Department at the State University of New York, Oswego.

Michel Ferrari is Associate Professor and Head, Center for Applied Cognitive Science, University of Toronto/Ontario Institute for Studies in Education.

Epistemology and Science Education

Understanding the Evolution vs. Intelligent Design Controversy

Edited by
Roger S. Taylor
State University of New York

and Michel Ferrari
University of Toronto

Routledge
Taylor & Francis Group
NEW YORK AND LONDON

First published 2011
by Routledge
270 Madison Avenue, New York, NY 10016

Simultaneously published in the UK
by Routledge
2 Park Square, Milton Park, Abingdon, Oxon OX14 4RN

Routledge is an imprint of the Taylor & Francis Group, an informa business

Typeset in Minion by Wearset Ltd, Boldon, Tyne and Wear
Printed and bound in the United States of America on acid-
free paper by Walsworth Publishing Company, Marceline, MO.

Library of Congress Cataloging in Publication Data
Epistemology and science education: understanding the
evolution vs. intelligent design controversy/edited by Roger S.
Taylor, Michel Ferrari.
p. cm.
1. Science—Study and teaching—Philosophy. I. Taylor, Roger S.
II. Ferrari, Michel, Ph. D.
Q181.E66 2010

507.1—dc22

2010020437

ISBN13: 978-0-415-96379-4 (hbk)
ISBN13: 978-0-415-96380-0 (pbk)
ISBN13: 978-0-203-83963-8 (ebk)

We would like to dedicate this book to our enormously supportive wives, Randi Taylor and Chandi Ferrari, without whom it would not have been possible.

Contents

Preface   ix
Acknowledgments   xvii

PART I
Epistemology   I

1. Demarcation in Science Education: Toward an Enhanced
   View of Scientific Method   3
   RICHARD A. DUSCHL AND RICHARD E. GRANDY

2. Evolution, Creation, and the Philosophy of Science   20
   PAUL THAGARD

3. Differences in Epistemic Practices among Scientists,
   Young Earth Creationists, Intelligent Design Creationists,
   and the Scientist-Creationists of Darwin's Era   38
   CLARK A. CHINN AND LUKE A. BUCKLAND

4. Ontological Assumptions about Species and Their
   Influence on Students' Understanding of Evolutionary
   Biology   77
   ALA SAMARAPUNGAVAN

5. Understanding Evolutionary Theory: The Role of
   Epistemological Development and Beliefs   95
   BARBARA K. HOFER, CHAK FU LAM, AND ALEX DELISI

6. Engaging Multiple Epistemologies: Implications for
   Science Education   111
   E. MARGARET EVANS, CRISTINE H. LEGARE, AND
   KARL S. ROSENGREN

PART II
Intelligent Design and Evolution   141

7. Accepting Evolution or Creation in People, Critters,
    Plants, and Classrooms: The Maelstrom of American
    Cognition about Biological Change   143
    MICHAEL ANDREW RANNEY AND ANASTASIA THANUKOS

8. Science and Religion: Ontologically Different
    Epistemologies?   173
    GALE M. SINATRA AND LOUIS NADELSON

PART III
Teaching Science   195

9. Toward a Cognitive Understanding of Science and
    Religion   197
    RYAN D. TWENEY

10. Teaching and Learning Evolution as an Emergent
    Process: The BEAGLE Project   213
    URI WILENSKY AND MICHAEL NOVAK

11. Teaching Evolution in a Historical Context: From the
    Wisdom of the Ancient Greeks to Genetic Algorithms 243
    MICHEL FERRARI, PETER LEE, AND ROGER S. TAYLOR

Conclusion   269

12. Teach the Demarcation: Suggestions for Science
    Education   271
    MICHEL FERRARI AND ROGER S. TAYLOR

    Notes on Contributors   286
    Index   291

Preface

This book explores the critical role of epistemological beliefs in the learning of science and how they are related to the issue of the teaching of science and evolution in the classroom. Several books have touched on this topic generally—including the philosophical and scientific aspects revolving around the evolution and intelligent design debate (e.g., Brockman, 2006; Dembski, 2004; Fuller, 2007; Pennock, 2006; Pennock & Ruse, 2009; Young & Edis, 2004) or providing biological information for teachers (Alters, 2005; Scott, 2004)—but none have focused on the cognitive and educational aspects of this complex issue. Thus, the target audience of our book ranges from cognitive and educational psychologists to science teachers and policy makers.

What accounts for this extraordinary lack of success in teaching and learning about biological evolution? Evolution is clearly a complex and abstract science construct; however, beyond the challenges inherent in teaching any difficult content, many students hold strong emotional commitments that they view to be in conflict with scientific explanations. The teaching of intelligent design in science classrooms has been offered as a way out of this apparent conflict. However, we will argue that the inclusion of intelligent design in the science curriculum does a disservice both to the integrity of science as a discipline and to the religious beliefs and personal commitments of learners.

In fact, 80 years after the Scopes Monkey Trial (Johnson, 1991; Scott, 2004), which firmly established the legality of teaching evolution in the science classroom, a conflict continues to brew which many believe threatens to undermine science instruction in American schools. However, unlike the earlier conflict in which science educators were required to justify the place of evolution in the classroom, the current conflict revolves around the nature of science itself (Fuller, 2007; Pennock, 2001; Pennock & Ruse, 2009; Young & Edis, 2004). Given the critical importance of scientific reasoning in the economic success of developed nations, it is deeply troubling that in May 2005 members of the Kansas State Board of Education proposed to change the definition of science to allow for the teaching of intelligent design in science classes. And they are not alone: other boards of education and government offices before and since have challenged the nature, content, and metaphysical presuppositions of science. One contributing factor to this effort is a significant dispute about the epistemology and nature of science and scientific writing among philosophers, sociologists, and historians of science (Schickore, 2008)—a dispute that finds echoes within the general populace.

In this book, we explore how epistemology of science and religion are related to the issue of public school teaching of science in general, and of biological evolution in particular. Kieran Egan (1997) is probably right to say that some of the perennial problems of public education stem from the fact that it has three competing mandates that do not always mutually support each other: (1) personal flourishing (becoming the best person you can be in light of your own talents and interests); (2) socialization (adapting well within a community, including vocational training); and (3) conveying hard won truths about the world that are not easy for individuals to uncover on their own (e.g., that the Earth orbits the sun and not the other way around as one might imagine by watching it apparently move across the sky, or that humans evolved from other simpler life forms). Clearly, to accomplish this third goal of public education is to help students become better at epistemic tasks like coordinating theory and evidence, evaluating sources of authority, resolving competing knowledge claims, and understanding the epistemic assumptions of particular disciplines. Within science this involves learning to appreciate the power of "scientific methods" of gathering empirical evidence, the meaning of "theory" and its relations to scientific representation, and the roles of falsifiability and tentativeness in the development of scientific knowledge (van Fraassen, 2008). Clearly, though, this third aim of education can sometimes conflict with the second, when scientifically discovered truths challenge or undermine cherished beliefs within a particular community. This is how we understand the controversy between Darwinian theory and intelligent design in the United States today.

Collectively, the chapters address the critical role of epistemological beliefs in learning science, including core epistemological differences between proponents of intelligent design and evolutionary scientists. The book includes chapters by pre-eminent educational psychologists and scholars of science education who were asked to report empirical research or make a theoretical contribution to the debate about science education, with a particular emphasis on the controversy over whether intelligent design deserves to be considered a science alongside Darwinian evolution.

Chapter Overview

The book is divided into three broad sections. Part I, Epistemology, deals with general issues of evolutionary science and the evolution of science, with a particular focus on its implications for science education. Part II, Intelligent Design and Evolution, explores the relations between creationism, intelligent design, and Darwinian evolution, and what they show about the nature of science and science education. Part III, Teaching Science, looks at authentic inquiry through model creation and refinement as a way of making more accessible to students in classrooms some of the core assumptions about science and the power of natural selection as an explanatory framework.

Part I: Epistemology

Duschl and Grandy address the nature of school science and how public debates about science provide a window to examine features about the nature of science that might be incorporated in teaching "ideas-about-science." New tools, technologies, techniques, and cognitive theories contribute to the progressive development of the scope of any scientific theory and, with refinements and debates among communities of scientists, constitute an enhanced view of the scientific method. Such a view recognizes the critical *epistemic* frameworks used when developing and evaluating scientific knowledge, and the *social* processes and contexts that shape how knowledge is discovered, communicated, represented, and argued. Duschl and Grandy propose an enhanced scientific method as a mechanism to support the processes of theory refinement, a mechanism that privileges the role of dialogic processes in the growth of scientific knowledge that extends the dominant "conduct experiments" view of scientific methods found in K-16 classrooms by placing emphasis on the social and epistemic dynamics that guide scientific inquiry.

Thagard specifically addresses debates about the nature and evaluation of scientific theories. What distinguishes science from non-science? What is a scientific explanation? How can we tell when a theory is better than its competitors? How can we tell if a theory is true? To answer these questions, his chapter draws on recent work in the philosophy of science as it applies to controversies about evolution and intelligent design, and discusses the philosophical and psychological implications of these questions for science education.

Chinn and Buckland specifically examine differences between the epistemic practices of scientists, young Earth creationists, intelligent design creationists, and the scientists of Darwin's era who supported creationism. Although some philosophers of science argue that creationism and evolutionary scientists reason differently and subscribe to very different epistemologies, others argue that evolutionists and creationists cannot be sharply distinguished according to their methodology or epistemology. In recent years, a number of sociologists of science have also argued that science is just one competing worldview among many, with no reason to trust science more than alternative views. In evaluating whether evolutionary scientists and creationists adopt similar or different epistemologies, Chinn and Buckland argue that it is critical to examine the actual epistemic practices of scientists and creationists. On the basis of a theoretical analysis of the knowledge change process, they identify seven dimensions of an epistemic practice: (a) its aims, (b) its explanations, (c) its methods, (d) its evidence, (e) the characteristics of inquirers, (f) the ways in which inquirers interact, and (g) the operations of the social institutions that inquirers form. Analyzing epistemic practices of scientists and creationists along each of these dimensions, Chinn and Buckland argue for a broad range of differences between the epistemic practices of scientists and the practices of two groups of contemporary creationists—young earth creationists and intelligent design creationists.

Samarapungavan examines how children's initial domain-specific ontological and epistemic beliefs about speciation affects conceptual change in the domain of evolutionary biology. Drawing upon results from a series of studies conducted with Dutch and American children, she argues that children's ontological beliefs—and especially their ontological essentialism with regard to species—have significant epistemic consequences. Specifically, they lead children to consider certain kinds of questions as being beyond the scope of biological inquiry, and certain biological phenomena (e.g., within species variability) as unimportant. Thus, the epistemic features of their initial beliefs cause children to miss or misconstrue the import of evidence in support of an evolutionary point of view. The analysis of children's in-group discussions also shows that some kinds of information are more persuasive to children with non-evolutionary points of view: for example, these children were more likely to consider the possibility of evolution when information about the fossil record was presented alongside information about how fossil age was determined, than when the fossil record information record was presented alone. Information about the methodological tools and approaches used by evolutionary biologists appears to be particularly valuable because it helps to change non-evolutionary children's epistemic beliefs about the boundaries of biological knowledge by showing how to empirically address questions that they initially considered unanswerable.

Hofer, Lam, and DeLisi explore a growing body of research demonstrating that students have both generalized epistemological worldviews and specific discipline-based epistemic beliefs that influence their learning of science. The failure of a vast number of Americans to accept basic premises of evolution, a foundational scientific theory, suggests inadequate training in scientific literacy and epistemic understanding. Based on several studies in her research lab, Hofer and her colleagues discuss why understanding students' epistemological beliefs is so important when teaching the theory of evolution and can account for students' difficulties with accepting evolution and their support for teaching intelligent design. They also explain why a model of conceptual change should include affective issues—especially critical for students for whom ideas about evolution implicate the self in complex ways that engage competing sources of epistemic authority (e.g., church, religious and scientific texts, parents, teachers, peers). They propose that teaching the epistemic assumptions of science and teaching is important to assure a high level of general scientific literacy needed for an educated citizenry.

Evans, Legare, and Rosengren present a taxonomy that situates people's beliefs about evolution within a larger framework of culture models and intuitive beliefs. For the cultural component they describe the potential tensions between scientific and supernatural epistemological beliefs. In addition to outright competition, they identify four patterns of co-existence between these beliefs (causal chains, target dependence, parallel reasoning, and juxtaposition). They also explore fusions and synthetic blends of intuitive and cultural beliefs, with the goal of identifying ways of bridging the gap between intuitive and scientific beliefs.

Part II: Intelligent Design and Evolution

Ranney and Thanukos detail two empirical studies regarding how undergraduates perceive evolution, along with a hypothesis (called Reinforced Theistic Manifest Destiny) about why America produces such perceptions. The first study used surveys and think-aloud protocols to examine whether undergraduates perceive evolutionary explanations differently for plant, human, and (non-human) animal phenomena. Results indicated that participants were more accepting of evolutionary explanations for plants than for humans; however, this "human reticence effect" was critically modulated by item characteristics and one's overall attitude toward evolution.

The second study surveyed undergraduate beliefs related to teaching evolution and/or creationism. It discerned differences among views on teaching about biological change, which often highlighted notions of pedagogical balance/fairness and freedom of thought/expression; "evolution advocates," "fence sitters," and other subgroups (e.g., "pluralists" and "no-evolution creationists") represent some clusters of college perspectives on the controversy.

Sinatra and Nadelson consider whether science and religion are at opposite ends of core epistemological continua. They note that science and religion are often confused as competing explanations of the same phenomena, which has led individuals to consider science and religion to be at odds, even discounting the validity of one or the other perspective. Recognition of the ontological differences between the epistemologies of religion and science may provide a way of distinguishing between these two worldviews. They note how recognition of the sometimes subtle distinctions between epistemic assumptions of science and religion may provide a means to resolve the controversy of teaching evolution. Evolution education should focus on overcoming misconceptions about evolution through promoting understanding of the nature of science and how the epistemic assumptions of science differ from other worldviews.

Part III: Teaching Science

Tweney's chapter is devoted to a cognitive understanding of science and religion. According to Tweney, because science is recent and still rare among human cultures, cognitive approaches to understanding science often appeal to historical events and the embodiment of science in the representations and practices of scientists, tying cognitive practices to specific cognitive contents as situated in their historical, cultural, and social contexts. Cognitive explanations of religious cognition have centered on evolutionary and cultural levels of explanation, but with relatively little attention to historicity. To make the comparison concrete, Tweney describes some of the scientific beliefs and concepts of Michael Faraday (1791–1867), to typical religious beliefs and practices. A complete understanding of Faraday's thinking requires cognitive historical methods for both kinds of beliefs and practices.

Wilensky and Novak address a key challenge of teaching about evolution—the inherent difficulty of understanding emergent processes. Emergent processes involve actions that simultaneously occur at two different levels, such as the micro level of genetics and the macro level of population distributions of organisms. One approach to tackling this problem is the use of agent-based software in which students can create and refine models of natural selection. They describe four cases of students grappling with these issues.

Ferrari, Lee, and Taylor pursue a very similar line of thought that looks at teaching evolution through genetic algorithms. However, they also tie their discussion back to a more general consideration of curriculum and the aims of science education, claiming that it should go beyond mere technical expertise and become one path to fostering wisdom. As they point out, many students may not initially accept the scientific theory of evolution by natural selection due, in part, to a fear that evolution undermines religious beliefs of central importance to their personal identity. A potential way around this difficulty is to teach natural science using a curriculum that *integrates* natural science, ethics, and logic. According to this approach, integral to medieval university science education, students would study *natural science* to understand empirical truths about human nature and what it means to be a human being in the natural world. They would also study *ethics* to know how to care for themselves and others within a community. Finally, they would study *logical reasoning* (or critical thinking) to know what beliefs can and cannot be held. Even mystical theology is open to those who wish to transcend science once they have mastered core concepts essential to understanding the natural world. This integrated approach to science education—in which biology is interwoven with a concern for ethics—undercuts a key appeal of intelligent design. Unless biological science addresses ethical concerns about human nature, it will continue to meet deep resistance among students and the general population.

Conclusion

In our closing chapter we draw out main themes from the preceding chapters to consider the nature of science and science education and the challenge of intelligent design for science education. We pay particular attention to how to teach the epistemological foundations of scientific explanations, and how these differ from religious explanations. We conclude that the intelligent design vs. Darwinian evolution controversy offers a rare chance to provide greatly needed instruction about epistemology and the philosophy of science within the context of high school science education. We also make recommendations for teachers and policy makers about how best to teach science so as to overcome misconceptions through a deep and well-rounded science education.

Overall, the chapters in this book explore the epistemology of science and religion and their relation to public school teaching of science, especially the science that supports a theory of biological evolution through natural selection. Clearly, this goal of public education requires that students become better at epistemic tasks like evaluating sources of authority, resolving competing knowledge claims, and coordinating theory and evidence. Just as clearly, this aim of education sometimes conflicts with scientifically discovered truths that challenge or undermine cherished beliefs within a particular community. Given the many challenges facing the world today, from global warming to the mass extinction of species and languages, it is particularly important in a democracy that the general population be well informed about the nature of science, and able to sift through competing claims about the evidence for particular problems and how to solve them. This is how we understand the importance of the controversy between Darwinian theory and intelligent design for science education in the United States and in the world today.

References

Alters, B. J. (2005). *Teaching Biological Evolution in Higher Education: Methodological, religious, and nonreligious issues.* Sudbury, MA: Jones and Bartlett.

Brockman, J. (Ed.). (2006). *Intelligent Thought: Science versus the intelligent design movement.* New York: Vintage.

Dembski, W. A. (Ed.). (2004). *Uncommon Dissent: Intellectuals who find Darwinism unconvincing.* Wilmington, DE: ISI Books.

Egan, K. (1997). *The Educated Mind: How cognitive tools shape our understanding.* Chicago, IL: University of Chicago Press.

Fuller, S. (2007). *Science vs Religion? Intelligent design and the problem of evolution.* Cambridge, UK: Polity Press.

Johnson, P. E. (1991). *Darwin on Trial.* Downers Grove, IL: InterVarsity Press.

Marks, J. (2003). *What it Means to be 98% Chimpanzee.* Berkeley, CA: University of California Press.

Pennock, R. T. (Ed.). (2001). *Intelligent Design Creationism and its Critics: Philosophical, theological, and scientific perspectives.* Cambridge, MA: MIT Press.

Pennock, R. T. (2006). *Tower of Babel: The evidence against the new creationism.* Cambridge, MA: MIT Press.

Pennock, R., & Ruse, M. (Eds.). (2009). *But Is It Science? The philosophical question in the creation/evolution controversy.* New York: Prometheus Books.

Schickore, J. (2008). Doing science, writing science. *Philosophy of Science, 75*, 323–343.

Scott, E. C. (2004). *Evolution vs. Creationism: An introduction.* Berkeley, CA: University of California Press.

Stove, D. (1995). *Darwinian Fairytales: Selfish genes, errors of heredity, and other fables of evolution.* New York: Encounter Books.

van Fraassen, B. C. (2008). *Scientific Representation: Paradoxes of perspective.* New York: Oxford University Press.

Young, M., & Edis, T. (2004). *Why Intelligent Design Fails: A scientific critique of the new creationism.* Rutgers, NJ: Rutgers University Press.

Acknowledgments

We would like to acknowledge all of the authors for their tremendous effort in helping to create this book.

Part I

Epistemology

Chapter 1

Demarcation in Science Education

Toward an Enhanced View of Scientific Method[1,2]

Richard A. Duschl and Richard E. Grandy

Introduction

What is science? What is not? What constitutes a scientific observation? A scientific theory? Scientific evidence? What are the limits of science? The ongoing century and a half debate about evolution theory and creationism, and in particular the recent revival of equal time in the classroom "teach the controversy" debate surrounding the idea of intelligent design, continues to stimulate conversations motivated by the preceding questions. For at its core isn't scientific inquiry about entertaining and debating competing ideas, models, and theories with the goal of sorting out the truth about how nature functions, how it is constituted, how it is construed. Creationist stances take just this "compare the theories" type of view when asking for "equal time" and for "teach the controversy." Demarcating science from non-science or even successful science from non-successful science is not a straightforward process, as developments in history and philosophy of science demonstrate (Thagard, 2007). Newer images of science grounded in naturalized philosophy challenge many of the standard criteria that have been used to demarcate science as a unique way of knowing.

Any characterization of scientific inquiry raises the question of whether science as a way of knowing is distinctive from other ways of knowing. Philosophers of science refer to this issue as the *demarcation* between science and other forms of inquiry (Eflin, Glennan, & Reisch, 1999). There are two related but somewhat distinct demarcation questions. First, some individuals see a distinction between legitimate science and activities that purport to be scientific but are not, for example, astrology, creation science, and so forth. Second, there are some who see a distinction between scientific inquiry and other forms of legitimate but non-scientific activities such as historical research or electrical engineering. Advocates of teaching the nature of science in science education programs feel that it not only is possible to make a sharp general demarcation, but that it is an important part of teaching science to teach that demarcation (Lederman, Abd-el-Khalick, Bell, & Schwartz, 2002; McComas & Olson, 1998; Osborne, Collins,

Ratcliffe, Millar, & Duschl, 2003). Others are skeptical that such a demarcation is possible.

One way to argue for demarcation is to claim scientific inquiry involves mechanistic explanations. This is clearly too narrow as magnetism and gravitation are not mechanical. Another is to argue that scientific explanations are causal. This suggestion has two problems; one is that it seems to rule out statistical explanations that are not necessarily causal. The second is that three centuries of debate over the nature of causation in philosophy have produced no consensus on what constitutes causation.

Another view is that scientific explanations/hypotheses must be testable. While this seems right in spirit, decades of attempts by philosophers to make this concept precise have also consistently failed. Yet another tack is to argue that the distinction between scientific and non-scientific hypotheses is real, but is not a matter for which we can formulate explicit rules for general application, for example, a scientific method. The only individuals able to appropriately make the distinction between testable and non-testable hypotheses are those who are deeply embedded in the practices of the specific science and have sophisticated knowledge. Today with the aid of powerful computers there are domains of science that do not begin inquiry with stating hypotheses but rather are guided by patterns of discovery from huge data sets (e.g., astronomy, human genome project).

We are not suggesting that it is impossible to distinguish scientific inquiry from pseudoscience. But we believe that to the extent that the distinction can be made, it has to be made locally, from the perspective of the particular field at a specific time. A naturalized approach to understanding science means that researchers observe what scientists do, not just what scientists say about what they do. The naturalized approach to the philosophy of science strongly suggests that the nature of scientific activities has changed over time and we expect change to continue. Knowledge of the relevant scientific principles and criteria for what counts as an observation are important elements in distinguishing science claims and developing demarcation capacities; for example, distinguishing science from pseudoscience. However, we are skeptical that a general demarcation criterion can be abstracted from the concrete historically situated judgments. And yet, in the context of creationism and evolution there is a desire to claim a demarcation on the grounds that the core theoretical belief system of one is religious and of the other is scientific. An alternative approach is to examine the scientific practices within a community of scientists—specifically, those scientific practices that as Thagard (2007) posits serve to broaden and deepen explanatory truths.

When Darwin's dangerous idea was first introduced the arguments he put forth in *The Origin of Species* regarding the mechanism of natural selection changed forever the relationship between science and religion, man and nature, and our interpretation of natural laws. In Kuhnian terminology, a scientific revolution had begun. Darwin's *The Descent of Man* only served to deepen the debate and widen the gulf between religious and scientific perspectives about the nature of science. The Great Synthesis in Biology introduced mechanisms to explain both the diversity of life and inherited stability of life. Molecular biology and population biology further deepened our understanding of the cellular level and organism level mechanisms that account for evolutionary and co-evolutionary dynamics. Such fine-tuning of the understanding of evolution theory, or any scientific theory for that matter, is a critically important component in the growth of scientific knowledge. New tools, technologies, techniques, and cognate theories contribute to the progressive development of the scope of a theory. However, the dialogic processes that take place between discovery and justification and that constitute the refinement of tool, technology, technique, and theory choice are often ignored in science classrooms and communications. Such dialogic processes, though, are critically important dynamics of the growth of scientific knowledge and of scientific revolutions. The between discovery and justification refinements and debates among communities of scientists constitute elements of an enhanced view of the scientific method. Such a view recognizes, where "received" views of the scientific method do not, the critical *epistemic* frameworks used when developing and evaluating scientific knowledge, and the *social* processes and contexts that shape how knowledge is discovered, communicated, represented, and argued. Failure on the part of the "intelligent design" to engage in epistemic and social processes is a fatal flaw.

The current "teach the controversy" debate being played out in classrooms, school districts, colleges, universities, and the courts serves as a strong reminder that the theory of evolution scientific revolution is alive and well and showing no signs of losing momentum. The century and a half dialog around *Darwin's Dangerous Idea* (Dennett, 1995) provides a window to examine the epistemological and ontological polemics in philosophy of science. For school science and public debates about science, it provides a window to examine features about the nature of science that might be incorporated in teaching "ideas-about-science." A goal of this chapter is to advocate for an enhanced scientific method, a view that privileges the role of dialogic processes in the growth of scientific knowledge. The enhanced scientific method view emerges from a consideration of seven core tenets about the nature of science put forth by the logical positivists, which we outline below (Grandy & Duschl, 2008).

Views about the Nature of Science

The science education research on learners' and teachers' views about the nature of science (NOS) is mixed (Ryan & Aikenhead, 1992; McComas & Olson, 1998; Driver, Leach, Millar, & Scott, 1996; Lederman et al., 2002; Lederman, 1999; Osborne et al., 2003; Smith & Wenk, 2006). When data are gathered employing survey instruments that probe learners' views of science outside of any specific context of inquiry, the results indicate that students do not develop accurate views about the theory revision and responsiveness to evidence nature of scientific knowledge. Driver et al. (1996) in a thorough investigation of 9–16 year olds found that the majority of pupils at all ages thought good science was that which involved investigations using phenomena or sense perception data; for example, seeing is believing. Few of the students held the more sophisticated model-based views of science. Smith and Wenk (2006) found similar results in a study of college freshman. The majority of students held an epistemology in which theories are understood as tested hypotheses. Missing were views seeing theories as complex explanatory frameworks that guide hypothesis testing. Windschitl (2004) also found similar results with preservice science teacher educators.

Osborne et al. (2003) conducted a study on what "ideas-about-science" should be part of the school science curriculum. Employing a Delphi study of experts' opinions, nine themes encapsulating key ideas about the nature of science were considered to be an essential component of school science curriculum. These nine themes when compared with the themes proposed by McComas and Olson (1998) show strong similarities (see Figure 1.1). What differences do exist reside in themes dealing with the extent to which cultural and social factors impinge on the practice of science and with the diversity of scientific thinking.

NOS Views from McComas & Olson (1998)
Scientific knowledge is tentative
Science relies on evidence
Scientists require replicability and truthful reporting
Scientists are creative
Science is part of social tradition
Science has played an important role in technology
Scientific ideas have been affected by their social and political milieu
Changes in science occur gradually
Science has global implications
New knowledge must be reported clearly and openly

Ideas-About-Science from Osborne et al. (2003)
Science and certainty
Analysis and interpretation of data
Scientific method and critical testing
Creativity
Science and questioning
Cooperation and collaboration in the development of scientific knowledge
Science and technology
Historical development of scientific knowledge
Diversity of scientific thinking

Figure 1.1 Views about nature of science (NOS) and "ideas-about-science" to teach in K-12 science.

This body of NOS research raises questions about whether the image of scientific inquiry found in the school science curriculum is sufficiently comprehensive. We will argue that there are important epistemic and social practices missing from the image of science presented by current NOS research (Grandy & Duschl, 2008; Eflin et al., 1999). A focus on investigative methods of science dominates the school science curriculum; not much emphasis is placed on dialectical processes that shape the role theory, evidence, explanation, and models have in the development of scientific knowledge. Such perspectives represent a more contemporary view of the science from scholars (cf. Giere, 1988, 1999; Solomon, 2001; Longino, 2002) "who portray science as a multidimensional interaction among the models of scientists, empirical observation of the real world, and their predictions" (Osborne et al., 2003, p. 715). What is missing, and what we have learned about the nature of science, is the important dialogic processes about what comes to count as the observations, measurements, data, evidence, models, theories, and explanations; dialogic processes that function between the contexts of discovery and justification and that represent a critical element of the nature of scientific inquiry. When we look at the dialectical and dialogic processes that contribute to the "intelligent design" position, we find, like the judge in Dover, PA decided, that "intelligent design" is not science.

Toward an Enhanced Version of a Scientific Method

Over the last 100 years new technologies and new scientific theories have modified the nature of scientific observation from an enterprise dominated by *sense perception*, aided or unaided, to a *theory-driven* enterprise. We now know that what we see is influenced by what we know and how we "look"; scientific theories are inextricably involved in the design and interpretation of experimental methods as well as the instruments and tools used to obtain data. Early in the 20th century, however, philosophers of science sought to establish the objectivity and rationality of scientific claims on the basis of language alone by (1) claiming a distinction between observational and theoretical languages based on grammar, (2) seeing theories as sets of sentences in a formal logical language, (3) using some form of inductive logic to provide formal criteria for theory evaluation, and (4) advocating that there is an important dichotomy between contexts of discovery and contexts of justification. The logical positivists also promoted tenets of science that saw scientists working (5) individually, (6) with criteria that are normative dimensions to scientific inquiry, and (7) with compatible theory choices that contributed to a cumulative and continually progressive process in the growth of scientific knowledge.

Twentieth century philosophy of science can be partitioned into three major developments: an experiment-driven enterprise, a theory-driven enterprise, and a model-driven enterprise. The experiment-driven enterprise gave birth to the movements called logical positivism or logical empiricism, shaped the development of analytic philosophy, and gave rise to the hypothetico-deductive conception of science. The image of scientific inquiry was that experiment led to new knowledge that accrued to established knowledge. How knowledge was discovered and refined was not on the philosophical agenda; only the final justification of knowledge was deemed important. This early 20th century perspective is referred to as the "received view" of philosophy of science.

This "received view" conception of science is closely related to traditional explanations of "the scientific method." The steps in the method are:

1. Make observations
2. Formulate a hypothesis
3. Deduce consequences from the hypothesis
4. Make observations to test the consequences
5. Accept or reject the hypothesis based on the observations.

The issue is to question the usefulness of scientific method frameworks that do not attend to the theory refinement dialogic practices embedded in science as a way of knowing. One must also question the usefulness of scientific method frameworks that do not attend to the epistemic practices inherent in constructing and evaluating models. Theory-building and model-building practices provide the contexts where epistemic abilities, social skills, and cognitive capacities are forged. Missing from the traditional five step hypothetico-deductive laboratory-based view of scientific method, and creationists' theories, are the important dialogic and epistemic processes involved in model and theory building.

Consideration for both the insights and limitations of logical positivism and early "Kuhnian" responses to logical positivism have expanded our perspectives about the nature of science, the growth of scientific knowledge, and the goals/limitations of science (see Godfrey-Smith, 2003; Zammito, 2004, for a comprehensive review). The seven tenets of science proposed by Duschl and Grandy (2008a, 2008b) characterize how the received view of the scientific method, one that is cast in terms of hypothetico-deductive views of the nature of science, has shifted. The revised tenets reflect the philosophical debates that have emerged since the introduction of Thomas Kuhn's seminal work *The Structure of Scientific Revolution* and, importantly, from the "Postscript" to the second edition where one finds the presentation of the disciplinary matrix as a response to his critics. The implication for the intelligent design "teach the controversy" position is that it fails to consider the ways with which, and manners through which, the dialogic processes are played out. In Thagard's (2007) terms, there is no deepening or broadening of explanatory truths over time.

Table 1.1 presents the seven "Traditional tenets from logical positivism" headings in column one. Columns two, three, and four respectively present

Table 1.1 Nature of Science (NOS): Seven Tenets

Traditional tenets from logical positivism	Received NOS views	Reasons for revision	Revised NOS views
1. There is an important dichotomy between contexts of discovery and contexts of justification.	Logical positivism's focus was on the final products or outcomes of science. Of the two end points, justification of knowledge claims was the only relevant issue. How ideas, hypotheses, and intuitions are initially considered or discovered was not relevant.	Theory change advocates value understanding how the growth of knowledge begins and proceeds. Perhaps the most important element Kuhn and others added is the recognition that most of the theory change is not final theory acceptance, but improvement and refinement.	The bulk of scientific inquiry is neither the context of discovery nor the context of justification. The dominant context is theory development and conceptual modification. The dialogic processes of theory development and of dealing with anomalous data occupy a great deal of scientists' time and energy.
2. The individual scientist is the basic unit of analysis for understanding science.	Logical positivists believed scientific rationality can be entirely understood in terms of choices by individual scientists.	Kuhn's inclusion of the scientific community as part of the scientific process introduced the idea of research groups or communities of practice as being the unit of scientific discourse. This shift from individual to group produced negative reactions from many philosophers. Including a social dimension was seen as threatening the objectivity and rationality of scientific development. Teams of scientists engage in investigations.	Scientific rationality can be understood in terms of dialogic processes taking place as knowledge claims and beliefs are posited and justified. Scientific discourse is organized within a disciplinary matrix of shared exemplars; for example, values, instruments, methods, models, evidence.

continued

Table 1.1 Continued

Traditional tenets from logical positivism	Received NOS views	Reasons for revision	Revised NOS views
3. There is an epistemologically significant distinction between observational and theoretical (O/T) languages based on grammar.	Logical positivism focused on the application of logic and on the philosophy of language to analyze scientific claims. Analysis void of contextual and contingent information produces a grammar that fixes criteria for observations.	The O/T distinction debate showed that our ordinary perceptual language is theory laden: what we see is influenced by what we believe. New theories leading to new tools and technologies greatly influenced the nature of observation in science and the representation of information and data.	What counts as observational shifts historically as science acquires new tools, technologies, and theories. Science from the 1700s to the present has made a transition from a sense perception dominated study of nature to a tool, technology, and theory-driven study of nature.
4. Some form of inductive logic would be found that would provide a formal criterion for theory evaluation.	There exists an algorithm for theory evaluation. Given a formal logical representation of the theory and data, the algorithm would provide the rational degree of confirmation the data confer on the theory.	Seeking an algorithm for a rational degree of confirmation is hopeless. Scientists working with the same data can rationally come to differing conclusions about which theory is best supported by given evidence. There is ongoing debate about how much variation is rational and how much is influenced by other factors.	Dialog over the merits of competing data, models, and theories is essential to the process of refining models and theories as well as accepting or rejecting them.

5. Scientific theories can most usefully be thought of as sets of sentences in a formal language.	Logical positivists advocated the position that theories are linguistic in character and could be described with deductive-nomological procedures.	Model-based views about the nature of science embrace, where hypothetico-deductive science does not, the dialogic complexities inherent in naturalized accounts of science. Scientific representations and explanations take many different forms: mathematical models, physical models, diagrams, computation models, and so forth.	Modern developments in science, mathematics, cognitive sciences, and computer sciences have extended the forms of representation in science well beyond strictly linguistic and logical formats. One widespread view is that theories should be thought of as families of models, and the models stand between empirical/conceptual evidence and theoretical explanations.
6. Different scientific frameworks within the same domain are commensurable.	Logical positivists sought to establish criteria that supported the claim that there are normative dimensions to scientific inquiry. The growth of scientific knowledge is a cumulative process.	Science communities are organized within disciplinary matrices. Shared exemplars help to define science communities. Scientific frameworks on different sides of a revolutionary change are incommensurable. Hypothesis testing takes place within more complex frameworks requiring more nuanced strategies for representing and reasoning with evidence.	Different scientific frameworks within the same domain share some common ground. But they can disagree significantly on methodology, models, and/or relevant data. The issue is the extent to which knowledge, beliefs, reasoning, representations, methods, and goals from one research domain map to another research domain. The social and epistemic contexts are complex indeed.

continued

Table 1.1 Continued

Traditional tenets from logical positivism	Received NOS views	Reasons for revision	Revised NOS views
7. Scientific development is cumulatively progressive.	Logical positivists held that the growth of scientific knowledge is cumulative and continually progressive. Scientists work with common theory choices.	Theory choice is an important dynamic of doing science and it influences how investigations are designed and conducted. On what grounds (e.g., rational vs. irrational) scientists make such choices is a matter for further research and debate.	The Kuhnian view that "revolutions" involve the abandonment of established guiding conceptions and methods challenges the belief that scientific development is always cumulatively progressive. New guiding conceptions inform what counts as an observation or a theory. Such changes reinforce beliefs that all scientific claims are revisable in principle. Thus, we embrace the notions of the "tentativeness" of knowledge claims and the "responsiveness" of scientific practices.

brief descriptions of the "Received NOS views," the "Reasons for revision," and the "Revised NOS views." The organization of the table's rows and columns is meant to highlight the reactions, objections, and insights the seven tenets raised. For each of the seven tenets we contrast the "Traditional" and the "Revised" views for the nature of science. Reading down the traditional "Received NOS views" column paints a picture of the commitments held by the logical positivists. Reading down the "Revised NOS views" column reveals commitments from those adhering to naturalized philosophical views. The "Revised NOS view" stresses the dialogic and dialectical processes/practices of science and does so with respect to conceptual as well as methodological changes in scientific inquiry.

It is important not to simply reject logical positivism without understanding it. If we do so we risk losing both some of the insights provided and perspectives on some of the oversimplifications that were involved. Similarly, the agenda here is not to reject the idea of scientific method out of hand, but rather to radically supplement it. The main points from Table 1.1 are placed in an order below that (1) reflects the improvement and refinement practices of scientific inquiry, and (2) provides a basis for an expanded scientific method and a critique of creation science:

- The bulk of scientific effort is not theory discovery or theory acceptance but theory improvement and refinement.
- Research groups or disciplinary communities are the units of practice for scientific discourse.
- Scientific inquiry involves a complex set of discourse processes.
- The discourse practices of science are organized within a disciplinary matrix of shared exemplars for decisions regarding the (a) values, (b) instruments, (c) methods, (d) models, and (e) evidence to adopt.
- Scientific inquiry has epistemic and social dimensions, as well as conceptual.
- Changes in scientific knowledge are not just in conceptual understandings alone; important advancements in science are also often the result of technological and methodological changes for conducting observations and measurements.
- What comes to count as an observation in science evolves with the introduction of new tools, technologies, and theories.
- Theories can be understood as clusters of models where the models stand between empirical/conceptual evidence and theoretical explanations.
- Theory and model choices serve as guiding conceptions for deciding "what counts" and are an important dynamic in scientific inquiry.
- Rubrics for a rational degree of confirmation are hopeless; dialog over merits of alternative models and theories is essential for refining, accepting, or rejecting them and is not reducible to an algorithm.

The expanded scientific method, then, would be inclusive, not exclusive, of the three sequential 20th century images of the nature of science: hypothetico-deductive experiment-driven science, conceptual change theory-driven science, and model based-driven science. The expanded scientific method recognizes the role of experiment and hypothesis testing in scientific inquiry, but emphasizes that the results of experiments are used to advance models and build theories. Thus, the expanded scientific method makes a further recognition that the practices of scientific inquiry involve important dialogic and dialectical practices that function across conceptual, epistemic, and social dimensions.

Demarcation Based on Practices

Looking across all seven tenets, the bold implication is the need to consider developing an enhanced notion for the scientific method. The enhanced scientific method is a view that recognizes the role of experiment and hypothesis testing but does so with a further recognition that the practices of scientific inquiry (1) have conceptual, epistemic, and social dimensions and (2) are epigenetic.

The enhanced view, though, goes well beyond the extant hypothetico-deductive view of scientific methods portrayed in K-16 classrooms:

1.   Make observations
2.   Formulate a hypothesis
3.   Deduce consequences from the hypothesis
4.   Make observations to test the consequences
5.   Accept or reject the hypothesis based on the observations.

We can see that although all of these five elements involve cognitive tasks, only the last involves an epistemic task. In contrast, many of the practices that are defined by the revised seven tenets of science as elements of scientific inquiry include social or epistemic elements. Consider how each of the seven tenets in Table 1.1 has implications for the design of school science with an example of how it might be implemented in a classroom.

 1. Contexts of theory development: Provide opportunities for students to engage in activities involving the growth of scientific knowledge; for example, respond to new data, to new theories that interpret data, or to both. Employ a dialectical orientation to school science to model how science and scientists are being *responsive* to anomalous data and worthy alternative conceptual frameworks when refining and modifying theory. The *responsive* label is pre-ferred over saying that scientific claims are at best only *tentative*, thus avoid-ing anti-science connotations that scientific claims being tentative are unsupported by evidence or scientific reasoning.

 2. Individual/group inquiry: Use distributed learning models during investigations—avoid when possible all students doing the same investigation, rather have individuals/small groups complete components of an inquiry and then report back to a larger group the data and the evidence obtained. Whole class discussions can then focus on a larger corpus of data and evidence in the development of explanations.

3. *Observation/theory:* Employ dialectical processes regarding which theoretical frameworks are being used as guiding conceptions when critiquing or making decisions about what data to collect, what questions to ask, what data to use as evidence, among others.

4. *Theory evaluation:* Engage learners in the development of criteria for theory/explanation evaluation. This includes making decisions regarding when it is plausible to pursue the development and interrogation of theory. Furthermore, there is the need to have learners consider alternative explanations and participate in dialogic activities that debate and argue the merits/ demerits of the alternative models and theories.

5. *Theory language:* Scientific explanations are not strictly linguistic statements. Scientists develop and use physical models, computational models, mathematical models, and iconic models, among others, to explain scientific investigations. So, too, should students be encouraged to develop and to use model-based approaches in scientific investigations and inquiry.

6. *Shared exemplars:* Provide attention to the theoretical or model-based frameworks that guide scientific inquiry. Establish shared goals by arranging inquiry around big ideas, driving questions, immersion units, and focusing meaning making on use of critical evidence, pivotal cases, and knowledge integration. Develop in students the idea that science is about engagement in theory change and model building and revision.

7. *Scientific progress:* Provide learners opportunities to engage in the examination of alternative explanations and guiding conceptions when developing accounts of phenomena and mechanisms. Allocate room in the curriculum for learners to engage in serious discussions about the criteria that are used to assess and make judgments about knowledge claims.

An enhanced scientific method incorporates new perspectives about the nature of science that recognizes the importance of dialectical and dialogic processes among the theory-building and model-building activities that inform the growth of scientific knowledge. Scientific ideas and information are rooted in evidence and guided by our best-reasoned beliefs in the form of the scientific models and theories that frame investigations and inquiries. All elements of science—questions, methods, evidence, and explanations—are open to scrutiny, examination, justification, and verification. *Inquiry and the National Standards in Science Education* (National Research Council, 2000) identifies five essential features of classroom inquiry:

- Learners are engaged by scientifically oriented questions.
- Learners give priority to **evidence**, which allows them to develop and evaluate explanations that address scientifically oriented questions.

- Learners formulate **explanations** from evidence to address scientifically oriented questions.
- Learners evaluate their explanations in light of alternative explanations, particularly those reflecting scientific understanding.
- Learners communicate and justify their proposed explanations.

The bold emphasis on evidence and explanation appears in the original text. Science, at its core, is about acquiring data and then transforming that data first into evidence and then into explanations. Preparation for making scientific discoveries and engaging in scientific inquiry is linked to students' opportunities to examine (1) the development or acquisition of the data and (2) the unfolding or transformations of data across the evidence–explanation continuum (Duschl, 2004). The enhanced scientific method perspective would add to the five features four other "features" that address opportunities to engage in the following dialogic processes and practices:

- Respond to criticisms from others
- Formulate appropriate criticisms of others
- Engage in criticism of own explanations
- Reflect on alternative explanations and not have a unique resolution.

Developments in scientific theory coupled with concomitant advances in material sciences, engineering, and technologies have given rise to radically new ways of observing nature and engaging with phenomenon. At the beginning of the 20th century scientists were debating the existence of atoms and genes; by the end of the century they were manipulating individual atoms and engaging in genetic engineering. These developments have altered the nature of scientific inquiry and greatly complicated our images of what it means to engage in scientific inquiry. Where once scientific inquiry was principally the domain of unaided sense perception, today scientific inquiry is guided by highly theoretical beliefs that determine the very existence of observational events (e.g., neutrino capture experiments in the ice fields of Antarctica). As we argue above, invoking the seven tenets of science frames science as a way of knowing around a set of epistemic and social practices.

The dialogic processes of theory development and of dealing with anomalous data occupy a great deal of scientists' time and energy. The logical positivist's "context of justification" is a formal final point—the end of a journey; moreover, it is a destination few theories ever achieve, and so overemphasis on it entirely misses the importance of the journey. Importantly, the journey involved in the growth of scientific knowledge reveals the ways in which scientists respond to new data, to new theories that interpret data, or to both. Thagard (2007) eloquently elaborates on the dynamics of these practices as they relate to achieving explanatory coherence. Advancing explanatory coherence, he argues, involves theories that deepen and broaden over time by respectively accounting for new facts and providing explanations of why the theory works. These general notions of theory refinement, articulation, deepening, and broadening are missing when we examine "intelligent design" and "creationist" points of view for teaching the controversy.

One of the important findings from the science studies literature is that not only does scientific knowledge change over time, but so, too, do the methods of inquiry and the criteria for the evaluation of knowledge change. The accretion growth model of scientific knowledge is no longer tenable. Nor is a model of the growth of knowledge that appeals to changes in theory commitments alone; for example, conceptual change models. Changes in research programs that drive the growth of scientific knowledge also can be due to changes in methodological commitments or goal commitments (Duschl & Grandy, 2008a, 2008b). Science studies examining contemporary science practices recognize that both the conceptual frameworks and the methodological practices of science have changed over time. Changes in methodology are a consequence of new tools, new technologies, and new explanatory models and theories that, in turn, have shaped and will continue to shape scientific knowledge and scientific practices.

As science has progressed as a way of knowing, yet another dichotomy has emerged, and it is one that is critically important for a contemporary consideration of the design of K-12 curriculum, instruction, and assessment. That dichotomy is the blurring of boundaries between science and technology and between different branches of the sciences themselves, yet another outcome of learning how to learn that challenges our beliefs about what counts as data, evidence, and explanations. Ackerman (1985) refers to such developments as the shifts in the "data texts" of science and warns that the conversations among contemporary scientists about measurement, observations, data, evidence, models, and explanations are of a kind that is quite foreign from the conversations found in the general population. Consequently, understanding discipline-based epistemic frameworks, as opposed to or in addition to learning-based epistemic frameworks, is critically important for situating school science learning, knowing, and inquiry (Kelly & Duschl, 2002; Hammer & Elby, 2003).

Pickering (1995) referred to this conflation when describing experiments in high-energy physics as the "mangle of practice." Zammito (2004, pp. 225–226) writes:

> Pickering's (1990) "practical realism" or interpretation of "science as practice" offers a robust appreciation for the *complexity* of science, its "rich plurality of elements of knowledge and practice," which he has come to call the "the mangle of practice." … As against the "statics of knowledge," the frame of existing theoretical ideas, Pickering (1990) situates the essence of scientific life in the "dynamics of practice," that is, "a complex process of reciprocal and interdependent tunings and refigurings of material procedures, interpretations and theories."

The enhanced dialogic practices' views of scientific method points out some of the ways proponents of "intelligent design" do not participate in or consider important epistemic and social practices of science. As Chapman (2006) points out in a critical review of the Dover, PA "Monkey trial," there are numerous examples of how scientific discourse and practices are perverted by proponents of "intelligent design" and "creationism." When you look carefully at creation science ideas and discourse, you find there is no journey, no mangle of practice, no complexity, no refinement of theory, and no deepening and broadening that leads to explanatory coherence. Herein lies the science/non-science demarcation between the theory of evolution and creation science ideas—on the basis of the practices of theory development and conceptual modification.

Notes

1. This research was supported by NSF grant REC #0343196 awarded to the authors. The opinions expressed in this article are those of the authors and do not necessarily reflect the views of the National Science Foundation.
2. Paper presented as part of the invited symposium "Examination of the Evolution vs. Intelligent Design Controversy: Opportunities for Epistemology and Philosophy of Science Education" at the annual meeting of AERA, April 9, 2006.

References

Ackerman, R. J. (1985). *Data, Instruments, and Theory: A Dialectical Approach to Understanding Science.* Princeton, NJ: Princeton University Press.

Chapman, M. (2006). God or gorilla: A Darwin descendant at the Dover Monkey Trial. *Harper's Magazine, February,* 54–63.

Dennett, D. (1995). *Darwin's Dangerous Idea: Evolution and the Meanings of Life.* New York: Touchstone.

Driver, R., Leach, J., Millar, R., & Scott, P. (1996). *Young People's Images of Science.* Philadelphia, PA: Open University Press.

Duschl, R. (2004). Assessment of inquiry. In J. M. Atkin & J. C. Coffey (Eds.) *Everyday Assessment in the Science Classroom.* Arlington, VA: NSTA Press.

Duschl, R., & Grandy, R., (Eds.) (2008a). *Teaching Scientific Inquiry: Recommendations for Research and Instruction.* Rotterdam, Netherlands: SensePublishers.

Duschl, R. A., & Grandy, R. E. (2008b). Reconsidering the character and role of inquiry in school science: Framing the debates. In R. Duschl & R. Grandy (Eds.) *Teaching Scientific Inquiry: Recommendations for Research and Instruction.* Rotterdam, Netherlands: SensePublishers.

Eflin, J., Glennan, S., & Reisch, G. (1999). The nature of science: A perspective from the philosophy of science. *Journal of Research in Science Teaching, 36*(1), 107–116.

Giere, R. (1988). *Explaining Science: A Cognitive Approach.* Chicago, IL: University of Chicago Press.

Giere, R. (1999). *Science without Laws.* Chicago, IL: University of Chicago Press.

Godfrey-Smith, P. (2003). *Theory and Reality: An Introduction to Philosophy of Science.* Chicago, IL: University of Chicago Press.

Grandy, R. E., & Duschl, R. A. (2008). Consensus: Expanding the scientific method and school science. In R. Duschl & R. Grandy (Eds.) *Teaching Scientific Inquiry: Recommendations for Research and Instruction.* Rotterdam, Netherlands: SensePublishers.

Hammer, D., & Elby, A. (2003). Tapping epistemological resources from learning physics. *Journal of the Learning Sciences, 12,* 53–91.

Kelly, G. J., & Duschl, R. (2002). *Toward a research agenda for epistemological studies in science education.* Invited paper presented at the annual meeting of National Association for Research in Science Teaching (NARST), April 2002, New Orleans, LA.

Lederman, N. G. (1999). Teachers' understanding of the nature of science and classroom practice: Factors that facilitate or impede the relationship. *Journal of Research in Science Teaching, 36,* 916–929.

Lederman, N., Abd-el-Khalick, F., Bell, R. L., & Schwartz, R. S. (2002). Views of Nature of Science questionnaire: Towards valid and meaningful assessment of learners' conceptions of the nature of science. *Journal of Research in Science Teaching, 39(6),* 497–521.

Longino, H. (2002). *The Fate of Knowledge.* Princeton, NJ: Princeton University Press.

McComas, W. F., & Olson, J. K. (1998). The Nature of Science in international science education standards documents. In W. F. McComas (Ed.) *The Nature of Science in Science Education: Rationales and Strategies* (pp. 41–52). Dordrecht: Kluwer.

National Research Council (2000). *Inquiry and the National Standards in Science Education.* Washington, DC: National Academy Press (www.nap.edu).

Osborne, J. F., Collins, S., Ratcliffe, M., Millar, R., & Duschl, R. (2003). What "Ideas-about-science" should be taught in school science? A Delphi study of the expert community. *Journal of Research in Science Teaching, 40(7),* 692–720.

Pickering, A. (1990). Knowledge, practice and mere construction. In *Deconstructing Quarks,* Special Issue of *Social Studies of Science, 20(4),* 682–729.

Pickering, A. (1995). *The Mangle of Practice: Time, Agency and Science.* Chicago, IL: University of Chicago Press.

Ryan, A. G., & Aikenhead, G. S. (1992). Students' preconceptions about the epistemology of science. *Science Education, 76,* 559–580.

Smith, C., & Wenk, L. (2006). Relations among three aspects of first-year college students' epistemologies of science. *Journal of Research in Science Teaching, 43(8),* 747–785.

Solomon, M. (2001). *Social Empiricism.* Cambridge, MA: MIT Press.

Thagard, P. (2007). Coherence, truth, and the development of scientific knowledge. *Philosophy of Science, 74,* 28–47.

Windschitl, M. (2004). Caught in the cycle of reproducing folk theories of "Inquiry": How pre-service teachers continue the discourse and practices of an atheoretical scientific method. *Journal of Research in Science Teaching, 41(5),* 481–512.

Zammito, J. H. (2004). *A Nice Derangement of Epistemes: Post-positivism in the Study of Science from Quine to Latour.* Chicago, IL: University of Chicago Press.

Chapter 2

Evolution, Creation, and the Philosophy of Science

Paul Thagard

Introduction

Debates about evolution and creation inevitably raise philosophical issues about the nature of scientific knowledge. What is a theory? What is an explanation? How is science different from non-science? How should theories be evaluated? Does science achieve truth? The aim of this chapter is to give a concise and accessible introduction to the philosophy of science, focusing on questions relevant to understanding evolution by natural selection, creation, and intelligent design. For the questions just listed, I state what I think is the best available answer and show how it applies to debates about evolution and creationism. I also indicate alternative answers that are preferred by other philosophers. I hope that the result will be useful for science educators and anyone else involved in controversies about evolution and creation.

What Are Theories and Explanations?

Theories Are Representations of Mechanisms

In ordinary speech, "theory" sometimes means an unsupported speculation, as in the phrase "just a theory." But many scientific theories are well established by a wealth of evidence; for example, relativity theory and quantum theory in physics, atomic theory in chemistry, genetic theory in biology, and the germ theory of disease in medicine. A theory is best understood as the representation of an explanatory mechanism, where a mechanism is a system of parts whose properties and interactions produce regular changes. A scientific explanation of something consists of showing how it results from the operations of a mechanism.

Consider a simple machine such as a manual can opener, whose parts usually include two handles hinged together at one end, a serrated wheel that cuts into the can, and a crank that operates gears that turn the wheel in order to remove the lid of the can. When you turn the crank, you exploit the properties of the parts such as their rigidity and their interactions such as the meshing of the gears to produce the desired change, cutting through the top of the can to remove the lid. Specifying this mechanism in terms of its parts, interactions, and resulting changes explains how cans have their lids removed. If the can opener is not working, its failure can usually be explained by defects in the mechanism, such as a broken crank.

I have described the can opener mechanism using words and sentences, but a fuller description would use visual representations such as pictures and diagrams. Perhaps while you were reading my verbal description you constructed a mental picture of using a can opener that made it easier for you to think about what the parts are and how they interact. An engineer might use mathematical representations that employ variables and equations to express concisely the forces and motions that enable the can opener to work. Thus representations of a mechanism on paper and in the mind can be verbal, pictorial, and/or mathematical.

Similarly, scientific theories represent mechanisms using a combination of ordinary words, pictures, and mathematics. For example, Newton mechanistically explained why bodies fall by describing their parts such as projectiles and planets, their interactions such as forces applied, and the resulting changes in speed and location. He used a combination of words, diagrams, and equations to show how motion results systematically from the interactions of objects. Table 2.1 concisely summarizes some of the important mechanisms employed in different areas of science, which vary in the kinds of representations they use. For example, physics uses more mathematical equations than cell biology, which uses more diagrams. The end result is the same, explaining how changes come about through systematic interactions of the parts of a system. What can count as a mechanism has changed in the history of science, from the simple parts and interactions of the Greeks, to Newton's ideas that allowed action at a distance, and to current views about complex dynamic systems such as those used in advanced robotics.

Table 2.1 Sketch of Some Important Mechanisms in Science

Science	Parts	Interactions	Changes
Physics	Objects such as projectiles and planets	Forces such as gravity	Motion
Chemistry	Elements, molecules	Mass, energy	Reactions
Geology—plate tectonics	Continents	Floating, collision	Continental drift, mountains, earthquakes
Neuroscience	Neurons, synapses	Electrochemical transmission	Brain activity, learning

Scientific theories often describe interacting mechanisms at different levels of organization. For example, the germ theory in medicine explains how people come down with influenza and other infectious diseases through the operation of microbes such as bacteria and viruses. Understanding these diseases requires attention to mechanisms that operate at several different levels, concerning social groups, organisms, cells, and molecules. Social groups are relevant to understanding such aspects of contagion as when you acquire a virus by shaking hands with someone you meet at a party. Relevant organisms are people's bodies and microbes that infect them, as when a virus infects your throat and makes it swollen. Viruses infect the cells in your throat through biochemical processes that enable them to bind with molecules on cell surfaces, invade the cells, and reproduce. Table 2.2 summarizes how medical theories explain disease by specifying mechanisms at interacting levels.

Levels are related in three ways, involving parts, interactions, and changes. The parts at one level are composed of parts at the next level down, and the interactions at the higher level are based on the interactions at the lower level, so that the changes at the higher level result from the changes at the lower level. For example, your sore throat results from infection by a virus (organism level) that occurs because the virus invades the cells in your throat (cell level) by means of chemical interactions with proteins on the cell surfaces (molecular level). A full understanding of disease requires specification of mechanisms at all relevant levels, including social groups, organisms, cells, and molecules.

Sources for the mechanistic account explanations and theories include: Bechtel (2006); Bechtel and Abrahamsen (2005); Bechtel and Richardson (1993); Craver (2007); Darden (2006); Machamer, Darden, and Craver (2000); Salmon (1984); Thagard (1999, 2006a, 2006b). Introductions to the philosophy of biology include Sterelny and Griffiths (1999) and Rosenberg and McShea (2007). Salmon (1989) reviews philosophical theories of scientific explanation.

Table 2.2 Levels of Mechanisms Relevant to Explaining Disease

Level	Parts	Interactions	Changes
Social groups	People	Contact	Contagion
Organisms	Bodies, microbes	Infection	Symptoms such as fever
Cells	Molecules such as proteins	Cell division, invasion	Cell growth, destruction
Molecules	Elements	Binding, reactions	Chemical reactions

Evolutionary Theory as Representation of Mechanisms

Similarly, evolutionary theory is best understood as the representation of mechanisms operating at several levels. Evolution by itself is not a mechanism, but rather a description of historical changes that Darwin described as "descent with modification." Humans and other species have developed from previous ones by modifying and preserving some of their characteristics. Darwin's great discovery was the mechanism of natural selection that explains how species can evolve by the competition to survive and reproduce by adapting to environments. In this mechanism, the parts are the different organisms in their environments, the interactions include feeding and reproduction, and the changes are the occurrences of members of species with different characteristics.

The great gap in Darwin's original theory of evolution by natural selection is that he lacked a good account of how variations occur in organisms and are passed on to their offspring. This gap was filled early in the 20th century by genetic theory which explained how characteristics can be inherited through the transmission of genes, and how variation can occur through genetic mutation. In the second half of that century, the molecular mechanisms for genetic transmission and variation became understood as the result of biochemical interactions such as those involving DNA and RNA. Thus evolutionary theory can be understood as representation of mechanisms operating at several different but interacting levels: natural selection, genetics, and molecular biology, as summarized in Table 2.3. Social mechanisms are indirectly relevant to evolutionary theory, through interactions of groups of organisms and interspecies competition. For the mechanisms of evolutionary theory, see textbooks such as Ridley (2003).

These mechanisms are interconnected through parts, interactions, and changes. Organisms consist of cells that include genes, which are sequences of DNA. The interactions of organisms derive partly from their genetic

Table 2.3 Mechanisms in Evolutionary Theory

Mechanism	Parts	Interactions	Changes
Natural selection	Organisms	Competition to survive and reproduce	Occurrence of characteristics; new species; extinction
Genetics	Genes, alleles	Mutation, protein production	Prevalence of genes
Biochemistry	Molecules such as DNA	Combination, chemical reactions	Structure of DNA

programming, based on the operations of DNA, RNA, and other molecules. Hence changes at the level of species and organisms can be understood partly in terms of changes in genes and molecules, allowing also for changes in physical environments (e.g., climate) and in social environments (e.g., culture).

Representation of mechanisms in evolutionary biology primarily uses words and sentences, but pictures and mathematics are also sometimes useful. Since Darwin, depictions of descent with modification have often used tree diagrams, such as Figure 2.1; see Novick and Catley (2007) for a discussion of hierarchical diagrams that depict evolutionary histories among species. It is hard to picture processes of natural selection and genetics, but graphs can be used to show the changing frequencies of characteristics and genes in a population of organisms. Cell and molecular biology frequently use diagrams to depict structures such as the parts of cells and amino acids that constitute DNA, as well as processes such as cell division and DNA recombination. Mathematical equations are also sometimes part of the representation of evolutionary mechanisms, especially in population genetics. For example, the Hardy–Weinberg law is an equation that specifies the relationship between the frequency of alleles and the genotype of the population. Hence evolutionary theory combines verbal, pictorial, and mathematical representations of mechanisms that include natural selection, genetics, and molecular interactions. Together, these mechanisms explain a wide array of biological changes such as the development of new species.

In contrast, the hypotheses of divine creation and intelligent design are clearly not mechanistic theories. Theorists such as Dembski (1999) postulate

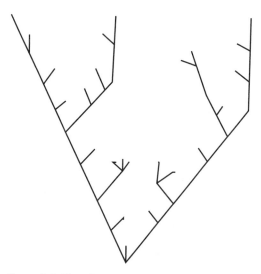

Figure 2.1 Visual representation of branching evolution of species: Darwin's tree of life, simplified.

that God created the universe, including the species on our planet, without giving any indication of how. Indeed, no such indication is possible, as God is a supernatural being, independent of time and space, whose effects on the world must occur in violation of basic laws of physics such as conservation of energy. By definition God cannot be part of a physical mechanism, so creationism cannot provide the kind of mechanistic explanation that has been the hallmark of science for centuries. Even if physical mechanisms were created by God, it remains totally mysterious how miraculous interventions could occur.

Alternative Views of Theories and Explanations

The mechanistic view of explanations and theories has become increasingly prominent in the philosophy of science in recent years, as the references in a previous subsection document. But it is by no means the only view, and to avoid dogmatism I will briefly point to alternatives. The classical view of theories developed by the logical empiricists is that a theory is a set of universal sentences ideally expressed in a formal language such as predicate calculus. From this perspective, evolutionary theory should be stated as a set of axioms, but no one has produced more than sketchy formalizations of natural selection and population genetics. On the classical view, an explanation is a deductive argument that looks like a proof in a formal system, showing how descriptions of phenomena to be explained follow logically from the axioms that constitute a theory. Sources of the logical empiricist account of theories and explanations include Hempel (1965, 1966) and Nagel (1961). Deductive explanations can sometimes be found in highly mathematical areas of science such as physics, but are rare in evolutionary biology. The classical view of explanation can be loosened by allowing that what is explained need only be made probable by a theory, but relevant probabilities are hard to find in applications of evolutionary theory. In contrast, the account of evolutionary theory and explanation in terms of representation and application of mechanisms fits well with scientific practice. On the "erotetic" view of explanation, an explanation is just an answer to a why question, but this view fails to differentiate good scientific explanations from fanciful answers.

An alternative to the classical view of theories is the semantic (set-theoretic) conception that rejected the idea of a theory as a specific linguistic formulation. On this conception, a theory is a structure that serves to pick a class of models out of a general class of models. Here a model is not anything concrete, but rather a mathematical abstraction consisting of a set of objects and relations among them. It can be used to make empirical claims that the models that constitute the intended applications of the theory are among the models picked out by the theory. To specify a theory, we need to define a predicate such as "x is a biological population" by stating in informal set theory a series of axioms characterizing those objects that fall under the predicate. A theoretical claim then says that biological populations in the real world are included in the abstract models defined by the set-theoretic predicate. Suppe (1977) includes discussions of the set-theoretic alternative, which was applied to biology by Thompson (1989). Unfortunately, such set-theoretic axiomatizations are as difficult to produce as the syntactic ones sought by the classical view of theories. In contrast, the much more informal view of theories as involving several kinds of representation does not require reconstruction of scientific practice.

How Is Science Different from Pseudoscience?

Science Has Typical Features

Debates about whether creationism and intelligent design theory are scientific would benefit from a strict definition of science that distinguish it sharply from non-science or pseudoscience. (By pseudoscience I mean a non-scientific enterprise that purports to be scientific.) Some philosophers have proposed criteria such as verifiability or falsifiability as distinguishing marks of science, but other philosophers have pointed out serious problems with these criteria. As I will discuss further below, precise versions of these criteria tend to rule out as scientific even sciences such as physics, whereas loose versions of them tend to include just about anything. It therefore looks hopeless to come up with a definition of science that would enable us to say that a field or theory is scientific if and only if it has properties A, B, and C. Some philosophers have concluded that the problem of demarcating science from pseudoscience is unsolvable (Laudan, 1983).

We should not, however, be surprised or dismayed by failure to define science exactly, because few concepts outside mathematics have precise definitions. To take a mundane example, my dictionary defines *restaurant* as a "public eating place," but this seems too loose: my department has a lounge where people bring their lunches, but it is not a restaurant, nor is a university residence cafeteria. Much research in cognitive science suggests that concepts are characterized, not by strict definitions, but by descriptions of prototypical features and standard examples.

For science, our most standard examples are physics, chemistry, and biology, so we can ask what features are most typical of them and their subfields. Identifying such features would not provide the necessary and sufficient conditions that are needed for a sharp definition, but could nevertheless provide a profile of science that could serve to discriminate it from pseudoscience. We can also develop a profile of pseudoscience by looking at the typical features of fields that have falsely purported to be scientific, such as alchemy and astrology. Table 2.4 provides such profiles of science and pseudoscience. Earlier attempts to demarcate science from pseudoscience by means of prototypical profiles include Thagard (1988) and Derksen (1993).

Table 2.4 Profiles of Science and Pseudoscience

Science	Pseudoscience
Explains using mechanisms.	Lacks mechanistic explanations.
Uses correlation thinking, which applies statistical methods to find patterns in nature.	Uses dogmatic assertions, or resemblance thinking, which infers that things are causally related merely because they are similar.
Practitioners care about evaluating theories in relation to alternative ones.	Practitioners are oblivious to alternative theories.
Uses simple theories that have broad explanatory power.	Uses nonsimple theories that require many extra hypotheses for particular explanations.
Progresses over time by developing new theories that explain newly discovered facts.	Stagnant in doctrine and applications.

It should be obvious that physics, chemistry, and biology over the past several hundred years have matched very well the profile for science. In contrast, astrology and graphology (analyzing people's personality from their handwriting) match much better the profile for pseudoscience. Astrology lacks mechanistic explanations, in that it has never been able to say how the alignment of the stars and planets could affect people's lives. Its generalizations such as that being born under the influence of the planet Mars will make a person warlike are based either on dogmatic assertions or on resemblance theories (the red planet resembles blood which is spilled in war). Astrologers ignore alternative explanations of people's personalities such as the genetic and social learning ones provided by modern psychology. Astrologers can always explain an event by coming up with an account of how a mixture of celestial influences affect one's fate. Finally, astrology has certainly been stagnant, failing to develop new theories and empirical applications over many hundreds of years. The contrast is dramatic with scientific fields such as physics, chemistry, and biology, all of which have had fabulous developments in new theories, instruments, empirical evidence, and technological applications over the same time period.

In sum, the problem of demarcating science from pseudoscience is manageable despite the lack of a strict definition of science. By attending to the differences in intellectual practice and historical development, we can develop profiles of science and pseudoscience that specify their prototypical features. We can then categorize a field or theory as scientific or pseudoscientific by matching it against the two profiles.

The Scientific Status of Evolution and Creation

Evolutionary theory, encompassing natural selection, genetics, and molecular biology, clearly fits the profile of science provided in Table 2.4. I have already described how it uses mechanistic explanations, and it makes generalizations about the properties of populations of organisms using statistical techniques rather than dogmatic assertion or thinking based on mere similarities. Beginning with Darwin's systematic comparison in *The Origin of Species* of his theory of evolution by natural selection with the dominant theory of his day, divine creation, evolutionary biologists have engaged in debates about alternative theories. Natural selection and genetics have great explanatory power described in the next section. Finally, evolutionary theory has clearly progressed in the century and a half since Darwin published the *Origin*, through the development of whole new fields such as genetics and molecular biology. According to the profile of science in Table 2.4, evolution is as scientific as any field you can name.

In contrast, creationism and its current version, intelligent design, fit well the profile of pseudoscience. We have already seen that they lack mechanistic explanations, and many of their claims are based on dogmatic assertions rather than on statistical analysis. The proponents of divine creation remain blind to the substantial explanatory successes of evolutionary theory, and address it only to be able to reject it in line with their religious motivations. As I discuss further in connection with theory evaluation below, creation theory can potentially explain anything, merely by adding the additional hypothesis that God wanted it to happen. The price, however, is great loss in simplicity, as such explanations require a separate hypothesis about God's plan for each fact explained. Finally, the theory that species originated through divine creation has not been progressive, having advanced little since the early 19th century. Given its dependence on religious doctrine rather than hypothesis generation based on empirical observation, such stagnation was inevitable. We should therefore have no hesitation in concluding that creationism and intelligent design theory are not scientific. On intelligent design, see also Sober (2007).

Alternative Views of Demarcation

Science textbooks often begin by saying that science proceeds by forming hypotheses, using them to make predictions, and then performing experiments to see whether the predictions are true. If the experiments fit the predictions, then the hypotheses are said to be confirmed (verified), but if the predictions fail then the hypotheses are disconfirmed (falsified). According to the philosophical movement called logical positivism, what makes science meaningful is verifiability: theories can be used to make predictions that can be verified (Ayer, 1946).

The principle that science is marked by verifiability has two major problems. First, no one ever managed to state the principle of verifiability in a precise and plausible way that excludes metaphysics (the main target of the logical positivists) without excluding science as well. Second, the principle itself seems to be unverifiable and hence meaningless metaphysics (according to the positivists) rather than scientific. Undoubtedly, science is concerned with forming hypotheses, making predictions, and performing experiments, but this practice cannot be codified into a strict definition that by itself demarcates science from non-science. Instead, I have included concern with evaluating the explanatory power of theories as one of the features of my profile of prototypical science, but verifiability should not be intended to perform the demarcation function all by itself.

Falsifiability is also often stated as *the* mark of a scientific theory, but has similar problems to verifiability. Karl Popper (1959) thought that confirmation of theories is too easy to come by, so what makes a field scientific is that its practitioners try to do experiments that could disconfirm their theories and thereby show them to be false. But even scientific theories are not capable of strict falsification, for the deduction of an observation statement from a theory always requires the use of auxiliary hypotheses, and it is always logically possible to reject one of these rather than the theory. For example, if your theory makes a prediction that is disconfirmed by experiment, you can always suppose that the experiment failed because of technical problems such as poor design or malfunctioning instruments, rather than because the theory was false. In the history of science, rejection of theories on the basis of failed predictions is extremely rare. When theories are rejected and taken to be falsified, it is because they have been replaced by theories with greater explanatory power. Hence rather than thinking of verification and falsification as two-place relations between hypotheses and observations, we should think of theory evaluation as a more complex competition between alternative theories that purport to explain the facts. Hence verification and falsification are only facets of scientific practice as indicated in the aspects of my profile citing concern with theory evaluation, not knock-down features of what makes a field scientific. Thus verifiability and falsifiability are poor criteria for demarcating science from pseudoscience, and hence useless by themselves in trying to distinguish evolutionary theory from creationism. Problems with using falsifiability as the mark of science were identified by Duhem (1954), Quine (1963), and Lakatos (1970).

How Are Scientific Theories Evaluated?

Theory Choice Is Inference to the Best Explanation

As I remarked in discussing the demarcation problem, the acceptance of a scientific theory is rarely based just on how well it makes predictions. Usually, there is more than one candidate theory for explaining the relevant data, and scientists need to pick the best one. Once a science is underway with an established theory, proponents of a new theory must show that it is superior. For example, Copernicus had to argue that his heliocentric theory provided a better fit with the observed motions of the planets than did Ptolemy's theory. Similarly, Lavoisier had to show that his oxygen theory of combustion provided a better explanation than the accepted phlogiston theory. Theory choice requires evaluating the available competing theories to determine which of them provides the best explanation of all the relevant data.

The two main criteria for evaluating theories are explanatory breadth and simplicity. One theory has more explanatory breadth than its competitor if it explains more classes of facts. For example, the theory that dinosaurs became extinct as the result of an asteroid hitting the Earth explains why there is an unusual layer of earth that was deposited around the time that dinosaur extinction occurred, a fact that other theories such as climate change cannot easily accommodate. Explanatory breadth needs to be balanced against another criterion, simplicity, which concerns how many special assumptions a theory has to make in order to accomplish its explanations. Lavoisier's oxygen theory had more explanatory breadth than the established phlogiston theory because it could explain why burning bodies gain rather than lose weight. But defenders of the phlogiston theory tried to save it by hypothesizing that the phlogiston supposedly given off during combustion had negative weight. This hypothesis helped the explanatory breadth of phlogiston theory at the cost of simplicity, introducing a special assumption. Similarly, the impressive explanatory breadth of the Ptolemaic theory came at the expense of simplicity, because it had to make assumptions about numerous epicycles for the planets in order to account for the observed motion.

Inference to the best explanation is not only used in science, but also in law, medicine, and everyday life. Your doctor's diagnosis is an inference about what disease provides the best explanation of your symptoms and test results. A detective's judgment that a suspect is responsible for a murder is based on the inference that this hypothesis is the best explanation of the available evidence. In addition to explanatory breadth and simplicity, the detective's confidence is often increased by being able to provide a motive such as anger or jealousy that explains why the suspect murdered the victim. Similarly, a scientific hypothesis gains support if in addition to explaining a variety of facts we can explain why the hypothesis is true. Such deeper explanations require identifying an underlying mechanism, as when Newton explained why planets revolve around the sun as the result of gravity, and atomic theory explained how oxygen combines with other elements to produce combustion. Hence the best scientific hypotheses should provide explanations that are broad (explaining a lot), deep (being themselves explained), and simple (requiring few additional assumptions). An additional factor relevant to picking the best explanation is how well a set of hypotheses fit with other accepted theories and facts. In sum, we accept a theory as the best explanation if it is more coherent with all available information than its alternatives. The view that theory evaluation in science is inference to the best explanation is defended by Thagard (1988) and Lipton (2004).

Evaluating Evolution and Creation

When creationists maintain that intelligent design theory should be taught in biology classes along with (or instead of) evolutionary theory, they assume that creationism is a reasonable alternative. There have been times in the history of science when the available evidence made it difficult to determine which of competing theories was best. For example, in the 18th century, it was not clear whether the wave theory of light or the particle theory was superior, since each could explain some observed phenomena that the other had trouble with. Teaching creationism along with evolutionary theory would be reasonable if it came even close to providing the best explanation of the relevant facts.

In the early 19th century, leading scientists as well as theologians extolled how divine creation beautifully explained biological facts. No alternative explanation of the complexity of life was available then, so it was reasonable to infer that creation was responsible for facts such as the diversity of species. In 1859, however, Darwin's *Origin* changed the situation radically, when he showed that evolution by natural selection provides a unified explanation of a broad range of facts involving the fossil record, the complexity of organs, extinction, and the geographical distribution of species. Since then, the explanatory superiority of evolution over creation has become increasingly evident, as evolutionary theory has progressed to explain more and more facts, for example the development of bacteria that are resistant to antibiotics. Moreover, evolutionary theory has been progressively deepened, as genetic theory came to provide a mechanism for inheritance and variability, and as molecular biology provided mechanisms for genetics.

In principle, divine creation could explain everything in biology including the appearance of evolution, by postulating that God wanted to set things up so it looked like species have evolved. But then creation theory fails on the criterion of simplicity, because it needs a special assumption about God's intentions and actions for each fact explained. Why, for example, did he set the world up in such a way that bacteria could become resistant to antibiotics? Because of the simplicity problem, and the lack of mechanistic explanations, it is fair to evaluate the explanatory power of creationism as very poor. Proponents of intelligent design maintain that only their approach can explain "irreducible complexity" found in nature, but natural selection and genetics have gone a long way to explaining organs as complex as the eye. Many people have the intuition that evolution by natural selection is not powerful enough to have produced the marvelous capacities of the human mind, but great advances have been made in understanding how mental processes are in fact brain processes. Moreover, much is known about how human brains evolved. Hence creationism and intelligent design have no explanatory advantages over evolutionary theory, and they have many disadvantages such as lack of mechanisms and inability to account without special assumptions for facts like the fossil record. Evolution is so superior to creation as the best explanation of a huge array of biological facts that it is not reasonable for science education to include intelligent design as an alternative view. A detailed theory of explanatory coherence with many scientific applications, including Darwin versus creation, is found in Thagard (1992). I provide a comparison of the explanatory coherence of materialist philosophy and science versus creationism and mind–body dualism in Thagard (2000).

If creationism is so inferior to evolution in explanatory coherence, why do so many people still espouse it? The answer is complex, involving both social factors such as the transmission of religious beliefs from parents to children, and psychological factors such as the emotional appeal of religious views about God, the afterlife, and morality. Many people believe that life would be pointless and amoral without the presence of God and the prospect of immortality. The story of divine creation fits well with appealing views about the non-material nature of the mind that make it capable of free will and existence beyond death. Creationism lacks scientific explanatory coherence, but it has enormous emotional coherence with many people's goals and everyday social experience (Thagard, 2006a). For many students, evolutionary theory has negative personal and social implications (Brem, Ranney, & Schindel, 2003). Hence pointing out the explanatory advantages of evolution over creationism rarely has any effect on the belief systems of true believers. A full alternative to the creationist world view requires not only evolutionary theory but also a materialist theory of mind and new philosophical theories about morality and the meaning of life (Thagard, 2010).

Alternative Views of Theory Evaluation

Many philosophers do not endorse the view I have presented that theory evaluation is inference to the best explanation. There are still proponents of the hypothetico-deductive view of confirmation, according to which a theory rises or falls based on the success or failures of its predictions (Hempel, 1965). I would argue that this view neglects both the comparative nature of theory acceptance and the prevalence of explanation rather than deductive prediction as the relation between theories and facts.

The most sophisticated alternative to inference to the best explanation is Bayesianism, which contends that theory evaluation is a matter of picking the most probable theory (Earman, 1992; Howson & Urbach, 1989). Probability is calculated via Bayes' theorem, which derives the probability of a hypothesis given the evidence from the result of multiplying its prior probability by the probability of the evidence given the hypothesis, all divided by the probability of the evidence. Use of Bayes' theorem is fine when we have objective information about probabilities, for example when we know the frequency with which someone has a symptom if they have a disease. But Bayes' theorem is very hard to apply objectively in cases such as evolution versus creation, because little is known about, for example, the probability of the fossil record given evolution versus its probability given creation.

Postmodernists would claim that the whole idea of rational theory evaluation is a myth: the theory with the most powerful proponents wins. Science is just a social construction. But the history of science is full of cases where objective theory evaluation has occurred because scientists have systematically compared competing theories with respect to how well they explain the evidence. For arguments against social constructivism, see Thagard (1999).

Is Science True?

Science Can Achieve Approximate Truth

It has become fashionable to try to reconcile science and religion by saying that they operate in different domains, or that they constitute separate but equal ways of knowing. Although creationist proponents of intelligent design make a show of giving empirical arguments for their views, the basis of these views is clearly religious faith rather than scientific observation and theorizing. Is there any reason to think that science is better than faith in arriving at the truth about the world? Critics of science sometimes discount it as just another kind of faith.

There are good reasons to be skeptical of claims that faith can be a reliable source of knowledge about the world. The first is that faith provides no way of choosing between different views. If you are going to base your religious beliefs on faith, which religion should you choose? Faith can be used to defend belief in Judaism, Islam, Hinduism, Buddhism, as well as many variants of Christianity, from Catholicism to Mormonism. Obviously they cannot all be right, and faith provides no way of evaluating them with respect to each other or more ancient forms of polytheism. Sociologically, it is evident that most people adopt a faith based on the family and community they grow up in, so faith appears to be an accident of birth and association rather than a source of knowledge.

The second reason to be skeptical about faith-based claims is that religion has a poor track record of arriving at reliable knowledge about the world. Classic examples include the rejection by the Catholic Church of the heliocentric theories of Copernicus and Galileo, and bible-based claims that the universe is only about 6,000 years old rather than the billions of years suggested by physical evidence. Religious faith has made only negative contributions to the vast amount of scientific knowledge that has accumulated over the past 400 years.

But is science actually any more successful at arriving at the truth? Some philosophers of science have advocated the "pessimistic induction" that all scientific theories eventually turn out to be false. Good examples of scientific theories that were widely accepted but later rejected include the humoral theory of disease, the caloric theory of heat, and ether theories of electromagnetism. Perhaps we should expect that current scientific theories will eventually bite the dust too. Even the two pillars of modern physics, relativity and quantum theory, are problematic in that they seem to be incompatible with each other; and scientists are attempting to use approaches such as string theory and quantum gravity to develop a new synthesis. If scientific theories are ephemeral, why should we take science as telling us how the world really is? Perhaps accepting a scientific theory, even one with a lot of evidence behind, involves a leap of faith not much different from religion.

The pessimistic induction about scientific theories, however, gives a distorted picture of the history of science. Most of the examples that support it are centuries old, whereas the 20th century witnessed a remarkable accumulation of knowledge in physics, chemistry, and biology. Relativity theory and quantum theory introduced conceptions not found in Newtonian mechanics, but Newton's theory of motion survives as a good approximation to the behavior of bodies that are not in intense gravitational fields or very small. Although explaining a lot is no guarantee of truth, as examples such as the wave theory of light show, theories that have not only broadened by explanation new classes of facts but also deepened by the discovery of underlying mechanisms have stood the test of time. Hence we can justify the cautiously optimistic induction that theories which have both broadened and deepened are at least approximately true (Thagard, 2007).

One of the major reasons for believing that scientific theories have some grip on truth is the huge success of technological applications. Enormously successful technologies such as computers, televisions, and DVD players are based on physical theories about electrons and electromagnetic waves. Effective drugs such as antibiotics and cholesterol-lowering medications are based on biological accounts such as bacterial theories of diseases and biochemical theories of metabolism. The best explanation of the technological applicability of such technologies is that the underlying theories are at least approximately true. Hence because of technological success and the past century's accumulation of scientific results, we have good reason to believe that scientific theories are often at least approximately true. Faith-based approaches have no such track record. For further defense of scientific realism, see Psillos (1999) and Thagard (1988, 1999, 2010).

The Truth of Evolution and Creation

Do we have any reason to believe that evolutionary theory is true? Beginning with Darwin, evidence has accumulated both that species have evolved and that natural selection is the major mechanism responsible for evolution. Genetics provided mechanisms for variability and inheritance, and molecular biology provided mechanisms for genetics. Thus evolutionary theory has broadened and deepened in the century and a half since Darwin began it, so my cautiously optimistic induction about the development of scientific knowledge applies to it: we have good reason to believe that evolutionary theory is at least approximately true. The truth of the theory of evolution is not so strongly supported by technological applications as modern physics, but there are at least a few developments such as genetic engineering that only make sense in the light of evolution.

In contrast, only faith supports the doctrine of divine creation, and we have already seen that faith is a highly unreliable guide to truth. There is no epistemological reason to suppose that science education needs to be based on faith as well as on the kinds of evidence collection, experimentation, and constrained theorizing that have served modern science so well. Softer views on the compatibility of religion and evolutionary theory include Gould (1999). Dawkins (2006) argues that science requires the rejection of religion.

Alternative Views of Scientific Truth

I have been defending the position called scientific realism, which says that science aims and often succeeds in developing theories that truly represent the world. Some philosophers reject realism in favor of instrumentalism, according to which we are only justified in saying that theories are useful tools for prediction, not that they are true. Van Fraassen (1980) defends a trenchant version of anti-realism that he calls constructive empiricism, and a later book argues for compatibility of this view of science with religious faith (van Fraassen, 2002). Some sociologists and historians reject realism in favor of social constructivism, which claims that there is no such thing as truth as the development of science can be explained purely by social forces. Proponents of social constructivism include Barnes (1985) and Latour and Woolgar (1986).

Conclusion

I have tried to provide a concise guide to current ideas in the philosophy of science that are highly relevant to debates about evolution and creation. Scientific theories are representations of explanatory mechanisms, so it is clear that creationism and intelligent design do not provide scientific explanations. There is no one feature that defines science, but, in addition to explanatory mechanisms, creationism lacks additional features that are characteristic of science, such as critical evaluation of competing theories. Scientific theories are evaluated by comparing the breadth and depth of their explanations, and theories of creation and intelligent design are severely lacking on both these dimensions. Finally, we have good reason to believe that evolutionary theory is at least approximately truth, because of the breadth and depth of its explanations. In sum, there is no reason to treat creation and intelligent design as serious competitors for the modern version of the theory of evolution by natural selection.

Acknowledgments

This research was supported by the Natural Science and Engineering Research Council of Canada. I am grateful to Roger Taylor and Michel Ferrari for helpful comments on an earlier draft.

References

Ayer, A. J. (1946). Language, truth and logic (2nd ed.). New York: Dover.
Barnes, B. (1985). About science. Oxford: Blackwell.
Bechtel, W. (2006). Discovering cell mechanisms: The creation of modern cell biology. New York: Cambridge University Press.
Bechtel, W., & Abrahamsen, A. A. (2005). Explanation: A mechanistic alternative. Studies in History and Philosophy of Biology and Biomedical Sciences, 36, 421–441.
Bechtel, W., & Richardson, R. C. (1993). Discovering complexity. Princeton, NJ: Princeton University Press.
Brem, S. K., Ranney, M., & Schindel, J. E. (2003). The perceived consequences of evolution: College students perceive negative personal and social impact in evolutionary theory. Science Education, 87, 181–206.
Craver, C. F. (2007). Explaining the brain. Oxford: Oxford University Press.
Darden, L. (2006). Reasoning in biological discoveries. Cambridge, UK: Cambridge University Press.
Dawkins, R. (2006). The God delusion. New York: Houghton Mifflin.
Dembski, W. (1999). Intelligent design: The bridge between science and theology. Downers Grove, IL: InterVarsity Press.
Derksen, A. A. (1993). The seven sins of pseudo-science. Journal for General Philosophy of Science, 24, 17–42.
Duhem, P. (1954 (Originally published 1914)). The aim and structure of physical theory (P. Wiener, Trans.). Princeton, NJ: Princeton University Press.
Earman, J. (1992). Bayes or bust? Cambridge, MA: MIT Press.
Gould, S. J. (1999). Rock of ages: Science and religion in the fullness of life. New York: Ballantine.
Hempel, C. G. (1965). Aspects of scientific explanation. New York: The Free Press.
Hempel, C. G. (1966). Philosophy of natural science. Englewood Cliffs, NJ: Prentice-Hall.
Howson, C., & Urbach, P. (1989). Scientific reasoning: The Bayesian tradition. Lasalle, IL: Open Court.
Lakatos, I. (1970). Falsification and the methodology of scientific research programs. In I. Lakatos & A. Musgrave (Eds.), Criticism and the growth of knowledge (pp. 91–195). Cambridge, UK: Cambridge University Press.
Latour, B., & Woolgar, S. (1986). Laboratory life: The construction of scientific facts. Princeton, NJ: Princeton University Press.

Laudan, L. (1983). The demise of the demarcation problem. In R. Cohen & L. Laudan (Eds.), *Physics, philosophy, and psychoanalysis* (pp. 111–127). Dordrecht: Reidel.

Lipton, P. (2004). *Inference to the best explanation* (2nd ed.). London: Routledge.

Machamer, P., Darden, L., & Craver, C. F. (2000). Thinking about mechanisms. *Philosophy of Science, 67*, 1–25.

Nagel, E. (1961). *The structure of science.* New York: Harcourt, Brace.

Novick, L. R., and Catley, K. M. (2007). Understanding phylogenies in biology: The influence of a Gestalt perceptual principle. *Journal of Experimental Psychology: Applied, 13*, 197–223.

Popper, K. (1959). *The logic of scientific discovery.* London: Hutchinson.

Psillos, S. (1999). *Scientific realism: How science tracks the truth.* London: Routledge.

Quine, W. V. O. (1963). *From a logical point of view* (2nd ed.). New York: Harper Torchbooks.

Ridley, M. (2003). *Evolution* (3rd ed.). Oxford: Blackwell.

Rosenberg, A., & McShea, D. W. (2007). *Philosophy of biology: A contemporary introduction.* Milton Park: Routledge.

Salmon, W. (1984). *Scientific explanation and the causal structure of the world.* Princeton, NJ: Princeton University Press.

Salmon, W. C. (1989). Four decades of scientific explanation. In P. Kitcher & W. C. Salmon (Eds.), *Scientific explanation (Minnesota Studies in the Philosophy of Science, vol. XIII)* (pp. 3–219). Minneapolis, MN: University of Minnesota Press.

Sober, E. (2007). What is wrong with intelligent design? *Quarterly Review of Biology, 82*, 3–8.

Sterelny, K., & Griffiths, P. E. (1999). *Sex and death: An introduction to the philosophy of biology.* Chicago, IL: University of Chicago Press.

Suppe, F. (1977). *The structure of scientific theories* (2nd ed.). Urbana, IL: University of Illinois Press.

Thagard, P. (1988). *Computational philosophy of science.* Cambridge, MA: MIT Press/ Bradford Books.

Thagard, P. (1992). *Conceptual revolutions.* Princeton, NJ: Princeton University Press.

Thagard, P. (1999). *How scientists explain disease.* Princeton, NJ: Princeton University Press.

Thagard, P. (2000). *Coherence in thought and action.* Cambridge, MA: MIT Press.

Thagard, P. (2006a). *Hot thought: Mechanisms and applications of emotional cognition.* Cambridge, MA: MIT Press.

Thagard, P. (2006b). What is a medical theory? In R. Paton & L. A. McNamara (Eds.), *Multidisciplinary approaches to theory in medicine* (pp. 47–62). Amsterdam: Elsevier.

Thagard, P. (2007). Coherence, truth, and the development of scientific knowledge. *Philosophy of Science, 74*, 28–47.

Thagard, P. (2010). *The brain and the meaning of life.* Princeton, NJ: Princeton University Press.

Thompson, P. (1989). *The structure of biological theories.* New York: State University of New York Press.

van Fraassen, B. (1980). *The scientific image.* Oxford: Clarendon Press.

van Fraassen, B. C. (2002). *The empirical stance.* New Haven, CT: Yale University Press.

Chapter 3

Differences in Epistemic Practices among Scientists, Young Earth Creationists, Intelligent Design Creationists, and the Scientist-Creationists of Darwin's Era

Clark A. Chinn and Luke A. Buckland

Introduction

In this chapter, we investigate differences in the epistemic practices of scientists and creationists. We compare and contrast the epistemic practices of scientists with those of three different groups of creationists: (a) young Earth creationists, (b) intelligent design creationists, and (c) the scientists who were creationists in the middle to late 1800s, around the time when Darwin published *The Origin of Species* in 1859. We address seven dimensions of epistemic practices, including both cognitive and social practices.

Debate over Epistemic Differences between Science and Creationism

United States courts have consistently ruled that creationism, including its current embodiment as intelligent design (ID), is not science and therefore should not be taught in science class (Matsumura & Mead, 2007). These rulings have found that creationism fails to exhibit the critical epistemic features of science. A judge in a creationist challenge in Arkansas, drawing on testimony by philosopher of biology Michael Ruse and others, ruled that creationism failed to meet the following criteria for scientific knowledge (Laudon, 1982, p. 16; see also Ruse, 1982a, 1982b, 2005): (a) Science is guided by natural law. (b) Science is explanatory by reference to natural law. (c) Science is testable against the empirical world. (d) Science is tentative and fallible; that is, it is subject to change if overturned by a growing body of anomalous evidence. (e) Science is falsifiable.

However, the view that there are fundamental epistemic differences between science and creationism has come under attack from at least three sources. The first source is mainstream philosophy of science. The philosopher Larry Laudan (1982) argued that Ruse's five demarcation criteria constitute bad philosophy of science. Laudan argued that many parts of science lack natural laws; indeed, given that Darwin lacked a full explanation of the source of variation on which natural selection operated, Ruse's criteria would rule Darwinian theory as nonscientific during its earlier years. Laudan also argued that creationism can be readily modified to meet three other criteria (testability, fallibility, and tentativeness): "...it would be easy for a creationist to say the following: 'I will abandon my views if we find a living specimen of a species intermediate between man and apes.' It is, of course, extremely unlikely that such an individual will be discovered. But, in that statement the creationist would satisfy, in one fell swoop, all the formal requirements of testability, falsifiability, and revisability" (Laudan, 1982, p. 18).

Laudan argued that creationism should be rejected not because it is untestable but because it *is* testable, it has been tested, and it has completely failed the test. He stated: "if any doctrine in the history of science has ever been falsified, it is the set of claims associated with 'creation-science'" (Laudan, 1982, p. 17). On this view, creationism can be viewed as "discarded science, dead science" (Kitcher, 2007, p. 12) rather than nonscience.

A second source of objections to the claim that evolution differs from creationism in any fundamental epistemic way comes from some sociologists and philosophers of science who are radical constructivists. These researchers argue that scientific practices offer no special access to what is true. For example, Harry Collins (1981, p. 3) noted the rise of the viewpoint that "the natural world has a small or nonexistent role in the construction of scientific knowledge." Andy Pickering (1984, p. 413) concurred that "there is no obligation upon anyone framing a view of the world to take account of what twentieth-century science has to say." On this account, scientific theories advance or decline based not on evidence but on social dynamics, political power plays, and clever rhetorical maneuvers that vanquish opponents (e.g., Ashmore, 1993; Picart, 1994). The spirit of radical constructivism is revealed in the scare quotes in the title of Wright's (1979) article: "The 'success' of medicine and the 'failure' of astrology."

This general epistemological stance provides legitimacy to the claim that creationism, and especially its most recent embodiment intelligent design, are genuine scientific theories that have been unfairly suppressed by scientists for strictly political and ideological reasons. Constructivist philosopher Steve Fuller testified in favor of the scientific status of intelligent design at the 2005 Dover, Pennsylvania, trial that addressed whether intelligent design could be taught in science classes (*Kitzmiller* v. *Dover Area School District*, 2005, Day 15, AM Session, Part 1).

The third source of claims that there are no essential epistemological differences between science and creationism comes from creationists themselves, particularly from advocates of intelligent design theory. Intelligent design creationists officially eschew reference to the traditional biblical sources of creationist belief, claiming that their movement is fully scientific, on equal footing with any other branch of science, and clearly preferable to its evolutionary alternative (e.g., Dembski, 2003). Thus, for example, intelligent design theorist Michael Behe wrote, "The discovery [of the design principle] rivals those of Newton and Einstein, Lavoisier and Schrodinger, Pasteur and Darwin" (Behe, 1996, p. 233).

As the preceding discussion demonstrates, there are several lines of argument that question whether the epistemic practices of creationists are different in any important way from those of scientists. In this chapter we investigate this issue by comparing and contrasting the epistemic practices of three groups of creationists—including intelligent design creationists—with the practices of scientists.

It is important to note that instead of addressing the traditional question of whether *theories* should be counted as scientific or nonscientific, we evaluate whether the *epistemic practices* of the proponents of the theory should be counted as scientific or nonscientific. Our view is that the science is best viewed as a complex of epistemic practices rather than as a set of theories (Haack, 2003). These practices include the processes, methods, activities, and institutional arrangements implicated in the development and justification of theories and the attainment of consensus (Goldman, 2006; Haack, 2003). The epistemic practices are governed by norms that specify appropriate ways of developing explanations, justifying theories, gathering evidence, developing arguments, publishing work, and so on.

Consequently, to determine the scientific status of intelligent design and other forms of creationism, we must examine the practices of their advocates. On this view, a form of creationism might be scientific or not, depending on the epistemic practices of its proponents. The same epistemic practices can yield different theories at different times, depending on the background theories and evidence available at the time. Indeed, we aim to demonstrate that much of the creationism of the 19th century *was* scientific, in that its proponents tended to engage in epistemic practices common to scientists then and now, whereas the creationism of today is not scientific, because its proponents do not.

Therefore, throughout this chapter we examine the *actual epistemic practices* of the practitioners and advocates of each of the four groups under study. For example, we examine not whether a theory is testable but whether the proponents of the theory actually test it. If the proponents of two theories differ on whether they actually test their theories in practice, there are critical differences in epistemic practice, regardless of what might be done in principle.

Three Groups of Creationists

In this chapter, we compare the epistemic practices of scientists with the epistemic practices of three groups of creationists. Generally, the term *creationism* refers to the viewpoint that a divine agency has created the world and its constituents—including plant and animal species. Creationism in this general sense includes creationists of many different religious faiths, some utterly opposed to the findings of modern science, and some who consider science, including evolutionary science, to be fully consistent with their religious views (i.e., theistic evolutionists). In what follows, we limit our use of the term *creationist* to Christian creationists who regard evolutionary theory as false and who believe that the existence and character of biological species can only be explained in terms of the intentional action of a divine creator.

We use the term *young Earth creationists* (YECs) to refer to creationists who regard the biblical story of Genesis as literally true. Young Earth creationists believe that God created each species in an act of special creation and that the Earth is very young (typically about 6,000 years old). Young Earth creationists have been prominent in the United States throughout the 20th century (Numbers, 1995, 2006).

Intelligent design creationists (IDCs) advocate a form of creationism presented as a fully scientific alternative to evolutionary theory. According to intelligent design (ID) theory, biological species can be explained only in terms of the intentional actions of a powerful and intelligent (but otherwise unspecified) personal agency. Intelligent design creationists officially accept both the old age of the Earth (approximately 4.5 billion years) and "microevolution"—small-scale changes within a species over time, as when a species of bacteria develops resistance to penicillin. A few (e.g., Michael Behe) even accept the thesis of universal common ancestry. However, IDCs universally contend that neither natural selection nor any other wholly natural phenomenon can account for the biological systems and structures observed in nature, and that these can be explained only through the operation of intelligent, intentional, personal agency.

Advocates of ID strongly dispute any classification of their theory as creationist. They are officially "agnostic regarding the source of design" and have "no commitment to defending Genesis, the Bible or any other sacred text" (Center for Science & Culture, n.d.). Indeed, some ID supporters are not Christian. However, when the leaders of the ID movement write for their religious supporters, many of them reveal their creationist roots. For example, in his book *Intelligent Design: The Bridge Between Science and Theology*, William Dembski (1999), a leading ID proponent, has written, "Intelligent design is just the Logos theology of John's Gospel restated in the idiom of information theory" (p. 84). In the same book, Dembski (1999) asserted that "the conceptual soundness of [any scientific theory] can … only be located in Christ" (p. 210). Phillip Johnson, a founder of the ID movement, wrote about ID in explicitly biblical and creationist terms: "The Intelligent Design movement starts with the recognition that 'In the beginning was the Word,' and 'In the beginning God created'" (Johnson, 2000, p. 5). Intelligent design leader Stephen Meyer advocated that "scientists and philosophers might be most receptive to systems of thought that find their roots in Biblical theology" (Meyer, 1986, p. 42). These and many other writings directed at religious audiences reveal the Christian, creationist commitments of the most prominent ID supporters (see also Forrest, in press). These kinds of statements are indicative of practices that assume the truth of religious tenets and scriptures, affording them epistemic priority over the empirical and theoretical consensus of the scientific community, regardless of the evidence. These statements also reveal that for significant leaders in the ID movement, the intelligent designer is the Christian God.

The third group of creationists comprises the scientists of Darwin's era who were creationists. We call these scientists *nineteenth-century scientist-creationists* (NCSCs). Unlike contemporary YECs and IDCs, NCSCs were fully accepted as scientists by the broader scientific community, and prior to the publication of *The Origin of Species*, they included most of the prominent scientists of the day. Within one to two decades of the publication, however, a majority of the biologists had converted to some version of evolutionary theory (although many rejected natural selection as a major evolutionary force). We think that examining the practices of early creationists who were accepted members of the scientific community will help illuminate the differences between science and contemporary creationism.

Dimensions of Epistemic Practices

To guide our analysis we draw on the work of Chinn and Samarapungavan (2005), who have located epistemic practices within a framework that includes both cognitive and social practices. The framework is organized around four dimensions of knowledge systems and three dimensions of inquirers and their social systems (see Table 3.1).

According to Chinn and Samarapungavan (2005), a scientific knowledge system is composed of at least four distinguishable dimensions: (a) its aims, (b) its explanations (as theories, models, or other high-level structures), (c) its methods, and (d) its evidence. There are epistemic practices associated with each of these dimensions, and one can ask how creationists and scientists differ in their practices along each dimension. Several illustrative questions that can be asked about practices related to each dimension are included in Table 3.1.

The second cluster of three categories in the framework focuses on three dimensions of inquirers and their social systems. The three dimensions are (a) characteristics of inquirers, (b) the ways in which inquirers interact, and (c) the social institutions that inquirers form. Characteristics of inquirers include their cognitive capacities and dispositions. Interactions among inquirers include interactions within research groups and interactions among groups at conferences and in other settings. Social institutions include academic societies and journals. Epistemic practices are associated with each dimension, and

Table 3.1 Dimensions of Epistemological Practices in Science

Dimension of epistemic practice	Examples of questions that can be asked about epistemic practices
Knowledge system	
Core aims of inquiry	• What are the core aims or goals (e.g., truth, empirical adequacy)?
Explanations	• What are the favored explanatory patterns?
	• How do the practitioners integrate their explanations with the broader structure of scientific knowledge?
	• Should explanations incorporate only material processes, or should supernatural or other nonmaterial processes be allowed?
Methods	• Do inquirers expose theories to data as part of their method?
	• What are the preferred methods of inquiry?
Evidence	• How is evidence used to generate and justify claims?
	• To what extent do accepted theories attempt to explain all available evidence?
Inquirers and their social systems	
Characteristics of individual inquirers	• Do individual inquirers reason in a disinterested manner?
	• What do individuals believe about their cognitive capacities, and how do these beliefs affect their practices of inquiry?
Social interactions	• What kinds of intragroup and intergroup interactions do teams of inquirers engage in, and how do these interactions yield knowledge claims?
Institutions	• How do institutions facilitate or impede knowledge development?

we can again ask how the practices of scientists associated with each dimension differ from the practices of each of the three groups of creationists. Table 3.1 provides examples of questions about epistemic practices associated with each dimension.

The categories in Table 3.1 are intended to be merely heuristic in nature. Epistemic practices cannot be neatly located in a single dimension; there is overlap between and interactions among dimensions. Nonetheless, we think that the dimensions help us identify a broad range of important issues that might be sources of interesting differences between scientists and the three groups of creationists that we examine.

In the remainder of the chapter, we will address each of the dimensions of epistemic practices in Table 3.1. For each dimension, we will consider one or more issues regarding epistemic practices related to that dimension. For each issue, we will analyze the practices of scientists, YECs, IDCs, and NCSCs. Table 3.2, near the end of the chapter, summarizes our conclusions about each epistemic dimension.

A theme that will recur several times in this chapter is our hypothesis that contemporary creationists (YECs and IDCs) are forced into certain epistemic practices due to the overwhelming empirical support for evolutionary theory. As many biologists (e.g., Dobzhansky, 1973; Mayr, 2001; Sober, 2008) have documented, evolutionary theory has vast, converging support from nearly every subfield of biology. There is a corresponding lack of evidential support for any version of creationism (Young & Edis, 2004; Petto & Godfrey, 1998). We think that this overwhelming evidential advantage for evolutionary theory over creationism can help explain some of the epistemic practices demonstrated by contemporary creationists.

Core Aims of Inquiry

The first dimension of epistemic practices at the knowledge level (Table 3.1) concerns the adoption of core aims of inquiry. We contend that there are major differences in the core aims adopted by evolutionary theorists and other contemporary scientists, on the one hand, and by all three groups of creationists, on the other.

Although the aims of particular scientists vary according to their personal, political, and philosophical commitments, a shared aim of most scientists is the development of descriptive and explanatory accounts of empirical data. Scientists who are metaphysical realists regard truth as their ultimate aim (Boyd, 1991). For anti-realists the aim is empirical adequacy (van Fraassen, 1980), and for proponents of a model-theoretic account of science, the goal is verisimilitude between models and reality (Giere, 1988, 2004). Scientists have other aims (e.g., seeking simplicity, seeking prestige, advancing social agendas), but even many of those philosophers who have emphasized these other aims agree that the preeminent goal of scientific inquiry is providing an adequate account of empirical data (e.g., Longino, 1990, 2002; Solomon, 2001; Kitcher, 1993).

In contrast to scientists, YECs explicitly avow the core aim of attesting to the truth of the inerrant Bible and spreading this truth to others. Although this goal reflects an orientation towards what YECs regard as truth, it certainly does not aim at truth as the best explanation of empirical data. This is partly because YECs cannot follow the data to any truth other than what is expressed in the Bible. So, for example, members of the Creation Research Society must sign a statement of affirmation that "The Bible is the written Word of God, and because we believe it to be inspired throughout, all of its assertions are historically and scientifically true in all the original autographs ...." (cited in Ruse, 1982b).

Intelligent design creationists might appear at first to share with scientists the truth-oriented goal of explaining the available biological data. However, a number of writings by IDCs indicate that this is not the case. The "Wedge Document" is a treatise attributed to Phillip Johnson, one of the founders of the ID movement. In the Wedge Document, Johnson describes the primary goal of IDC as the overthrowing of materialistic science. Two specific goals are listed (Center for the Renewal of Science and Culture, n.d.): (1) "To defeat scientific materialism and its destructive moral, cultural and political legacies." (2) "To replace materialistic explanations with the theistic understanding that nature and human beings are created by God." We emphasize that the Wedge Document is not a manifesto of a fringe group of IDCs but is rather the document that has framed the ongoing practices of the Discovery Institute, the preeminent ID institution in the world (Forrest, 2001 & in press). The two goals concern the moral, political, and cultural transformation of society and the infusion of theistic belief into science; they therefore represent a significant departure from the core scientific goal of explaining empirical data. Moreover, as the statements of leading IDCs quoted earlier indicate, many IDCs treat their religious commitments as epistemically foundational. This means that the practices of theory-building and the weighing of empirical evidence cannot overturn the religious beliefs associated with these commitments.

Many NCSCs appear to have held combined goals of both truth and religious piety. Part of religious piety was upholding the role of God as creator and retaining the special exalted status of humans as created in God's image. Prior to the development of evolutionary theory, most NCSCs did not perceive a conflict between their religious goal of piety and their scientific goal of explaining natural phenomena. There was also no perceived divergence between the Bible and biology, as scientists generally considered William Paley's argument from design as decisive on empirical grounds (Ruse, 1999). According to Paley, organic structures such as eyes are so complex and so obviously well designed for their function that the best explanation for their existence requires inference to a designer; Paley considered it as inconceivable that such a finely built device as the eye could be the product of any cause other than intentional design. In his younger years, Darwin, too, found this argument to be compelling (Browne, 1995). Contemporary creationist versions of this argument have changed nothing essential.

After the publication of Darwin's theory, with its carefully marshaled evidence and detailed arguments, most scientists accepted common ancestry of species (Mayr, 1982). At this time, the goals of piety and empirical adequacy came into conflict. This sometimes surfaced in signs of individual turmoil about the extent to which Darwin's ideas should be accepted, as in the case of Charles Lyell, who vacillated in his acceptance of evolution (Ruse, 1999). Many scientists found evolution difficult to accept because they perceived it as lowering the special status of human beings (Ruse, 1999). Still, most biologists eventually resolved the conflict by adopting the theory (common ancestry) that they believed was better supported by the evidence, even though this theory contradicted certain of their prior religious commitments. Thus, for these scientists, the aim of aligning explanations with evidence seems to have been preeminent.

In summary, among the four groups we consider, we find that contemporary scientists and NCSCs adopt accounting for empirical data as their preeminent aim. To varying degrees, all three groups of creationists regard retaining a central role for God in creation as a preeminent or at least co-equal aim. For YECs and IDCs, this aim officially supersedes any aims of empirical adequacy.

Explanations

The second dimension of epistemic practices consists of the epistemic practices used to develop explanations. When constructing explanations, practitioners are guided not only by their core aims (e.g., accounting for empirical data, in the case of scientists), but also by the explanatory ideals that specify the ideal forms that explanations take. Practitioners' explanatory practices are guided by these explanatory ideals, which can be regarded as secondary aims.

We consider three epistemic practices related to this dimension. First, what are the practitioners' favored explanatory patterns? Second, how do the practitioners integrate their theory with the broader structure of scientific knowledge? Third, should explanations involve only naturalistic material entities and processes?

Favored Explanatory Patterns

Evolutionary theorists typically explain patterns of species distribution and biological variation using a core set of explanatory patterns involving common ancestry, natural selection, gene flow, and the generation of genetic variation through mutations and genetic drift (Dawkins, 1976; Kitcher, 1982, 1993; Mayr, 2001). The theory is advanced through the refinement and articulation of these patterns and processes, and their application to new and poorly understood questions. Contested areas of evolutionary theory and gaps in current explanations (such as relative role of natural selection versus genetic drift, determinants of rate of evolutionary change, and the balance between mutation and selection related to neutral theory, etc.) are regarded by biologists as ripe for further research and for more detailed articulation and revision of the core explanatory patterns. Thus, scientists also favor efforts to increase the detail of their explanations.

Young Earth creationists link their explanations directly to the story of Genesis. On their view, the existence of species, their geographic distributions, and their functional adaptations are to be explained by separate acts of special creation by a supernatural deity; geological events are to be explained by the six days of creation and Noah's flood (Witham, 2002). The practice of YECs reveals a systematic failure to meet the scientific explanatory ideal of developing detailed explanations. They assert that particular biological phenomena (such as the complex structures of the eye) are (a) not explained by the theory of evolution and (b) in principle not explicable through natural means. Instead, intentional design by a divine agency (a process which cannot be articulated in more detail than is provided by the Bible) is taken as the default explanation for the phenomenon (Denton, 1985; Morris & Parker, 1987).

The theoretical explanations offered by IDCs conform to the general pattern of the YECs'. They extend the YECs' arguments about macroscopic bodily systems such as eyes to microbiological systems such as the bacterial flagellum. In a way exactly analogous to the traditional YEC argument that only God's intervention could explain the structure and formation of the vertebrate eye, ID proponent Michael Behe has argued that only an intelligent designer can account for what he claims to be the "irreducible complexity" of a flagellum (Behe, 1996). In contrast to YECs' unequivocal identification of the designer with the Christian deity, IDCs officially make no claims about the nature, characteristics, or intentions of the designer or the design process.

The avoidance of specific hypotheses sharply distinguishes the explanatory practices of IDCs from those of scientists. Unlike scientists, IDCs do not attempt to specify the processes that produce observed phenomena. For example, while inferring the operation of an intelligent agent from the structure of the eye, IDCs do not attempt to develop explanations to account for the multitude of alternate eye designs, the many varied imperfections of eye design, the existence of useless eyes in cave-dwelling organisms, and so on. Similarly, they say nothing about the intentions and processes that the designer might follow to yield the observed fossil distribution or the geographic distribution of species. While insisting that the existence of an intelligent designer is revealed in the structure and kinds of biological systems, IDCs decline to spell out the processes by which the designer might have produced the phenomena observed by biologists; Behe asserts in his *Darwin's Black Box* that "The question of the identity of the designer will simply be ignored by science" (Behe, 1996, p. 251). This stance stands in very stark contrast with scientists' treatment of design hypotheses in any other domain. For example, forensic evidence suggesting that a deadly explosion was an intentional, criminal act naturally leads to further inferences about who perpetrated the crime and how they may have accomplished it. Also, evidence that scientists had detected electromagnetic signals from intelligent life elsewhere in the universe would certainly encourage the development and testing of further hypotheses about the nature and identity of the purportedly intelligent agency. The IDCs' systematic failure to develop and test hypotheses about the sources and methods of design therefore constitutes a practice that diverges very strongly from that of scientists.

Although unwilling to provide specific explanations of their own, IDCs demand that evolutionary theorists provide detailed, evidence-based accounts for any and all biological phenomena. When evolutionary theorists do provide such accounts, IDCs are typically unsatisfied, making extravagant explanatory demands of evolutionary theory to which their own accounts appear immune. For instance, the prominent IDC advocate Phillip Johnson denies that *Diarthrognathus* (a fossil species with a double-jaw joint) presents any significant support for the Darwinian account of the transition from reptiles to mammals because "there are many important features by which mammals differ from reptiles besides the jaw and ear bones, including the all-important reproductive systems" (Johnson, 1993, p. 76). To require that every internal change be documented through the fossil record places unrealistic demands on evolutionary biologists, given the established fact that most body systems (e.g., the reproductive) do not fossilize well. Intelligent design creationists thus demand impossibly detailed explanations from evolutionists but exempt their own theory from any such requirement. This is a stark epistemic asymmetry at the heart of modern creationism.

In contrast to YECs and IDCs, scientists are in the business of trying to fill gaps in knowledge with new explanations as well as augmenting old explanations with more detailed and well-evidenced alternatives (Kuhn, 1962; Kitcher, 1993). Scientists typically do not declare that an explanatory gap is unfillable, let alone that the gap should be therefore explained in terms of a supernatural or intelligent cause that cannot be subject to further theoretical articulation.

The insistence of IDCs that the actions of the designer are not open to explication stands in sharp contrast to the views of at least some NCSCs. The geologist Charles Lyell, for example, believed that God created species according to law-like regularities, although he did not specify what these regularities were (Ruse, 1999). The biologist Richard Owen attempted to formulate principles by which similarities in (divinely designed) anatomical structure could be explained (Rupke, 1994). The biologist Louis Agassiz explained observed fossil patterns by positing that God eradicated earlier eras' species in repeated acts of mass extinctions, each followed by a new round of creation (Lurie, 1988). A number of NCSCs believed that God acted in the geological, physical, and biological realms through natural law, though the natural laws of biology had yet to be discovered (Ruse, 1999).

Thus, although NCSCs shared with modern YECs and IDCs a belief that an intelligent being was the cause of speciation, at least some of them shared with Darwin and modern evolutionists a belief that science could provide detailed, regularized explanations for speciation, even if this meant describing regularities through which divine creation was effected. In contrast to YECs and IDCs, many NCSCs of Darwin's era were committed to providing positive theoretical explanations to account for as wide a range of biological phenomena as possible.

Compatibility with Other Theories

A second epistemic practice of modern science is that scientists develop new explanations that are compatible with other, well-established theoretical knowledge. Indeed, the network of links among different scientific theories (in terms of common explanatory patterns, shared methodologies, interdisciplinary citations, etc.) is one of the most impressive features of modern science (e.g., Haack, 2003; Kitcher, 1993). In terms of this practice, modern evolutionary theory is very well integrated with current theories of biology, geology, physics, and cosmology. For example, evolutionary theory is consistent with the constraints independently generated by geological theories (of how geological structures form and about the age of those formations). Similarly, evolutionary theory is fully consistent with physical theories of radioactive decay that are used to determine ages of fossils and rocks.

In sharp contrast to scientists, YECs must reject large swathes of modern science as strongly incompatible with the young age of the Earth. Indeed, they must throw out almost all scientific theory that is explicitly or implicitly committed to a universe older than 6,000 years. This includes a rejection of radiometric dating techniques, and their associated physics and chemistry, most of modern geology, astronomy, and astrophysics, much of archeology, anthropology, and history, much of genetics, and so on. Integrating young Earth creationism into the larger network of science would require throwing out the large majority of accepted scientific theory, effectively wrecking the coherence and unification of the larger body of knowledge.

In contrast to YECs, IDCs accept the old age of the Earth and the many disciplines that are committed to it. Intelligent design creationism is designed so as to be consistent with the non-biological disciplines, and even with large areas of biology. Intelligent design creationists typically accept what they call Darwinian "microevolution" (i.e., small-scale changes within species due to natural selection). However, even though intended to be compatible with the broader tapestry of science, ID creationism does exhibit notable inconsistencies with extra-biological disciplines. For example, critics of prominent ID theorist William Dembski have argued that his version of ID theory depends crucially on a view of entropy that scientists have shown to be at odds with current theories of thermodynamics (Stenger, 1998). Moreover, Dembski has relied on flawed statistical and probabilistic procedures (Shallit, 2002; Wolpert, 2003; Fitelson, Stephens, & Sober, 1999).

Of course, there are many instances in which successful scientific theories that were once inconsistent with the findings of allied scientific disciplines were subsequently vindicated. For example, in the post-*Origin* years, the theory of evolution by natural selection was at odds with the geophysics of the day (Ruse, 1999). Lord Kelvin concluded on the basis of calculations of the rate of cooling of the Earth that the Earth was around 100 million years old—not old enough for the slow process of natural selection to engender the full panoply of species. Only later, with the discovery of radioactivity as an additional source of heat, was the age of the Earth pushed back to billions of years. This example illustrates that successful theories often convert initial conceptual difficulties to later conceptual successes.

Creationists often argue that they should be accorded the same opportunity to solve their conceptual problems (Dembski, 1998). However, creationism has already been granted several centuries of financial and intellectual support. Even with access to the methods and tools of contemporary science, creationism still fails to present a detailed positive account of the range of available evidence (Kitcher, 2007), and creationists are no closer to a theory of design than they were two centuries ago. The complete failure of many previous attempts to resurrect design as a successful scientific explanation provides no reasonable grounds for hope for any future success.

Methodological Naturalism

Although we have argued that ID is compatible with many branches of science, there is a significant sense in which IDCs are at odds with every scientific discipline. As we noted earlier, the Wedge Document lays out the goals and strategies of the ID movement, indicating that the central aim of the overall ID movement is "nothing less than the overthrow of materialism" (cited in Forrest & Gross, 2004, p. 30). Thus, despite the claims of some IDCs to be in congruence with contemporary non-biological science, their own account of their practice as primarily a battle against the naturalistic explanations of modern science appears to diverge very strongly from the practice of the wider scientific community.

Young Earth creationists share this rejection of materialistic explanations. In the words of prominent YEC website *Answers in Genesis*, "we need to point out what's wrong with such anti-God philosophies as evolution, humanism, materialism, naturalism, and long-age ideas" (McKeever, 2008). Young Earth creationists Henry Morris and Gary Parker (1987) similarly wrote, "If materialist philosophy is confused with science, the search for truth is sharply limited" (p. 182).

In contrast to IDCs and YECs, an explanatory ideal of contemporary scientists is that explanations must employ material mechanisms and avoid non-material causes such as divine intervention or vital forces (Ruse, 1982a; Forrest, in press). Restricting the search for explanations to natural (as opposed to supernatural or other non-material) explanations is known as *methodological naturalism*. Methodological naturalism is best considered not as a method but as an explanatory ideal espoused by contemporary scientists.

Although it is beyond the scope of this chapter to argue this in detail, we contend that methodological naturalism has gained ascendancy because of its great success as an explanatory strategy across many scientific disciplines (Kitcher, 1993). In earlier periods of science, non-material explanations were viewed by scientists as legitimate. But in field after field, non-material explanations have given way based on a strong preponderance of empirical evidence favoring material explanations. Material evolutionary explanations provide a superior explanation of biological evidence than divine creationism (Sober, 2008). Vitalistic explanations of biological functioning were abandoned in favor of more successful biochemical explanations of cell and body function (Mayr, 1982). Explanations of abnormal human behavior in terms of demonic possession have been replaced by naturalistic theories of mental illness. Scientific interest in the occult dissipated when phenomena could not be replicated and highly touted occult phenomena were proved to be fraudulent (Brandon, 1983). The history of science shows that there has been no *a priori* commitment by scientists to naturalistic, material explanations. Rather, it is the widespread empirical success of methodological naturalism that has led to the abandonment of the theistic, vitalistic, and occult explanations that were fully acceptable to scientists in earlier periods.

Our view therefore accords with the IDCs' claim that there is nothing necessarily unscientific about the inference to design. We thus agree with the ID movement that it is in principle possible that early scientists *might* have discovered evidence that life, human life, or even the character of physical law is the product of intelligent design. Nevertheless, the consensus among scientists is that the evidence overwhelmingly supports an evolutionary explanation over that of design, and that the historical success of methodological naturalism is grounds for continuing to pursue the naturalist strategy. The systematic failure to account for this evidence is thus a strikingly unscientific feature of the practice of both YECs and IDCs.

Like YECs and IDCs, NCSCs also advanced a non-materialistic explanation of the origin of species. However, these scientists worked before the development of strong evidence supporting the current scientific consensus that material explanations are successful at explaining observations of the natural world. Creationism and vitalism were both vibrant scientific theories in the 1800s (Mayr, 1982). Thus, although NCSCs appear to have shared in many of the beliefs of modern IDCs, they did so at a time when non-naturalistic explanations were considered an acceptable part of scientific practice. We therefore argue that the practice of these NSCSs was fully scientific, on the grounds that a practice can be considered scientific at one period and unscientific in another, as determined by the background body of theory, evidence, and methodology. And, with the increased empirical success of methodological naturalism, the epistemic norms governing acceptable scientific practice themselves changed to include a reliance on materialistic explanations as an explanatory ideal.

In summary, we have concluded that scientists differ sharply from YECs and IDCs on three explanatory ideals. First, scientists but not YECs or IDCs seek naturalistic, material explanations due to the track record of empirical success afforded by such explanations. Second, scientists strive to develop increasingly detailed explanations; YECs and IDCs resist providing any such detailed explanations themselves but demand that evolutionary biologists provide them. Many NCSCs favored detailed explanations, but—consistent with the broader scientific knowledge of the time—did not favor purely material explanations. Third, on the explanatory ideal of seeking consistency with other scientific theories, scientists and NCSCs seek broad consistency, whereas YECs do not. Intelligent design creationists aim to be consistent with the larger tapestry of scientific knowledge, but, as we noted, their practice is not consistent with the methodological naturalism of modern scientists.

Methods

Until this point, we have examined epistemic practices related to aims and explanatory ideas. In this section, we discuss a third set of epistemic practices at the knowledge level (Table 3.1): *methods* of investigation. We discuss two questions about epistemic practices related to method. First, do the theorists in each group expose their theories to data? Second, what do the theorists in each group regard as appropriate scientific methods?

Exposing Theories to Data

A hallmark of scientific practice is that scientists expose theories to data. Exposing theories to data entails both that researchers actively gather data and that the data gathered could serve to disconfirm their theoretically-generated expectations. This does not mean that scientists act as naïve Popperian falsificationists; in reality, scientists do not typically abandon their favored explanations in response to one or even several disconfirming studies (Chinn & Brewer, 1993; Lakatos, 1970). However, accumulating anomalies eventually lead to theory change (Kuhn, 1962; Donovan, Laudan, & Laudan, 1998), and scientists typically do gather data that have the potential to falsify their theories. For example, evolutionary biologists made major changes to their theories in the early 20th century, as new data on evolutionary processes were provided by geneticists, population ecologists, and paleontologists (Mayr, 1982). Many scientists who had denied some part of evolutionary theory (e.g., the efficacy of natural selection) changed their minds and adopted what has become known as the modern synthesis (Mayr, 1982).

Despite the existence of the Creationist Research Institute, the Discovery Institute, and other well-funded institutions devoted to the promotion of "creationist science," creationists (including both YECs and IDCs) have launched no new lines of research or research programs (Forrest & Gross, 2004; J. Lynch, 2008, 2009). Creationism does make a variety of strong predictions which could be investigated and which, if confirmed, would present serious empirical problems for evolutionary theory (Laudan, 1982). The difficulty for creationists is that their predictions are so clearly contradicted by the already-existing evidence. For example, YECs predict a distribution of fossils that would be explicable in terms of Noah's flood, a prediction that is completely at odds with the actual fossil evidence. Intelligent design creationists predict that cellular structures have irreducible complexity, meaning that no functions will be found for the molecular subcomponents of structures such as flagella—a core IDC prediction that has been disconfirmed (Shanks & Joplin, 1999; Miller, 2004). Perhaps because their predictions are already refuted by a large body of evidence, creationists do not engage in the regular and extensive fossil hunting, genetic analyses, microbiological experiments, biogeographic studies, or many other lines of research that could support or contradict their position (Forrest & Gross, 2004). Michael Behe, the most prominent IDC biologist, stated at the 2005 Dover ID trial that he did not carry out tests of ID theory, because "I myself would prefer to spend time in what I would consider to be more fruitful endeavors" (*Kitzmiller* v. *Dover Area School District*, 2005, Day 12, PM Session, Part 1). Other ID supporters have similarly failed to publish either in established scientific journals or even in their own journal; an academic journal set up to publish ID research in 2002 had ceased publishing by 2005 after a mere 10 issues (as shown on September 30, 2010 at www.iscid.org/pcid.php).

It appears to us that NCSCs varied in the extent to which they exposed their theories to data. Many of the arguments made by NCSCs were over the interpretation of already-known data. There were, however, deliberate attempts to test the competing theories. For example, Galton carried out blood transfusion experiments to test Darwin's (incorrect) pangenesis theory of heredity (Ruse, 1999). Louis Agassiz sought to collect samples of all native fish from all of the world's river systems to gather evidence that would undermine evolutionary theory (Lurie, 1988). Richard Owen attempted to counter evolutionary theory by carrying out detailed comparisons of the skeletons of primates with the skeletons of humans (Rupke, 1994). He also procured a just-discovered archaeopteryx fossil in 1862 to study its implications for evolution and creationism (Chambers, 2002). Overall, although the extent to which NCSCs tested their ideas may have been less than that of contemporary scientists, NCSCs did conduct a steady stream of relevant research.

Preferred Methods

A second epistemic practice pertaining to methods is the nature of the preferred methods. Scientists collectively employ a very wide array of methods. No one method is universal, and methodological pluralism characterizes the field of biology as a whole. In particular, evolutionary biologists use a diverse array of methods to investigate evolutionary issues. Paleontologists analyze the morphology of fossils. Geneticists compare DNA sequences of different species. Experimentalists examine generational changes in fruit flies in response to environmental variation. Both experimentation and abductive reasoning about the historical causes of events are legitimate forms of scientific inquiry, and both are actively pursued by evolutionary researchers.

The primary method that YECs employ to determine what they believe to be true about the world is to consult the Bible. We have already noted that members of the Creation Research Society must swear upon membership that the sole arbiter of truth is the Bible. The Bible is in fact considered to be the wellspring of all true scientific knowledge. For example, according to the founder of a prominent creationist organization, *Answers in Genesis*, "There is no mystery surrounding dinosaurs if you accept the Bible's totally different account of dinosaur history" (Ham, 2007).

Young Earth creationists have repeatedly pressed for a methodological demarcation between "experimental" research (involving actual manipulation of variables) and "historical" or "forensic" research (involving inference about the past, such as inferences about geological strata or fossils). Young Earth creationists view experimental methods as legitimately scientific, but "have a very different perspective when it comes to forensic science (origins, prehistory)" (Schafersman, 2008; see also Numbers, 2006). The argument seems to be that only experimental research allows predictions and tests of predictions. Scientists reject this distinction, noting that scientists can make predictions about data that are unknown to them, even if the data were produced by past events. For example, scientists can predict that certain kinds of fossils will be found in previously unexplored fossil beds in Cretaceous sediments, even though the fossils were formed millions of years ago.

Although IDCs do not, in principle, exclude any widely accepted form of scientific research, the methodology that IDCs actually use in practice is an extremely limited mode of investigation with little or no actual data gathering. Intelligent Design Creationists' main method, common to all modern creationists, is to identify biological structures and systems (e.g., the flagellum, the immune system, the eye, etc.) that allegedly could not have arisen by naturalistic evolutionary processes. An "irreducible complexity" is ascribed whenever a structure is composed of multiple integrated components such that, were any particular component missing, the structure would appear unable to fulfill its prior biological function. From this IDCs conclude that the structure could not have functional ancestral intermediates, and thus could not evolve via a gradualist evolutionary process. In applying this method, IDCs perform no experiments to verify their claims regarding missing structures, nor do they extensively search the literature for alternate possible functions, nor do they propose and test hypotheses regarding potential alternatives. Their method instead relies very heavily on their own intuitions about what seems to be too complex to explain. In the case of William Dembski's application of the method, the intuitions are accompanied by arcane mathematical calculations, described by Shallit (2002) as "pseudo-mathematics" (p. 93).

The general preferred methods of NCSCs overlapped a great deal with those of current evolutionary theorists. These scientists did not interpret the

Bible literally, nor did they look to the Bible as a source of scientific knowledge (Ruse, 1999). They did not subscribe to the contemporary YEC view that historical investigations have inherently less scientific legitimacy than other branches of research; indeed, many of them engaged in productive historical research in geology. Although the NCSCs did subscribe to arguments that were very similar to those of modern creationists regarding the character of complex structures, they did not focus their argumentation on the issue of complexity alone. They rather engaged with evolutionists on the full range of available data, and most eventually adopted a belief in common ancestry on the basis of the data and arguments emerging from these investigations (Ruse, 1999).

In summary, contemporary scientists use a plethora of methods to expose their theories to data, and NCSCs generally did the same. Young Earth creationists and IDCs do not collect data to test their theories and rely on identifying biological structures they believe to be too complex to explain through evolution. Young Earth creationists additionally disallow historical forms of research.

Empirical Evidence

The fourth dimension of epistemic practice at the knowledge level (Table 3.1) focuses on the ways in which empirical evidence is used (if at all) to generate and justify theories. On this epistemic dimension, we think there are critical differences between both groups of contemporary creationists, on the one hand, and both groups of scientists, on the other.

In science, evolutionary theory provides a unifying framework which accounts for disparate data in many, many arenas of biology. Darwin's *The Origin of Species* noted the power of evolutionary theory to account for observations of adaptation and deficiency, of various forms of variation and biogeographical distribution, the fossil record, morphology and comparative anatomy, embryology, and so on. These independent lines of evidence have, since Darwin's time, been multiplied, as the modern evolutionary synthesis propounded by biologists including Theodosius Dobzhansky and Ernst Mayr unified disparate bodies of evidence (including Mendelian and population genetics, biogeography, ecology, morphology, cytology, and systematics) under evolutionary theory in the 1930s and 1940s (Mayr, 1982; Smocovitis, 1996). For example, George Gaylord Simpson brought paleontology fully within the evolutionary account, and G. Ledyard Stebbins integrated a variety of findings from botany within evolutionary theory (Mayr, 1982). Evolutionary theory has continued to expand the diverse lines of evidence that it accounts for (Sober, 2008).

With such broad and deep support by multiply-convergent data, it would certainly be irrational for scientists to respond to occasional anomalies, challenges, and explanatory gaps by giving up on the theory in favor of either a biblical alternative or the bare hypothesis of intelligent design. Nonetheless, evolutionary researchers have responded to claimed anomalies advanced by YECs and IDCs. For example, Miller (2004; see also Shanks & Joplin, 1999) has shown—contrary to Behe's claims that the structure of the flagellum is irreducibly complex—that smaller components of the flagellum exist functionally in other species, often with other functions. Contrary to the popular creationist claim that the eye is irreducibly complex, evolutionary biologists have provided evidence for many steps in the repeated evolution of eyes and have shown the functional benefits of proto-eyes and eyes in earlier stages of development (Gregory, 2008). Further, the history of paleontology can be read as a history of identifying intermediate species that creationists claimed did not and could not exist. Nearly every year brings stunning new discoveries of intermediate forms.

The history of evolutionary theory has exhibited great responsiveness to data. For example, during the years of the evolutionary synthesis in the 1930s and 1940s, many biologists were rapidly persuaded by new evidence that there was a great deal more genetic variation within species than had been previously believed (Mayr, 1982). Similarly, the Lamarckian view—still popular in the 1930s—that acquired characteristics could be inherited was abandoned fairly quickly when a body of contrary evidence appeared (Mayr, 1982). Today there remains active debate, disagreement, and the occasional changing of minds within the communities engaged in evolutionary research. Recent research has, for example, persuaded some evolutionary theorists of the importance of random genetic drift as a mechanism of speciation, separate from natural or sexual selection (Mayr, 2001). Evolutionary scientists thus actively gather many different kinds of empirical data which they use to guide and constrain theory revision (Kitcher, 2007).

We conjecture that many of the reasoning and rhetorical strategies chosen by YECs and IDCs result from the overwhelming evidentiary support for evolutionary theory over the creationist alternatives. When the evidence is so overwhelming arrayed against a position, the moves available to its proponents are limited, inviting recourse to sophistry, obfuscation, and misrepresentation. Thus, the "flood geology" promulgated by YECs makes many claims that ignore or radically reinterpret a vast array of data. For instance, the claim that the pattern of drowning from Noah's flood accounts for the stratification of species in the fossil record is dramatically inconsistent with fossil distributions worldwide.

In a similar way, in IDCs' arguments about microbiological structure, they rampantly ignore multiple lines of evidence. For example, Behe has claimed that "the scientific literature has no answers to the question of the origin of the immune system" (1996, p. 138), that "*no one on earth has the vaguest idea how the coagulation cascade came to be*" (1996, p. 97, italics in original), and even that "no publication in the scientific literature … describes how molecular evolution of any real, complex, biochemical system either did occur or even might have occurred" (1996, p. 185). These claims ignore a large body of work on the precursors to current clotting and immune systems, on the natural origin of complex biochemical and metabolic systems such as the Krebs cascade, and on the computational and biochemical modeling of self-organizing systems (Kauffman, 1993; Ussery, 2004; Weber & Depew, 2004). There are thousands of articles in PubMed on "evolution and immunology," over 2,000 of which were already published even when Behe wrote the 1996 book quoted above (Ussery, 2004, p. 55).

In addition to ignoring the mass of data for evolutionary theory, creationists very often fail to backtrack when their data or lines of reasoning are shown to be incorrect. Instead, they continue to repeat their errors. Young Earth creationists have, for example, continued to promote the juxtaposition of dinosaur tracks and human footprints in the Paluxy River bed in Texas, despite the fact that these have been shown to be a hoax (Miller, 1984). Arguments that evolution is "just a theory," "completely random," "incompatible with the laws of thermodynamics," "disproven by the fossil record," and "contradicted by the fact of altruism" (among *many* others) all have a long history, and they spring up anew regardless of how many times their many failings are pointed out (Kitcher, 1982). The perseverance of discredited claims has become such a problem that a theme has arisen within creationism itself which tries to limit the proliferation and use of old and definitively discredited arguments and claims, in an attempt to resuscitate the intellectual respectability of creationism (e.g., Ham, 2009; Sarfati, n.d.).

Intelligent design creationists exhibit a similar pattern. Thus, for example, although Dembski produces a steady stream of (mostly popular) writings, he has consistently failed to address what many regard as the key criticisms of his account—for example, those of Elsberry and Shallit (2004), who showed that his "explanatory filter" failed to distinguish apparent from actual "complex specified information" and failed to avoid false positives, and that his use of "No Free Lunch" theorems involved multiple unjustified assumptions about uniformity. At the Dover trial, when Behe was presented with a stack of books and journals contradicting his claim that there is no published literature on the evolution of the immune system, Behe simply "did not budge" (Weiss, 2005, p. 3).

We think that the strategy of ignoring large masses of evidence is a key epistemic move that differentiates scientists from contemporary creationists. Many of the other epistemic deficiencies may flow from this core difference. For example, even dim awareness of the array of evidence against creationism (e.g., the failure to find human remains mixed with fossils in any Paleozoic or Mesozoic strata ever explored) might make a creationist funding agency wary of spending millions of dollars quarrying a Mesozoic fossil bed to find the first such human remains. This would also explain creationism's predilection for fighting its battles in the media and public domains, rather than in science journals. Critical reviewers can be expected to demand that ignored data be taken into consideration; journalists and the public are typically ignorant of the relevant evidence, and can thus be counted on never to make such demands. Indeed, to laypersons and non-biologist scientists who are unaware both of the evidence for evolutionary theory and of the complex genetic and developmental mechanisms that can effect changes in organisms, public appeals to the argument from design can be very effective.

We have argued that evolutionary theorists have shown themselves to be responsive to converging lines of empirical evidence, whereas both YECs and IDCs have had to actively ignore an enormous body of empirical evidence. We think that NCSCs were more like evolutionary scientists—constrained by data in a way that is not true of current creationists. Most biologist NCSCs adopted a belief in common ancestry within a decade or two of the publication of Darwin's *Origin* (Ruse, 1999). While the relative importance of natural selection remained controversial, this seems reasonable, given that the evidence for natural selection as the main mechanism of evolution was much weaker than the evidence for common ancestry (Mayr, 1982). Examination of the reactions of individual 19th century scientists sometimes shows individuals adopting components of evolutionary theory with great reluctance, but unable to come to other conclusions because of the weight of evidence. For example, Lyell was extremely uncomfortable with abandoning the special status of humans, but he felt compelled by the evidence of the geographical distribution of species to adopt many elements of Darwin's theory (Wilson, 1970). Even Richard Owen, lampooned by history as making himself look foolish in fighting evolution, appears to have adopted some components of Darwin's theory (Rupke, 1994).

Characteristics of Inquirers

So far, we have examined four dimensions of epistemic practices at the knowledge level along which evolutionary scientists and creationists differ: core aims, explanatory ideals, methods, and the use of evidence. Next we turn to the three dimensions of epistemic practices related to characteristics of human inquirers and the social systems that inquirers form. The three dimensions of epistemic practices we discuss are practices related to the characteristics of individual inquirers, practices of social groups, and practices of institutions (see Table 3.1).

In this section, we examine questions about epistemic practices that are located largely at the level of individual inquirers. First, to what extent do individuals reason in a disinterested manner? Second, what do individuals believe about their cognitive capacities, and how do these beliefs affect their practices of inquiry?

Disinterestedness

A traditional view of science is that scientists pursue inquiry in accordance with the norm of disinterestedness (Merton, 1942). This would mean that scientists generally avoid allowing personal considerations (such as friendships, personal antipathies, or excessive adherence to prior theories) to influence their judgments about what is true, valid, or supported by the evidence.

Among both 19th century evolutionists and NCSCs, this norm was far from ascendant. Over a period of many years, prior to publication of *The Origin of Species*, Darwin carefully nurtured friendships with important scientists, aiming to build some support for his ideas in advance of publishing them (Browne, 1995, 2002; Ruse, 1999). In his letters, Darwin appealed to the claims of friendships, not just to the evidential claims of a superior theory (Browne, 1995, 2002). Further, both evolutionists and NCSCs seem to have been influenced by personal animus in the post-*Origin* debates. Darwin's tenacious defender Thomas Huxley developed a very personal feud with the anatomist Richard Owen, and it appears that some of Owen's public opposition to evolution may have stemmed from this animus (Ruse, 1999). In addition, scientists believed that violations of the norms of gentlemanly behavior were sufficient grounds for dismissing ideas—in clear contradiction to the supposed norm of disinterestedness. The French biologist Mivart published the best synthesis of anti-Darwinian arguments in 1870, but his impact was lessened because he committed the ungentlemanly social blunder of insulting one of Darwin's sons, which reduced his credibility with his fellow scientists (Gruber, 1960; Ruse, 1999).

Scientists are therefore not immune from the influence of personal interests. However, despite the clear influence of personal interests, most NCSCs did over a period of years either abandon their core creationist beliefs or find a way to reconcile their theistic commitments with the facts of evolution. They were sufficiently disinterested to be able to eventually abandon the theory to which they were initially committed. In contrast, contemporary YECs and many IDC leaders expressly disavow any possibility of disinterested appraisal of evidence through statements of their *a priori* commitment to creationism. As ID proponent Jonathan Wells (1996) wrote, quoting John Henry Newman, "Christians believe in design because they believe in God, not in a God because they see design.... [T]heir belief in God then leads them to the conclusion that living things are designed" (Forrest, in press). This is an explicit and complete disavowal of the norm of disinterestedness, or indeed of any need to examine evidence at all.

Beliefs about Human Cognitive Capacities and Consequences for Practices of Inquiry

Scientists believe that humans are capable of arriving at knowledge of the world through their sensory interactions with the world. At the same time, scientists are well aware of human capacity for falling into error. Consequently, they deploy a broad variety of techniques to make their findings more trustworthy, including many different techniques to guard against biased observations and inferences (e.g., masked and automated observation, inferential statistics) (Haack, 2003). Scientists also conduct systemic investigations directed at the effects of methodological variations in order to uncover possible sources of error (Mayo, 1996). They thus seek actively to identify and eliminate sources of methodological error (Mayo, 1996).

Young Earth creationists sometimes express a profound distrust of the human capacity to arrive at accurate knowledge of the world. Their distrust arises from the doctrine that humans have fallen from grace, and as fallen, sinful creatures, their cognitive capabilities to know the world are severely and incorrigibly compromised. As Robert E. Kofahl put it: "The Fall resulted in the corruption and ruin of every human capacity and attribute, including his intellect, affections, moral capacity and will" (Kofahl, 2008). On this view human reason cannot attain knowledge, which can only be attained through the word of God as revealed in the scriptures.

In one respect, by accepting much of the findings of modern science, IDCs also accept that humans have the capacity to arrive at least at some limited forms of knowledge (although knowledge of the details of the designer and the design process is ruled as unattainable). In another respect, it appears to us that IDCs hold a heavily overconfident view of their own cognitive capabilities. The argument for design rests on the assumption that personal intuitions about which biological structures are irreducibly complex or minimally functional are a reliable guide to the truth. It seems that if IDCs cannot personally envision a way in which complex function could arise naturally, then they conclude that the complexity cannot have arisen naturally (see Dawkins, 1996). This argument from ignorance seems to us to be an argument based on personal hubris.

Like contemporary scientists, many NCSCs believed that humans had the cognitive capacity to understand the laws of nature. Many believed that God had designed the world to run according to laws that humans were capable of discovering (Ruse, 1999). Many who believed in design believed that design might proceed in a law-like way, which scientists could comprehend.

In summary, scientists and all three groups of creationists fall short of the norm of perfect disinterestedness. But scientists do display enough disinterestedness to sometimes abandon favored beliefs. Young Earth creationists explicitly reject the disinterested evaluation of evidence in their non-negotiable commitment to creationism. Intelligent design creationists profess to be engaged in the disinterested examination of evidence, but their writings for religious audiences frequently indicate that their support of ID follows from their non-negotiable religious commitments. Contemporary scientists and NCSCs both act in accordance with a belief that humans can understand nature through their senses, albeit with many techniques used to minimize bias and error. In contrast, YECs' profound distrust of human capacities means that truth can be learned only through revelation. Intelligent design creationists seem to have an overconfident trust in their intuitions about what materialistic science will be unable to explain, and they use no independent checks to guard against bias in these intuitions.

Social Interactions

The second dimension of epistemic practices related to inquirers concerns the practices by which individuals interact with each other. The question is how interactions within and between research teams (e.g., discussions at lab group meetings, informal conversations in hallways or at conferences, or interactions in formal panels at conferences) affect knowledge creation.

With respect to science, a growing body of historical, philosophical, anthropological, sociological, and psychological research has documented social interactions that promote or impede the development of scientific knowledge (e.g., Dunbar, 1993; Kitcher, 1993; M. Lynch, 1985; Knorr-Cetina, 1999). For example, Dunbar (1993) has found that knowledge generation is enhanced when scientists working in research teams treat anomalous empirical results seriously as possible indicators of new findings, rather than as merely signaling methodological errors. These studies have documented the importance of particular research team interactions in the generation and validation of scientific knowledge.

In contrast to scientists, contemporary creationists (both YECs and IDCs) have not, as we have discussed, engaged in original research. Thus, it is not possible for researchers to analyze their social interactions in research teams. However, examination of YEC practices reveals the preeminence of a form of discourse common on cable news but relatively rare in contemporary science: eristic debate (cf. Tannen, 1998; Walton, 1996). Eristic debate is debate intended to win rhetorical points at all costs, with no real interest in the careful consideration of the evidence. Many YECs have mastered this form of discourse (e.g., Hovind, 2009). Debates are geared not to investigate evidence or its interpretation, but to score rhetorical points in front of an audience mainly uninformed about evolutionary theory and the evidence supporting it. Because the audience is uninformed, it is easy to capitalize on their ignorance in ways that are wholly dishonest. Here is an observation by scientist Richard Trott (1999), commenting on the talking points in a presentation by well-known YEC Duane Gish:

> … Gish stated that there are no fossil precursors to the dinosaur *Triceratops*. Gish has been telling this myth for at least 12 years now. However, it is absolutely untrue. Ceratopsian precursors of *Triceratops* include, for example, *Monoclonius* and *Protoceratops*. This lineage appears in proper sequence in the fossil record. It shows the expected developmental change in body size, size of the bony frill, and number of horns. Unfortunately, it

is likely that none of Gish's audience was aware that his statement was completely contrary to fact. Gish promulgated similar falsehoods about the fossil record all night long.

We have argued that creationism is contradicted by a vast body of evidence, which explains the epistemic move of ignoring vast tracts of data that cannot be explained. Here Gish goes a step further by averring that these data do not exist. This can be extremely effective with naïve audiences but elicits a very different reaction from knowledgeable experts.

To our knowledge, IDCs generally avoid such blatant lies about scientific evidence, as one of the goals of their movement is to engage in scientific forms of discourse and to be accepted into the scientific community. However, as we discussed earlier, the most famous IDCs have refused to acknowledge criticisms and contrary evidence even when it is placed before them. In contrast, evolutionary scientists have repeatedly responded to purported IDC examples of irreducibly complex microbiological structures by producing old and new empirical studies that confute the IDC claims (e.g., Young & Edis, 2004; Matzke, 2009; Miller, 2009; Shanks & Joplin, 1999). We are interested in the question of the extent to which the discourse of IDC debates differs from the discourse of scientists participating in debates or panels at professional meetings, but we are unaware of any research on the language of scientists or IDCs at such meetings, discussions, or debates.

Some NCSCs engaged in very heated public debates following the publication of Darwin's theory, as did the evolutionary defenders of Darwin's theory. However, those debates that came closest to the character of modern YEC debates involved creationists who were not scientists, such as Bishop Wilberforce. Although public debates between evolutionists and NCSCs seem to have focused on interpretations of evidence, the rhetoric and tone was often extremely venomous (Chambers, 2002; Rupke, 1994). Once again, without more information about the debates of contemporary scientists, it is difficult to know the extent to which evolutionists and NCSCs of the 1800s were similar to or different from contemporary scientists.

Institutions

The third dimension of epistemic practices is at the level of the institutions that individuals create. We are interested in the epistemic practices that emerge at the institutional level.

Scientists form scholarly institutions led and overseen by experts within their field. These institutions frequently publish journals edited by scholars with relevant expertise. Peer review is one important mechanism by which the institutions of science aim to maintain the integrity of the research they conduct. Importantly, universities and other professional institutions allow scientists to earn a living practicing science.

In the 1800s, NCSCs were just beginning to form professional societies with a contemporary character. During this time it also became more common for people to successfully earn a living as a scientist. Prior to this time, many scientists earned their living in other ways, such as working as clergymen (e.g., Walters & Stow, 2001). Ruse (1999) has argued that the decrease in scientists dependent on the Church for their livelihood helped make it possible for scientists to support evolution after Darwin published *The Origin of Species* in 1859.

As discussed earlier, the YEC Creationist Research Institute requires prospective members to sign a profession of faith. This presents a clear contrast with modern scientific societies, institutions, and research groups, which do not require that scientists sign professions of faith as a precondition for membership.

The ID community is closely associated with an institute called the Discovery Institute. The Discovery Institute is not a center of new empirical research in biology; and, as we have noted, IDCs have not launched empirical research initiatives to investigate their claims. With only two or three exceptions (e.g., Meyer, 2004—a review article published in a minor proceedings), the publications of IDCs at the Discovery Institute do not appear in the peer-reviewed scientific literature. Instead, they are published mainly in special-interest creationist and Christian publications which are not aimed at an audience of scientists. The Center for Science & Culture (CSC), a program of the Discovery Institute, touts on its website a journal of research related to ID, *Progress in Complexity, Information, and Design* (CSC, n.d.); however, as mentioned earlier, as of September 30, 2010, the journal's website indicated that only 10 issues were published from 2002 to 2005 (and only three after 2003), and no issues have been published since.

Most of the activities of the Discovery Institute are social and political, including working to promote ID and to encourage laws encouraging criticism of evolution and allowing intelligent design to be discussed in science classrooms. There are scientific organizations that engage in some (perhaps limited) political lobbying activities; one example is the American Psychological Association (APA). However, the APA also publishes many of the leading academic journals in every major branch of psychology. The Discovery Institute has no such journals of new empirical research. In addition, we note that the Discovery Institute recently named conservative film critic and radio talk-show host Michael Medved as one of its board members. Scientific societies do not name film critics or journalists without scientific training to serve on their boards.

Scientific societies expect their recognized fellows to be accomplished scholars with many publications and clear expertise in their specialty. However, this is not true at the Discovery Institute. Paul Chien is a biologist whose publications listed on the Discovery Institute website on September 30, 2010, were *The Cambrian Explosion* and *Biology's Big Bang*, both books about paleontology. The Wedge Document cited him as the group's expert in pale-ontology. Yet Chien has no degree or journal publications of any kind in pale-ontology (Forrest & Gross, 2004), and has described his own interest in this area as "a hobby" (cited in Forrest & Gross, 2004, p. 63). That Chien would be named a fellow under these conditions reveals a very different approach to institution building than is evident in science. It also reveals a different view of professional expertise.

The fact that the Discovery Institute has sought to promote ID through social and political action rather than through expert empirical research is in line with IDCs' apparent view of the epistemic practices of institutions. Intel-ligent design creationists argue that biologists ignore ID theory not because it fails to meet epistemic standards of scientific inquiry, but because their prior atheistic and materialist commitments engender an "open hostility" to ID, which prevents IDCs from obtaining a fair hearing (Center for Science & Culture, n.d.). (This does not explain, however, why IDCs cannot sustain pub-lication of their own research journal.) This view that scientists are simply ideologues appears to be the same view of science taken by radical social con-structivists (discussed at the outset of this chapter), who claim that science is not, in reality, a process of developing theories that fit evidence but rather a political game played by exerting political muscle. Although we cannot provide detailed arguments here, we take the contrary view that although political interests and affiliations do influence scientists, over the long term it is the weight of the evidence that most strongly influences whether theories, methods, and practices succeed or fail (Kitcher, 1993).

We conclude that there are large differences between the institutional prac-tices of scientists and those of both groups of creationists. We believe that these differences arise naturally from the very different aims of the various groups. Scientific institutions work to develop empirically supported know-ledge through peer-reviewed publications. In contrast, creationist institutes appear to be formed primarily to promote religious beliefs in the social and political arena, and they appear to believe that scientific institutions are just as political as they themselves are. They also view professional expertise differ-ently from scientists.

Conclusions

In this chapter, we have analyzed the epistemic practices of scientists, young Earth creationists, intelligent design creationists, and the scientist-creationists of the early to mid 1800s. Our approach has been to examine epistemic prac-tices related to aims, explanations, methods, evidence, individual inquirers, social interactions among groups of inquirers, and the institutions con-structed by these individuals. We have maintained that it is pointless to con-sider what a group of theorists *might* conceivably do to evaluate the scientific validity of their theories and practice. Instead, it is necessary to examine their actual epistemic practices. For example, if advocates of a viewpoint do not expose their ideas to data, there are likely powerful reasons why they do not do so, even if they conceivably could do so.

Our conclusions for each of the four groups in each of the seven epistemic dimensions are summarized in Table 3.2. In this section, we draw out some of the main themes.

The first conclusion is that the epistemic practices of YECs are starkly and diametrically opposed to the epistemic practices of scientists at nearly every point. It is difficult to imagine a set of epistemic practices more divergent from those of scientists. The differences seem to stem from an absolute commitment to the Bible as the source of truth and a concomitant devaluation of the capabilities of human reason. It is easy to understand why YECs do not expose ideas to data. Given the view that the Bible is infallible, there could be no possible data that might contradict it, and given the profound unreliability of human reasoning, there is no real reason to seek further evidence. Dogmatic certainty about the literal truth of Genesis leads to the radical reinterpretation of any anomalous data and a permanent unwillingness to engage in real, substantive debate.

Our second set of conclusions focuses on the epistemic practices of IDCs. In comparison to YECs, IDCs have moved closer to science on several epistemic practices.

- *Explanatory ideals.* Intelligent design creationists develop theories that are not explicitly theistic (though they are implicitly so). Intelligent design is also compatible with most non-biological sciences (though not all).
- *Method.* Intelligent design creationists do not reject historical or forensic methods of inquiry.
- *Evidence.* They appear to be less guilty of blatantly distorting scientific evidence.
- *Human capabilities.* They do not believe that reason is incapable of arriving at any truths.

Against this, however, IDCs adopt a number of epistemic practices that are completely opposed to those of science.

- *Aims.* Their central aims are religious and political (replacing materialism with a worldview permeated with Christian theism) rather than truth-seeking.
- *Explanatory ideals.* They offer no detailed positive explanation of *any* phenomena (while demanding that evolutionists provide unrealistically detailed explanations for *all* phenomena). They also reject methodological naturalism.
- *Methods.* They do not actually expose their ideas to data and rather rely

Table 3.2 Summary of Similarities and Differences in Epistemic Practices

Dimension of epistemic practice	Group			
	Scientists	Young Earth creationists	Intelligent design creationists	Scientist-creationists of the 1800s
Knowledge system Core aims of inquiry	• The preeminent aim is accounting for empirical data.	• The preeminent aim is knowing the truth of the Bible and spreading that truth.	• Accounting for empirical data is a stated goal, but the preeminent aim of many leaders is the overthrow of "scientific materialism" and replacing it with a theistic worldview.	• Held combined goals of accounting for empirical data and maintaining religious piety. When these goals came into conflict, most opted for evolutionary explanations that accounted for the data.
Explanations	• Develop increasingly detailed explanatory accounts. • Develop explanations with strong compatibility with rest of science. • Favor materialistic explanations due to their history of empirical success.	• Develop explicitly theistic explanations based on Genesis. • Develop explanations with very strong incompatibility with rest of science. • Oppose purely materialistic explanations.	• Develop implicitly theistic explanations; develop no positive explanation of data related to speciation but demand that evolutionary scientists do so. • Compatible with most non-biological sciences. • Oppose purely materialistic explanations.	• Some were committed to providing law-like explanations of data in terms of God and natural law. • Developed explanations that (at the time) were compatible with the rest of science. • Opposed purely materialistic explanations.

Methods	• Expose theories to data. • Employ diverse methods, including but not limited to experimental and historical abductive methods.	• Do not gather data and conduct tests; seek truth by reading the Bible. Knowledge must be consistent with a literal reading of the Bible. • Reject historical methods.	• Generally do not gather data and conduct tests. Instead, they challenge evolutionary scientists to explain complex structures for which they themselves cannot think of an evolutionary explanation. • Accept use of historical as well as experimental methods.	• Varied in the extent to which they exposed theories to data. • Accepted use of historical as well as experimental methods.
Empirical evidence	• Scientists are constrained by empirical evidence. Many theories, including evolutionary theory, explain many diverse lines of evidence.	• Must ignore or radically interpret almost all diverse lines of empirical evidence. • They often continue to cite evidence shown to be false.	• Must ignore or radically interpret almost all diverse lines of empirical evidence.	• Scientist-creationists were constrained by data.

continued

Table 3.2 Continued

Dimension of epistemic practice	Group			
	Scientists	Young Earth creationists	Intelligent design creationists	Scientist-creationists of the 1800s
Inquirers and their social systems				
Characteristics of individual inquirers	• Fall short of the ideal of disinterestedness, but do give up strongly held beliefs in the face of evidence. • Believe that humans are cognitively capable of reaching knowledge through empirical investigations but that many techniques are needed to guard against error.	• Core commitment to creationism precludes disinterested interpretation of data. • Believe that humans are fallen and sinful and incapable of attaining knowledge through empirical investigations.	• Implicit commitment to creationism precludes disinterested interpretation of data. • Believe that humans are cognitively capable of reaching knowledge through empirical investigations, but knowledge of any mechanisms or laws of creation is not possible. • Are overconfident of their ability to judge whether non-design explanations are reasonable.	• Did not exhibit a high degree of disinterestedness, but did give up strongly held beliefs in the face of evidence. • Many believed that humans can attain knowledge through empirical investigations, including knowledge of the laws by which God operated in the biological world.

Social interactions	• Some social interactions assist the development of knowledge. • Present evidence in response to challenges.	• Eristic debate is common.	• Eristic debate is not common. • Sometimes continue to make assertions that are refuted.	• Eristic debate occurred.
Institutions	• Institutions comprise experts in conducting inquiry who comport to standards of scientific inquiry and peer review. • Science is professionalized.	• The institutions are religious institutions that enforce formal professions of faith.	• Institutions are organized for social and political action rather than scientific inquiry. "Experts" need not have traditional expertise. • Peer-reviewed publication is rare; institutions do not sponsor academic journals. • Science is viewed as operating in a wholly biased manner.	• Increasing professionalization of science helped make it possible for scientists to accept common ancestry and (in some cases) natural selection.

on the argument from ignorance as their main (often sole) form of reasoning about data.

- *Evidence.* Just as much as YECs, they must ignore or radically interpret almost all diverse lines of empirical evidence supporting evolutionary theory.
- *Institutions.* Their institutions are organized for political action, not for developing, testing, and refining theories through peer-reviewed empirical research. Moreover, professional expertise in a discipline is not valued in the way it is valued within the institutions of science.

Laudan (1982) seemed to think that it would be possible for a re-cloaked creationism to mimic the epistemic practices of science. Our analysis indicates that IDCs have not succeeded in mimicking scientific practice on most of the epistemic dimensions we have examined. Would it be possible for them to go further, and to adopt more of the epistemic practices of science? We think that they cannot, because there exists a foundational conflict between their core aims and the aims of science, and because the overwhelming evidence for common ancestry and natural selection requires them to adopt epistemic practices at odds with the evidence-based practices of science.

As we have argued, an important goal of many IDCs is the overthrow of secularism and materialism in society; evolution is a target because it constitutes "a major prop for naturalism in philosophy and for agnosticism in religion" (Johnson, 1994). However, the materialist explanation provided by evolutionary theory has great explanatory power, explaining many empirical phenomena in diverse disciplines. Many or most of these data are inimical to any intelligent design theory (e.g., manifold instances of bad design, the observed geographical distribution of species, and so on). Consequently, IDCs must ignore or downplay all the data that evolutionary theory does successfully explain. Because they refuse to specify the design processes, they are able to make no positive predictions that can be tested. All that is left, epistemically, is to present phenomena that they claim evolution cannot explain and hope that evolutionists will not be able to explain these phenomena. (They must also hope that evolutionists have not *already* provided an explanation of which they are ignorant!) When evolutionists meet the challenge, IDCs must shift to a new phenomenon and demand that *now* evolutionists explain *this* phenomenon. This has the ironic consequence of strengthening evolutionary theory each time that the challenge is met.

In our view, the reason why IDCs cannot succeed in adopting the epistemic practices of modern science is closely related to the reason why NCSCs *could* adopt most of the epistemic practices of modern scientists despite their creationist beliefs. In the 1800s, even after Darwin, evidence for common ancestry and (especially) natural selection was not nearly as strong as it is today. One could oppose part or even all of Darwin's theory without ignoring vast tracts of evidence. It was still reasonable to conduct tests, as there was no overwhelming weight of evidence to make such tests seem futile. For example, there was as yet no experimental or even direct correlational evidence for natural selection. Hence, there were fertile areas in which meaningful research could be conducted.

One other difference between IDCs and many NCSCs is particularly important. Many NCSCs considered that it would be possible to describe some laws by which divine creation of species occurred. Perhaps this suggests that piety was less central to NCSCs than was the quest for truth. Certainly their theology was different from that of modern creationists, in that they believed that divine intervention was amenable to empirical investigation and scientific explanation. The fact that most NCSCs eventually adopted at least some of Darwin's views suggests that their goal of piety was less central than the goal of truth, or that their view of piety was not inconsistent with their view of evolutionary principles.

Taken together, these conclusions suggest to us that knowledge of vast arrays of evidence in a field is an underappreciated aspect of scientific expertise. Consider the situations in which laypeople read about evidence that AIDS is not caused by HIV or evidence that global warming is not caused by humans. If the laypeople find themselves persuaded by these arguments, educators might lament their failure to think critically about the evidence. But the problem may not be so much that laypeople are unskilled at criticizing evidence–theory connections; in fact, the particular studies that are selected for presentation may seem to strongly support the contrarian claims. Instead, the problem may be simply that laypeople are unaware of the vast body of evidence that AIDS *is* caused by HIV and that global warming is in fact caused by humans. The failure in reasoning may be the failure to consider that they have seen too little evidence to judge for themselves. If this argument is correct, it means that an important part of education in evolution should be to present large amounts of evidence bearing on evolutionary theory, so that students do come to appreciate the weight of evidence in support of the theory.

References

Ashmore, M. (1993). The theatre of the blind: Starring a Promethean prankster, a phoney phenomenon, a prism, a pocket and a piece of wood. *Social Studies of Science, 23*, 67–106.

Behe, M. J. (1996). *Darwin's black box.* New York: Free Press.

Boyd, R. (1991). On the current status of scientific realism. In R. Boyd, P. Gasper, & J. D. Trout (Eds.), *The philosophy of science* (pp. 195–222). Cambridge, MA: MIT Press.

Brandon, R. (1983). *The spiritualists: The passion for the occult in the nineteenth and twentieth centuries.* New York: Knopf.

Browne, J. (1995). *Charles Darwin: Voyaging.* Princeton, NJ: Princeton University Press.

Browne, J. (2002). *Charles Darwin: The power of place*. Princeton, NJ: Princeton University Press.

Center for Science & Culture. (n.d.). Top questions. Retrieved July 12, 2009, from www.discovery.org/csc/topQuestions.php

Center for the Renewal of Science and Culture. (n.d.). The wedge strategy. Retrieved July 12, 2009, from www.public.asu.edu/~jmlynch/idt/wedge.html

Chambers, P. (2002). *Bones of contention: The fossil that shook science*. London: John Murray.

Chinn, C. A., & Brewer, W. F. (1993). The role of anomalous data in knowledge acquisition: A theoretical framework and implications for science instruction. *Review of Educational Research, 63*, 1–49.

Chinn, C. A., & Samarapungavan, A. (2005, July). *Toward a broader conceptualization of epistemology in science education*. Paper presented at the biennial meeting of the International History, Philosophy, and Science Teaching Conference, Leeds, United Kingdom.

Collins, H. M. (1981). Stages in the empirical programme of relativism. *Social Studies of Science, 11*, 3–10.

Dawkins, R. (1976). *The selfish gene*. Oxford: Oxford University Press.

Dawkins, R. (1996). *The blind watchmaker: Why the evidence of evolution reveals a universe without design*. New York: Norton.

Dembski, W. A. (1998). *The design inference: Eliminating chance through small probabilities*. New York: Cambridge University Press.

Dembski, W. A. (1999). *Intelligent design: The bridge between science and theology*. Downers Grove, IL: InterVarsity Press.

Dembski, W. A. (2003). Still spinning just fine: A response to Ken Miller. Accessed July 12, 2009, at www.designinference.com/documents/2003.02.Miller_Response.htm

Denton, M. (1985). *Evolution: A theory in crisis*. Bethesda, MD: Adler & Adler.

Dobzhansky, T. (1973). Nothing in biology makes sense except in the light of evolution. *American Biology Teacher, 35*, 125–129.

Donovan, A., Laudan, L., & Laudan, R. (1998). *Scrutinizing science: Empirical studies of scientific change*. Baltimore, MD: Johns Hopkins University Press.

Dunbar, K. (1993). How scientists really reason: Scientific reasoning in real-world laboratories. In R. J. Sternberg & J. Davidson (Eds.), *Mechanisms of insight* (pp. 365–395). Cambridge, MA: MIT Press.

Elsberry W., & Shallit, J. (2004). Playing games with probability: Dembski's complex specified information. In M. Young & T. Edis (Eds.), *Why intelligent design fails: A scientific critique of the new creationism* (pp. 121–138). New Brunswick, NJ: Rutgers University Press.

Fitelson, B., Stephens, C., & Sober, E. (1999). How not to detect design—A review of William Dembski's *The Design Inference*. *Philosophy of Science, 66*, 472–488.

Forrest, B. (2001). The wedge at work: How intelligent design creationism is wedging its way into the cultural and academic mainstream. In R. T. Pennock (Ed.), *Intelligent design creationism and its critics: Philosophical, theological and scientific perspectives* (pp. 5–53). Cambridge, MA: MIT Press.

Forrest, B. (in press). The non-epistemology of intelligent design: Its implications for public policy. *Synthese*.

Forrest, B., & Gross, P. R. (2004). *Creationism's Trojan horse: The wedge of intelligent design*. Oxford: Oxford University Press.

Giere, R. N. (1988). *Explaining science: A cognitive approach.* Chicago, IL: University of Chicago Press.

Giere, R. N. (2004). How models are used to represent reality. *Philosophy of Science, 71,* 742–752.

Goldman, A. (2006). Social epistemology, theory of evidence, and intelligent design: Deciding what to teach. *Southern Journal of Philosophy, 44,* 1–22.

Gregory, T. R. (Ed.). (2008). *The evolution of eyes.* Special issue of *Evolution: Education and Outreach.* New York: Springer.

Gruber, J. W. (1960). *A conscience in conflict: The life of St. George Jackson Mivart.* Philadelphia, PA: Temple University Press.

Haack, S. (2003). *Defending science: Between scientism and cynicism.* Amherst, NY: Prometheus Books.

Ham, K. (2007). *The new answers book: What really happened to the dinosaurs.* Retrieved July 12, 2009, from www.answersingenesis.org/articles/nab/what-happened-to-the-dinosaurs

Ham, K. (2009). *Arguments we think creationists should not use.* Retrieved July 12, 2009, from www.answersingenesis.org/home/area/faq/dont_use.asp

Hovind, K. (2009). *Creation science evangelism.* Retrieved July 12, 2009, from www.drdino.com/

Johnson, P. E. (1993). *Darwin on trial* (2nd ed.). Downers Grove, IL: InterVarsity.

Johnson, P. E. (1994). Introduction. In J. Buell & V. Hearn (Eds.), *Darwinism: Science or philosophy?* Richardson, TX: Foundation for Thought & Ethics. Retrieved July 12, 2009, from www.veritas-ucsb.org/reading/BuDSP.html

Johnson, P. E. (2000). Forward. In R. G. Bohlin, *Creation, evolution, and modern science: Probing the headlines that impact your family* (pp. 5–6). Grand Rapids, MI: Kregel Publications.

Kauffman, S. (1993). *The origins of order: Self-organization and selection in evolution.* New York: Oxford University Press.

Kitcher, P. (1982). *Abusing science: The case against creationism.* Cambridge, MA: MIT Press.

Kitcher, P. (1993). *The advancement of science: Science without legend, objectivity without illusions.* New York: Oxford University Press.

Kitcher, P. (2007). *Living with Darwin: Evolution, design, and the future of faith.* New York: Oxford University Press.

Kitzmiller v. Dover Area School District. (2005). Dover, Pennsylvania Intelligent Design Case. Retrieved July 12, 2009, from www.talkorigins.org/faqs/dover/kitzmiller_v_dover.html

Knorr-Cetina, K. (1999). *Epistemic cultures: How the sciences make knowledge.* Cambridge, MA: Harvard University Press.

Kofahl, R. E. (2008). *Creation essays: Where does knowledge come from?* Retrieved July 12, 2009, from www.parentcompany.com/creation_essays/essay1.htm

Kuhn, T. S. (1962). *The structure of scientific revolutions.* Chicago, IL: University of Chicago Press.

Lakatos, I. (1970). Falsification and the methodology of scientific research programmes. In I. Lakatos & A. Musgrave (Eds.), *Criticism and the growth of knowledge* (pp. 91–196). Cambridge, UK: Cambridge University Press.

Laudan, L. (1982, Fall). Commentary: Science at the bar. *Science, Technology, and Human Values, 41,* 16–19.

Longino, H. E. (1990). *Science as social knowledge: Values and objectivity in scientific inquiry.* Princeton, NJ: Princeton University Press.

Longino, H. E. (2002). *The fate of knowledge.* Princeton, NJ: Princeton University Press.

Lurie, E. (1988). *Louis Agassiz: A life in science.* Baltimore, MD: Johns Hopkins University Press.

Lynch, J. M. (2008). The year in ID: 2007 edition. Retrieved July 12, 2009, from http://scienceblogs.com/strangerfruit/2007/12/the_year_in_id_2007_edition.php

Lynch, J. M. (2009). The year in ID: 2008 edition. Retrieved July 12, 2009, from http://scienceblogs.com/strangerfruit/2009/01/the_year_in_id_2008_edition.php

Lynch, M. (1985). *Art and artifact in laboratory science: A study of shop work and shop talk in a research laboratory.* London: Routledge & Kegan Paul.

Matsumura, M., & Mead, L. (2007). *Ten major court cases about evolution and creationism.* National Center for Science Education. Retrieved July 12, 2009, from http://ncseweb.org/taking-action/ten-major-court-cases-evolution-creationism

Matzke, N. (2009). God of the gaps...in your own knowledge. Luskin, Behe, & blood-clotting. Retrieved July 12, 2009, from http://pandasthumb.org/archives/2009/01/god-of-the-gapsin-your-own-knowledge-luskin-behe-blood-clotting.html

Mayo, D. G. (1996). *Error and the growth of experimental knowledge.* Chicago, IL: University of Chicago Press.

Mayr, E. (1982). *The growth of biological thought: Diversity, evolution, and inheritance.* Cambridge, MA: Harvard University Press.

Mayr, E. (2001). *What evolution is.* New York: Basic Books.

McKeever, S. (2008). Feedback: Should we keep them from seeing? Teaching discernment to children. Retrieved July 12, 2009, from www.answersingenesis.org/articles/2008/03/28/feedback-keep-from-seeing

Merton, R. K. (1942). A note on science and democracy. *Journal of Legal and Political Sociology, 1,* 115–126.

Meyer, S. C. (1986). Scientific tenets of faith. *Perspectives on Science & Christian Faith, 38,* 40–42.

Meyer, S. (2004). The origin of biological information and the higher taxonomic categories. *Proceedings of the Biological Society of Washington, 117,* 213–239.

Miller, K. R. (1984). Scientific creationism versus evolution: The mislabeled debated. In A. Montagu (Ed.), *Science and creationism* (pp. 18–63). Oxford: Oxford University Press.

Miller, K. (2004). The flagellum unspun: The collapse of "irreducible complexity." In W. A. Dembski & M. Ruse (Eds.), *Debating design: From Darwin to DNA* (pp. 81–97). New York: Cambridge University Press.

Miller, K. (2009). Smoke and mirrors, whales and lampreys. Retrieved July 12, 2009, from http://blogs.discovermagazine.com/loom/2009/01/02/smoke-and-mirrors-whales-and-lampreys-a-guest-post-by-ken-miller/

Morris, H. M., & Parker, G. E. (1987). *What is creation science?* El Cajon, CA: Master Books.

Numbers, R. L. (1995). *The early writings of Harold W. Clark and Frank Lewis Marsh.* New York: Garland Publishing.

Numbers, R. L. (2006). *The creationists: From scientific creationism to intelligent design* (expanded ed.). Cambridge, MA: Harvard University Press.

Petto, J. P., & Godfrey, L. R. (Eds.). (1998). *Scientists confront intelligent design and creationism.* London: W.W. Norton & Company, Inc.

Picart, C. J. S. (1994). Scientific controversy as farce: The Benveniste–Maddox counter trials. *Social Studies of Science, 24*, 7–37.

Pickering, A. (1984). *Constructing quarks: A sociological history of particle physics.* Chicago, IL: University of Chicago Press.

Rupke, N. A. (1994). *Richard Owen: Victorian naturalist.* New Haven, CT: Yale University Press.

Ruse, M. (1982a, Summer). Creation-science is not science. *Science, Technology, and Human Values, 7*, 72–78.

Ruse, M. (1982b, Fall). Response to commentary: *Pro judice. Science, Technology, and Human Values, 7*, 19–23.

Ruse, M. (1999). *The Darwinian revolution: Science red in tooth and claw* (2nd ed.). Chicago, IL: University of Chicago Press.

Ruse, M. (2005). The Darwinian revolution, as seen in 1979 and as seen twenty-five years later in 2004. *Journal of the History of Biology, 38*, 3–17.

Sarfati, J. (n.d.). Arguments creationists should not use. Retrieved July 12, 2009, from www.creationontheweb.com/content/view/2996/

Schafersman, S. (2008). The disjunctive duality of science distinction: A new argument from the Institute for Creation Research. Retrieved July 12, 2009, from www.texscience.org/reviews/icr-duality-science.htm

Shallit, J. (2002). William Dembski, no free lunch. *Biosystems, 66*, 93–99.

Shanks, N., & Joplin, K. H. (1999). Redundant complexity: A critical analysis of intelligent design in biochemistry. *Philosophy of Science, 66*, 268–298.

Smocovitis, V. B. (1996). *Unifying biology: The evolutionary synthesis and evolutionary biology.* Princeton, NJ: Princeton University Press.

Sober, E. (2008). *Evidence and evolution: The logic behind the science.* Cambridge, UK: Cambridge University Press.

Solomon, M. (2001). *Social empiricism.* Cambridge, MA: MIT Press.

Stenger, V. J. (1998). Physics, cosmology and the new creationism. In J. P. Petto & L. R. Godfrey (Eds.), *Scientists confront intelligent design and creationism* (pp. 131–149). London: W.W. Norton & Company, Inc.

Tannen, D. (1998). *The argument culture: Stopping America's war of words.* New York: Ballantine Books.

Trott, R. (1999). Duane Gish and creationism. Retrieved July 12, 2009, from http://talkorigins.org/faqs/gish-rutgers.html

Ussery, D. (2004). Darwin's transparent box: The biochemical evidence for evolution. In M. Young & T. Edis (Eds.), *Why intelligent design fails: A scientific critique of the new creationism* (pp. 48–57). New Brunswick, NJ: Rutgers University Press.

van Fraassen, B. C. (1980). *The scientific image.* Oxford: Oxford University Press.

Walters, S. M., & Stow, E. A. (2001). *Darwin's mentor: John Stevens Henslow 1796–1861.* Cambridge, UK: Cambridge University Press.

Walton, D. N. (1996). *Argumentation schemes for presumptive reasoning.* Mahwah, NJ: Erlbaum.

Weber, B. H., & Depew, D. J. (2004). Darwinism, design, and complex systems dynamics. In W. A. Dembski & M. Ruse (Eds.), *Debating design: From Darwin to DNA* (pp. 173–190). New York: Cambridge University Press.

Weiss, M. (2005, November 6). War of ideas fought in a small-town courtroom: Intelligent design theory vs. the science of evolution at center of Pennsylvania trial. *San Francisco Chronicle.*

Wells, J. (1996). Issues in the creation–evolution controversies. *The World & I, 11,* 294–305.

Wilson, L. (1970). *Sir Charles Lyell's scientific journals on the species question.* New Haven, CT: Yale University Press.

Witham, L. (2002). *Where Darwin meets the Bible: Creationists and evolutionists in America.* New York: Oxford University Press.

Wolpert, D. (2003). William Dembski's treatment of the No Free Lunch Theorems is written in jello. *Mathematical Reviews.* Review 2003b:00012.

Wright, P. W. G. (1979). A study in the legitimisation of knowledge: The 'success' of medicine and the 'failure' of astrology. In R. Wallis (Ed.), *On the margins of science: The social construction of rejected knowledge* (pp. 85–101). Keele: University of Keele.

Young, M., & Edis, T. (Eds.). (2004). *Why intelligent design fails: A scientific critique of the new creationism.* New Brunswick, NJ: Rutgers University Press.

Chapter 4

Ontological Assumptions about Species and Their Influence on Students' Understanding of Evolutionary Biology

Ala Samarapungavan

Introduction

This chapter is a theoretical and empirical synthesis of our past research on knowledge acquisition in the domain of evolutionary biology (Chinn & Samarapungavan, 2006; Samarapungavan, 2004; Samarapungavan & Malikowski, 1992; Samarapungavan & Wiers, 1994, 1997). Although the research reviewed here focuses on the scientific domain of evolutionary biology, I discuss our findings in terms of "theories of speciation" because a vast majority of our research participants have non-normative beliefs (i.e., beliefs that do not conform to current scientific theory) about the nature and origin of species.

Our research is constrained by the guiding assumption that the structure of concepts and the nature of reasoning and learning vary across domains of knowledge (Carey & Spelke, 1994). A second assumption is that people (both children and adults) understand natural phenomena through the lens of explanatory frameworks (Samarapungavan & Wiers, 1997) constructed from a synthesis of their everyday phenomenological experiences as well as cultural information (Brewer & Samarapungavan, 1991; Carey, 1991; Gopnik & Wellman, 1994). The content and structure of such belief systems serve to organize and interpret experience. A vast body of empirical research has shown that children's initial concepts of the natural world differ dramatically from scientific theories in their conceptual content (Carey & Spelke, 1994; Chi, Slotta, & de Leeuw, 1994; diSessa, 1993; Wiser, 1988; Vosniadou & Brewer, 1992, 1994; Samarapungavan, Vosniadou, & Brewer, 1996). Therefore, accounts of knowledge acquisition need to explain how people might come to acquire the formal scientific theories that are so distant from their initial representations of the world.

Evolutionary biology serves as a paradigm case for exploring the factors that influence the course of conceptual development. Research indicates that even four-year-olds have concepts about the nature of biological species (Inagaki & Hatano, 2004; Kelemen, 2004). For instance, Kelemen (2004) suggests that children may be intuitively predisposed to construct design-based explanations for the origin of species. By elementary school, children also develop ideas about mechanisms of speciation: how species originate, and whether and how they change over time (Evans, 2000; Samarapungavan & Wiers, 1997; Samarapungavan, 1997, 2004). In other words, children acquire beliefs about speciation even before they receive any formal biological instruction on the topic in school.

To complicate matters, evolutionary theory is not necessarily the most prevalent or salient cultural account of speciation that is available to students through the course of their conceptual development (Brem, Ranney, & Schindel, 2003; Lawson & Worsnop, 1992; Ruse, 1988; Sinclair, Pendarvis, & Baldwin, 1997). Variants of creationism (Moreland & Reynolds, 1999) may be presented as competing explanations for speciation both informally (e.g., through conversations with parents or friends) and formally (e.g., in the course of formal religious instruction). The prevalence of competing cultural models for speciation also leads to variability in the extent and quality of formal instruction in evolutionary biology (Brem et al., 2003). Past research indicates that many adults reject evolutionary theory altogether and others, who are willing to entertain evolutionary explanations, show significant misunderstandings about many aspects of evolution (Bishop & Anderson, 1990; Brem et al., 2003; Chi, 2005; Clough & Wood-Robinson, 1985; Mazur, 2005; Samarapungavan & Malikowski, 1992; Sinatra, Southerland, McConaughy, & Demastes, 2003). The reasons for the current state of affairs with regard to the understanding of evolutionary biology are manifold and undoubtedly include socio-cultural factors such as religious belief (Mazur, 2005; Evans, 2001), the pedagogical treatment of evolution in formal schooling (Lerner, 2000), as well as personal predispositions such as openness to conceptual change (Sinatra et al., 2003).

The research described here examines one set of factors: the interplay between domain-specific ontological and epistemic beliefs as children construct and revise their ideas about species and speciation. Specifically, we suggest that by elementary school, children construct explanatory frameworks in terms of which they think about species and speciation. The term "explanatory framework" is used to describe the system of beliefs that children draw upon to answer questions about speciation (see Samarapungavan & Wiers, 1997 for details). Explanatory frameworks are not fully pre-specified theories in that the core beliefs of a single framework may be compatible with a variety of specific solutions to problems of speciation. The frameworks are not necessarily parsimonious. Multiple mechanisms for speciation may be proposed within a single framework as long as these mechanisms are not mutually inconsistent and do not contravene the core beliefs of the framework. Historical theories of speciation have been characterized by a lack of parsimony. In *The Origin of Species* (1872, last edition) Darwin proposes mechanisms such as the modification of features through use, or by direct environmental influence, in addition to natural selection to explain speciation. One important aspect of explanatory frameworks is that they carry ontological and epistemological commitments that influence how novel problems are treated. In the next section, I will describe our findings with regard to naïve explanatory frameworks.

Naïve Explanatory Frameworks for Speciation

The speciation research was initiated in the Netherlands and I have since extended that research to American children and adolescents. We use individual semi-structured interviews to collect data from participants. The basic methodology was developed in our studies with Dutch elementary school children (Samarapungavan & Wiers, 1994, 1997) and has been adapted to different age groups and cultural groups. Individual semi-structured interviews are used to gauge participants' beliefs about speciation (see Samarapungavan & Wiers, 1997 for a complete description of interview items). The interviews are comprised of several sets of questions that deal with the following concepts: (1) the nature and origins of the first life forms; (2) changes in the distribution of species populations through (a) the evolutionary differentiation of new species, and (b) the extinction of existing species; (3) species-specific characteristics: (a) function and origins, and (b) modifiability over time; and (4) within species variation.

Each conceptual area is tested with multiple questions to provide converging evidence for children's concepts and to enable the researchers to examine the internal consistency of children's beliefs. Some questions require only verbal responses but others require participants to reason with pictures or drawings. The participants were asked *factual questions* (e.g., Q3: Were there always people on Earth?), *questions that required explanations* of biological phenomena (e.g., Q9a: How did people first appear on Earth?) and *questions that called for predictions or inferences to novel situations* (e.g., Q12a: If you teach a mother dog how to jump through a hoop and this mother dog has puppies, will these puppies be born knowing how to jump through a hoop?).

Our research indicates that lay people have a variety of explanatory frameworks for speciation. In particular, Dutch elementary school children who have had no formal instruction in evolution have predominantly non-evolutionary, or micro-evolutionary, frameworks (Samarapungavan & Wiers, 1994, 1997). In contrast, Dutch adolescents and adults tend to have macro-evolutionary frameworks which are approximations of either Lamarckian or Neo-Darwinian theory in evolutionary biology (Samarapungavan, 1997; Samarapungavan & Malikowski, 1992). The specific speciation frameworks can be grouped into three broad classes of explanatory frameworks:

(i)   *Non-evolutionary frameworks* treat species essences as immutable (an ontological assumption about species). Consequently, such frameworks rule out the possibility that new species can evolve from existing ones or that the biological characteristics of species can be transformed over time. However, such frameworks also emphasize the importance of species-specific biological features in meeting adaptation or survival needs. Interestingly, children with such frameworks believe that while species essences are immutable the environment does change over time. Changes in the environment render some species features maladaptive causing the species to become extinct. Only those species whose initial features continue to be adaptive over time survive in the face of environmental change. Implicit in such frameworks appears to be the notion of perfect fit or design, such that each species-specific feature (e.g., the wings of an ostrich) has a vital adaptation or survival function relative to its environment.

We found three types of non-evolutionary frameworks that differed only in their assumptions about species origins. *Pure essentialist frameworks* do not address the question of species origins and operate on a working assumption that current species have always existed on Earth. *Spontaneous generation frameworks* posit that all species originated "full blown" through spontaneous generation from life seeds or soil particles at some earlier point in the history of the Earth. The above frameworks do not propose that God created the species. Each of these non-evolutionary frameworks has counterparts in the history of biological theory (see Mayr, 1982), although the children's frameworks differ from their historical counterparts in their explanatory focus on extinction. In contrast, *creationist frameworks* invoke creation by God to explain species origins. We found that 49% of Dutch elementary school children (Samarapungavan & Wiers, 1994, 1997) and 83% of American school children (Samarapungavan, 1997) had non-evolutionary frameworks for speciation. One interesting difference between Dutch and American elementary school children was that only 9% of Dutch children had creationist frameworks and the others explicitly ruled out the notion that species were created by God. Consider the response of eight-year-old Suzanne, who has a pure essentialist framework, to our question about the biblical account of species origins (asked after she said that species have always existed on Earth and do not change over time):

E: So what do you think of the Bible's explanation [for species origins]?
S: I do not know, I do not believe it at all but I also do not know how else the world came into being. I know it is strange that suddenly there is the Earth with all these animals and all. I don't believe that God or someone just suddenly put them here but I do not really have a better explanation myself. I do not think anyone does.

In contrast to Dutch children, a much higher percentage of American elementary school children (90%) provided creationist accounts (Samarapungavan, 1997). Evans (2000, 2001) has also found a predominance of creationist explanations for origins of species among American school children.

(ii)   *Micro-evolutionary frameworks* allow for small changes in the exemplar prototype within species boundaries. They assume that while species essences do not change over time, the exemplars which instantiate a species may vary somewhat in response to adaptational pressures. Among Dutch elementary school children, we found a unique micro-evolutionary framework that has no historical counterpart. We call this the *dinosaur essentialist framework*. Twenty-three percent of Dutch children had this framework (Samarapungavan & Wiers, 1997) while no American children did. Dinosaur essentialists say that in the beginning, the Earth was populated by the dinosaur ancestors of modern species. These children believe that the initial dinosaur exemplars of modern species underwent micro-adaptational changes in response to a changing environment. They describe only two kinds of changes: (a) dinosaur ancestors diminish in overall scale (become smaller), and (b) dinosaur ancestors possess more body hair/rougher skin (e.g., mammoth to elephant). These beliefs lead children to predict that for any modern species, there exists a unique dinosaur ancestor which is simply a large scale prototype with the exaggerated features of the modern species in question. An excerpt from the response of Richard (eight years old) illustrates key aspects of dinosaur essentialist responses.

E: What did the first animals look like? Were they similar to the animals that exist today or different?

R: Different. Our dinosaur forerunners were huge … Some had lots of hair like the mammoth.

E: Were there animals in the beginning that do not exist any more?

R: All. There are no dinosaurs left.

E: What happened to them?

R: The climate began to change. It became hot and dry and there was less food … so … they began to change. They became smaller and smaller until they became the animals of now …

E: So how did the climate and the food make them become smaller?

R: Don't know exactly. As it became warmer, they changed slowly. The mammoth … it began to lose its hair … turned into an elephant, so it became extinct.

Six percent of American children had a micro-evolutionary framework not found among Dutch children, that of hybridization. These children proposed that certain features such as skin color, wing size, tail length, and type of hair could change through interbreeding between different breeds of a species (Samarapungavan, 1997).

(iii) Macro-evolutionary frameworks. These frameworks hold that new species emerge through evolutionary differentiation from pre-existing ones. We found only one variant of these frameworks among Dutch and American elementary school children. Eight percent of Dutch children and 6% of American children had a Lamarckian framework which explained macro-evolution in terms of teleological or need-driven adaptation and the inheritance of

acquired characteristics. However, adolescents and adults had other variants such as theistic evolution (in which evolution unfolds according to a divine plan) and Neo-Darwinian or scientific frameworks (Samarapungavan, 1997, 2004; Samarapungavan & Malikowski, 1992).

The ontological and conceptual assumptions of explanatory frameworks give rise to different epistemological commitments. Examples of how such assumptions lead children to construct theoretical boundaries by distinguishing between unanswerable and answerable questions are provided in Table 4.1.

Table 4.1 Differences in Epistemic Status Assigned to Different Kinds of Questions by Dutch Children

---

Epistemic category: First questions (appropriate but unanswerable)
Jacco (11 years)
E: How did people first appear on Earth?
J: It's the same as with the animals. No one can know that! That will always be a puzzle.

Epistemic category: Inappropriate questions (do not make "sense")
Jacco (11 years)
E: How do you think giraffes came to have their long necks?
J: It [i.e., the neck] did not come into being! It was always there. I don't understand what you mean by that.

Epistemic category: Cutting-edge questions (need to be answered by theory)
Fiona (12 years)
E: Why do ostriches have wings?
F: Good question! I guess all birds have wings and they are birds. But then why is it, their wings don't work for them? That is a difficult question.
E: Yes. What do you think the answer might be?
F: I don't know. I doubt that it has been found out. Maybe if real experts study them, they will find that wings have some other use as well.

Epistemic category: Personal ignorance (answers are in domain of public knowledge)
Rachel (10 years)
E: Let us start with the giraffes. Can you tell me what the ancestors of the giraffes were?
R: Oh! I have forgotten what they are called. It is a dinosaur giraffe with a difficult name.
E: Can you try and remember the name?
R: No. But I would know if I went to the museum. They have dinosaur bones there with all the names.

Epistemic category: Trivial or unimportant questions
Jacco (11 years)
E: Why do people have different color of eyes or hair? For example, why do some people have blue eyes and others green or brown eyes?
J: Why? That is a silly question. That sort of thing is not important. I must say I never really gave it a thought.

Source: Samarapungavan and Wiers (1994).

To illustrate this point, we can compare the pure essentialist and dinosaur essentialist frameworks. The explanatory focus of pure essentialist frameworks centers on two related biological questions. The first question concerns the reasons for the survival or extinction of entire species populations in the course of biological history. The second question, which follows from the first, concerns the identification of adaptive functions for the known characteristics of existing species. Pure essentialists believe that while species themselves do not change over time, their environment does. The fate of a species is determined by the extent to which its immutable characteristics are functional relative to the changing environment.

In contrast, the central problem for the dinosaur essentialist framework is one of explaining micro changes within species boundaries from the original "dinosaur" exemplar of a species to its current exemplar (e.g., the "dinosaur man" to the modern man). This focus is accompanied by a unique concept of extinction. For these children, extinction refers not to the dying out of a species category, but to the physical transformation by which the ancestral or "dinosaur" species exemplar becomes the current species exemplar through a gradual process of scale reduction. Such differences in ontological assumptions and explanatory focus are used by children to define the *boundaries of biological knowledge* and differentiate between core phenomena and peripheral phenomena.

Pure and dinosaur essentialist children appear to distinguish between first questions that are beyond the scope of biological theory, "cutting-edge" or unsolved problems which fall within the scope of biological theory, and "facts" which they may be personally ignorant of, but which (they believe) exist in the domain of public knowledge (see Table 4.1 for examples). Children with pure essentialist frameworks often treat questions about the initial origins of species as philosophical "first questions" that are in principle unanswerable (see Suzanne's response above) and questions about the origins of species-specific characteristics as inappropriate or "not sensible." For example, one Dutch child was asked a series of questions about how various species-specific properties such as the long neck of the giraffe came to be. Here is his response to a question about the peacock's tail: "I can tell you that the peacock's tail helps him to attract wives. And now you will surely ask me how this tail originated. It just is that way. Peacocks always had long tails just like giraffes always had long necks." Questions about the adaptive functions of biological features, however, are treated as problems amenable to solution (see Table 4.1 for examples).

Studies with adolescents and adults often point to religious beliefs as a barrier to accepting evolution. While this is undoubtedly true, religious belief is not the only barrier to accepting evolution. Our research with Dutch children (Samarapungavan & Wiers, 1994, 1997) indicates that even young children who explicitly reject creationist explanations for the origins of species bring an essentialist perspective to problems of speciation. Research on categorical reasoning in naïve biology supports the idea that lay people, including children, approach biological problems such as those of species identity and inheritance through a lens of ontological essentialism (Ahn et al., 2001).

The ontological and epistemic assumptions embedded in naïve explanatory frameworks are likely to influence the course of future learning. These issues are being investigated in my ongoing research with high school and college students. I will discuss some preliminary findings below.

Trajectories of Conceptual Change

An exploratory study was conducted with American adolescents to examine how their initial frameworks might influence their understanding of evolution (Samarapungavan, 2004; in preparation). While more detailed studies are currently underway, the results of the exploratory study suggest ways in which the initial frameworks students bring to learning constrain their interpretation of information about evolution. Twenty-four American students (13–14 years of age) attending a small Midwestern charter school volunteered to participate in an after school learning experiment. The students had not received any formal instruction in evolution prior to the study. Pre- and post-interviews were used to examine how students' prior beliefs with regard to speciation changed over the course of the experiment. The study was conducted on school premises after school hours. The students worked in small groups (four students per group) to answer a set of speciation-related questions as they read and discussed a unit on evolution from a high school biology text book used by their school (Towle, 2000). Groups were assigned randomly. The group work was conducted under the guidance of a trained experimenter/teacher.

Students met in their pre-assigned groups for 10 sessions lasting an hour each. The sessions were spread out over a five-week period with each group scheduled for two sessions a week. Data from small group discussions were audio-taped and transcribed. A researcher also observed each session and took field notes. During the first session, students were first asked to draw timelines and family trees to represent their ideas about the biological history of species and to share these and discuss them in their small groups. In the second session, the students were given individual copies of the text on evolutionary biology to read and instructed that their group task was to use information given in the text to answer the following questions: (1) What did the earliest species look like? (2) How did these first species originate? (3) Do species change over time? If yes, how do they change? (4) Explain what causes changes in species over time. Each subsequent session followed the following format: Students started by deciding which questions they would work on and identifying which text segments they wanted to read or re-read in preparation for their discussions. The evolution text available to the students contained individual sections on the origins of life, theories of evolution and the evidence for them, speciation, and the evolution of populations and human evolution. The first half of each session was dedicated to reading and research while the second half was dedicated to small group discussion of questions. During each session students were encouraged to explicitly discuss areas of agreement and disagreement and to identify things that were not clear in the text. The teacher facilitated group discussion and monitored student work to ensure that they stayed on task.

Consistent with our own prior work and that of others cited above, eight of the 24 students above had non-evolutionary frameworks and 11 students had micro-evolutionary frameworks at the start of the study. These 19 students believed that species were created by a divine entity, although those with micro-evolutionary frameworks also believed that species could undergo micro-adaptations leading to the emergence of new breeds within a species. Of the five students who had macro-evolutionary frameworks (i.e., they believed that current species evolved from very simple original life forms), four students provided Lamarckian or teleological accounts of the mechanisms of speciation. Only one student with a macro-evolutionary framework suggested principles of natural selection as the mechanism for the origin of species. This student was able to apply principles of natural selection to explain cases of micro-evolution (e.g., variations in fur pigmentation in bear species) but could not describe or even name a single example of macro-evolution through natural selection.

Post-instructional interviews showed that although many students' explanations of speciation had shifted over the course of the study, they were still very different from the explanations provided in the framework of evolutionary biology. Of the eight students who started out with non-evolutionary frameworks, seven indicated at the end of the study that they thought micro-evolutionary adaptations were possible. These students thought that such adaptations could occur through natural selection but also through use and disuse and direct environmental influence (Lamarckian mechanisms). One student did not change his mind at all. Eight of the eleven students who started out with micro-evolutionary frameworks did not accept macro-evolution even after instruction but they did accept natural selection as one possible source of micro-evolution along with other mechanisms such as the Lamarckian mechanisms mentioned above. Three students did shift to macro-evolutionary frameworks in that they believed that new species and species characteristics could develop over time through natural selection. However, none of these could provide an example of how such change might occur. In this sense, their understanding of natural selection was primarily a verbalism that could not be connected to macro-evolutionary phenomena in any meaningful way. Consider the post-interview responses of Rebecca below.

E: What is evolution?
REBECCA: Natural selection of random variations.

E: Can you explain that a little more?
REBECCA: Selection?
E: How does it work?
REBECCA: Survival of the fittest.
E: Can you explain how that leads to biological change?
REBECCA: You mean like variations?
E: Can you give me an example of how something changes over time through natural selection?
REBECCA: Uh—like maybe if you are a bear ... you can hide better if your fur is whiter. So—uh—you might live longer. So—uh—over time there would be more bears left with whiter fur.
E: So remember, you told me that the earliest living things were tiny sea creatures? Can you give me an example of how a new life form or species might evolve?
REBECCA: No.
E: How about something like flight in birds?
REBECCA: Oh! Don't know.

Responses of the kind above show that even after instruction, many students have only a surface understanding of evolutionary theory. In the next section, I will elaborate upon some of the conceptual and epistemic challenges for students learning evolutionary theory for the first time.

Conceptual and Epistemic Barriers to Learning about Evolution

Constructs of Evidence

One of the things that emerged from the analysis of group discussions (Samarapungavan, 2004; in preparation) was that many of the conventional lines of evidence offered for evolution are poorly understood by students. For example, mere awareness of fossils and the existence of a fossil record was a poor predictor of students' explanatory frameworks. All 24 students in the learning experiment described above knew that "fossils" existed and that the fossil record showed that some animal populations which existed a long time ago (e.g., dinosaurs, mammoths) were now extinct. The problem is that students typically knew little more than this and "constructed" the details of the fossil record to fit the outlines of their general beliefs about speciation. Further, they had no real sense of the timelines of biological, geological, and cosmological history and how these related to each other. Consider how fossils feature in the responses of four students who were considering how species had changed over time.

MARGARET: Dinosaur fossils were the first ... umm normal ones ... umm ... are later.

ELLIOT: How do we know this?

JAY: Bones [inaudible] bigger.

ERIN: WHAT! No guys ... the first fossils were small.

ELLIOT: Hey, but ... our fossils ... we, they're ... are easily crushed.

JAY: Yeah! Crushed by the humungous dinosaurs [bangs his fist on the table].

Jay's comment leads the group into a discussion about what the fossil record shows and how the age of fossils is determined. Erin suggests that the dating of fossils is based on the study of sedimentation (in what layer of sediment they are found). Elliot counters that this is not likely to be a reliable process. He says, "What if the layers were mixed up? ... You got earthquakes, and floods, and people digging stuff up. If you got a fossil somewhere, doesn't mean it's always there."

These findings are in line with our earlier work (Samarapungavan & Wiers, 1994, 1997) with elementary school children and stand in contrast to Evans' (2000) findings that fossil knowledge is negatively correlated with non-evolutionary explanations in school-age children. One possible explanation for the divergence in findings is that our measures are more open ended and more likely to reveal participants' non-normative interpretations of the fossil record. Additionally, unlike Evans (2000) we include participants' beliefs about dinosaur fossils in our analysis because these beliefs reveal key aspects of their explanatory frameworks for speciation. While I agree with Evans' assumption that a scientific understanding of the fossil record should make students more likely to understand and accept evolutionary theory, our results suggest that achieving such an understanding would require sustained and focused instruction and discussion. For example, it is not enough for students to know simple facts about fossils (e.g., they are the remains of plants and animals that died, or that they are very old and date back to prehistoric times) as this kind of knowledge is compatible with a vast array of views about speciation. A compelling case for evolutionary theory rests on understanding the details of the fossil record as well as how fossil data fits with theoretical knowledge and empirical evidence across scientific disciplines such as geology, biogeography, comparative anatomy, and developmental biology.

The students' discussions of species origins (Samarapungavan, 2004; in preparation) illustrate how epistemic constructs about the boundaries of knowledge, generated from their initial frameworks, affect the course of learning. In the excerpt below, Samantha rejected the question about initial species origins as an "original cause" question. She further justified her position by saying that there was no empirical evidence that one could use to evaluate original cause explanations. Other group members concurred that questions about initial species origins appeared to be unanswerable because they could not be settled by appeal to empirical evidence.

SAMANTHA: How it all began? ... Can't tell ... it's just theory ... no evidence.

DINA: How come?

SAMANTHA: 'Cause ... there's nothing to study ... no fossils. We go to church and all. But no offense ... I don't really think that God just made the world, like in one go.

MARIO: You're not explaining anything!

JAY: I agree with Sam. God ... is not a scientific explanation.

DINA: Yes. But ... how they come from nothing ... that's a problem!

Even students with evolutionary frameworks, like Dina above, often considered questions about initial species origins to be philosophical first questions that are beyond the scope of biological theory. A common misconception that underlies such assumptions is that fossils are the only or the main source of empirical evidence with regard to biological history. Students pay scant attention to other relevant lines of scientific research such as prebiotic chemistry (Rothschild & Manicelli, 2001; Lazcano & Miller, 1996).

Inability to Visualize or Model Macro-Evolutionary Change

Our earlier research with Dutch elementary school children (Samarapungavan & Wiers, 1997) indicates that they regarded questions about the origins of species-specific characteristics as "strange" or incorrectly worded. Because these children believed that a species' features are part of its immutable essence, such questions were not "sensible" to them. Although many of the American adolescents (Samarapungavan, 1995) were willing to accept the notion that existing features could vary in magnitude through use and disuse, they could not think of a mechanism to explain how a novel feature originated. Even after instruction on evolution, many students doubted the notion that natural selection of random variations could suffice to account for speciation. This is illustrated in the discussion excerpt below.

MARGARET: Hey ... about Darwin, I get it but ... like I think ... it's not really all proved yet. How does it actually happen?

JAY: Variation ... I mean selection, explains ... uh ... breeds. I mean, there are dark people in Asia where it's hot ... pale here. [pause] Us from chimps? OK, maybe—'cause they're really pretty smart. They can sign and all. But how d'you go from a teeny germ thing to King Kong?

The students' general inability to envisage examples of macro-evolutionary change coupled with a lack of attention to variability and its role in natural selection constituted a major barrier to their full acceptance of evolutionary theory, especially with regard to macro-evolution. Examples of natural selection presented in the course of biology instruction are often micro-evolutionary in nature. For instance, some innovative programs to teach evolution through inquiry provide students with data on variations in the finch beaks to consider (Reiser et al., 2001). While such programs help students understand the principles of natural selection on a micro-evolutionary scale, they are less likely to be successful in moving students to an acceptance of macro-evolution. Recently, Catley (2006) has made similar arguments about the necessity of focusing more on macro-evolutionary change in science instruction. Most students cannot imagine a sequence of morphological development that would correspond to the emergence of a complex novel biological characteristic. Although such accounts do exist, for instance for the human eye, students are rarely given an opportunity to consider them systematically during the course of instruction.

Much of this chapter has focused on ways in which students' pre-instructional explanatory frameworks for speciation might constrain their learning of evolutionary biology. In the final section, I will consider some dimensions of instruction that might facilitate conceptual change.

Facilitating Conceptual Change

One way to think about conceptual change is to relate the idea of explanatory frameworks to the notion of a conceptual ecology (Demastes, Good, & Peebles, 1995). Our findings (Samarapungavan, 2004; Samarapungavan & Malikowski, 1992; Samarapungavan & Wiers, 1997) are compatible with those of Demastes et al. (1995), in that we also find that various kinds of evolutionary and non-evolutionary beliefs co-exist, especially in the frameworks of adolescents and adults. Indeed, as observed in Samarapungavan and Wiers (1997) and earlier in this chapter, Darwin himself invoked several mechanisms for evolutionary change in addition to natural selection in his work (such as development through use and disuse). Our research suggests that students' trajectories of conceptual development for evolution reflect habits of local and typically unconscious synthesis of information presented in instruction such that the core principles of the prior frameworks (e.g., divine creation or biological essentialism) are preserved. To argue for the existence of explanatory frameworks is not to argue for a Kuhnian (1962) "theory replacement" model of conceptual change. Thagard (1990, 1991), using examples from the history of science, has shown how theoretical frameworks can undergo evolutionary development. From the perspective of instructional design, I suggest that it is particularly useful to think of conceptual ecologies in terms of socio-cultural space. In the realm of speciation, scientific and non-scientific ontological, conceptual, and epistemic principles compete to occupy a niche in students' minds.

The framework of evolutionary biology currently provides the major, indeed the only, scientifically fruitful and valid account of speciation. In many domains of science, the instructional goals of public education would align routinely with the normative scientific theories of the discipline. However, Mazur (2005) has noted that Americans are far more likely to reject evolutionary theory than citizens of Europe and of many non-European nations. Analyzing data from the General Social Survey (GSS) Mazur found that 53% of American respondents judged a statement that humans had evolved from earlier species to be untrue. After conducting a multivariate analysis of the effects of a number of demographic variables including education, age, geographic location, political philosophy, and cultural affiliation, he concluded that religiosity (church affiliation and attendance) was the single most important predictor of non-acceptance of evolution. However, educational level was also a significant factor, with college-educated adults being more likely to believe in evolution. Mazur (2005) concluded that his findings support arguments that a combination of "strong religion and weak education" (p. 61) is the most likely cause of resistance to evolutionary theory in the United States. There are few areas of science where the central explanatory principles and findings of scientific theory are so directly at odds with the religious beliefs of large segments of the American public.

The pervasiveness of the tensions between religious belief and scientific theory are played out both directly and indirectly in the arena of public education. Among the more direct manifestations of these tensions are the legal fights to try to force the teaching of religious theories of speciation such as "creation science" or "intelligent design" on a co-equal footing with evolution in public schools. There are more subtle manifestations as well. From a review of state standards, Lerner (2000) concludes that as many as a third of all states have adopted watered down or ambivalent standards for teaching evolution. Additionally, teachers often have negative perceptions of evolutionary theory, especially with regard to its social and personal implications (Griffith & Brem, 2004).

The research discussed above suggests that the successful teaching of evolution will require a comprehensive and systematic approach which addresses the many cognitive and epistemic stumbling blocks to conceptual change among both future teachers and their students. In terms of domain-specific knowledge, the results of our prior research suggest that students need to understand the full range of empirical evidence for evolution from studies of biodiversity and biogeography, molecular biology and genetics, embryology and developmental biology, as well as the fossil record (Samarapungavan & Wiers, 1994, 1997; Samarapungavan & Malikowski, 1992; Samarapungavan, 1995, 2004). Most students currently fail to comprehend the breadth and inter-relatedness of evidence for evolutionary theory. Additionally, students need to consider multiple examples of macro-evolutionary change.

I suggest that students' tendency for local and piecemeal synthesis of scientific information about evolution in ways that preserve pre-existing core beliefs prevents them from truly appreciating the magnitude and scope of the differences between their own knowledge and evolutionary theory. A recent study by Asterhan and Schwarz (2007) shows that students who engaged in argumentation and debate while learning evolutionary theory showed gains in conceptual understanding and long-term retention over a control group that had access to the viewpoints of other students but did not engage in argumentation. Instructional approaches that help students fully articulate, compare, and evaluate their concepts with those of evolutionary theory by the epistemic standards and norms of science are more likely to facilitate conceptual change.

In the course of my research, I have had occasion to observe how evolution is taught in several middle and high school classrooms. I have often been struck by the fact that even teachers who accept the theory of evolution as an organizing principle of biology limit their defense of the theory to presenting well-known examples in support of evolution and rarely focus on the shortcomings of alternative explanations. I recently asked a teacher, who was recounting a barrage of "counter-examples" from design put forth by a creationist-minded student, why he did not respond by asking the class to consider some of Gould's (1980) examples of poor design. The teacher responded that it was wrong to attack students' religious beliefs.

The response is symptomatic of one of the key problems in teaching evolutionary theory in American classrooms. Competing alternatives to evolution often have subtle competitive advantages in conceptual ecology. In this instance, even though "good design" was offered as counter-evidence to the evolutionary principle of natural selection, the notion of good design itself was immune from critical examination. The ability to examine and debate the *weaknesses* as well as the strengths of competing models is a core epistemic characteristic of science. From a socio-cultural perspective, if we are to take the idea of conceptual ecology seriously, we must consider ways in which alternate cultural models compete for a niche in our students' minds. The design of science instruction should allow students to seriously explore and evaluate a range of explanations against the norms and practices of *science*. As we noted in an article on teaching as persuasion (Chinn & Samarapungavan, 2001), there is a difference between understanding a scientific theory and believing it to be true. While no instructional strategies can guarantee that students will believe in evolution, ensuring that students fully understand evolutionary theory and its advantages for scientists in terms of coherence, non ad hocness, and evidentiary support, over any purported alternative that is currently offered, should be the goal of science instruction.

Conclusions

Research on children's and adolescents' pre-instructional frameworks for speciation helps explain why many fail to fully understand and accept evolutionary biology even after formal instruction. Specifically, our research suggests that in trying to bring about conceptual change, instruction must address not only the domain-specific content of students' alternate beliefs but also the ontological and epistemic constructs that are associated with such beliefs and influence how students evaluate and select information that is presented to them.

References

Ahn, W., Kalish, C., Gelman, S. A., Medin, D. L., Luhmann, C., Attran, S., Coley, J. D., & Shafto, P. (2001). Why essences are essential in the psychology of concepts. *Cognition, 82*, 59–69.

Asterhan, C. S., & Schwarz, B. (2007). The effects of monological and dialogical argumentation on concept learning in evolutionary theory. *Educational Psychology, 99*(3), 626–639.

Bishop, B. A., & Anderson, C. W. (1990). Student conceptions of natural selection and its role in evolution. *Journal of Research in Science Teaching, 27*, 415–428.

Brem, S. K., Ranney, M., & Schindel, J. (2003). Perceived consequences of evolution: College students perceive negative personal and social impact in evolutionary theory. *Science Education, 87*(2), 181–206.

Brewer, W. F., & Samarapungavan, A. (1991). Child theories versus scientific theories: Differences in reasoning or differences in knowledge? In R. R. Hoffman & D. S. Palermo (Eds.), *Cognition and the symbolic processes: Vol. 3. Applied and ecological perspectives* (pp. 209–232). Hillsdale, NJ: Erlbaum.

Carey, S. (1991). Knowledge acquisition: Enrichment or conceptual change? In S. Carey & R. Gelman (Eds.), *The epigenesis of mind* (pp. 257–292). Hillsdale, NJ: Erlbaum.

Carey, S., & Spelke, E. (1994). Domain-specific knowledge and conceptual change. In L. A. Hirschfeld & S. A. Gelman (Eds.), *Mapping the mind* (pp. 169–200). New York: Cambridge University Press.

Catley, K. M. (2006). Darwin's missing link—A novel paradigm for evolution education. *Science Education, 90*(5), 767–783.

Chi, M. T. H. (2005). Commonsense conceptions of emergent processes: Why some misconceptions are robust. *Journal of the Learning Sciences, 14*(2), 161–199.

Chi, M. T. H., Slotta, J. D., & de Leeuw, N. (1994). From things to processes: A theory of conceptual change for science learning. *Learning and Instruction, 4*, 27–43.

Chinn, C. A., & Samarapungavan, A. (2001). Distinguishing between understanding and belief. *Theory Into Practice, 40*(4), 235–241.

Chinn, C. A., & Samarapungavan, A. (2006, April). *Deep epistemological differences between creationists and evolutionary scientists*. Paper presented at the Annual Meeting of the American Educational Research Association (AERA), San Francisco, CA.

Clough, E. E., & Wood-Robinson, C. (1985). How secondary students interpret instances of biological adaptation. *Journal of Biological Education, 19*, 125–130.

Darwin, C. (1872). *The Origin of Species*. London: John Murray.

Demastes, S. S., Good, R. G., & Peebles, P. (1995). Students' conceptual ecologies and the process of conceptual change in evolution. *Science Education, 79*(6), 637–666.

diSessa, A. (1993). Toward an epistemology of physics. *Cognition and Instruction, 10*, 105–225.

Evans, E. M. (2000). The emergence of beliefs about origins of species in school-age children. *Merrill-Palmer Quarterly, 46*(2), 221–254.

Evans, E. M. (2001). Cognitive and contextual factors in the emergence of diverse belief systems: Creation versus evolution. *Cognitive Psychology, 42*, 217–266.

Gopnik, A., & Wellman, H. M. (1994). The theory theory. In L. A. Hirschfeld & S. A. Gelman (Eds.), *Mapping the mind* (pp. 257–293). New York: Cambridge University Press.

Gould, S. J. (1980). *The panda's thumb.* New York: Norton.

Griffith, J. A., & Brem, S. K. (2004). Teaching evolution: Pressures, stress and coping. *Journal of Research in Science Teaching, 41*, 791–809.

Inagaki, H., & Hatano, G. (2004). Vitalistic causality in young children's naïve biology. *Trends in Cognitive Science, 8*, 356–362.

Kelemen, D. (2004). Are children "intuitive theists"? *Psychological Science, 15*(5), 295–301.

Kuhn, T. S. (1962). *The structure of scientific revolutions.* Chicago, IL: University of Chicago Press.

Lawson, A., & Worsnop, W. A. (1992). Learning about evolution and rejecting a belief in special creation: Effects of reflective reasoning skill, prior knowledge, prior belief and religious commitment. *Journal of Research in Science Teaching, 29*, 143–166.

Lazcano, A., & Miller, S. L. (1996). The origin and early evolution of life. *Cell, 85*, 793–798.

Lerner, L. S. (2000). Good and bad science in US schools. *Nature, 407*, 287–290.

Mayr, E. (1982). *The growth of biological thought.* Cambridge, MA: Harvard University Press.

Mazur, A. (2005). Believers and disbelievers in evolution. *Politics and the Life Sciences, 23*(2), 55–61.

Moreland, J. P., & Reynolds, J. M. (Eds.). (1999). *Three views on creation and evolution.* Grand Rapids, MI: Zondervan Publishing.

Reiser, B. J., Tabak, I., Sandoval, W. A., Smith, B. K., Steinmuller, F., & Leone, A. J. (2001). BGuILE: Strategic and conceptual scaffolds for scientific inquiry in biology classrooms. In S. M. Carver & D. Klahr (Eds.), *Cognition and instruction: Twenty-five years of progress* (pp. 263–305). Mahwah, NJ: Erlbaum.

Rothschild, L. J., & Manicelli, R. L. (2001). The origin of life in extreme environments. *Nature, 409*, 1092–1101.

Ruse, M. (Ed.). (1988). *But is it science? The philosophical question in the creation/evolution controversy.* New York: Prometheus.

Samarapungavan, A. (1995, April). *Establishing boundaries for explanatory frameworks: Children's epistemologies in context.* Paper presented at the Annual Meeting of the American Educational Research Association (AERA), San Francisco, CA.

Samarapungavan, A. (1997, March). *Changing beliefs about the scope and boundaries of biological knowledge: The role of context in epistemic development.* Paper presented at the Annual Meeting of the American Educational Research Association (AERA), Chicago, IL.

Samarapungavan, A. (2004, December). *Domain specificity, ontology, and epistemology, constraints on conceptual change.* Paper presented to the National Research Council/National Academies of Science, Washington, DC.

Samarapungavan, A. (in preparation). *Misconstruing the evidence: Student 'readings' of the fossil record.*

Samarapungavan, A., & Malikowski, M. (1992). Knowledge acquisition in evolutionary biology. *International Journal of Psychology, 27–28*, 589.

Samarapungavan, A., Vosniadou, S., & Brewer, W. F. (1996). Thinking about the earth, sun, and moon: Indian children's cosmologies. *Cognitive Development, 11*, 491–521.

Samarapungavan, A., & Wiers, R. (1994). Do children have epistemic constructs about explanatory frameworks: Examples from naive ideas about the origin of species. In A. Ram & K. Eiselt (Eds.), *Proceedings of the Sixteenth Annual Conference of the Cognitive Science Society* (pp. 778–783). Hillsdale, NJ: Erlbaum.

Samarapungavan, A., & Wiers, R. (1997). Children's thoughts on the origin of species: A study of explanatory coherence. *Cognitive Science, 21*(2), 147–177.

Sinatra, G. M., Southerland, S. A., McConaughy, F., & Demastes, J. W. (2003). Intentions and beliefs in students' understanding and acceptance of biological evolution. *Journal of Research in Science Teaching, 40*(5), 510–528.

Sinclair, A., Pendarvis, M. P., & Baldwin, B. (1997). The relationship between college zoology students' beliefs about evolutionary theory and religion. *Journal of Research and Development in Education, 30*, 118–125.

Thagard, P. (1990). Concepts and conceptual change. *Synthese, 82*(2), 225–274.

Thagard, P. (1991). The conceptual structure of the chemical revolution. *Philosophy of Science, 57*, 183–209.

Towle, A. (2000). *Modern biology.* Austin, TX: Holt, Rinehart & Winston.

Vosniadou, S., & Brewer, W. F. (1992). Mental models of the earth: A study of conceptual change in childhood. *Cognitive Psychology, 24*, 535–585.

Vosniadou, S., & Brewer, W. F. (1994). Mental models of the day/night cycle. *Cognitive Science, 18*, 123–183.

Wiser, M. (1988). The differentiation of heat and temperature: History of science and novice expert shift. In S. Strauss (Ed.), *Ontogeny, phylogeny, and historical development* (pp. 28–48). Norwood, NJ: Ablex.

Chapter 5

Understanding Evolutionary Theory

The Role of Epistemological Development and Beliefs

Barbara K. Hofer, Chak Fu Lam, and Alex DeLisi

Introduction

There are likely many explanations for the difficulty students have in comprehending and accepting evolutionary theory. This chapter addresses a set of reasons that we believe need further research and more attention by educators, particularly at the college level. We focus on what psychologists have termed "personal epistemology" (Hofer & Pintrich, 1997, 2002), individual conceptions of knowledge and knowing.

In this chapter, we provide a conceptual overview of personal epistemology and examples of empirical evidence from our research on how students' beliefs about knowledge and knowing are related to their comprehension and acceptance of the theory of evolution. Our goal is to contribute to building conceptual models of students' grasp of this important issue so that our educational systems may be more effective in teaching scientific literacy.

Learners' Epistemologies and Evolutionary Theory

A growing body of research demonstrates that students have both generalized epistemological worldviews and specific discipline-based epistemic beliefs (Hofer, 2006) and that these are related to learning and education (Hofer, 2001). One of the goals of a college education is to assist student advancement in both these areas, so that they become better at the epistemic tasks of coordinating theory and evidence, evaluating sources of authority, and resolving competing knowledge claims, as well as developing an understanding of the epistemic underpinnings of particular disciplines. Within science this involves learning, for example, an understanding of the scientific method and empirical processes, the meaning of "theory," what counts as evidence, and the roles of falsifiability and tentativeness in the development of scientific knowledge.

The failure of a vast number of Americans to accept the basic premises of evolution, an accepted scientific theory, is a complicated issue, but part of the problem may be inadequate training in scientific literacy and an underdeveloped epistemic understanding of science. Furthermore, school boards in a number of states have advocated the inclusion of "intelligent design" in their curricula. Refutation of this position has been problematic for many otherwise well-educated individuals, particularly for those who seem to believe that all views on this issue merit equal consideration. In epistemic terms, such a stance would be indicative of what has been termed "multiplism," a stance that all such "opinions" are equally valid and no means exist for justification (Kuhn, Cheney, & Weinstock, 2000). Moving students from this position of multiplism toward an evaluativist stance represents significant strides toward critical thinking and helps create an educated citizenry that can make informed decisions about such significant issues.

Personal Epistemology: An Overview

Researchers who have investigated student beliefs about knowledge and knowing have explored this through multiple paradigms. The two most prominent of these are a developmental approach (Baxter Magolda, 1992, 2004; King & Kitchener, 1994, 2004; Kuhn, 1991; Kuhn et al., 2000; Perry, 1970, 1981), which suggests that individuals move through a somewhat structured and predictable progression in their path toward epistemological understanding, and the epistemic beliefs approach (Perry, 1970; Schommer, 1990; Schommer-Aikins, 2004; Schraw, Bendixen, & Dunkle, 2002), which is predicated on the assumption that individuals' beliefs are multidimensional and that the beliefs are more or less independent. Others have explored the construct as one of more fine-grained resources (Elby & Hammer, 2001; Louca, Elby, Hammer, & Kagey, 2004), as a metacognitive process (Hofer, 2004; Kitchener, 1983; Kuhn, 1999), or as theories that are more coherently organized than a loose set of beliefs (Hofer & Pintrich, 1997), for example. For the purposes of this chapter, we focus on the two most central approaches, epistemological development and epistemic beliefs.

Epistemological Development

Those who view personal epistemology as a developmental process typically chart a progression of the evolving coordination between the objective and subjective aspects of knowing (Kuhn et al., 2000; Kuhn & Weinstock, 2002), with an endpoint that represents a coordination of the two. The number of stages in any particular developmental scheme ranges from three to nine, but in its most simplified form, the developmental progression across the schemes appears similar.

Very young children appear to experience the world from a position of *egocentric subjectivity* (Burr & Hofer, 2002), evidenced by a lack of understanding that others might have differing knowledge of the world than they do. The attainment of theory of mind (Wellman, 1990; Wellman, Cross, & Watson, 2001), typically between the ages of three and five, ushers in the awareness of differing belief and knowledge states among individuals, and children begin to see an objective "truth" that exists apart from false beliefs (Wildenger, Hofer, & Burr, in press). This new emphasis on objectivity characterizes a developmental phase often called *dualism* or *absolutism*, and the hallmark is a black-and-white view of knowledge as highly certain, dichotomous, unambiguous, and handed down from authority.

Absolutism breaks down when individuals begin to acknowledge the possibility of multiple claims, but as yet see no means for adjudicating them. This period of *multiplicity* is characterized by subjectivity and the belief that one claim is likely to be as good as another. Knowledge is uncertain and tentative, and the role of authority diminished and questionable, as most assertions are viewed as opinions, with equal validity. In early studies, this worldview often characterized college sophomores, and it is no doubt a familiar perspective to anyone who has taught adolescents.

Learning that there are means for evaluating truth claims, that theory and evidence can be coordinated, and that the subjective and objective can be reconciled are hallmarks of burgeoning *evaluativism* (Kuhn et al., 2000), the final stage in the sequence. Although those intellectual achievements would seem to be congruent with the aims of a college education, studies suggest that only a small percentage of adults actually achieve all the intellectual accomplishments of this level, casting serious concern about whether we have an educated citizenry capable of making the judgments necessary for either a successful democracy or optimal well-being.

Epistemic Beliefs

Epistemological development, as it was initially conceived in a series of studies on reflective judgment (King & Kitchener, 1994), skills of argument (Kuhn, 1991), and epistemological reflection (Baxter Magolda, 1992), presumed synchronous development and domain generality. By contrast, those who investigate conceptions of knowledge and knowing as a set of beliefs have been more likely to argue that the various dimensions of epistemology can be more or less independent (Schommer, 1990), although this has received few empirical tests.

The exact dimensions of these beliefs vary by scheme, with some debate about whether beliefs about learning and intelligence are to be included, or whether the beliefs should be restricted to those about knowledge and knowing. Across both the epistemological development and the epistemic beliefs literature, four dimensions appear consistently that are also congruent with a philosophical definition of epistemology (Hofer & Pintrich, 1997). These include the *certainty* and *simplicity* of knowledge (which comprise the *nature of knowledge*) and the *source* and *justification* for knowing (which comprise the *nature of knowing*). Briefly, views of knowledge range from certain to tentative and evolving, and from a belief of knowledge as discrete bits of information to an understanding that ideas are complex and interwoven. The dimension of source of knowing involves both personal experience and insight as well as the role of external authority and this dimension progresses toward an eventual sense of constructed understanding in which knower and known are reconciled. Justification involves how one moves from an acceptance that does not require justification to a position of evaluating knowledge and authority, and supporting knowing with evidence.

Personal Epistemology and Domain Specificity

The original research on epistemological development was predicated on assumptions of domain generality. One's stance toward knowing and knowledge was presumed to transcend the topic or field. Recent work, however, has suggested that even young children, and certainly older ones, can make distinctions between domains of fact and opinion. For example, they understand the relative degree of certainty involved in judgments of aesthetic preference or taste versus facts about the physical world (Kuhn et al., 2000; Mason & Boscolo, 2004; Wainryb, Shaw, Langley, Cottam, & Lewis, 2004; Wildenger et al., 2010).

Domain-specific levels of epistemic beliefs, however, have focused on domains as the equivalent of academic disciplines (Muis, Bendixen, & Haerle, 2006). A series of studies, both within-subject and between-subject, have examined whether students hold beliefs that differ by discipline. Results of a within-subject study suggest that students hold the same structure of epistemic beliefs across disciplines but that there are mean differences in their views of the disciplines by dimension; for example, knowledge is perceived as more certain in natural science than in psychology (Hofer, 2000). As noted by Muis et al. (2006) in their review of the literature, measurement sensitivity is a critical factor when investigating such differences, and studies that utilize domain-general measures have been less likely to pick up these distinctions (Schommer & Walker, 1995). The difference may appear subtle—for example, a domain-general item of "Truth is unchanging" is adapted to "Truth is unchanging in this field" in the domain-specific studies, but this is a meaningful and significant difference, as sensitivity to context and discipline seems to influence outcomes. This seems particularly critical in studies of evolution and other aspects of scientific understanding, with explicit attention to learning within science.

Other researchers have pursued epistemic beliefs that are particular to the disciplines, such as beliefs about math (Muis, 2004), history (Wineburg, 1998), or science (Conley, Pintrich, Vekiri, & Harrison, 2004; Samarapungavan, Westby, & Bodner, 2006; Sandoval, 2005). At the most basic level, research on disciplinary beliefs can involve understanding students' naïve beliefs about knowledge and knowing in the disciplines that may be an impediment to learning, for example, whether history is viewed as a list of dates, mathematics as knowing when to use the right formula, or science as a collection of facts that are already known and simply need to be memorized. Research on disciplinary beliefs, however, is a burgeoning area with research pertinent to instruction at all levels.

One of the recurrent dimensions in several domain-general epistemic beliefs measures and in domain-specific measures of science beliefs is the degree to which knowledge is perceived as certain. Although students may find knowledge in chemistry more certain and unchanging than in psychology, they need to develop an appreciation for scientists' understanding of the tentative and evolving nature of knowledge, the degree to which claims can be known for certain, and what constitutes valid evidence. In the absence of such a nuanced understanding, and bolstered by personal epistemic beliefs that value certainty, students may perceive evolutionary theory as invalid in the absence of complete "proof."

The Relation between Personal Epistemology and Learning

In terms of epistemological development, students are likely to view their education and the learning process through the prism of their current epistemic worldview, to the degree that such a lens is generalized, or perhaps to the degree to which it is operative within a particular domain. As Perry (1970) and others have noted, students who are absolutists would expect for an instructor to have discrete bits of knowledge and to transmit them in a way that provides for direct transfer, and such authority would be accepted without challenge. Multiplists, by contrast, are likely to acknowledge more complexity but to see any expressed conflicts as diversity of opinion; viewed from this position, authorities are simply good at articulating their views. Those at higher levels on any of the schemes work more actively to reconcile their own position with that of experts, and to construct knowledge in a way that provides for more immediate understanding rather than simple received truth. They are likely to develop a more nuanced understanding of how evidence can be used to support various claims, and how such evidence can be evaluated, as well as how expertise and authority vary and how they can be assessed.

Research on epistemological development and the skills of argumentation (applied to topics such as global warming and genetically modified food) indicates that advanced epistemological understanding predicts skills of argumentation, such as the use of counter-arguments and rebuttals with justification (Mason & Scirica, 2006). In general, research has shown a correlation between epistemological level and both education and expertise (Hofer, 2001).

Although the Mason and Scirica (2006) study employed a written instrument (Kuhn et al., 2000), epistemological development has been assessed most often through interview methodology, making large-scale studies of the relation between developmental level and various aspects of learning less frequent. Students' epistemic beliefs, however, have typically been measured through Likert-type questionnaires, simpler to administer than individual interviews, and this has led to a growing range of studies indicating that epistemic beliefs are related to learning in important ways. Epistemic beliefs have been shown to influence text comprehension (Schommer, 1990), strategy use, cognitive processing (Kardash & Howell, 2000), and conceptual change (Andre & Windschitl, 2003; Mason, 2003; Mason & Boscolo, 2004; Qian, 2000; Windschitl & Andre, 1998), for example. Students' beliefs influence how they approach the learning process: those who think of knowledge as simple, certain bits of information are likely to use memorization strategies, and this in turn leads to less depth of learning and lower achievement (Schommer, Crouse, & Rhodes, 1992). Thus the investigation of epistemic stances, from both the developmental and beliefs perspective, is an important factor to examine in interpreting current issues in the controversy around evolutionary theory, given the problems that have arisen in student understanding and acceptance of this important scientific construct. Epistemic stances might be implicated in the learning of evolution, for example, in regard to whether a student expects absolute certainty of knowledge, whether they understand what "tentative" implies in regard to the nature of science, and in their openness to challenging and altering their conceptual misunderstandings.

Acceptance of Evolution and the "Intelligent Design" Controversy

From the perspective of science education, there are serious concerns when a large percentage of individuals in the United States fail to either understand or accept the theory of evolution, view it as incompatible with other beliefs, and promote the teaching of "intelligent design" as a comparable educational counterpoint to the theory of evolution. Statistics on this phenomenon abound. A national survey found that 42% of those surveyed said that humans and other living things have existed in their present form since the beginning of time (Pew Forum on Religion and Public Life, 2005). Of the 46% who agree that life has evolved over time, just over half (and 26% of the overall sample) subscribed to a Darwinian account of this process, with 40% of those who accepted evolution also saying that evolution was guided by a supreme being for the purpose of creating humans and other life forms as they exist today, a view consistent with intelligent design. Such views, not surprisingly, were highly correlated with religious affiliation, political affiliation, age, gender, education, and region of the country. College graduates, for example, were twice as likely to accept the natural selection theory of evolution as those who did not attend college (40% vs. 18%). This finding shows that well over half the nation's college graduates, however, fail to accept a theory that is foundational in the natural sciences.

Beliefs about one's own certainty of the knowledge of life's origins also appeared influential in this study. Those who identify with creationism were roughly twice as likely to be certain about the origins of life as those who accept the explanation of evolution (63% are very certain vs. 22%), and those who take the Bible literally—as an all-powerful source of authority—are most likely to be very certain about their knowledge.

In this same study, support for teaching of creationism well exceeds those who actually believe in creationism, with 64% reportedly in favor that it should be taught in the schools, perhaps evidence of an epistemic position that these are merely opinions deserving of equal time. And who should decide whether creationism is taught? This is a critical question in terms of the source of authority, an important aspect of epistemic beliefs, and reflects a view of what counts as knowledge and who is most qualified to determine this. The dominant view is that parents should have this authority (41%), followed by scientists and science teachers (28%), and school boards (21%). This varies, however, depending on point of view on the topic, with creationists favoring parents (56%) and those who accept evolution favoring scientists (47%) as the authority on this topic.

These are dramatic examples of why we need to pay more attention to underlying epistemological assumptions in these issues—beliefs about certainty of both knowing and knowledge, issues of justification and source of authority, and, of course, what counts as evidence in such concerns. Researchers have an enormous task ahead to better understand how individuals with many years of schooling have come to such positions about science and scientific authority.

Initial research on linking the issue of evolution with student epistemologies was conducted by Sinatra and colleagues, who examined students' understanding of evolution, general epistemic beliefs, and cognitive dispositions (Sinatra, Southerland, McConaughy, & Demastes, 2003). They found that epistemic beliefs, as measured with a subset of scales from a domain-general instrument, were related to an acceptance of human evolution; students with more sophisticated beliefs in regard to the certainty of knowledge and the questioning of authority were more likely to accept the theory of evolution, although epistemic beliefs were not related to understanding. As noted by the authors, the measure used to assess beliefs was a domain-general one, however, and may not have been sensitive to the issue of beliefs in science.

Ongoing Research on Epistemology, Evolutionary Theory, and Intelligent Design

In our lab we have recently conducted several studies examining how students' epistemological development and beliefs are related to their understanding and acceptance of evolutionary theory. Our goal here is to provide an overview of some of the early findings, rather than a full report of the research.

In our first study we began by surveying all incoming first-year students at a highly selective liberal arts college about their ideas regarding the theory of evolution in order to gain a sense of how this population compared to those surveyed in national studies, and in order to provide baseline data and create a profile of entering students. We did this by adding a few "local" questions to the national survey that a large number of U.S. first-year students complete before arriving at college. The Cooperative Institutional Research Program (CIRP) Freshman Year Study is conducted at nearly 400 institutions annually and has been a rich source of data about student values and attitudes. Adding questions about the origins of life drawn from the national study by the Pew Forum on Religion and Public Life (2005) as our additional local questions appeared to be a good way to better understand the ideas of entering college students. This approach has the particular advantage that the students complete this questionnaire during orientation, prior to the start of classes, and that we were able to survey the entire population.

In this study we had 534 students (52% female) with a mean SAT of 1,350. Among these students 62% endorsed evolution through natural selection, compared to 26% of adults in the national study and the 40% of college graduates nationally. We also found that 22% subscribed to a view compatible with intelligent design (humans evolved over time guided by a supreme being), 5% supported creationism, and 10% reported that they didn't know. Students were remarkably certain about these beliefs, with 66% reporting they were completely or nearly so, and only 11% reporting below the midpoint on a five-point certainty scale. Few claimed to be highly knowledgeable, however, with only 36% reporting above the midpoint on a five-point scale. They are certain about what they don't claim to know very well, which presents a considerable challenge for college educators.

Moreover, lack of support for the theory of evolution was positively correlated with strength of religious convictions, spirituality, certainty of this viewpoint, similarity to parents' views, and the expectation that religious beliefs and convictions were likely to strengthen during college. Those who were low in support for evolution also had lower self-reported knowledge and SAT math scores. If this is reflective of college students elsewhere, this means that a good percentage of college students arrive unaccepting of a basic scientific theory, not particularly knowledgeable about it, and clinging to both the certainty of those views and the expectation that their convictions and values will strengthen.

These findings not only suggest the importance of strong science education, but indicate the need for studies that help define models for achieving conceptual change and an epistemic appreciation of science. These data also suggest that educators need to think carefully about how to support individuals as they make a transition in their scientific understanding of the world in cases where this may also involve concomitant changes in beliefs about self, religion, and authority.

In our second study, we were interested in replicating aspects of the Sinatra et al. (2003) study, altering other aspects, and adding additional questions that appear pertinent in light of current controversies. In particular, in contrast to the Sinatra et al. study, we wanted to utilize a general text about evolution, rather than the measures of specific examples of evolution used in that study, to use a domain-specific measure of epistemic beliefs rather than a domain-general one, and to add questions about the teaching of intelligent design, the meaning of the word "theory," and questions about epistemic stance toward the acceptance of others' opinions (as an indicator of multiplism). We also were interested in considering some of the affective components noted in Gill's model of conceptual change (Gill, 2004), as a basis for future studies on the nature of change during the college years in regard to understanding evolutionary theory. We wanted to know the degree to which evolution is an issue that implicates the self. Is there a personal investment in this issue? Does it have emotional salience?

Participants

In our first administration of this second study, 89 students (40% males) from 30 different majors completed the study. Among them, 39% were first-year students, 47% sophomores, 6% juniors, and 7% seniors. All had taken biology in high school. Although 21% said they were majoring or were likely to major in natural science, 14% reported that they did not plan to take a natural science course in college.

Procedure

In this survey we utilized a web-based format, with a variety of instruments, as well as questions we designed, including several open-ended questions so that we might access student thinking about these issues. Students first read a passage from *National Geographic* that explained and described evolution. They then answered questions about the comprehensibility of the text, and then completed an assessment that measured their acceptance of the theory of evolution. We also asked them to describe the meaning of the word "theory" in their own words, and to explain their thoughts about the acceptance of evolution. We asked them how certain they were about the theory and how certain they thought scientists were, and asked them to choose a statement that best fit their point of view about the origin of life. Students were asked how similar their views were to their parents, if they experienced any conflict, and, if so, to describe the conflict and to discuss how they managed it. We also inquired about intelligent design and whether they thought it should be taught in schools and to explain their thinking on the topic, and we asked about the relevance of the topic and its personal significance. We then asked for level of agreement with the statement, "In regard to the theory of evolution, each person is entitled to his or her own opinion" and provided a space for open-ended comments where they were asked to explain their response. Measures that followed included a 20-item instrument on the acceptance of evolution, a set of six examples of evolution that they had to interpret as a measure of understanding, a belief identification measure, and measures of domain-specific epistemic beliefs about science, need for cognition, and religiosity. We also collected demographic information, such as political affiliation, major, number of science courses taken, and time spent learning about evolution in their high school classes.

Findings

In this study, 87% of participants reported that evolution seems to be a mostly (49%) or completely (37%) accurate account of how human beings were created or developed. Pressed further to identify with a set of statements about the origins of life, however, only 51% endorsed evolution without the involvement of a supreme being. Although only 5% endorsed creationism, 37% of the participants believed evolution was set in motion by a supreme being, and another 7% said that the supreme being continues to shape or override the evolutionary process. More than a quarter (27%) reported experiencing some conflict in their beliefs, and this is a group we have begun studying further. In terms of whether the topic of evolution is personally meaningful, three-quarters (76%) of the participants said that evolution is either somewhat or very important to them personally, and nearly half (45%) reported that it is somewhat or very emotionally significant. Clearly this is a topic of interest and meaning to most, and this is not surprising considering the attention the media has given to evolution. This also provides evidence that we need to think beyond a "cold" model of conceptual change (Gill, 2004; Pintrich, Marx, & Boyle, 1993), acknowledging the affective components of learning when considering pedagogical strategies for teaching evolution.

Among the students in this particular study, acceptance of evolution was correlated with understanding of the theory, a finding that has not been consistent across studies (e.g., Sinatra et al., 2003), and both understanding and acceptance were correlated with self-reported knowledge of the topic. In terms of epistemological development, multiplists (those who think one opinion is as good as another) were less likely to accept evolution than those who were in transition between multiplism and evaluativism. That transitional group was less likely to accept evolution than were evaluativists, the group most likely to accept the theory. We found only one dualist, and two who were categorized as between dualism and multiplism; this would suggest that the challenge for college faculty in terms of the promotion of epistemological development might be how to provide students with the tools and the supported practice to learn to move beyond multiplism and to begin evaluating competing claims.

We also used a domain-specific level of epistemic beliefs, and found that sophistication in the dimension of certainty of science beliefs was correlated with need for cognition (Cacioppo & Petty, 1982), and with the importance and emotional significance of the theory of evolution, but not with acceptance or understanding. Many students do not view knowledge in science as certain; this may in fact be somewhat of a problem as it leads them to question the validity of evolutionary theory, given their interpretation of uncertainty. Students need a nuanced understanding of this construct and of how claims are supported and falsified in science.

A surprising finding was that acceptance was positively correlated with conflict about the theory. Our initial assumption had been that those who were less accepting would be the ones most conflicted, but this was not the case, as those who did not accept evolutionary theory appeared to experience less conflict than those who did. So if cognitive conflict is necessary for conceptual change, educators may have to find a way to induce it among those not accepting of evolution—and yet these are the students who also reported the lowest need for cognition and who said they are least likely to take science courses of their own volition. However, we do not know if some of the students who reported conflict at the time of this study were those who had already changed their views on evolution since arriving in college. We are now conducting further studies to investigate this process, as we are particularly interested in how students resolve competing claims from important sources of authority in their lives and suspect this is one of the epistemic challenges for students in regard to this issue.

Understanding of evolution was not related to the self-reported amount of time that students' high school curriculum devoted to teaching about evolution, although the time spent learning the topic in high school was related to how knowledgeable they thought they were. Taking a college course on evolution, however, was strongly related to understanding. This suggests both the importance of improving high school science education and the need for continuing to address these issues at the college level.

Issues of "Theory"

One aspect that is often discussed in relation to students' misconceptions about evolutionary theory is the meaning of the word "theory." In the context of this study, where the survey heading and particular questions themselves referred to the "theory of evolution," we asked students to tell us in their own words what they think is the meaning of the word. We analyzed these on a qualitative basis and identified multiple categories: 6% said that it was an idea or hunch; 12% said that it was an idea or hypothesis that could be tested; 25% said that it is a partially proven or unproven idea about something, but often widely accepted; and 23% said that it is a hypothesis that has been corroborated by research. Another 28% mentioned explanation, but in a limited or truncated manner, and 7% gave an elaborated definition consistent with scientific thinking. So it is no surprise that students are dubious about evolutionary theory as an explanatory mechanism if they don't understand the intended scientific meaning of "theory." In our follow-up studies with larger samples we are investigating how these conceptions of theory are related to students' thoughts about evolution and to science course-taking, among other constructs.

Teaching of Intelligent Design

Asked whether intelligent design should be taught in schools, 21% agreed that it should. The belief that it should be taught, not surprisingly, was correlated with spirituality and religion. They justified this in the following ways:

"We have to teach students to think critically and present them with both sides of a controversial subject."

"If there is more than one theory, both should be taught. It is better to present all the information available and let the students make their own decision about what to believe."

"Freedom of religion means having a knowledge of all possibilities. Also, evolution is still strictly a theory, so there is no reason for it to be the only one taught."

"The theory of evolution is not any more proved than the idea of intelligent design."

"Creationism has been around for thousands of years, while Darwin did his work just under 200 years ago."

These quotes illustrate the connections between epistemic stance, understanding of the meaning of theory in a scientific science, and support for the teaching of intelligent design. Clearly much work is needed to assist students in disentangling a variety of misconceptions.

Conclusions and Future Directions

A central conclusion of the preliminary analyses we have reported is that even well-educated college students continue to have misconceptions about evolution, the meaning of the term "theory," and the role of schools in teaching scientific knowledge. In addition, the theory of evolution is a personally significant issue for many, and is related to a host of constructs central to conceptual change, including epistemic understanding.

We have begun to speculate about other related issues that may help guide future studies, as well as prompt reflection by educators. One of these is that we have pondered whether students schooled in the current climate have confused tolerance and relativism. We suspect that in very well-meaning ways they may have overgeneralized messages about multiculturalism and tolerance of others' beliefs. They may have extended their acceptance of others' perspectives to include issues that merit deeper consideration and for which there is empirical support. Skillful argumentation, refutation, and the marshalling of significant evidence to support contradictory claims, once a central aspect of higher education, may be eschewed by students who find this inappropriate or offensive to others. This needs further examination and pedagogical attention.

Second, we find the inconsistent results in other studies regarding the relation between understanding and acceptance of evolution to be of considerable interest, although we did find a positive correlation in our research. A disconnect between understanding and acceptance has led us to inquire about instructors' goals in this regard. Our preliminary conversations with college science faculty members suggest that the two are often separated pedagogically in the teaching of evolutionary theory, reportedly out of respect for students' religious beliefs. This separation does not appear to be the case on other topics that are difficult to both understand and accept, for example, counterintuitive laws of physics, or explanations for the seasons. Thus far, we are unable to find scientific parallels of topics where educators would be satisfied if students could demonstrate an understanding but not be concerned about whether the students accepted the theory as the most valid explanation for a set of phenomena. Why is evolution so different? Is this a cultural phenomenon in the United States where educators are particularly cautious when religion is involved, or is this more pervasive? This has led us to an interest in studying teachers' beliefs further, as well as fostered our continued interest in pursuing cross-cultural research on this topic to understand how cultures define such debates and introduce pedagogical caution.

We have several other issues we wish to pursue in future studies. We are currently conducting another study to further investigate issues of self, identity, and emotional salience for students. As noted earlier, we want to better understand how students resolve competing sources of epistemic authority. Raviv and colleagues (Raviv, Bar-tal, Raviv, Biran, & Sela, 2003) found that teachers perceive themselves as being more of an epistemic authority than students consider them to be, and also believe that students see them as more of an epistemic authority than is actually the case. When authorities conflict (e.g., pastors, parents, teachers, peers), whom do students believe and what do they accept? Currently we are conducting a longitudinal study with a larger group and more range across college years and post-graduation.

This research has a number of implications, and on multiple levels. We hope it can be used to help inform science educators in particular about attending to epistemic stance in the process of teaching about evolution. Our goal is to continue to contribute to conceptual models that map the complex components that inhibit, impede, or enhance student understanding of this important topic. We also hope such research can be useful to those thinking about how college education prepares an informed citizenry. Teaching students not only how to evaluate competing knowledge claims but the importance of doing so must become a key component of liberal arts and science education.

References

Andre, T., & Windschitl, M. (2003). Interest, epistemological belief, and intentional conceptual change. In G. M. Sinatra & P. R. Pintrich (Eds.), *Intentional conceptual change* (pp. 173–197). Mahwah, NJ: Erlbaum.

Baxter Magolda, M. B. (1992). *Knowing and reasoning in college: Gender-related patterns in students' intellectual development.* San Francisco, CA: Jossey-Bass.

Baxter Magolda, M. B. (2004). Evolution of a constructivist conceptualization of epistemological reflection. *Educational Psychologist, 39,* 31–42.

Burr, J. E., & Hofer, B. K. (2002). Personal epistemology and theory of mind: Deciphering young children's beliefs about knowledge and knowing. *New Ideas in Psychology, 20,* 199–224.

Cacioppo, J. T., & Petty, R. E. (1982). The need for cognition. *Journal of Personality and Social Psychology, 42,* 116–131.

Conley, A. M., Pintrich, P. R., Vekiri, I., & Harrison, D. (2004). Changes in epistemological beliefs in elementary science students. *Contemporary Educational Psychology, 29,* 186–204.

Elby, A., & Hammer, D. (2001). On the substance of a sophisticated epistemology. *Science Education, 85,* 554–567.

Gill, M. G. (2004). Changing preservice teachers' epistemological beliefs about teaching and learning in mathematics. *Contemporary Educational Psychology, 29,* 164–185.

Hofer, B. K. (2000). Dimensionality and disciplinary differences in personal epistemology. *Contemporary Educational Psychology, 25,* 378–405.

Hofer, B. K. (2001). Personal epistemology research: Implications for learning and teaching. *Educational Psychology Review, 13*(4), 353–383.

Hofer, B. K. (2004). Epistemological understanding as a metacognitive process: Thinking aloud during online searching. *Educational Psychologist, 39*(1), 43–55.

Hofer, B. K. (2006). Beliefs about knowledge and knowing: Integrating domain specificity and domain generality. *Educational Psychology Review, 18,* 67–76.

Hofer, B. K., & Pintrich, P. R. (1997). The development of epistemological theories: Beliefs about knowledge and knowing and their relation to learning. *Review of Educational Research, 67,* 88–140.

Hofer, B. K., & Pintrich, P. R. (Eds.). (2002). *Personal epistemology: The psychology of beliefs about knowledge and knowing.* Mahwah, NJ: Erlbaum.

Kardash, C. M., & Howell, K. L. (2000). Effects of epistemological beliefs and topic-specific beliefs on undergraduates' cognitive and strategic processing of dual-positional text. *Journal of Educational Psychology, 92,* 524–535.

King, P. M., & Kitchener, K. S. (1994). *Developing reflective judgment: Understanding and promoting intellectual growth and critical thinking in adolescents and adults.* San Francisco, CA: Jossey-Bass.

King, P. M., & Kitchener, K. S. (2004). Reflective judgment: Theory and research on the development of epistemic assumptions through adulthood. *Educational Psychologist, 39,* 5–18.

Kitchener, K. S. (1983). Cognition, metacognition, and epistemic cognition. *Human Development, 26,* 222–232.

Kuhn, D. (1991). *The skills of argument.* Cambridge, UK: Cambridge University Press.

Kuhn, D. (1999). Metacognitive development. In L. Balter & C. S. Tamis-LeMonda (Eds.), *Child psychology: A handbook of contemporary issues* (pp. 258–286). Philadelphia, PA: Psychology Press.

Kuhn, D., & Weinstock, M. (2002). What is epistemological thinking and why does it matter? In B. K. Hofer & P. R. Pintrich (Eds.), *Personal epistemology: The psychology of beliefs about knowledge and knowing* (pp. 121–144). Mahwah, NJ: Erlbaum.

Kuhn, D., Cheney, R., & Weinstock, M. (2000). The development of epistemological understanding. *Cognitive Development, 15,* 309–328.

Louca, L., Elby, A., Hammer, D., & Kagey, T. (2004). Epistemological resources: Applying a new methodological framework to science instruction. *Educational Psychologist, 39,* 57–68.

Mason, L. (2003). Personal epistemologies and intentional conceptual change. In G. M. Sinatra & P. R. Pintrich (Eds.), *Intentional conceptual change* (pp. 199–236). Mahwah, NJ: Erlbaum.

Mason, L., & Boscolo, P. (2004). Role of epistemological understanding and interest in interpreting a controversy and in topic-specific belief change. *Contemporary Educational Psychology, 29,* 103–128.

Mason, L., & Scirica, F. (2006). Prediction of students' argumentation skills about controversial topics by epistemological understanding. *Learning and Instruction, 16*(5), 492–509.

Muis, K. R. (2004). Personal epistemology and mathematics: A critical review and synthesis of research. *Review of Educational Research, 74,* 317–377.

Muis, K. R., Bendixen, L. D., & Haerle, F. C. (2006). Domain generality and domain specificity in personal epistemology research: Philosophical and empirical reflections in the development of a theoretical model. *Educational Psychology Review, 18,* 3–54.

Perry, W. G. (1970). *Forms of intellectual and ethical development in the college years: A scheme.* New York: Holt, Rinehart & Winston.

Perry, W. G. (1981). Cognitive and ethical growth: The making of meaning. In A. Chickering (Ed.), *The modern American college* (pp. 76–116). San Francisco, CA: Jossey-Bass.

Pew Forum on Religion and Public Life. (2005). *Public divided on origins of life.* Washington, DC: Pew Forum on Religion and Public Life.

Pintrich, P. R., Marx, R. W., & Boyle, R. A. (1993). Beyond cold conceptual change: The role of motivational beliefs and classroom contextual factors in the process of conceptual change. *Review of Educational Research, 63*(2), 167–199.

Qian, G. (2000). Relationship between epistemological beliefs and conceptual change learning. *Reading and Writing Quarterly, 16,* 59–74.

Raviv, A., Bar-tal, D., Raviv, A., Biran, B., & Sela, Z. (2003). Teachers' epistemic authority: Perceptions of students and teachers. *Social Psychology of Education, 6,* 17–42.

Samarapungavan, A., Westby, E. L., & Bodner, G. M. (2006). Contextual epistemic development in science: A comparison of chemistry students and research chemists. *Science Education, 90*(3), 468–495.

Sandoval, W. A. (2005). Understanding students' practical epistemologies and their influence on learning through inquiry. *Science Education, 89*(4), 634–656.

Schommer, M. (1990). Effects of beliefs about the nature of knowledge on comprehension. *Journal of Educational Psychology, 82,* 498–504.

Schommer, M., Crouse, A., & Rhodes, N. (1992). Epistemological beliefs and mathematical text comprehension: Believing it is simple does not make it so. *Journal of Educational Psychology, 82,* 435–443.

Schommer, M., & Walker, K. (1995). Are epistemological beliefs similar across domains? *Journal of Educational Psychology, 87*(3), 424–432.

Schommer-Aikins, M. (2004). Explaining the epistemological belief system: Introducing the embedded systemic model and coordinated research approach. *Educational Psychologist, 39*(1), 19–29.

Schraw, G., Bendixen, L. D., & Dunkle, M. E. (2002). Development and evaluation of the Epistemic Belief Inventory (EBI). In B. K. Hofer & P. R. Pintrich (Eds.), *Personal epistemology: The psychology of beliefs about knowledge and knowing* (pp. 261–275). Mahwah, NJ: Erlbaum.

Sinatra, G. M., Southerland, S. A., McConaughy, F., & Demastes, J. W. (2003). Intentions and beliefs in students' understanding and acceptance of biological evolution. *Journal of Research in Science Teaching, 40*(5), 510–528.

Wainryb, C., Shaw, L. A., Langley, M., Cottam, K., & Lewis, R. (2004). Children's thinking about diversity of belief and in the early school years: Judgments of relativism, tolerance, and disagreeing persons. *Child Development, 75,* 687–703.

Wellman, H. M. (1990). *The child's theory of mind.* Cambridge, MA: Bradford/MIT Press.

Wellman, H. M., Cross, D., & Watson, J. (2001). Meta-analysis of theory-of-mind development: The truth about false belief. *Child Development, 72,* 655–684.

Wildenger, L., Hofer, B. K., & Burr, J. E. (2010). Epistemological development in very young knowers. In L. D. Bendixen & F. C. Haerle (Eds.), *Personal epistemology in Pre-K to 12 education: Theory, research and educational implications.* Cambridge, UK: Cambridge University Press.

Windschitl, M., & Andre, T. (1998). Using computer simulations to enhance conceptual change: The roles of constructivist instruction and student epistemological beliefs. *Journal of Research in Science Teaching, 35*(2), 145–160.

Wineburg, S. (1998). Reading Abraham Lincoln: An expert/expert study in the interpretation of historical texts. *Cognitive Science, 22,* 319–346.

Chapter 6

Engaging Multiple Epistemologies

Implications for Science Education

*E. Margaret Evans, Cristine H. Legare, and
Karl S. Rosengren*

Introduction

> It might seem contradictory to believe that humans were created in their
> present form at one time within the past 10,000 years and at the same
> time believe that humans developed over millions of years from less
> advanced forms of life. But, based on an analysis of the two side-by-side
> questions asked this month about evolution and creationism, it appears
> that a substantial number of Americans hold these conflicting views.
>
> (Gallup, June 11, 2007, p. 4)

In a 2007 Gallup poll, 24% of Americans endorsed beliefs in both evolution
and creationism, with another 41% believing that creationism is true and evolution is false. Of the rest, 28% believe that evolution is true and creationism
is false (June 11, 2007). This result echoes earlier findings among parents and
their adolescent children in the Midwest, with about a third of the sample
endorsing both creationist and evolutionist views (Evans, 1994/95, 2000a,
2000b, 2001). Our focus in this chapter is on this phenomenon. What are the
conceptual processes that underlie the endorsement of seemingly mutually
inconsistent epistemologies? To address this issue we draw upon research in
three related areas—beliefs about illness, death, and origins—and link these
findings to recent work on the development of intuitive theories of biology
and psychology. Although evolution is typically treated as if it were distinctly
different from other areas of biological reasoning, we highlight similarities in
the reasoning of children and adults across these three areas. In this process,
we examine the different ways in which individuals engage multiple epistemologies and the circumstances that foster such an engagement. We conclude
by drawing out the implications of this line of research for informal and
formal science education.

Most of the media focus on the evolution–creationist controversy tends to
report it as a clash of belief systems, an either/or debate, with notable atheists,
such as Dawkins, taking up one side of the debate and notable creationists,
exemplified by the biblical literalists, taking the opposing view (Scott, 2005).

Similarly, the focus of most Gallup polls conducted over the last 20 years (in the United States) has been on evolution and creationism as competing beliefs, particularly with respect to the origin of humans (Gallup, 2007). The pattern of results has remained relatively unchanged over that time period. Dawkins' position, that humans evolved without the help of a supernatural being, is regularly endorsed by about 13% of the sample, with the biblical version of human origins endorsed by 46%. Yet, typically, a substantial portion of these samples (about 36%) accepted evolution, while also acknowledging a role for God. How is it possible to endorse such seemingly incompatible belief systems? Without more detailed analyses it is difficult to know exactly how these beliefs were reconciled, but one strong possibility is that they endorsed theistic evolution, the belief that God is a supernatural agent who set up the naturalistic conditions under which evolution occurred (Evans, 1994/95, 2001, 2008; Scott, 2005). In this scenario, variations of which are endorsed by theologians from most non-fundamentalist Western religions (Ruse, 2005), God is the final or ultimate cause, with evolutionary causes at a more proximal point on the causal chain. This contrasts with the view of biblical literalists who believe that God was directly involved in the creation of humans and other species (Scott, 2005). The latter version, with God as the proximate cause, is the definition of creationism that we use in this chapter.

Furthermore, theologians who endorse religious and evolutionary explanations for the origins of species are not alone; many contemporary scientists also reconcile these belief systems in similar ways. Gould, the evolutionary biologist, described them as "nonoverlapping magisteria" (Gould, 1997), each of which plays a crucial role in human affairs. For geneticist Frances Collins, God "exists outside of space and time" (Biema, 2006). In these types of epistemological blends, most notably championed by evolutionary biologist Ken Miller (1999), a devout Catholic, religion and science are viewed as complementary, not competing views of the world. This analysis suggests that there are a range of complementary rather than competing belief systems about science and religion (see www.templeton.org/belief, for some intriguing examples).

These different ways of engaging multiple epistemologies appear to be relatively common among scientific, philosophical, and religious leaders who have been forced to confront the apparent contradictions, but this mode of reasoning has yet to be investigated in much detail in the lay public. The traditional analysis suggests that these different worldviews can be viewed as competitive *ways of knowing*, with science and religion in a battle for the *truth*, or as complementary but distinct epistemological stances. Our investigations of the beliefs of lay adults and children suggest, however, that there are additional models that could bind these beliefs in coherent explanatory frameworks. In our analyses we recognize two broad sources of belief (Sperber, 1996), the first derived directly from the sociocultural context, via the media and cultural institutions, and the second, intuitive beliefs, which are largely untutored and derived from our everyday reasoning (Atran & Sperber, 1991). We begin by reviewing some work on intuitive beliefs about the natural world, which, we claim, underlie the culturally endorsed epistemological stances. Moreover, from this work on an intuitive epistemology it would appear that epistemological blends and shifts between epistemological stances are commonplace and part and parcel of the causal flexibility that characterizes human thought (Gutheil, Vera, & Keil, 1998; Poling & Evans, 2002).

Intuitive Theories

Over the course of a day children and adults use a wide variety of explanatory models to reason about the outcome of various events, such as the disappearance of a cookie in a cookie jar, the shattering of a drinking glass on a ceramic tile, or the lack of movement in a robin lying on the front walk. In many instances a single explanation adequately captures the causal structure of the event. Because of his past habits and love of cookies it is surmised that Dad raided the cookie jar, that the drinking glass broke because it fell to the floor and glass is more fragile than tile, and the robin is not moving because it has died. In these situations explanations from the realms of three different foundational theories, those of intuitive psychology (theory of mind), intuitive physics (or mechanics), and intuitive biology, adequately capture plausible and likely causes of the three events (Wellman & Gelman, 1998). Although it would be possible to talk about each of these events using other types of explanations, such as magic or the will of God, these do not seem as straightforward as those provided by intuitive psychology, physics, and biology.

In their everyday lives children and adults shift between these different forms of causal understanding (Schult & Wellman, 1997), though at times causal explanations from one of these domains pop up in one of the other domains. For example, an individual might say that his car "was hurt" in an accident as if the car was a biological organism that could be injured and perhaps "heal." Or another individual might say her car "doesn't want to start" as if the car has a mind of its own that determines whether it starts or not. In other instances individuals may take widely divergent worldviews, perhaps religious and scientific ones, and combine them to create a coherent model of the world. Still others might be quite happy to compartmentalize these different worldviews to describe different phenomena or use these different perspectives in distinctly different contexts. One of the goals of this chapter is to examine those circumstances when children and adults maintain a sharp boundary between different types of explanations, when individuals allow seemingly contradictory explanations to co-exist, and when individuals blend these contradictory explanations into a relatively coherent framework.

In the next sections, we explore how children and adults navigate between different causal explanations for biological phenomena. Although multiple forms of explanation can be used to explain a variety of psychological and physical phenomena, we focus here on biology because of the central problem of understanding how children and adults reason about evolutionary processes. First, we provide evidence, using examples from our own research, that individuals, from both Western and non-Western samples, combine or shift between natural and supernatural explanations to explain phenomena that address fundamental existential questions: *illness, death*, and *origins*. In the process we comment on several factors that serve to trigger these novel alignments. Finally, we shall argue, again using research data, that although different individuals approach evolutionary reasoning from very different perspectives, by and large their explanations fall into characteristic patterns.

Using Multiple Epistemologies to Reason about Biological Phenomena

The issue of how children and adults coordinate natural and supernatural belief systems regarding biological phenomena is a broad one that, we propose, is of universal concern. On the one hand, there is no society we are aware of that wholly excludes supernatural beliefs. Even within highly educated, industrialized modern communities, at least some individuals endorse supernatural beliefs, ranging from God to ghosts to astrology (Evans, 2000b; Zusne & Jones, 1989). On the other hand, there is no society we are aware of that wholly excludes natural beliefs. Even within highly traditional, non-industrialized communities, at least some individuals endorse folk-biological beliefs (e.g., regarding inheritance, Astuti, Solomon, & Carey, 2004, and death, Astuti & Harris, 2008). Thus, access to natural and supernatural explanatory frameworks is a universal psychological experience, and coordinating these different belief systems is a general cognitive problem. People in all societies are faced with the task of conceptualizing potentially contradictory belief systems about biological phenomena.

One approach to investigating the relationship between different epistemologies is to focus on content areas in which both natural and supernatural explanations are prevalent (Evans, 2001). Although there are potentially a number of different content areas that are particularly apt to draw on divergent explanatory systems, focusing on individuals' understanding of the illness, death, and the origins of species are specific areas where the prevalence of multiple explanations may be quite common. These concepts also share a number of properties that may enhance the likelihood of drawing on different types of explanation. First, a central aspect of these phenomena is that they often involve unobservable causes such as microorganisms and genes. Second, each of these content areas is associated with strong emotions. For illness and death these emotions arise from the loss or potential loss of loved ones. For the concept of origins, the emotions surround the belief that humans are somehow special and different from other organisms (Evans, 2001) or that acceptance of evolution is associated with a range of negative outcomes (e.g., Evans, 2008; Brem, Ranney, & Schindel, 2003). These emotions, whether due to existential crises about humans' role in the universe or due to the loss or potential loss of loved ones, may serve to elicit those intuitive explanations most intimately concerned with human affairs, namely an intuitive psychology. Finally, both illness and death are associated with particular rituals that are embedded in specific cultural contexts and practices that predate our current scientific understanding of these concepts and which continue to co-exist alongside our scientific knowledge. In the case of origins, different cultures clearly treat the status of humans as elevated compared to other species, and an evolutionary account of origins calls this cultural understanding into question.

A Taxonomy of Cultural and Intuitive Beliefs

Before delving into the studies, we first outline a proposal for a taxonomy of beliefs, which is portrayed in a simplified graphic (see Table 6.1) that is

Table 6.1 A Proposed Taxonomy of Cultural and Intuitive Beliefs: Explaining Origins, Death, and Disease

	Cultural beliefs		Intuitive beliefs	
	Science	Supernatural	Intuitive biology	Intuitive psychology
Cultural beliefs Science Supernatural	Quadrant A Competing cultural models i. Science dominant ii. Supernatural dominant Co-existence cultural models i. Causal chain ii. Target dependent iii. Parallel iv. Juxtaposition		Quadrant C Synthetic blends Fusion of intuitive and cultural beliefs, with intuitive beliefs dominating	
Intuitive beliefs Intuitive biology Intuitive psychology	Quadrant B Overlay models Cultural model overlay, intuitive model underlay (or foundation)		Quadrant D Competing intuitive models i. Intuitive psychology dominant ii. Intuitive biology dominant Co-existence intuitive models i. Causal chain ii. Target dependent iii. Parallel iv. Juxtaposition	

divided into four quadrants, each of which represents a different combination of cultural and intuitive beliefs. This graphic will be used to frame the specific models presented in each quadrant. To make the problem of creating such a taxonomy tractable, we have reduced the problem space by focusing on scientific and supernatural perspectives, construed broadly, for cultural beliefs, and only on intuitive biology and psychology for intuitive beliefs.

We start with the cultural models, found in Quadrant A of Table 6.1: these characterize the different ways in which individuals might represent both scientific and supernatural beliefs. The model most often cited in the media is a competitive one in which one mode dominates and the other is dismissed, though its presence is acknowledged. A key example here is Dawkins' championing of evolutionary explanations and his contention that supernatural explanations are childish (Dawkins, 1995). Reconciliations of these two extremes are presented in a variety of *co-existence* models. In a *causal chain*, described earlier, a supernatural cause might precede the scientific cause, as in theistic evolution. Yet another possibility is the *target-dependent* model, in which one form of reasoning is reserved for a particular entity or domain, and other forms of reasoning for other entities or domains. For example, some individuals treat humans, but not other animals, as created by God (Evans, 2001). This type of reasoning also captures Gould's (1997) concept of non-overlapping magisteria, where religion and science occupy separate realms, the one supernatural and the other natural, and are used to explain different phenomena, such as the meaning of life versus what constitutes life. Collins' belief that God exists outside time and space may also fit here (Biema, 2006). A third co-existence model is one where individuals hold two very different types of beliefs that are used to explain the same or highly similar phenomena. One example of this model is provided by Subbotsky (2000, 2001) who has shown that both children and adults provided the right context will deny the existence of magic, a form of supernatural reasoning, but will behaviorally exhibit evidence of credulity toward magic for the same seemingly impossible event. We refer to this form of co-existence reasoning as a *parallel reasoning* model in which two different epistemological beliefs are used by the same individual to explain the same or similar outcome. A final form of the co-existence model has been labeled as *juxtaposition reasoning* (Legare & Gelman, 2008; Piaget, 1928). In this model two different forms of reasoning may be used, but not necessarily in any systematic or well-integrated manner.

For intuitive beliefs, found in Quadrant D, the competitive and co-existence models are now used to refer to an intuitive biology and intuitive psychology. As described earlier, the latter provide natural, everyday or commonsense explanations for natural phenomena, from human behavior to growth and development, to evolutionary change. Given the emphasis of this chapter on biological phenomena, we do not directly address claims that an intuitive psychology might also yield religious beliefs (Boyer, 1993; Evans & Wellman, 2006; but see Atran, 2002). Characterizing the ways in which intuitive and cultural beliefs might blend is more difficult. For the moment we acknowledge two broad types, one in which cultural beliefs *overlay* a foundation of intuitive beliefs (Table 6.1, Quadrant B), with cultural beliefs dominating, and the other in which cultural and intuitive beliefs may fuse, in *synthetic blends*, with intuitive beliefs dominating (Table 6.1, Quadrant C). These differ from co-existence models, in that the latter refer to combinations of cultural beliefs (Quadrant A) or of intuitive beliefs (Quadrant D), but not cultural–intuitive blends.

In the next section, we discuss relevant research pertaining to understanding of illness, proceed to talk about death, and then continue with a discussion of research examining explanations of origins. These examples demonstrate how this taxonomy can be applied to different problems in different contexts. We use these examples to suggest that reasoning about evolution is in many ways similar to reasoning about certain other types of biological phenomena that involve existential issues.

Using Multiple Epistemologies to Reason about Illness

Most diseases are caused by an amalgamation of several factors (Thagard, 1998). Anthropological evidence from both industrialized and developing countries indicates that illness is not always interpreted exclusively in biological terms (Green, 1999). Instead, a combination of biological, social, and supernatural explanations are available to explain the process of illness transmission (Brandt & Rozin, 1997; Shweder, Much, Mahapatra, & Park, 1997). For humans, the transfer of illness typically involves a human vector and can therefore be interpreted as interpersonal as well as biological (Nemeroff & Rozin, 2000). Due to the awareness of malicious human action in promoting suffering, especially in contexts of oppression and inequality, people often assume human causes of illness. Among deeply impoverished groups, those who improve their socioeconomic status are subject to witchcraft accusations. In many regions of sub-Saharan Africa and the Caribbean, anthropological reports suggest that supernatural explanations in terms of witchcraft, as well as biological explanations, are both used as explanatory frameworks for illness (Ashforth, 2005; Farmer, 1999).

Co-existence of Beliefs: Biological and Witchcraft Attributions of Illness in South Africa

The co-existence of natural and supernatural belief systems can be investigated most clearly in cultural settings where both these belief systems are prevalent. The AIDS crisis in South Africa provides such a context. In South Africa, multiple approaches to illness are available, including traditional folk medicine, faith healing, and modern biomedical services (Schlebusch & Ruggieri, 1996).

Perhaps the most prominent supernatural explanation for AIDS in South Africa is that of witchcraft, or the practices of persons with malicious intent to cause harm through the use of harmful substances and invisible supernatural forces (Ashforth, 2005). Witchcraft is often associated with *muthi* (*sejeso* in Sesotho), or the malicious manipulation of herbs and other substances, and is believed to cause a wide variety of misfortunes ranging from unemployment and interpersonal discord to illness and death. The civilizing agenda of both the colonial and apartheid regimes viewed any beliefs and practices associated with witchcraft as irrational and primitive. This perspective clearly is one of competing epistemologies with an attempt of the established regimes to drive out the competing epistemology. Education based on Western science and Christianity was viewed as a necessary prerequisite for ameliorating and replacing such beliefs. However, traditional health practices do not necessarily disappear with modernization or education (Ashforth, 2005; Niehaus, 2001). In South Africa, a country of 47 million people, there are nearly 500,000 traditional health practitioners, healers, and prophets working outside the formal biomedical system and 25,000 medical doctors. This is equivalent to one traditional healer for every 80 people in contrast to one medical doctor for every 1,600 people. Notably, the medical doctor to patient ratio in the United States is 1:375. Traditional healers serve to interpret and counteract perceived cases of witchcraft, and provide indirect evidence that millions of South Africans attribute misfortunes to witchcraft (Ashforth, 2001, 2005; Niehaus, 2001).

How do intuitive biological (including scientific) explanatory systems co-exist with non-scientific, supernatural explanatory frameworks? There are several broad possibilities. One is that the natural and supernatural realms remain distinct, alternative views of the world recruited to explain distinct phenomena, contexts, and events as in the target-dependent model described earlier. For example, regarding illness, natural explanations may be used to explain transient illnesses such as colds, and supernatural explanations may be used to explain severe illnesses such as AIDS. A second possibility is that natural and supernatural frameworks are used jointly in a blended or synthetic fashion to explain the same phenomena. On this latter possibility, the integration of the frameworks might be quite loose (a person may appeal to both natural and supernatural explanations, but without consideration of how they would interact) as in the juxtaposition model, or instead may combine precisely (a person may treat natural causes as proximate, but supernatural causes as ultimate: e.g., contaminated blood causes illness, but bewitchment causes a person to come into contact with the contaminated blood), as in the causal chain model.

However, given the seemingly contradictory nature of natural and supernatural explanatory frameworks, it is also feasible that they compete. A major implication of the competition model is that the acquisition of a biological explanation could gradually supplant a supernatural explanation, which exists only in the absence of an accurate and coherent biological explanation. Thus, supernatural explanations for illness might exist as a "placeholder" for biological information, which, once acquired, replaces supernatural explanations (Mitchell, 1965).

Legare and Gelman (2008) examined the co-existence of natural and supernatural explanations for illness and disease transmission from a developmental perspective. The participants (5-, 7-, 11-, and 15-year-olds and adults; $N = 366$) were drawn from two Sesotho-speaking, South African communities, where Western biomedical and traditional healing frameworks are both available. In Studies 1 and 2, participants were given the opportunity to endorse or reject a variety of biological and supernatural explanations for AIDS. Results indicated that although biological explanations for illness were endorsed at high levels in that participants of all age groups endorsed biological explanations for at least one vignette, witchcraft was also often endorsed. Bewitchment explanations for at least one vignette were endorsed by 47% of 5-year-olds, 59% of 7-year-olds, 47% of 11-year-olds, 34% of 15-year-olds, and 100% of adults. Importantly, bewitchment explanations were not the result of ignorance of biological causes. Thus, they existed alongside, and were not replaced by biological explanations.

Studies 1 and 2 also showed that while endorsement of witchcraft explanations for AIDS was high among adults, it was significantly lower among adolescents. Hence, there were considerably fewer co-existence responses among adolescents. One plausible explanation for this difference between adolescents and adults is that adolescents in school have had more exposure to educational programs concerning the biological causes of AIDS and these have been successful in reducing their belief in explanations based on witchcraft. This would be an important result for both theoretical and practical reasons. First, from a theoretical point of view it provides evidence that natural and supernatural frameworks do not always co-exist. They can be brought into conflict with one another. More specifically, it implies that adolescents who receive information about the viral basis of AIDS are subsequently less prone to endorse explanations based on witchcraft. Second, from a practical point of view, it suggests that adolescents who have a more thorough medical understanding of AIDS will be more likely to have a realistic and accurate appreciation of what constitutes risky behavior as well as the preventive steps that can be taken.

This study also indicated several ways that individuals reconcile and reason about seemingly incompatible belief systems. In Study 3, adolescent and adult participants provided explanations for vignettes that provided a substantial amount of contextual information about characters who had been afflicted by AIDS. There were four conditions that varied in the kind of explanatory system that was primed: biological only, bewitchment only, both biological and bewitchment, and neither. Results indicated that although biological explanations are the default explanatory system for interpreting AIDS, when attention is drawn to socially risky behavior believed to put one at risk for witchcraft attacks (lack of generosity or jealousy), participants give primarily witchcraft explanations for AIDS. Additionally, the data from this study provided evidence that biological and bewitchment explanations can co-exist in at least three distinct ways in this cultural context: juxtaposition reasoning, parallel reasoning, and causal chain reasoning (see Table 6.1). Each reasoning type is a different solution to the problem of how to combine biological and bewitchment belief systems to explain illness.

Juxtaposition reasoning accommodates multiple belief systems, though not in a clearly integrated manner (i.e., it is not clear what role each domain plays). An example of juxtaposition reasoning was provided by one informant who suggested that AIDS was caused by "Witchcraft, which is mixed with evil spirits, and having unprotected sex." Parallel reasoning provides the greatest separation between biology and witchcraft. More specifically, the same illness is believed to have either natural or supernatural origins that are entirely non-interactive. Adults using parallel reasoning maintain that although AIDS has a biological explanation, witchcraft can cause an equally deadly disease that mimics AIDS. For example, "Witchcraft can cause a disease that looks like AIDS" or "To medical doctors it seems like AIDS but it is not. The spell was supposed to look like AIDS." The notion of "supernatural AIDS" is arguably a reaction to the information people receive from AIDS education programs indicating explicitly that witchcraft does not cause AIDS, while nonetheless maintaining witchcraft as an explanatory system for illness and misfortune generally (Niehaus, 2001). Causal chain reasoning appears to be the most coherent co-existence reasoning pattern because it takes into account which aspects of the causal chain should be attributed to each explanation type. This kind of reasoning addresses the "how" versus "why" distinction in causal explanations. Most typically, the proximate cause is identified as unprotected sex, whereas the final cause is believed to be witchcraft. For example, witches are believed to be capable of distorting your sense of good judgment or putting an AIDS-infected person in your path. This series of studies provides strong evidence for the co-existence model of natural and supernatural explanatory frameworks.

Returning to the overview of different ways of combining biological and supernatural explanations (see Table 6.1), in this discussion of AIDS transmission the focus has been on culturally derived beliefs (see Table 6.1, Quadrant A). Witchcraft and biological or natural explanations of AIDS are both embedded in cultural models sanctioned by the purveyors of folk medicine and biomedical services. Participants in these studies endorsed competing and co-existence models of AIDS transmission, combining the latter forms of explanation in diverse ways. Likewise, in the following discussion of beliefs about death, the role of cultural beliefs is examined in detail, but this time in a Western context with children from different ethnic backgrounds.

Using Multiple Epistemologies to Reason about Death

Like illness, death can be explained using a variety of different types of explanations. We can discuss death in terms of the cessation of biological processes or in the case of humans and some other higher organisms we can discuss death in terms of the cessation of psychological processes. This is another example of target-dependent reasoning, but in this case it involves foundational theories of biology and psychology. We can also think of death in terms of a third intuitive theory, physics or mechanics, when we refer to the physical body that is left after death and the space that it occupies. But these forms of explanation seem distant, far removed from the emotionally laden situation that arises when an individual experiences the death of a loved one. This may be one reason why explanations based on intuitive biology or other foundational theories often give way to religious and spiritual explanations of death.

New research has investigated children's understanding of death in the context of the larger cultural discourse around death (Gutiérrez, Vasquez, Anderson, Rosengren, & Miller, 2007; Rosengren, Gutiérrez, & Miller, 2009). In the United States, death is rarely discussed openly with children, rather it is something that is generally avoided, with parents routinely shielding their children from images and experiences related to death (Aries, 1974). In contrast, in Mexico, death is celebrated, viewed as part of the fabric of everyday life, with children participating as partners in rituals and traditions surrounding death, such as the Day of the Dead celebration (Lomnitz, 2005). In Mexican culture images of death that would be viewed as macabre in the United States are common in the lives of children. How do children in these neighboring, but very different, cultures experience death and come to understand it?

Traditionally, based on Piaget's research and theory (Piaget, 1929), children were thought not to have a very sophisticated or biological understanding of death until as late as 9 or 10. Piaget clearly assumed a competitive model with respect to different epistemologies, believing that scientific reasoning eventually won over earlier forms of reasoning that were pre-causal and non-scientific. This view, still relatively widely held by practitioners working with children, suggests that the strong emotions surrounding death make it particularly difficult for children to understand the finality of death. Researchers such as Speece and Brent (1984) have identified a number of additional subconcepts that children appear to have some difficulty grasping, including causality (death is brought about by particular causes), universality (all living things eventually die), and irreversibility (once a living thing dies it cannot come back to life). More recent work suggests that children understand important aspects of these subconcepts by as young as four years of age and potentially earlier, especially if death is discussed with respect to entities such as plants that are far removed from humans (Nguyen & Gelman, 2002), or the focus is on animals rather than humans, or if the questions focus on the cessation of biological rather than psychological behaviors (Harris & Giménez, 2005; Poling & Evans, 2004b). This more current work has tended to suggest that children have a fairly accurate understanding of death from a biological perspective by a relatively young age (four to six years) (Slaughter & Lyons, 2003).

The relatively sophisticated understanding of death, reported by cognitive developmental researchers, contrasts sharply with reports from parents that their children have substantial misconceptions about death (Nguyen & Rosengren, 2004). This research suggests that parents believe their children to have particular difficulty with the concepts of the finality and irreversibility of death. In their analysis of children's understanding of death, Nguyen and Rosengren (2004) suggest that these misconceptions should perhaps be construed as "alternative conceptions" that combine biological conceptions of death with those based on religious or spiritual explanations. Research by Harris and Giménez (2005) has also found that children often endorse both biological and religious conceptions of death. In their research they found these forms of reasoning vary by context (secular versus religious) and age, with older children exhibiting more evidence for the co-existence of these two different types of beliefs. It is likely that in both of these research studies instances of causal chain or juxtaposition reasoning were present.

Rosengren and colleagues have been investigating children's reasoning about death more directly in interviews with children and their parents (Rosengren et al., 2009). These researchers have also investigated how death is presented in books commonly read to children. What this research has revealed, as Aries originally suggested (1974), is that children in the United States are often shielded from death and death-related experiences by parents and the larger culture. For example, in an analysis of 100 common books read to young children, only three had any mention of death (Gutiérrez, 2006).

When children are exposed to death, a wide range of explanations of death seem to be provided to them. These explanations often involve a single causal model that may be purely natural or scientific (e.g., when you die, your body stops working), or purely religious (e.g., when you die you go to heaven). Other explanations provided by parents or in books adopt a co-existence model of death that resembles the causal chain reasoning discussed earlier (e.g., when you die your body stops working, but your soul goes to heaven). In an analysis of parents' comments to children's questions, as well as an in-depth study of literature especially designed for children who have lost a loved one, these researchers have found that divergent forms of explanation are commonly provided in the same book or parental response to children's questions. Thus, many children appear to be exposed to multiple forms of explanation for death throughout childhood. This exposure to multiple forms of explanation is likely the case for other aspects of biological reasoning such as illness and origins.

How do children interpret this seemingly contradictory information? To answer this question Rosengren et al. (2009) have been coding three- to five-year-old children's responses to an in-depth interview about biological processes. The interview focuses on children's understanding of life processes (e.g., growth, illness, what makes something alive?) and children's understanding of death. These researchers explicitly investigated children's understanding of the subconcepts of death (finality, universality, causality, and irreversibility) as well as children's understanding of the continuity of life processes following death. What they have been finding is that children's understanding of these concepts varies as a function of age, religiosity of the family of origin, and cultural background. Specifically, younger children, those from more highly religious families, and those from Mexican-American families tend to treat many life processes as continuing after death. In Mexican-American families this effect remains significant even after controlling for religiosity, suggesting an effect of culture above and beyond any effect of religion. In some ways it may not be that surprising that in religions and cultures that support afterlife beliefs, children think that more life processes continue after death, but this finding contrasts sharply with traditional cognitive developmental accounts of children's understanding of death.

Our analysis of individual children suggests that about half of the white middle-class children adopt a dominant biological approach to explaining life and death. Only a small number of children in this sample appeared to adopt a dominant religious approach to death, mentioning God or some sort of religious entity throughout the interview. The remaining children provided some form of co-existence reasoning, in some cases using juxtaposition reasoning and others target-dependent reasoning. Children in this later group used primarily biological explanations for death, unless explicitly asked questions that probed about the afterlife or spirituality, in which case the children provided a religious explanation. A final group of children appear to combine explanations into a more integrated or blended approach that incorporates both everyday views of biology with religious or spiritual ones. For example, one child talked about how her mother who had recently died was tired. Further questioning revealed that the child thought that her mother was standing all day long on a cloud in heaven, and that this must be physically tiring. In this case, an intuitive biology is merged with the cultural notion of heaven into a synthetic blend (see Table 6.1, Quadrant C).

Thus, as early as ages three to five years, children are beginning to use multiple epistemologies, sometimes in competition, sometimes to complement one another, and in other cases synthesizing them into a single, coherent explanatory system. Future research should explore the source of these individual differences. While it is likely that some are due to how parents socialize children, it is also likely that certain child characteristics influence whether a child adopts a single consistent model, a co-existence model, or attempts to unify seemingly contradictory ideas into a blended model.

Regardless of cultural context, the research summarized to date indicates that the endorsement of apparently competing epistemologies is commonplace in both Western and non-Western contexts. So far, the major emphasis has been placed on culturally derived sources of belief, which suggests that religious and scientific ideas may replace intuitive beliefs about death or illness, or provide a cultural overlay (see Table 6.1, Quadrant B). In addition to the co-existence models already described for AIDS transmission, this analysis of death concepts reveals a *target-dependent* model, with the soul treated differently than the body. These target-dependent models can operate at the entity level (human versus animals) and at the domain level (intuitive biology versus intuitive psychology). The following analysis of beliefs about the origin of species builds on these co-existence models and extends the discussion to include intuitive beliefs.

Using Multiple Epistemologies to Reason about the Origin of Species

Cultural Models: Supernatural and Scientific

As many as 30% of the U.S. population, from a range of religious backgrounds, endorse a literal interpretation of the Bible in which God plays a direct role in the origins of species (Doyle, 2003), the core creationist viewpoint presented in this chapter. Creation science and intelligent design provide the most coherent contemporary models of this viewpoint, at least in the United States. Although supernatural beliefs about the origins of living kinds prevail in most cultures (Campbell, 1972), predating evolutionary ideas (Mayr, 1982), these models emerged relatively recently, in the late 20th century (Evans, 2001; Morris & Parker, 1982; Numbers, 1992). Unlike creation scientists, who adhere closely to the biblical description of origins, intelligent design theorists accept current views of the age of the Earth. Both creation scientists and intelligent design theorists, however, deny naturalistic explanations for the origins of species (Scott, 2005). This point was made most forcefully by Judge John Jones III in the recent Dover trial. He concluded that intelligent design could not be taught in the science classroom because it was, at base, a non-materialistic, supernatural perspective (Mervis, 2006). The creationist viewpoint contrasts markedly with a post-Darwinian evolutionary perspective in which all living beings share a (tangled) common ancestry of natural origins (Doolittle, 2000).

In the Introduction, we briefly reviewed some of the ways in which theologians from non-fundamentalist religions and some evolutionary biologists reconcile supernatural and scientific explanations of the origin of species, in various co-existence models (see Table 6.1). Next, we provide evidence that such blends are also endorsed by members of the public. Finally, we shall use these models as a starting point for a consideration of the ways in which culturally derived and intuitive models might be combined.

Co-existence Models of Evolutionary and Creationist Origins

An interesting example of a target-dependent co-existence model is the provision, by creationists, of different explanations for micro- and macro-evolution. Darwinian evolution consists, essentially, of two related processes, micro-evolutionary or small-scale evolution and macro-evolutionary or large-scale evolution. The former refers to changes in gene frequencies within a population, whereas the latter refers to large-scale changes that result in ancestor and descendent species of markedly different phenotypes, the origin of new species (Futuyma, 1998). While creationists may accept that micro-evolution is a biological process, they routinely reject the idea that macro-evolution is also a biological process, as in the following example:

> The evolution of HIV is not disputed by creationists. The only complaint that creationists have ... is the confusing use of the term evolution to describe both variation within a species and the origin of new kinds of life.
>
> (Jones, 2005)

The rationale offered to justify this model is that variation within a population (a micro-evolutionary process) is not only observable, but is also consistent with the claim that God built diversity into the DNA of each living kind (Evans, 2008; Greenspan, 2002; Morris & Parker, 1982). Macro-evolutionary processes require, however, not only acceptance of a timescale that is inconsistent with biblical accounts, but also acceptance of transitional forms (some of which are inferred rather than observed), and, most critically, acceptance of the idea that new forms of life may emerge from earlier forms (Evans, 2008). According to creationists, each living kind has a unique essence (DNA) bestowed by the direct hand of God, thus it cannot have descended from or be the ancestor of a different living kind (Whitcomb, 1988).

There are several examples of this kind of reasoning among members of the public. According to one natural history museum visitor, God built diversity into the DNA of the original wolf-dog pair that made it onto Noah's Ark (Evans, 2008):

> Ok, I believe ... um ..., God created a pair, a male and female of everything with the ability to diversify. So I guess what I meant at the time of the flood, [...] they had the genetic background to be able to diversify into all of the, like for instance, dogs, and all the different kinds that we have. And so ... um .... does that help? Just a creationistic view.
>
> (Evans et al., 2010)

In this kind of argument, the variation originally locked into the DNA of one pair of canine ancestors is now manifest in diverse dogs, from dingoes to dachshunds, which are adapted to life in different parts of the world. Thus, dachshunds and dingoes comprise one living kind that share a common essence, bestowed by God. This appears to be an example of a target-dependent model with supernatural and scientific explanations of macro- and micro-evolution, respectively. God placed each living kind on Earth and local adaptations resulted in the variation observed in canines across the world. If these two processes were clearly linked in the mind of this individual, then this would be considered a causal chain model rather than a target-dependent one.

A second example of a target-dependent co-existence model is the differential treatment of the human versus other animals. This model is widespread (Evans, 2000b, 2001). In a recent interview study, 30 adult natural history museum visitors were asked to explain evolutionary problems about seven different species (they were not told these were evolutionary problems). When the human was the target, 28% of them included creationist explanations. Only 6% were consistently creationist for the other species, which ranged in size from a diatom to a whale (Diamond & Evans, 2007). In a more in-depth study of this type of pattern, 115 6–12-year-olds, and their parents, from both biblical literalist and theistic evolutionist families (defined by parental belief system) were asked about the origins of humans, non-human mammals (e.g., deer), and animals that undergo metamorphosis, such as frogs and butterflies. All age groups were more likely to accept (pre-Darwinian) macro-evolutionary explanations (it came from a different kind of animal) for animals that were taxonomically distant from the human, and least likely to accept evolutionary explanations for the human (Evans, 2008; Evans, Rosengren, Szymanowksi, Smith, & Johnson, 2005). This kind of nuanced investigation is rare in national polls, where the human is the most typical target of surveys.

Why is the human treated so differently? One possible explanation is the children do not realize that the human is an animal (Carey, 1985). This possibility was investigated in the same study by asking children which of the above species were animals (Evans et al., 2005). There was an effect both of age and of community of origin. Overall, younger children were less likely to agree that the human was an animal (all agreed that the other species were animals). Additionally, children from biblical literalist families, regardless of age, were less likely than children from theistic evolutionist families to agree that the human was an animal. Further, children's acceptance of the human as an animal predicted their acceptance of evolutionary origins, independently of other relevant factors (Evans, 2008).

Overlay Models: Cultural and Intuitive Beliefs

In addition to revealing the ways that members of the lay public combine religion and science into relatively coherent target-dependent co-existence models, these two examples also reveal something of the underlying intuitive belief systems that constrain an understanding of evolution. A crucial element of an intuitive biology is the belief in the relative immutability of species, called essentialism (Gelman, 2003). This intuition is magnified in a cultural context, in that creationists will not accept the idea of common ancestry because it violates the essentialist principle that each living kind has a unique unchanging essence. Biblical literalism explicitly supports this viewpoint (Evans, 2000b, 2001). On the other hand, in the second example, we see that this intuitive essentialism can be modified by exposure to evidence of within-species change, provided the cultural context supports this position (Evans, 2008). These researchers predicted that pre-Darwinian evolutionary explanations of the origin of species were more likely to be accepted for species that underwent metamorphosis, because such dramatic biological change might modify essentialist beliefs in the continuity and stability of species; this turned out to be the case (Evans et al., 2005; Rosengren, Gelman, Kalish, & McCormick, 1991). The human, on the other hand, elicits an intuitive psychology, which arouses emotions and is accompanied by a natural resistance to the idea that humans are subject to the same biological processes that constrain the rest of the animal world: Humans are privileged (Evans, 2001; Poling & Evans, 2004b). Both of these examples imply that evolutionary and creationist ideas, initially at least, are superimposed on a foundation of intuitive beliefs, which both constrain and potentially make possible these cultural forms (see Table 6.1, Quadrant B).

These observations suggest that there are many ways in which intuitive beliefs constrain the expression of evolutionary ideas. On the face of it, evolutionary ideas are strongly counterintuitive, in that they require that we abandon or modify essentialist ideas in the stability of species and that we treat the human as another kind of animal (Evans, 2008). How are these strong intuitions overcome? One possible route is explored by examining the nature of synthetic blends and their potential role as transitional concepts from purely intuitive to purely cultural concepts.

Synthetic Blends and Intuitive Beliefs

In synthetic blends (Table 6.1, Quadrant C), intuitive or everyday beliefs are fused with culturally available ideas from science and religion (Poling & Evans, 2004a; Vosniadou, Vamvakoussi, & Skopeliti, 2008). An overarching goal of this section is to characterize the different ways in which these intuitive and cultural beliefs are combined, and to identify those transitional forms that might serve to bridge the gap between intuitive and scientific beliefs.

In one study, open-ended interviews about evolution were carried out with a sample of 32 adult natural history museum visitors. This study provided a window into the thinking of members of the general public who are both interested in natural history and are more likely to have completed college than the public at large (Evans et al., 2010). This group was less likely than other members of the lay public to endorse creationist ideas. Moreover, by and large their creationist ideas were confined to the human. In addition to the human, the visitors were presented with scenarios describing evolutionary change in six other organisms, from HIV to whales, and asked to explain what had happened. Importantly, they were told only that they would be asked about "some new scientific discoveries about living things" (the term evolution was not mentioned) as this allowed an assessment of whether the visitors would spontaneously recognize these as evolutionary problems. Responses were coded as multiple themes under (Darwinian) evolutionary, intuitive, or creationist reasoning patterns.

Surprisingly, not one visitor consistently used evolutionary reasoning across all seven organisms. Overall, visitors endorsed a synthetic blend with 72% combining evolutionary and intuitive themes from those two reasoning patterns, and another 28% also including creationist reasoning. The whale, finch, and human were more likely to elicit Darwinian evolutionary themes, whereas the HIV and the fly, ant, and diatom were more likely to elicit intuitive themes. Only 34% of the visitors used evolutionary reasoning in the majority of their responses; for over half of the visitors, intuitive reasoning was the dominant pattern.

The key to understanding conceptual change is to make sense of the nature of these synthetic blends and, in particular, the nature of visitors' intuitive beliefs. To this end, a detailed analysis of visitors' concepts ensued (Evans et al., 2010). We shall comment on two key themes in this chapter. Consistent with other research (see Evans, 2008 for a summary), the study revealed that visitors' intuitive concepts of biological change included need-based (or goal-directed) reasoning, with the change described as directed toward the goal of enabling the organism to adapt to a changed environment. This is one of a family of *teleological* themes found in folk-biologies the world over and, along with essentialism, this kind of reasoning characterizes an intuitive biology (Medin & Atran, 2004). In the study of museum visitors, just described, need-based reasoning from an intuitive biology was distinguished from the desire-based, intentional or mental-state reasoning characterizing an intuitive psychology (Evans et al., 2010).

Although both an intuitive psychology and an intuitive biology involve purpose or goals, a core feature of teleological reasoning, the underlying reason differs. This is illustrated using examples from the Galapagos finch problem (Evans et al., 2010). In an intuitive biology the underlying goal is one of survival: of necessity the organism needs to change in order to survive in a particular environment. This is accomplished through physiological means. In the following synthetic blend, this visitor clearly recognized that the finch problem was one of evolutionary change. However, the visitor provided a non-Darwinian mechanism, derived from an intuitive biology, to explain the change: "evolution for survival … well, in order to survive, their body parts had to adjust to certain things … so the beak grew longer in order to deal with the tougher seeds." In the next example a mental state is invoked, indicating that the change comes about through intentional means, from an intuitive psychology: "in order to eat the seeds" the finch "had to try to work harder, probably, to develop their beaks." By distinguishing between these two intuitive modes, Evans et al. (2010) were able to get a better handle on the nature of these concepts and their relationship with the other themes. Whereas need-based reasoning was prevalent, elicited in more than 44% of the responses, fewer than 20% of the responses involved intentional reasoning. The pattern of endorsement of these two themes was examined in greater detail in a follow-up study that included children as well as adults.

Thirty adults and 34 11–18-year-olds visited an exhibition on contemporary evolution research with the same seven organisms. As they were recruited for this study, it was not possible to disguise the fact that the exhibition was on evolution (Spiegel et al., 2009). In the questionnaire, eight closed-ended explanations, derived from major themes found in the first study, were attached to each of the seven original scenarios. For each scenario, visitors could express their degree of agreement with each explanation.

Following the visit to the evolution exhibition, and regardless of age, demographic characteristics, and interest in the organism, there was a significant increased agreement with all three evolutionary explanations, across all organisms. However, agreement with the goal-directed explanation (needed to change) also increased. At the same time there was significant decrease in visitors' agreement with the intentional explanation (wanted to change). Children were less likely to endorse evolutionary explanations and more likely to endorse intentional explanations than adults. Visitors for whom evolution was compatible with their religion were more likely to endorse evolutionary and goal-directed reasoning. Visitors for whom evolution was incompatible with their religion were less likely to endorse evolution, and more likely to endorse creationism (created that way). Although there was no wholesale conversion to an evolutionary explanation, visitors did increase their endorsement of evolutionary explanations, while decreasing intentional and creationist explanations. Importantly, need-based reasoning appeared to act as a bridge between intuitive and evolutionary explanations (Spiegel et al., 2009)

In the first study, need-based reasoning was negatively correlated with the micro-evolutionary theme of natural selection, but uncorrelated with the macro-evolutionary theme, common descent (Evans et al., 2010). Further investigation of this pattern of findings suggested that while many visitors accepted the idea of evolution, as indicated by their endorsement of common descent, only some of them grasped the Darwinian mechanism of natural selection; instead, they provided a need-based mechanism of change. The synthetic blend of common descent and need-based reasoning was found in the second study, as well (Spiegel et al., 2009). On the other hand, for visitors who understood natural selection, which is best tested in an open-ended format, need-based explanations of evolutionary change were no longer used, hence the negative correlation between these two themes. Moreover, this pattern sheds light on one of the co-existence models described earlier. In the lay public's mind the acceptance or rejection of evolution seems to refer to the macro-evolutionary principle, common descent, but not to natural selection. It appears that members of the public can accept, or, if they are creationist, reject, macro-evolutionary concepts, while misunderstanding (or even understanding) the Darwinian mechanism of evolutionary change (Evans, 2008). In terms of public understanding, the two evolutionary principles are somewhat orthogonal, even though for the evolutionary biologist they are seamlessly connected.

What about intentional reasoning? There was nothing in the exhibition to suggest that such reasoning was incorrect. Yet, older visitors, in particular, were less likely to endorse this theme after the gallery visit. The exhibition appears to have had the effect of fine-tuning visitors' explanatory repertoire, helping them to discriminate between survival or need-based reasoning and intentional or mental-state reasoning. Once they have realized that the organism's survival depends on a particular change, and that this change cannot come about through conscious effort, then they may be ready to grasp the principle of natural selection.

Children, however, were less influenced by the exhibition, even though children as young as five years are capable of distinguishing between those themes, reasoning, for example, that animals breath because they *need to* not because they *want to* (Poling & Evans, 2002). Past research has shown that children are more susceptible to intentional themes, in part because their grasp of an intuitive psychology is undergoing rapid change over the preschool through elementary school years (Evans, 2008). Moreover, they are more likely to explain biological change in intentional terms, particularly if they have been raised in communities that support such interpretations and if they are questioned about macro-evolutionary themes (e.g., where did the very first X come from?), rather than within-population change (Evans, 2000a, 2001, 2008).

These findings suggest that anthropomorphizing nature in an exhibition or in school curricula should have a particularly deleterious effect on children's scientific reasoning, even if it makes the topic more attractive. This hypothesis was tested in a recent study with an experimental manipulation of the language used to tell children stories about evolutionary change in birds (Legare, Evans, & Lane, 2010). One story used need-based language, another intentional language, and the third, natural selection. The outcome variable was children's endorsement of need, intention, and natural selection themes and their use of such language when asked to repeat the story back to the experimenter. There was a main effect of story type with the intentional story eliciting intentional themes, particularly in younger children. Need-based and natural selection stories were equally likely to elicit need-based and natural selection reasoning at all ages. This finding provides further converging evidence that need-based reasoning may be a crucial intermediary concept, easing the transition from intuitive to evolutionary reasoning.

Synthetic Blends: Bridging the Transition from Intuitive to Cultural Explanations

Across the three domains of illness, death, and origins, we have peeled back the cultural layers to expose their intuitive foundations, and, in effect, revealed the process of conceptual change, in reverse. Table 6.1 provides a developmental model. At an early point in development, children have at hand a repertoire of intuitive beliefs that makes their world comprehensible. These concepts give stability, coherence, and purpose to what would otherwise be a bewildering and incomprehensible environment. These intuitive concepts (Quadrant D, Table 6.1) persist into adulthood where they play the same role in adult reasoning, when adults are confronted with unfamiliar problems. As children (and adults) assimilate cultural concepts, from God to atoms to evolution, they construct synthetic blends (Quadrant C, Table 6.1), fusing newly acquired ideas to familiar intuitions, which makes the cultural concepts more tractable. Gradually, these cultural concepts appear to become detached from their intuitive base (Quadrants B–A, Table 6.1), at least in experts (though this is debatable). The studies with museum visitors indicate, however, that, without consistent reinforcement, synthetic blends are normative and represent the understanding that most lay adults will have of evolution and, probably, of most complex scientific topics. Even experts revert to such synthetic blends when talking to students or writing for the general public (Evans, 2008). Evolutionary theory is particularly problematic, because it is highly counterintuitive, denying even the appearance of stability and purpose to the natural world. Not surprisingly, then, it has an effective cultural competitor. Co-existence models of religion and evolutionary science provide a solution to this problem, at least for many theologians and scientists.

Some Unanswered Questions

This series of studies demonstrate that children from diverse cultural contexts come into the classroom with a range of approaches that involve combinations of very different explanatory models (see Table 6.1). While this is true of illness and death we also see this with respect to understanding the origins of living kinds. In our view, one of the real dangers of introducing creationism or intelligent design alongside evolution in the classroom is that it is likely to induce some children to create models that contradict the actual science. On the other hand, as described earlier, leading theologians and scientists have combined religious and scientific epistemologies in ways that leave evolutionary theory intact. Is this the way to approach this issue in the classroom? This would seem to be beyond the scope of the science classroom, but such discussions might well have a role in the broader curriculum.

Why do some children and adults adopt a single explanatory approach when confronted with competing epistemologies? Why do other children and adults treat different epistemologies as complementary rather than competing worldviews? Why do still other individuals blend different intuitive and cultural epistemologies into a single synthetic approach? Our research has begun to answer these questions and suggests that age and experience coupled with language and contextual influences operate at a relatively global level to influence the normative reasoning patterns within particular groups or cultures. That is, when children and adults live within a culture where multiple epistemologies are common, they are more willing to embrace what often seem to be contradictory explanations to reason about illness, death, and the origin of species. We have reported evidence in support of this from research conducted examining explanations for AIDS in South Africa, research on death in children in the United States and Mexico, and from children in the United States from religious and non-religious backgrounds with respect to both death and the origin of living things. While this research suggests that age and context influence the overall use of different epistemologies, and whether they compete, complement, or are combined, we still do not have a complete understanding of why certain individuals adopt one explanatory model over another, choose to treat them in a complementary fashion, or blend them into a single, relatively coherent model. Here we provide some ideas of what might influence an individual to adopt one or the other of these approaches.

Adoption of a blended approach may differ from adopting a single epistemology, or using complementary ones. Co-existence cultural models may require more cognitive effort to bring together views that seem on the face of it to be in direct competition or even incompatible. For adults, we suggest that some sort of conflict triggers the effort to create a coherent, integrated model of different epistemologies. This kind of conflict has often been reported by individuals with strong Christian fundamentalist beliefs who are brought into direct contact with scientific evidence that directly contradicts those views (Numbers, 1992; Poling & Evans, 2004b). Peter Woo, a biochemist, who now shares Collins' co-existence beliefs, described this conflict as he entered university where "my Christian faith was seriously challenged and replaced by tormenting, depressing doubt." Eventually, he achieved a reconciliation of his faith and the scientific evidence with the realization that "the nature and the existence of God are beyond the scope of science and human intellect" (Woo, 2004).

A conflict may also trigger this pattern in young children. For example, the death of a loved one may force children to combine different explanations experienced at home, school, and church to reach a single, blended, explanation that provides meaning to a traumatic event. These might be co-existence cultural models or synthetic blends of intuitive and cultural beliefs. But even in these cases, which epistemologies will enter into the mix is clearly dependent upon those the individual is exposed to in their family of origin and broader culture.

In many cases, however, this might not be a conscious process. As described earlier, as students struggle to grasp unfamiliar scientific concepts, they are likely to assimilate them to familiar intuitive concepts that, at least, offer one coherent model. Students may not be aware that their understanding of the science is rooted in their intuitive epistemologies. Moreover, these synthetic blends might be helpful or a hindrance. At least for evolution, the research reported here suggests that as students fine-tune their explanatory repertoire, the jettisoning of intentional concepts, while retaining need-based concepts, might provide a bridge to a more scientific understanding. The core question here is whether making students aware of this unconscious process would help them achieve a more coherent scientific model.

Implications for Informal and Formal Evolution Education

We have chosen to discuss three different areas of biological understanding— illness, death, and origins—to highlight the similarities across these different areas. That is, each involves learning about unseen processes that have important outcomes and may exact an emotional cost. Each is often learned in the context of competing explanatory models. Each also involves the acquisition of intuitive knowledge prior to onset of formal schooling. Thus, there appear to be some general issues and processes that cut across these three areas of knowledge. In this sense, teaching about evolution should perhaps be done in a manner that is similar to the teaching of other biological concepts, though teachers should be attentive to those issues that are most likely to elicit existential concerns.

What are the implications for science educators? First, educators clearly face a difficult task. Children will enter their classrooms with very different ways of handling information. Some will approach the information from a single unified causal model. But for others the model may not be scientific at all, as they embrace strong religious or supernatural beliefs. In many situations, the parents themselves may resolve the educational quandary by simply removing the child from public education and enrolling them in a school that complements their beliefs. Other children likely enter the classroom with explanatory models that co-exist, using one in a particular context and the other one in a different context. In traditional classrooms the context may provide ample support to enable a consistent scientific model to expand and flourish, so children who enter with this mix of explanations may not present much of a problem.

The evidence presented in this chapter indicates, however, that two of the co-existence models present a unique challenge to evolution educators. If the classroom instruction or exhibition focuses on non-human animals and micro-evolutionary processes, students are likely to be comfortable with the information in that it does not appear to elicit existential fears. However, once macro-evolutionary themes are introduced, especially those involving the human, then these conflicts are more likely to arise. As several researchers have noted, the absence of macro-evolution from the typical classroom results in students with little understanding of the links between these two processes (e.g., Catley, 2006). Ironically, the reverse pattern is likely to be found in natural history museums, which house the evidence for macro-evolution (Diamond & Scotchmoor, 2006). One feasible solution is to focus on non-human animals, but link micro- and macro-evolutionary processes from the earliest years. Dinosaurs are often incorporated into the typical second-grade curriculum, but children have little sense of their evolutionary history, even if they can classify them with ease (Evans, 2000a). By linking the evolutionary history of dinosaurs to that of modern birds, macro-evolution is introduced in a way that maps onto children's fascination with dinosaurs. Similarly, the middle-school curriculum includes health. Why not link this to evolutionary explanations of why people get sick (Nesse & Williams, 1996)? In sum, evolutionary reasoning should be introduced early and tied to compelling topics, throughout the curriculum.

Educators should also work to harness children's and adults' intuitive beliefs about the world (Carey, 2000). This involves reinforcing those beliefs that conform to scientific understanding, and directly confronting ones, such as the essentialist view of species, that conflict with known science. Children who adopt a blended or synthetic form of explanation may present a very difficult challenge for teachers, depending on the nature of the blending. Also, if we are correct in thinking that some of these synthetic models arise out of cognitive or emotional conflict they may be more strongly held and more difficult to challenge. On the other hand, some synthetic blends, such as the use of need-based reasoning to explain evolutionary change, appear to be crucial bridges to an evolutionary understanding. Students' acceptance of the idea of common ancestry, even if accompanied by need-based reasoning, is a significant step toward a full grasp of evolutionary theory. These small steps should not be seen as failures of instruction but as small victories. In either of these cases, identifying students' reasoning patterns is a crucial first step. This could then be followed by a process of intentional conceptual change (see Sinatra & Pintrich, 2003), in which students are made aware of their own thinking processes and of their use of language when explaining scientific processes.

As we have shown, children and adults alike are adept at shifting between explanatory modes. This causal flexibility facilitates different ways of handling what are often viewed as incompatible and conflicting worldviews and integrating these with intuitive beliefs. It is not simply that they hold alternative concepts, but these conceptions are rooted in different ways of understanding how things in the world work. It is not enough to classify these as misconceptions; it is also necessary to understand the underlying explanatory systems that support these systems of belief.

Acknowledgments

The material on evolution is based, in part, upon studies supported by the National Science Foundation with grants to: Evans (PI) & Rosengren (#0411406), Diamond (PI), University of Nebraska State Museum of Natural History (#0229294), and to Weiss (PI), New York Hall of Science, & Evans (#0540152).

References

Aries, P. (1974). *Western attitudes towards death: From the middle ages to the present.* Baltimore, MD: Johns Hopkins University Press.

Ashforth, A. (2001). An epidemic of witchcraft? The implications of AIDS for the post-apartheid state. In H. Moore & T. Sanders (Eds.), *Magical interpretation, material realities* (pp. 184–225). London: Routledge.

Ashforth, A. (2005). *Witchcraft, violence, and democracy in South Africa.* Chicago, IL: University of Chicago Press.

Astuti, R., & Harris, P. L. (2008). Understanding mortality and the life of the ancestors in rural Madagascar. *Cognitive Science: A Multidisciplinary Journal, 32,* 713–740.

Astuti, R., Solomon, G. E. A., & Carey, S. (2004). Constraints on conceptual development: A case study of the acquisition of folk biological and folk sociological knowledge in Madagascar. *Monographs of the Society for Research in Child Development, 69* (3. Serial No. 277).

Atran, S. (2002). *In gods we trust: The evolutionary landscape of religion.* New York: Oxford University Press.

Atran, S., & Sperber, D. (1991). Learning without teaching: Its place in culture. In L. Landsman (Ed.), *Culture, schooling, and psychological development* (pp. 39–55). Norwood, NJ: Ablex.

Biema, D. V. (2006, November 13). God vs. Science. *Time, 168,* 48–55.

Boyer, P. (1993). *The naturalness of religious ideas: Outline of a cognitive theory of religion.* Los Angeles/Berkeley, CA: University of California Press.

Brandt, A., & Rozin, P. (Eds.). (1997). *Morality and health.* New York: Routledge.

Brem, S. K., Ranney, M., & Schindel, J. (2003). Perceived consequences of evolution: College students perceive negative personal and social impact in evolutionary theory. *Science Education, 87,* 181–206.

Campbell, J. (1972). *Myths to live by.* New York: Viking Penguin, Inc.

Carey, S. (1985). *Conceptual change in childhood.* Cambridge. MA: MIT Press.

Carey, S. (2000). Science education as conceptual change. *Journal of Applied Developmental Psychology, 21,* 13–19.

Catley, K. M. (2006). Darwin's missing link—A novel paradigm for evolution education. *Science Education, 90,* 767–783.

Dawkins, R. (1995). Putting away childish things. *Skeptical Inquirer, 19*(1), 31–36.

Diamond, J., & Evans, E. M. (2007). Museums teach evolution. *Evolution, 61*(6), 1500–1506.

Diamond, J., & Scotchmoor, J. (2006). Exhibiting evolution. *Museums and Social Issues, 1,* 21–48.

Doolittle, W. (2000). Uprooting the tree of life. *Scientific American, 282*(2), 90–95.

Doyle, R. (2003, March). Sizing up evangelicals: Fundamentalism persists but shows signs of moderation. *Scientific American, 228*, 37.

Evans, E. M. (1994/95). *God or Darwin? The development of beliefs about the origin of species.* Dissertation Abstracts International Section A: Humanities & Social Sciences; Vol. 558-A Feb 1995 2335 AAM9500920: University of Michigan.

Evans, E. M. (2000a). The emergence of beliefs about the origins of species in school-age children. *Merrill-Palmer Quarterly: A Journal of Developmental Psychology, 46*, 221–254.

Evans, E. M. (2000b). Beyond Scopes: Why creationism is here to stay. In K. Rosengren, C. Johnson, & P. Harris (Eds.), *Imagining the impossible: Magical, scientific and religious thinking in children* (pp. 305–331). Cambridge, UK: Cambridge University Press.

Evans, E. M. (2001). Cognitive and contextual factors in the emergence of diverse belief systems: Creation versus evolution. *Cognitive Psychology, 42*, 217–266.

Evans, E. M. (2008). Conceptual change and evolutionary biology: A developmental analysis. In S. Vosniadou (Ed.), *International Handbook of Research on Conceptual Change* (pp. 263–294). New York: Routledge.

Evans, E. M., Rosengren, K. S., Szymanowksi, K., Smith, P. H., & Johnson, K. (2005, October). *Culture, cognition, and creationism.* Biennial Meeting of the Cognitive Development Society, San Diego, CA.

Evans, E. M., Spiegel, A., Gram, W., Frazier, B. F., Tare, M., Thompson, S., & Diamond, J. (2010). A conceptual guide to museum visitors' understanding of evolution. *Journal of Research in Science Teaching, 47*, 326–353.

Evans, E. M., & Wellman, H. M. (2006). A case of stunted development? Existential reasoning is contingent on a developing theory of mind. [Commentary on *The folk psychology of souls*]. *Brain and Behavioral Sciences, 29*, 471–472.

Farmer, P. (1999). *Infections and inequalities: The modern plagues.* Berkeley, CA: University of California Press.

Futuyma, D. J. (1998). *Evolutionary Biology* (3rd ed.). Sunderland, MA: Sinauer Associates.

Gallup. (2007). *Majority of republicans doubt theory of evolution: More Americans accept theory of creationism than evolution,* from www.galluppoll.com/content/?ci=27847

Gelman, S. A. (2003). *The essential child: Origins of essentialism in everyday thought.* Oxford: Oxford University Press.

Gould, S. J. (1997). Nonoverlapping magisteria. *Natural History, 106*, 16–22.

Green, E. (1999). *Indigenous theories of contagious disease.* Walnut Creek, CA: AltaMira Press.

Greenspan, N. S. (2002). Not-so-intelligent design. *The Scientist, 16*(5), 12.

Gutheil, G., Vera, A., & Keil, F. C. (1998). Do houseflies think? Patterns of induction and biological beliefs in development. *Cognition, 66*, 33–49.

Gutiérrez, I. (2006). *Portrayals of death in children's literature.* Unpublished Masters Thesis. University of Illinois.

Gutiérrez, I., Vasquez, A., Anderson, K. N., Rosengren, K. S., & Miller, P. J. (2007). A comparison of children's concept of death in two cultures. Poster presented at the Biennial Meeting of the Society for Research in Child Development, Boston, MA.

Harris, P. L., & Giménez, M. (2005). Children's acceptance of conflicting testimony: The case of death. *Journal of Cognition and Culture, 5*, 143–164.

Jones, D.-W. (2005, December). *Smart sponsors*, from www.scienceagainstevolution. org/v10i3f.htm

Legare, C. H., Evans, E. M., & Lane, J. (2010). Anthropomorphizing nature: What effect does it have on children's understanding? (Manuscript under review).

Legare, C. H., & Gelman, S. A. (2008). Bewitchment, biology, or both: The co-existence of natural and supernatural explanatory frameworks across development. *Cognitive Science: A Multidisciplinary Journal, 32*, 607–642.

Lomnitz, C. (2005). *Death and the idea of Mexico*. New York: Zone Books.

Mayr, E. (1982). *The growth of biological thought: Diversity, evolution, and inheritance.* Cambridge, MA: Harvard University Press.

Medin, D. L., & Atran, S. (2004). The native mind: Biological categorization and reasoning in development and across cultures. *Psychological Review, 111*(4), 960–983.

Mervis, J. (2006, January 6). Judge Jones defines science—and why intelligent design isn't. *Science, 311*, 34.

Miller, K. R. (1999). *Finding Darwin's God*. New York: Harper Collins.

Mitchell, J. (1965). The meaning of misfortune for urban Africans. In M. Fortes & G. Dieterlen (Eds.), *African systems of thought* (pp. 192–203). London: Oxford University Press.

Morris, H. M., & Parker, G. E. (1982). *What is creation science?* El Cajon, CA: Master Books.

Nemeroff, C., & Rozin, P. (2000). The makings of the magical mind: The nature and function of sympathetic magical thinking. In K. Rosengren, C. Johnson, & P. Harris (Eds.), *Imagining the impossible: Magical, scientific, and religious thinking in children* (pp. 1–34). Cambridge, UK: Cambridge University Press.

Nesse, R. M., & Williams, G. C. (1996). *Why we get sick: The new science of Darwinian medicine*. New York: Vintage Books.

Nguyen, S., & Gelman, S. A. (2002). Four and 6-year-olds' biological concept of death: The case of plants. *British Journal of Developmental Psychology, 20*, 495–513.

Nguyen, S., & Rosengren, K. S. (2004). Parental reports of children's biological experiences and misconceptions. *International Journal of Behavioral Development, 28*, 411–420.

Niehaus, I. (2001). Witchcraft in the new South Africa: From colonial superstition to postcolonial reality. In H. Moore & T. Sanders (Eds.), *Magical interpretations, material realities* (pp. 184–225). London: Routledge.

Numbers, R. L. (1992). *The creationists: The evolution of scientific creationism*. New York: Knopf.

Piaget, J. (1928). *Judgment and reasoning in the child*. London: Routledge & Kegan Paul.

Piaget, J. (1929). *The child's conception of the world*. London: Routledge & Kegan Paul.

Poling, D. A., & Evans, E. M. (2002). Why do birds of a feather flock together? Developmental change in the use of multiple explanations: Intention, teleology, essentialism. *British Journal of Developmental Psychology, 20*, 89–112.

Poling, D. A., & Evans, E. M. (2004a). Religious belief, scientific expertise, and folk ecology. *Journal of Cognition and Culture: Studies in the Cognitive Anthropology of Science, 4*, 485–524.

Poling, D. A., & Evans, E. M. (2004b). Are dinosaurs the rule or the exception? Developing concepts of death and extinction. *Cognitive Development, 19*, 363–383.

Rosengren, K. S., Gelman, S. A., Kalish, C., & McCormick, M. (1991). As time goes by:

Children's early understanding of biological growth. *Child Development, 62,* 1302–1320.

Rosengren, K. S., Gutiérrez, I. T., & Miller, P. J. (2009, April). Encountering death: The use of multiple explanatory models by young children and their parents. Paper presented at the Biennial Conference for the Society for Research in Child Development, Denver, CO.

Rosengren, K. S., Miller, P. J., Gutiérrez, I. T., Chow, P., Schein, S., & Anderson, K. A. (2009). Children's understanding of death: Toward a contextual perspective. Manuscript in preparation.

Ruse, M. (2005). *The evolution–creation struggle.* Cambridge, MA: Harvard University Press.

Schlebusch, L., & Ruggieri, G. (1996). Health beliefs of a sample of black patients attending a specialized medical facility. *South African Journal of Psychology, 26,* 35–38.

Schult, C. A., & Wellman, H. M. (1997). Explaining human movements and actions: Children's understanding of the limits of psychological explanation. *Cognition, 62,* 291–324.

Scott, E. C. (2005). *Evolution vs. creationism: An introduction.* Berkeley, CA: University of California Press.

Shweder, R. A., Much, N. C., Mahapatra, M., & Park, L. (1997). The "big three" of morality (autonomy, community, divinity) and the "big three" explanations of suffering. In A. Brand & P. Rozin (Eds.), *Morality and health* (pp. 119–169). New York: Routledge.

Sinatra, G. M., & Pintrich, P. R. (2003). *Intentional conceptual change.* Mahwah, NJ: Erlbaum.

Slaughter, V., & Lyons, M. (2003). Learning about life and death in early childhood. *Cognitive Psychology, 46,* 1–30.

Speece, M. W., & Brent, S. B. (1984). Children's understanding of death: A review of three components of a death concept. *Child Development, 55,* 1671–1686.

Sperber, D. (1996). *Explaining culture: A naturalistic approach.* Oxford: Blackwell.

Spiegel, A., Evans, E. M., Frazier, B. F., Hazel, A., Tare, M., Gram, W., & Diamond, J. (2009). Changing museum visitors' concepts of evolution. Manuscript submitted for publication.

Subbotsky, E. V. (2000). Phenomenalistic perception and rational understanding in the mind of an individual: The fight for dominance. In K. Rosengren, C. N. Johnson, & P. L. Harris (Eds.), *Imagining the impossible: Magical, scientific, and religious thinking in children.* Cambridge, UK: Cambridge University Press.

Subbotsky, E. V. (2001). Causal explanations of events by children and adults: Can alternative causal models coexist in one mind? *British Journal of Developmental Psychology, 19,* 23–46.

Thagard, P. (1998). Explaining disease: Correlations, causes, and mechanisms. *Minds and Machines, 8,* 61–78.

Vosniadou, S., Vamvakoussi, X., & Skopeliti, I. (2008). The framework theory approach to the problem of conceptual change. In S. Vosniadou (Ed.), *International handbook of research on conceptual change* (pp. 3–34). New York: Routledge.

Wellman, H. M., & Gelman, S. A. (1998). Knowledge acquisition in foundational domains. In D. Kuhn & R. S. Siegler (Eds.), *Handbook of child psychology 5th edition: Vol. 2: Cognition, perception, and language* (pp. 523–573). New York: John Wiley & Sons.

Whitcomb, J. C. (1988). *The world that perished: An introduction to biblical catastrophism*. Grand Rapids, MI: Baker Book House.

Woo, P. W. K. (2004, August). *Science, intellect, and the rationale of Christian faith*, from www.ccmusa.org

Zusne, L., & Jones, W. H. (1989). *Anomalistic psychology: A study of magical thinking*. Mahwah, NJ: Lawrence Erlbaum Associates.

Part II

Intelligent Design and Evolution

Accepting Evolution or Creation in People, Critters, Plants, and Classrooms

The Maelstrom of American Cognition about Biological Change

Michael Andrew Ranney and Anastasia Thanukos

Introduction

Early in our joint investigations of individuals' cognitions about evolution, a Japanese visiting professor asked a wide-eyed question during a lab meeting: "Excuse me, but did you say that some Americans do *not* believe in evolution?" His amazement was infectious. When we asserted that somewhat less than 50% of U.S. adults accept evolution (e.g., Miller, Scott, & Okamoto, 2006), we were as surprised by his reaction as he was by the situation. He wanted to know what else there was to accept, so we explained that it was roughly the Old Testament's Genesis story. When asked what the Shinto creation myth was, he eventually recalled, "Two gods were fighting and people resulted," but he could recall no particulars of how animals and plants arose. This episode, and less anecdotal evidence, led one of us (Ranney, 1998 & in press) to a conjecture about an answer to an oft-posed puzzle (e.g., Miller et al., 2006), which we will call the U.S. "divergence" question: Why does the United States lag so far behind comparable nations in its acceptance of evolution? The episode also highlights another element of cognition about evolution: human-centrism.

The U.S.'s modest embrace of evolution has been salient on the landscapes of both public opinion polls and biology education (e.g., Bishop & Anderson, 1990). Although this may amuse some citizens (even some scientists) from peer nations, the import of the U.S. evolutionary divergence goes well beyond science education (even plausibly engaging global climate change issues; Ranney, in press).

This chapter's central goal is to add richness to our collective knowledge of how people understand (and *could* understand) evolution. We take two approaches toward the goal, with the bulk of the chapter focusing on the concretely evidential and the rest providing a broad theoretical perspective in support. We first offer novel empirical evidence (two experiments and some survey data) that we hope both problematizes and enlightens discussions about the cognition of evolution. A conjectural answer to the oft-posed question from above is then explicated in sweeping geopolitical terms. Our empirical results cohere with this conjecture about the relatively modest U.S. acceptance of evolution, but they stand on their own regardless of the conjecture's veracity.

Below, we describe two empirical ventures that address some of the landscape of how U.S. undergraduates think about the complex arena of evolution. Study 1's experiments address some interesting asymmetries in how undergraduates approach evolution in the realm of plants—compared to that of humans. Study 2 focuses on the relationships between undergraduate views regarding evolution and creationism—and which of these ought to be taught in U.S. schools.

Study 1: Perception of Evolution across the Tree of Life

A key aspect of evolutionary theory's appeal is its power to explain biological phenomena over many scales and situations using the same set of relatively simple mechanisms (see Ferrari & Chi, 1998, etc.). Darwin's two great ideas, natural selection and common ancestry, form an illuminating lens for analyzing and understanding virtually any aspect of biology. The basic process of natural selection is essentially the same, whether the evolving population is made up of cells in a Petri dish, asexual fungi, colonial coral, cognitively adept humans, fruit flies, or elephants. Similarly, the concept of common ancestry helps us understand widely divergent observations, from the vestigial "finger" bones in a whale's fin to the genetic code's chemical consistency.

Evolutionary theory's universality makes it the keystone of modern biology, yet the broader U.S. population seems to accept evolution piecemeal and in select situations. Human evolution, for example, may be (or often is) a sticking point. Surveys (e.g., Almquist & Cronin, 1988; Gallup Organization, 2001; People For the American Way Foundation, 2000) typically find that roughly half of the U.S. (e.g., Gallup Organization, 2001) rejects evolution as an explanation of human origins and development. However, these studies' implications are somewhat unclear because many implicitly frame human evolution as a controversy, defining evolution and creationism with respect to humans (e.g., People For the American Way Foundation, 2000) or failing to ask about anything except human origins and evolution (e.g., Gallup Organization, 2001). While others have examined this area, no study has explicitly compared the acceptance of human evolution to that of plant or animal evolution.

The evolution education literature includes a few studies with findings directly related to students' views of evolution in different organisms. Jenson, Settlage, and Odem (1996) found that U.S. students do not consistently and appropriately apply the concept of natural selection across different, non-human organisms. Brem, Ranney, and Schindel (2003) found that many U.S. students favoring creationism believed that only non-human species had evolved. Evans, Stewart, and Poling (1997) found that U.S. parents are less likely to explain human origins to their children in terms of evolution than they are to explain dinosaur origins in terms of evolution. Others, though, found that human origins might be an evolutionary touchstone for students. Bizzo (1994) found that many Brazilian high school students use humans as a central reference for evolution and tend to view the evolutionary process as motivated by a conscious effort—one that can only be mustered by "higher" animals like humans, leaving organisms like plants in evolutionary limbo. A study performed at the University of California, Berkeley (Ranney, 1998) found that, when asked to write about evolution in general, the 30 undergraduates often spontaneously mentioned human evolution, and occasionally mentioned animal evolution, yet *never* mentioned plant evolution. These studies are consistent with the idea that people's views of evolution vary across organisms, but do not explain how or why.

To help illuminate this issue, Study 1 examines how accepting people are of evolution in different organisms (plants, animals, and humans)[1] and what factors into these acceptance levels (e.g., conceptions of evolution, affective constraints, and religious concerns) through two investigations. In both, participants responded to Likert-scale items asking about their agreement with evolutionary explanations for features of plants, animals, and humans. One investigation explored basic patterns with a set of surveys. The other used think-aloud protocols (TAPs) to explore participants' reasoning about plant and human evolution items. Full explanations of the materials, methods, results, coding schemes, and data transformations for these experiments are in Thanukos (2002). A brief summary of key points follows.

Surveys: Patterns across the Tree of Life

Seventy-six University of California at Berkeley undergraduates completed a Likert-rating survey and a demographics survey for psychology course credit. The Likert survey included 21 items probing acceptance of evolution in plants, animals, and humans—for example: "Scientists have found parts of fossilized animals that are very similar in form to a modern horse species. Evolutionary relationships are a major cause of this similarity." Students were asked to rate their agreement with the second sentence ascribing an evolutionary cause to the feature on a scale of −4 (totally disagree) to +4 (totally agree). The 21 items were divided into three sections containing isomorphic items on plant, animal, and human evolution.[2] Figure 7.1 summarizes the topics of the seven items in each section. Five of these (*adaptation framework items*) describe an adaptation or population characteristic and suggest that natural selection is the cause of this adaptation or characteristic; two (*similarity framework items*) describe a similarity between two organisms and suggest that common

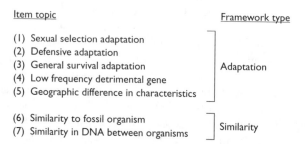

Item topic   Framework type

(1) Sexual selection adaptation
(2) Defensive adaptation
(3) General survival adaptation   Adaptation
(4) Low frequency detrimental gene
(5) Geographic difference in characteristics

(6) Similarity to fossil organism   Similarity
(7) Similarity in DNA between organisms

Figure 7.1 Summary of item topics and framework types. Adaptation items reference microevolutionary phenomena (evolution within a species) and similarity items reference macroevolutionary phenomena (evolution above the species level).

ancestry and subsequent evolution are causes of this similarity. Within each section, items were randomly ordered for each participant.

The demographics survey probed students' attitudes toward creationism and evolution. Based on a free-response item about the reality of evolution ("Do you believe that evolution, as you have described it, accurately depicts what happens in the real world? If not, what parts of it are incorrect?"), participants' attitudes toward evolution were coded as negative (at minimum, expressed doubts about whether human evolution happened), neutral (described some exceptions to the evolutionary process or some lack of confidence in their response), or positive (expressed no doubts at all about evolution or allowed for minor exceptions, such as a deity starting life but evolution taking over thereafter; see Thanukos, 2002 for item and coding details).

Here, we reflect on the results of three analytic threads (Analyses 1, 2, and 3): (1) a repeated measures analysis for organism type (plant, animal, or human), (2) a 3 (attitude toward evolution) × 3 (organism type) ANOVA, with organism type as a repeated measure, and (3) a repeated measures analysis for organism type and framework type (adaptation or similarity), including and excluding participants who were negative toward evolution.[3]

Think-Aloud Protocols (TAPs): Explanations for the Patterns

After training on non-evolutionary "warm-up" items to familiarize them with TAPs, 24 other students (from the same pool) received stimuli identical to *either* the plant *or* the human Likert items described above, but were asked to read each item aloud and to think aloud while rating it.[4] (Item orders were randomized for each participant, and responses were audiotaped.) They then completed the demographics survey on their attitudes toward creationism and evolution described above.

A TAP coding scheme was designed to include categories for all phrases or ideas appearing in two or more responses or that were particularly salient to differences between plants and humans (Table 7.1). Each Likert item was scored for the presence/absence of all categories in the scheme; thus, a response could be scored for multiple categories. A trained second individual coded 10% of the total data set, yielding an inter-rater reliability of greater than 97%.

Chi-square tests on the full data set compared the number of references made to specific categories across treatment (i.e., those receiving plant or animal items) groups. Several references to a category by a person were treated the same as a single reference to that category. So, for example, we compared the number of people in the plant treatment group who did and did not mention the relatedness of organisms to the number of people in the human treatment group who did and did not.

Results and Discussion

Our samples were more positive toward human evolution than the U.S. public. A national poll found that only 27% of the U.S. think that evolution is at least a "mostly accurate account of how humans were created and developed" (People For the American Way Foundation, 2000), yet on our surveys, averaging each participant's human evolution section rating yielded a set of acceptance scores with a high median: +2.50 on a –4 to +4 scale. Of course, Berkeley undergraduates are likely similar to Americans with college degrees, who are less likely to reject human evolution in favor of strict creationism than the general population. Of college graduates, 25% reject human evolution; 47% of all Americans do (ThinkQuest, 1999).

Plant Evolution Is More Acceptable Than Human Evolution

Despite participants' relatively high level of acceptance of human evolution, the surveys found plant evolution to be more acceptable than human evolution, which we will term the *human reticence effect*. Analysis 1 identified a borderline-significant main effect of organism type [$F(2,150) = 3.24$, $p = 0.05$], which was strengthened in other analyses when more variables were included in the model. Participants' mean response across plant items was marginally significantly higher than that for the human items ($p < 0.1^5$; see Table 7.2, part I). Animal items were not rated differently than plant items or human items. This finding is not unexpected, given that many sources indicate human evolution to be dubitable for many Americans.

But why is that the case? It is plausible that human evolution conflicts with some people's worldviews—the sets of beliefs and ideas that shape our interpretations of the world. For example, some religious groups afford humans "exempt" status when it comes to evolution, but accept other organisms' evolution (Scott, 2000). On a less religious note, for some, acceptance of

Table 7.1 Frequency Distribution of References from Think-Aloud Protocols (TAPs), Displayed by Response Coding Scheme Categories. Numbers of references are collapsed across all items.

Coding scheme category	References from human treatment group (and %)	References from plant treatment group (and %)	Total number of references	References by different participants (and % of 24)
Availability, familiarity, and confidence				
Have Knowledge—has learned about the topic	15 (60%)	10 (40%)	25	16 (66.7%)
Lack of Knowledge—didn't know enough or about something	9 (36%)	16 (64%)	25	16 (66.7%)
Lack of Knowledge About Plants—didn't know about plants	0 (0%)	4 (100%)	4	4 (16.7%)
Unsure—felt unsure or not confident while responding	11 (42.3%)	15 (57.7%)	26	13 (54.2%)
Specific examples				
Human Example—referenced case of human evolution not in item	4 (50%)	4 (50%)	8	8 (33.3%)
Animal Example—referenced case of animal evolution not in item	4 (50%)	4 (50%)	8	5 (20.8%)
Plant Example—referenced case of plant evolution not in item	0 (0%)	1 (100%)	1	1 (4.2%)
Factors acknowledging evolutionary relationships over time				
Related Organisms—species are closely related or have common ancestor	22 (88%)	3 (12%)	25	14 (58.3%)

Similar DNA—since the species have similar DNA, they must be closely related	4 (57.1%)	3 (42.9%)	7	5 (20.8%)
Organism Hasn't Changed—organism has not changed much over evolutionary timescales	0 (0%)	4 (100%)	4	4 (16.7%)
References to natural selection or the products of natural selection				
Selection—causes death or leads to fewer offspring	9 (64.3%)	5 (35.7%)	14	14 (58.3%)
Adaptiveness—trait is adaptive for the organism	35 (44.9%)	43 (55.1%)	78	24 (100%)
Non-adaptiveness—trait is not adaptive for the organism	11 (91.7%)	1 (8.3%)	12	8 (33.3%)
Other factors likely to decrease the plausibility of an evolutionary explanation				
No Relationship Between—no relationship between evolution and the scenario in the item	3 (37.5%)	5 (62.5%)	8	7 (29.2%)
Innate Characteristic—trait is innate	3 (100%)	0 (0%)	3	3 (12.5%)
Human Interference—trait is a result of human interference on other species	0 (0%)	4 (100%)	4	2 (8.3%)
Environmental Influences—trait is a result of environmental influence	5 (50%)	5 (50%)	10	9 (37.5%)

Table 7.2 Summary of Effects and Interactions. Participants' acceptance of evolutionary explanations (i.e., their Likert ratings) for the survey, broken down by section and participant characteristics. The transformed mean column reports the mean of the transformed data, first averaged within section, framework type if appropriate, and participant; the next column reports the standard deviation of the same data. The final column reports the median of the untransformed data, first averaged within section and participant. Only responses to the items listed in Figure 7.1 are included in these analyses.

	Transformed data		Untransformed median
	Mean	(Standard deviation)	
I. Section			
Plant	103.9[a]	(44.7)	2.4
Similarity framework	104.5	(52.5)	2.5
Adaptation framework	105.9[b]	(46.2)	2.5
Animal	100.9	(48.1)	2.3
Similarity framework	109.1	(54.7)	2.5
Adaptation framework	99.6	(49.9)	2.2
Human	93.3[a]	(54.8)	2.5
Similarity framework	110.7[c]	(61.7)	3.0
Adaptation framework	88.5[bc]	(54.1)	2.2
II. Attitude toward evolution and section			
Negative attitude (n = 8)	38.8[de]	(41.1)	−0.4
Plant	56.9[f]	(39.6)	0.9
Animal	49.7	(49.5)	0.0
Human	9.9[f]	(9.0)	−1.4
Neutral attitude (n = 12)	92.4[d]	(48.2)	1.9
Plant	95.1	(51.1)	2.1
Animal	95.9	(42.1)	2.0
Human	86.2	(54.2)	1.5

Positive attitude (n = 56)	109.5^e	(44.1)	2.6
Plant	112.5	(39.9)	2.6
Animal	109.3	(45.0)	2.4
Human	106.8	(47.8)	2.7

Note

Transformed means marked in the table above with paired superscripts are significantly or marginally significantly different from each other, as per the following tests of mean difference (e.g., the two superscripted b's above indicate that the adaptation framework items for plants yielded a higher mean acceptance of evolutionary explanations than did the adaptation framework items for humans): a, $t(75) = 2.17$, mean diff $= 10.60 \pm 9.72$, $p < 0.1$; b, $t(75) = 3.48$, mean diff $= 17.43 \pm 9.98$, $p < 0.05$; c, $t(75) = 5.32$, mean diff $= 22.25 \pm 8.33$, $p < 0.01$; d, $t(58) = 4.47$, mean diff $= 53.57 \pm 24.00$, $p < 0.01$; e, $t(190) = 7.40$, mean diff $= 70.69 \pm 18.85$, $p < 0.01$; f, $t(7) = 3.82$, mean diff $= 47.06 \pm 29.12$, $p < 0.05$.

human evolution may entail loss of a sense of "their spiritual nature and their capacity for moral reasoning" (Evans, 2000), less sense of purpose, lower feelings of self-determination, and increased justification for racism and selfishness (Brem et al., 2003).[6]

Think-aloud protocols did not identify clear references to such religious and non-religious "conflicting worldview" reasons for the human reticence effect (Table 7.1), and the demographics survey did not include measures of religiosity. Still, other data show that some students hesitate to express such misgivings in experimental settings: in a paired discussion task based on similar stimuli, one explicated that she was trying not to mention her own religious reservations about evolution (Thanukos, 2002). Further, TAPs can only detect conscious influences (Ericsson & Simon, 1993). It is possible that worldview conflicts play a role in ratings, but remain unreported.

Think-aloud protocols, though, did identify several more scientific, less worldview-related factors that might help explain low ratings of the acceptance of evolutionary explanations. These include (see Table 7.1) learning and other *environmental influences* (i.e., a trait is better explained by an environmental factor—e.g., soil quality or learning—than by evolution) and *human interference* (i.e., humans, not evolution, manipulated another species' trait). Though more proximate than ultimate explanations for a particular trait, such reasons are certainly scientifically acceptable. Hence, scientifically valid arguments (and not just worldview conflicts) can *lower* the acceptance of evolutionary explanations for particular traits.

While many factors may help explain human reticence (e.g., recent research on life-status by Goldberg & Thompson-Schill, 2009, and on science standards by Mead & Mates, 2009), the finding had subtleties: patterns of acceptance varied depending upon item order and item topic, and these factors interacted with participants' attitudes toward, and experience with, evolution. We examine two "modulations" of the human reticence effect.

Modulation 1: Those generally less accepting of evolution were least accepting of human evolution. The human reticence effect seemed largely attributable to this group.

Analysis 2 on the survey data revealed a significant interaction between organism type and attitude toward evolution ($F[4,146] = 2.77$, $p < 0.05$; Figure 7.2).[7] Those negative toward evolution (eight participants) were less accepting of evolutionary explanations for human items than for plant items ($p < 0.05$; see Table 7.2, part II). In contrast, those positive (56 participants) and neutral (12 participants) toward evolution showed no differences in their acceptance of evolutionary explanations for plant, animal, and human items.

This coheres with Evans et al.'s (1997) finding that some are less likely to evolutionarily explain human origins, compared to other species' origins (dinosaurs, in this case—organisms of much intrinsic interest; e.g., Kaufman,

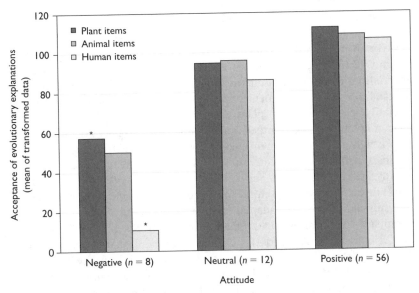

Figure 7.2 The interaction between organism type and attitude toward evolution. As expected, those positive and neutral toward evolution are more accepting of evolution in all organisms than are those negative toward evolution. However, only for those negative toward evolution is there a significant difference between acceptance of plant and human evolution, as indicated by the asterisks ($p<0.05$).

Ranney, Lewis, Thanukos, & Brem, 2000). Although Evans et al. identified this trend in fundamentalist Christians, there is likely an overlap between this group and our students who had negative evolution attitudes. Study 1 extends Evans et al.'s results by broadening the sorts of situations in which evolution is seen as a poor explanation of human history or characteristics. Additionally, Evans et al. examined evolution solely as an explanation for species origins (i.e., macroevolution); however, this study was concerned with other aspects of evolution, too (i.e., adaptation within a species—microevolution).

The human reticence effect was given many possible explanations above, but this modulation seems most consistent with the idea that human evolution conflicts with individuals' worldviews. The "negative attitude" group's stronger pattern would be expected if their (perhaps more religious or anthropocentric) worldviews diverged from those of people positive or neutral toward evolution.

Modulation 2: Participants positive and neutral toward evolution (68 participants) were unusually accepting of evolutionary explanations when items emphasized the relationships/similarities between humans and other species—and for these items, exhibited a "reverse" human reticence effect.

Analysis 3 on the survey data revealed a section by framework type interaction $(F[2,150] = 8.88, p < 0.001)$,[8] with items referencing human evolutionary relationships (human similarity items) rated higher than items explaining humans' adaptive traits via evolution (human adaptation items; $p < 0.01$; see Table 7.2, part I), but with plant similarity items not rated differently from plant adaptation items. In other words, human evolutionary relationships are surprisingly acceptable to many people. We will term this finding the "human origins acceptance effect." Interestingly, this effect is strengthened when those negative toward evolution are excluded $(F[2,134] = 10.83, p < 0.001$; Figure 7.3).[9] Those positive and neutral toward evolution rated plant items higher than human items for the adaptation items $(p < 0.05)$, but rated human items marginally significantly higher than plant items for the similarity items $(p = 0.10$; see Table 7.3, part I).[10] On the other hand, those negative toward evolution did not differentiate between adaptation and similarity items in this way; they rated human items low in general and lower than plant items for adaptation items $(p < 0.05)$ and marginally so for similarity items $(p = 0.058$;

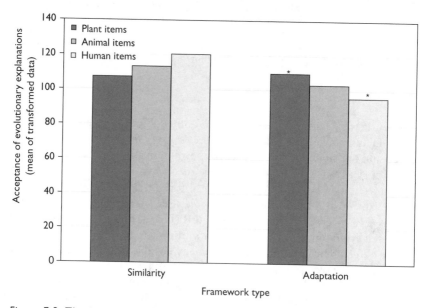

Figure 7.3 The interaction between organism type and framework type for those positive and neutral ($n = 68$) toward evolution. Plant evolution is more acceptable than human evolution for the adaptation items, as indicated by the asterisks ($p < 0.05$), but the same is not true for the similarity items. (Recall that each participant rated two similarity items and five adaptation items.)

Table 7.3 Interaction Associated With Framework Across Different Attitudes. Participants' acceptance of evolutionary explanations (i.e., their Likert ratings) for the survey, broken down by attitude toward evolution, framework type, and section. The first column reports the mean of the transformed data, first averaged within section, framework type, and participant; the second column reports the standard deviation of the same data. The final column reports the median of the untransformed data, first averaged within section, framework type, and participant. Transformed means marked with paired superscripts are significantly or nearly significantly different from each other.

	Transformed data		Untransformed median
	Mean	(Standard deviation)	
I. Positive and neutral attitudes			
Similarity framework			
Plant	109.8[a]	(50.9)	2.5
Animal	116.2	(51.3)	3.0
Human	123.0[ab]	(52.9)	3.0
Adaptation framework			
Plant	111.3[c]	(43.8)	2.6
Animal	105.1	(46.8)	2.3
Human	97.2[bc]	(50.1)	2.4
II. Negative attitudes			
Similarity framework			
Plant	59.2[d]	(47.2)	1.0
Animal	48.8	(47.3)	-0.3
Human	6.7[d]	(10.3)	-3.5
Adaptation framework			
Plant	60.2[e]	(42.3)	1.0
Animal	53.4	(54.6)	0.2
Human	14.2[e]	(15.3)	-1.3

Note

a, $t(67) = 2.17$, mean dif $= 13.17 \pm 12.14$, $p = 0.102$; b, $t(67) = 5.83$, mean dif $= 25.77 \pm 8.83$, $p < 0.01$; c, $t(67) = 2.67$, mean dif $= 14.07 \pm 10.53$, $p < 0.05$; d, $t(7) = 3.02$, mean dif $= 52.65 \pm 41.20$, $p < 0.1$; e, $t(7) = 3.62$, mean dif $= 46.02 \pm 30.02$, $p < 0.05$.

see Table 7.3, part II). Since our sample included rather few negative attitude participants, here we focus largely on plausible explanations for the more robust patterns exhibited by the positive and neutral participants.

It is interesting that for those positive and neutral toward evolution, the idea of human macroevolution (that we share recent common ancestors with other apes—ideas tapped by the human similarity items) may be more acceptable than that of human microevolution (that many human features are adaptive and were built by natural selection within a population—ideas tapped by the human adaptation items). This human origins acceptance effect (coined above) is the reverse of anti-evolution groups' views that reject macroevolution (particularly human origins), even when they accept microevolution (Scott, 2000). Other studies provide no hints of such a diverging acceptance pattern regarding macro- and microevolution in groups more positive toward evolution.

There are many possible explanations for this human origins acceptance effect, but we particularly examine one: that for those *not* negative toward evolution, (1) prior knowledge impacts similarity items' ratings more than adaptation items' ratings, and (2) prior knowledge of human evolution is greater than that of plant evolution. Supposition 1 is plausible due to the nature of the similarity and adaptation items. Adaptation items describe population characteristics and ascribe them to natural selection. Similarity items suggest that two organisms share a similarity because of common ancestry and subsequent evolution. For those savvy about natural selection, the plausibility that natural selection caused a trait may be easily assessed without much prior knowledge of the scenario (i.e., "just so" stories are easy to make up, even in the absence of detailed content knowledge); but for items involving a proposed evolutionary relationship between two species, one might feel the need to know more details to assess the tightness of the relationship. That is, there is no substitute for specific content knowledge and familiarity with the organisms when it comes to assessing the plausibility or closeness of an evolutionary relationship between two lineages.

Several lines of evidence indicate that people know more about humans' (than plants') evolutionary relationships (supposition 2 above). In TAPs, interspecies relationships were mentioned much more often for human than plant items ($\chi^2[1, n = 24] = 10.97$, $p < 0.005$, Fisher exact $p < 0.005$; see Table 7.1). Informal observations provide further support. Popular science articles often note that chimpanzees are *Homo sapiens'* closest living relatives, and the discovery (and media coverage) of new hominid relics is frequent—yet one rarely sees plant evolutionary relationships noted in a newspaper. Perhaps the human–chimp tie is so common that it has become uncontroversial for those without strong contrary commitments, and knowledge of human evolutionary relationships may be an area of relative confidence. Few people, though, hear about plant evolutionary relationships. Indeed, the relationships among many plant taxa are poorly resolved, while human evolutionary relationships are better understood. Further, secondary education biology textbooks often centrally describe human evolutionary relationships, while plant evolutionary relationships (if present) are often relegated to introducing the plant physiology and chemistry chapter (e.g., DiSpezio, Linner-Luebe, Lisowski, Skoog, & Sparks, 1994; Wright, Coble, Hopkins, Johnson, & Lahart, 1993). In sum, many arguments suggest that plants' evolutionary relationships are less familiar than humans'.

A further explanation for the human origins acceptance effect is that many people who are not negative toward evolution may find human adaptation (as opposed to human origins) more troubling than plant adaptation. As this explanation may be counterintuitive, we elaborate: The idea that human behavioral and physical characteristics result from evolution may conflict with participants' worldviews and experiences—even for those who are not negative toward evolution. Viewing humans as subject to evolution suggests that we *are* animals (not just their relatives). Further, if accepting evolution correlates with a lower sense of self-determination (Brem et al., 2003), viewing human traits (especially behavioral traits, many of which we like to think we control) as adaptations should be even more tied to a void of self-determination. This lack of self-control may conflict with one's experiences as a decision-maker. Plant adaptation, though, may present fewer conflicts. This idea (we'll call it "human agential experience") coheres with TAP results that show that participants in the human condition are much more likely to reference an organism's trait not being adaptive than those in the plant condition ($\chi^2[1, N = 24] = 6.75$, $p < 0.01$, Fisher exact $p < 0.05$; see Table 7.1). Thus, people may view human traits as less tuned for survival than plant traits.

Yet another explanation for a lessened willingness to tell adaptive "just so" stories for human traits may be that our familiarity with humans constrains our adaptive stories, compared to those we might create for (less familiar) plants. Plant ignorance may allow us *more* ways to tell adaptive tales about them. In contrast, both human adaptive story constraints (the difficulties of making up a "just so" story for humans when one knows humans well) and human agential experience (our reluctance to ascribe adaptive explanations for personal traits) could help explain the human origins acceptance effect and frequent references to non-adaptiveness in the human condition during TAPs.

Summary and Implications

Table 7.4 summarizes a subset of the factors hypothesized to affect one's acceptance of an evolutionary explanation. These factors need not be directly competitive and may simply reflect the various thought modes, unconscious influences, and interactions that play roles in the complex domain of evolution—with its personal, social, and scientific ramifications (Brem et al., 2003). For example, one's rating might simultaneously reflect plant unfamiliarity,

Table 7.4 Summary of Factors Hypothesized to Influence Ratings. The major factors identified as potentially increasing or decreasing a partici- pant's acceptance of an evolutionary explanation for a feature.

Factors increasing acceptance	Factors decreasing acceptance
More *positive* attitude toward evolution	More *negative* attitude toward evolution
Topic's *consistency* with worldview	Topic's *conflict* with worldview
Higher familiarity/availability of topic	*Lower* familiarity/availability of topic
Perceived *adaptiveness* of feature	Perceived *non-adaptiveness* of feature
Perceived *lack of influence* of the environment on the feature	Perceived *influence* of the environment on the feature

religious commitments, and a recently read news piece on human evolution. Our data show that many considerations and modes of thought are invoked for judgments on evolution.

This study posed two main questions, for which answers are now clearer. Question 1: Do students differentially accept evolution across organisms? Answer: They do, and some groups accept human evolution less than plant evolution. Question 2: Are students' views of evolution in different organisms consistent over different evolutionary scenarios? Answer: No, the acceptance of evolution across organisms varies depending on whether evolutionary rela- tionships (e.g., via similarity) or evolutionary adaptations are emphasized.

We found other interesting, novel results. Students distinguished between organisms' origins and adaptation (respectively reflected in their similarities and apt traits)—two aspects of evolution not previously examined in social science research. We also found that evolutionary attitudes across organisms are less obvious than one might imagine (e.g., many accept human evolution *less* than plant evolution) and may be strongly mediated by personal charac- teristics (e.g., general attitude toward evolution) and the aspect of evolution referenced (adaptation vs. common species origins).

For the population studied herein, at least some aspects of human evolu- tion may not represent a very thorny social issue: many students were famil- iar, and not uneasy, with humans' evolutionary ties to other animals. In this way, the media's influence may have yielded a positive effect by reinforcing this idea. However, people may accept human adaptation less, perhaps because it conflicts with their experiences as decision-makers or implies that they *are* animals (and not just related to animals).

Our results are consistent with the idea that the acceptance of evolutionary explanations is influenced by many factors—notably, familiarity (Table 7.4). Implications of familiarity's role ought to encourage defenders of evolution, suggesting that further efforts to explain evolution via media outlets may make its aspects more familiar and acceptable. Increasing evolution's familiarity may entail a markedly different approach than increasing its understanding (which does not seem much related to equivalent increases in accepting evolution; e.g., Bishop & Anderson, 1990; Demastes, Settlage, & Good, 1995; cf. Shtulman & Calabi, 2008). Increasing evolutionary familiarity might involve, for example, citing evolution whenever relevant, inhibiting publications from avoiding references to evolution, and highlighting evolution's wide acceptance among scientists. In contrast, increasing the understanding of evolution may involve more challenging educational interventions.

Beyond the basic conclusions of this study, we highlight a finding that we will return to toward the end: As others have noted about the approach of some religious groups toward evolution (e.g., Miller et al., 2006; Scott, 2000; Scott & Matzke, 2007), many of our participants acted as if humans have a special exemption from evolutionary processes—or are "above the game"—as suggested by the human reticence effect. We note that many people find adaptation in humans to be more troubling than in plants. We will return to speculations regarding why U.S. residents, compared to those of peer nations, are more likely to confer evolutionary exemptions upon themselves.

First, though, let us consider another line of research from our laboratory (with Jennifer Schindel) that provides evidence regarding a proximal issue: How do U.S. undergraduates' various levels of evolutionary acceptance play out in terms of a core element of national consciousness—namely how should our schools address the origins and diversity of life?

Study 2: U.S. Undergraduate Views Related to Teaching Evolution and Creationism

To better understand relationships among students' views about pedagogy and biological change, a series of written surveys were given to 113 paid University of California at Berkeley undergraduates (Schindel & Ranney, 2001). Four clusters of questions were presented, two of which we discuss here. Each student selected, from a given set of five statements in each cluster, the statement that best expressed his/her opinion; the student followed the choice with three written elaborations: (a) paraphrasing the chosen statement, (b) explaining how the statement matched his/her own opinions, and (c) explaining how the statement differed from his/her opinion. Quantitative and qualitative analyses were performed on objective and open-ended responses, respectively.

Question 1's five alternative statements regarded the origins and development of life on Earth, running a continuum from one typical of non-theistic evolutionists to one typical of no-evolution creationists; intermediate statements included those representative of theistically initiated evolution, deity-intervening evolution, and all-but-human evolution (i.e., human exceptionalism). Question 2's five alternatives focused on schools teaching about creation and/or evolution, running a continuum from one typical of evolution-only adherents to one typical of creation-only adherents (and one for those who believe *neither* should be taught); intermediate statements included the notion that both should be taught in schools (but need not be in the same class), and that both should be taught *side-by-side* in schools.

The objective choices and written responses received both intensive quantitative analyses and qualitative analyses; for instance, logistic regression statistical analyses were employed, and undergraduates' writings were subjected to a 14-code protocol scoring rubric—with code-titles such as "Let students decide" and "Equal time: 50/50." These analyses suggested the presence of three main groups of respondents (the third of which seemed least coherent as a cluster) and a fourth, residual, group. The groups generally become increasingly less likely to prefer the teaching of evolution in schools (and generally less likely to accept evolution), as ordered in what follows.

The first group, the "evolution advocates," believe that only evolution should be taught in schools; the group includes an atheistic subgroup that Schindel and Ranney (2001) termed "evolution warriors." Strongly evolutionist in their beliefs, they prototypically refer to church–state separations, and some focus on teaching evolution as teaching "proven facts." If creation *were* to be taught, they often suggest a particular, separate, non-science course (like philosophy).

The second group, the "fence-sitters," are more likely to believe that evolution and creation should both be taught, although not necessarily in the same class. They are less likely to name a course in which creation should be taught than do evolution advocates. Fence-sitters are also more likely than evolution advocates to find a role for a supreme being who intervenes in the evolutionary process, and they tend to focus on the pedagogical importance of multiple views.

The third, "side-by-side," undergraduate group subsumes two subgroups, due to a shared interest in teaching evolution and creation together—albeit for different reasons. The "pluralist" subgroup resembles the fence-sitters in focusing on the importance of diversity and freedom of thought. In contrast, the "no-evolution creationist" subgroup is motivated by the belief that species did not evolve, and thus that students need to receive alternatives to evolution.

The final, fourth, group of college students preferred excluding the teaching of evolution altogether. These (usually creationist) "evolution exclusionists" either believed that only creation ought to be taught *or* that neither evolution nor creation ought to be taught.

In general, our findings indicate that undergraduates' views are not mere reflections of either their beliefs or the strengths of a particular theory. Ranking the objective responses from the two questions on separate evolution-to-creation continua indicated that the more one accepted evolution, the more one wished evolution to be preferentially taught (Spearman's $r = 0.263$, $p < 0.01$; e.g., "No supreme being plays a role in evolution" was associated with "Only evolution should be taught in schools"; $x^2(1) = 6.67$, $p < 0.01$); however, the 0.263 correlation is hardly close to 1. Notions of fairness and freedom of thought/expression led the majority of the participants (71% of them, all coming from the fence-sitters and side-by-siders groups) to believe that schools should teach both evolution and creation (cf. Brem et al., 2003). The most frequently tallied of the 14 written response categories (30% of responses) was the one that included responses indicating that multiple or all views/sides should be taught.

An interesting element among the undergraduates' responses was that they seemed to view evolution and creation as inherently in conflict (consistent with prior work by Kaufman, Thanukos, Ranney, Brem, & Kwong, 1999; also see below). For instance, in contrast to the rhetoric one often hears associated with evolution and biology education, only three of the 113 participants volunteered that evolution and creation should *not* be viewed as incompatible. Regardless of where individuals fell on the continuum of evolutionary–creationist acceptance, most of our participants seemed to view evolution and religion as competitive or even incompatible. This is one of the reasons that the undergraduates would so often advocate letting students decide for themselves between the "two sides." Some even suggested that students choose the *one* view that is right for them, which is perhaps a multiplist epistemological perspective on evolution.

This study reveals that many U.S. residents—perhaps most of them—view evolution and religion as incompatible (see more evidence of this below), regardless of where they fall on a spectrum of "atheistic evolutionists" to "anti-evolution creationists." This conflict may not be logically necessary (as many flavors of God-believing, evolution-accepting Americans, including some prominent biologists, naturally point out), but it follows from the scientific principle of parsimony: given that species (including humans) arose, it is more likely that one process (i.e., evolution or creation) was involved than multiple processes (i.e., evolution and creation). (This point will be elaborated upon later.) However, people seem more nuanced with their educational preferences. They are more willing to balance children's educational needs by allowing a multiplicity of views about the origins and diversity of life.

We now return to some conjectural theorizing to help connect and contextualize results from the two studies. In doing so, we discuss why Americans seem more likely to consider themselves special, why that reflects a modest national evolutionary orientation (which is one in a reasonably coherent configuration of salient ways in which the U.S. is an outlier nation; e.g., Paul, 2005), and why so many in the U.S. would even entertain teaching creation alongside evolution in schools.

The Received View of the U.S. Divergence Phenomenon

As befits evolution—a realm of inquiry that involves historical analysis—answers to the divergence question tend to revolve around history. In brief, what Ranney (in press) calls the "received view" of U.S. divergence, although not often made this explicit (cf. Scott, 2004, 2006), is as follows: A society founded upon both (a) isolated frontier needs and (b) immigrants seeking religious (and speech, etc.) freedoms yielded (c) rather fiercely decentralized governmental (e.g., school district) and religious control, leading to (d_1) fundamentalist Christian groups, (d_2) anti-evolutionism in school curricula, and—because of (d_1), etc.—(e) rather low evolutionary acceptance among U.S. adults (relative to peer nations).

This received view has some problems, though (Ranney, in press). First, its adherents often focus largely on religion because (b) and (d_1) are among the precursors for (e), the U.S. divergence phenomenon. However, reasons for the U.S.'s religious mixture—and its anomalous religious fervor (given its security and wealth; Norris & Inglehart, 2004)—are far from clear and open to many other interpretations. Indeed, Norris and Inglehart effectively negate part of the received view—that religious pluralism and a lack of regulation yield greater national religiosity, as the U.S. is again a distinct outlier on that score (also see Paul, 2005). Furthermore, creationist fundamentalism is not the only source of resistance to scientific thinking; for instance, Griffin (2007) suggests that people often try to satisfy goals about affect, rather than accuracy (so one's goals interact with one's scientific beliefs, in contrast to them being readily compartmentalized separate spheres). In addition, religion (even conjoined with a frontier history, to the degree that the U.S. is more "frontier" than other nations) is only one way that the U.S. diverges from peer nations; its society has also had a dramatically different geopolitical, social, and economic development (cf. Paul, 2005). Further still, the received view uses a century-old fundamentalist religious framing (i.e., The Twelve Fundamentals, booklets from 1910 to 1915; Scott, 2006, p. 450; also see Scott & Matzke, 2007). Finally, by focusing more on the laggard (i.e., the U.S.) than the advanced, the received view largely ignores other possible answers to the U.S. divergence question—a question that should *also* be phrased, "Why have peer nations accepted evolution more readily than the U.S.?"

The RTMD (Reinforced Theistic Manifest Destiny) View of the U.S. "Divergence"

Ranney (initially mentioned in Ranney, 1998, and elaborated in Ranney, in press) offers a conjectural answer to the divergence question; as it helps frame our results, it is described here to the degree space allows. The conjecture expands the received view, offering more predictive power. In a nutshell, the received view seems to lack an updated geopolitical perspective that includes national reinforcements regarding theistic manifest destiny—particularly feedback about war and (perhaps less so) economics. The expansive conjecture, now called reinforced theistic manifest destiny theory (RTMD; Ranney, in press), focuses on how nations are militarily, economically, or otherwise reinforced regarding their collective desires (e.g., for stature, security, and prosperity)—and on how the reinforcements impact nations' theistic (and related) beliefs. World War II (WWII) represents a central RTMD event, as it (and/or World War I) markedly affected virtually all of the 34 nations in Miller et al.'s (2006) recent and striking evolution survey. The U.S. ranked only 33rd of these nations in evolutionary acceptance—results that are core data for RTMD as it employs 20th century military, economic, and geopolitical history to generally account for several of the ways in which the U.S. is, societally (e.g., Paul, 2005), an outlier among its otherwise more natural peer nations.

Only the gist of RTMD can be provided here (but it is expanded upon in Ranney, in press). The theory includes intentionally colloquial, national-identity, stochastic, and metaphorical constructs, such as a nation being an "organism" "reinforced" for a war or (as below) that a nation's "god" "won" a war for them (e.g., the "national god" of the U.S. in both WWI and WWII vs. that of Germany). Of course, a victorious nation may formally have many religions and/or multiple "gods." A more obvious caveat is that RTMD is a (fairly historical) theory, and all theories—even ones about gravity—are likely to be inaccurate in detail, and perhaps even in gist.

Given these caveats, RTMD theory's gist is: (1) From 1859 (Darwin's publishing *On the Origin of Species*) to 1917, the U.S. was not alone in being slow to accept evolution, but likely slower than Europe, due to factors noted in the received view. (2) Since WWI, WWII, and beyond, the U.S. has been uniquely reinforced as a military and (less so) an economic victor, helping maintain or enhance in its populace mutually supportive notions of religiosity, belief in an afterlife, and manifest destiny. (3) These effects further retarded the U.S.'s acceptance of evolution (and perhaps retarded the U.S.'s acceptance that humans are at least partially causing global climate change; see Ranney, in press, and data from Leiserowitz, 2007; also see remarks by Dr Gavriel Avital, chief scientist of Israel's Education Ministry, in which he both connects and explicitly doubts the plausibilities of evolution and global climate change; Kashti & Rinat, 2010).

The RTMD theory accounts for a good deal of evidence—from anecdotes to formal data sets. For instance, a Japanese colleague (different from the one mentioned above) noted that Japan's textbooks excluded Shinto creation myths after WWII, when its emperor effectively renounced Imperial divinity. Reinforced theistic manifest destiny theory suggests that the Japanese "god" lost, and that Japan understood this as a reinforcement about how its theistically linked manifest destiny had ebbed. The theory further suggests that this is why Japan ranks high in accepting evolution—fourth of 34 (Miller et al., 2006). In contrast, the big victor of WWII, the U.S., ranks 33rd—sandwiched between the only two countries surveyed that have major non-Christian influences: Cyprus (32nd) and Turkey (34th).

Reinforced theistic manifest destiny theory's cognitive competition model is supported by national and international data—as well as elements of logic. For empirical support, if one examines data from the 13 nations in common among Norris and Inglehart's (2004) corpus and Miller et al.'s (2006) corpus (including the U.S., Japan, and much of Europe), one notes that countries that rank high in accepting evolution rank low in (a) believing in an afterlife and (b) believing in God (i.e., strong *negative* correlations result; both r's $= -0.8$; $p < 0.001$; Paul, 2005, noted a related theism–evolution anti-link across 11 nations). In terms of logic, recall that RTMD holds that the U.S. is more likely, among peers, to view God as "on its side," and this inhibits the atheistically correlated evolutionary view. Virtually no atheists are creationists; this conjunction is basically an empty cell in the 2×2 matrix when one crosses "evolution vs. creation" with "theism vs. atheism." The cell's void helps drive the theism–evolution anti-correlation (i.e., the competition). Consistent with this logic, Preston and Epley (2009) recently reported data consistent with an automatic opposition between "God" and "science"—including an experiment that highlighted scientific origins (namely, the big bang and primordial soup notions).

Reinforced theistic manifest destiny theory is also supported by some verbal report data. Ranney (in press) notes that many people, if not most— even those with postgraduate biology degrees—prefer biological evolution to *not* be "true." Typically, when asked for their reasoning, people essentially replied: "Duh; God!" That is, while not formally contradictory, a creation-spawning deity at least indirectly competes with evolution in explaining species because parsimony suggests that one *or* the other is in force (and less likely both—just as parsimony can suggest that the K-T extinctions were due to an asteroid *or* volcanoes, rather than both; also see Preston & Epley, 2009). In connectionist modeling terms (e.g., Ranney & Schank, 1998), parsimony means that reducing the relative probability of evolution increases the relative probability of a deity, which increases the relative probability of life after death—which seems to be a major motivational reason to prefer the absence of evolution. In short, most people prefer evolution not to be true due to its undesirable coherence with "just moldering in the grave." Similarly, the five evolutionary impact areas Brem et al. (2003) studied and found to be relative "downers" if evolution were true—namely, plausibly reducing spirituality, self-determination, and a sense of purpose, while enhancing (otherwise heaven-inhibiting) selfishness and racism—implicitly engage the idea of an afterlife as a kind of "just desserts."

Many of the post-WWII dynamics of Japanese, German, and U.S. (and others') beliefs in an afterlife also seem consistent with RTMD's competition model (Ranney, in press). Data about the East/West German divide (Kutschera, 2008), data across English-speaking nations (Norris & Inglehart, 2004; Paul, 2005), combat death data (e.g., Fischer, Klarman, & Oboroceanu, 2007), and many historical considerations (e.g., some in Ruse, 2005, but many more—about invasions, the absence of invasions, military occupations, and economics) also cohere with the notion that a U.S.-benevolent deity preferentially shepherds its citizens to a good afterlife (Ranney, in press).

Because the received view of U.S. divergence focuses more on description than generativity, it is unclear what it predicts. Reinforced theistic manifest destiny theory, though, offers predictions about the potential for changes in the U.S.'s (and other nations') public acceptance of evolution (Ranney, in press), and predicts many relationships that are empirically testable in controlled settings. Across multiple surveys, Ranney (in press) has already observed a good number of RTMD-compatible correlations (or negative correlations, as appropriate) among beliefs about evolution, creation, theism, nationalism, the afterlife, and global climate change. (Also consistent with RTMD, our laboratory has found our atheistic participants to be the least nationalistic and the most accepting of evolution—while being part of the vanguard of accepting global climate change.) Laboratory manipulations—such as manipulating nationalistic emotions—may affect ratings on five or more related dimensions (e.g., evolutionary acceptance and even the idea that our planet's temperature increases are largely being caused by human activities). The theory thus has implications for individual cognition, U.S. diplomacy, and purported U.S. anti-intellectualisms (e.g., Ranney, in press).

If one believes that one's nation is the best—morally, militarily, or due to God's selective grace—one is likely to de-activate acceptance among discordant elements, such as evolution, to yield greater explanatory coherence (cf. Ranney & Schank, 1998; see Lombrozo, Shtulman, & Weisberg, 2006 for some links among morality, science, and evolution). This inhibition should be especially heightened for *human* evolution, leading to human exceptionalism (see the studies above, and Miller et al., 2006; Scott, 2000; etc.)—after all, a nation's non-humans (e.g., shrubs and owls) rarely go off to war. Therefore, we would expect people in the U.S. to be more comfortable with explanations about evolutionary changes in plants than in humans. Although Study 1's results were much richer than just this human reticence effect, this element of RTMD's predictive character was borne out.

Why Evolution Matters: Possible Implications of Human-Centrism and the RTMD View

Knowledge or understanding without acceptance is inert—it is rather like how we may understand a lot about Zeus (or the galaxy from the Star Wars films) but do not act on that knowledge because we reject its veracity. Is it all right that many in the U.S. "understand but reject" biological evolution—as if it would rarely, if ever, entail action? We were recently at an evolution-cognition conference at which a group of about 50 were asked why students' acceptance of evolution is important. (This question is revisited at this piece's end.) Even though many in the room knew the question was coming, it was greeted initially with silence and then responses that implicitly deflected the question. When the question was reiterated, the few responses were unimpressive and well-worn ones, such as why one should take all the pills one's physician prescribes. Virtually all of the voiced responses involved within-species changes and did not directly address questions of possible extinction(s), "die-offs," or dramatic lifestyle changes for humans. In short, none of the reasons for accepting evolution seemed to rival its potential import regarding environmental stewardship—for instance, regarding anthropogenic global climate change.

In contrast, RTMD explicitly addresses how thoughts about evolution connect to those about climate change. There may be common cause(s) between the U.S.'s over-representative contribution to Earth's warming and the country's peer-divergence in evolutionary acceptance (and theistically related beliefs). A nation that fails to fully understand or accept evolution may be less likely to readily act in ways to reduce the expected mass extinction of species (Wake & Vredenburg, 2008)—possibly including we humans. (A 4°C rise may yield over a 90% human "cull" (Vince, 2009)—yet Poling & Evans' 2004 data suggest that many U.S. adults do not even believe human extinction is *possible*.) Evolutionary non-acceptance would hardly be the sole cause of the U.S.'s carbonic overindulgence, but a society that more fully understands that environmental changes (whether atmospheric or biospheric) drive extinctions would likely act more quickly to reduce its international pollution asymmetry. We note that Brazil, site of mass Amazonian deforestations, also has a rather modest evolutionary acceptance rate (which RTMD may also account for). If most models of global climate change are apt, then the divergence problem (cf. Europe) may hardly be a "merely academic" concern.

Ultimately, the received view model (see (a)–(e) above), which helps explain pre-WWI U.S. religiosity, must be elaborated on and extended by RTMD differently for each particular nation's history. For nations like the U.S. that appeared to win WWI and WWII (and perhaps other wars)—especially when accomplished with rather mild trauma—RTMD conjectures: (1) that pre-WWI notions of humans as special (e.g., to a deity and/or as a species) were reinforced (as were the usual human optimism biases; Lovallo & Kahneman, 2003), and (2) that this specialness notion is suggested to have slowed both the acceptance of evolution, as well as—more speculatively—the U.S. acceptance of human-generated climate changes. For nations that were most scathed by wars, though, it is conjectured that notions of human specialness were inhibited, leaving national cultures that were more likely to accept evolution and perhaps even (at least partially) human-driven global climate change.

Beyond what is cited above, the U.S. is also an outlier nation in not ratifying the international Kyoto protocol on climate change and in delaying action on the protocol's successor—suggesting a harmful collective denial. Ranney (in press) notes several ways in which the high U.S. religiosity (Norris & Inglehart, 2004), fanned by RTMD influences, may have caused some subsets of U.S. society to, by act or thought, ignore global climate change. Given that Earth's warming may cause many catastrophes, if RTMD is correct, it seems critical for science educators to redouble their efforts to inform students and U.S. citizens about biological evolution. Otherwise, biospheric changes may lead to an evolutionary path quite different from the one pre-industrial Earth was on (e.g., CO_2 levels were just 73% of recent levels in the year 1750; Intergovernmental Panel on Climate Change, 2007). Further, RTMD theory has implications for classroom practice, as it suggests that teaching about global climate change (or even the ills of nationalism, perhaps) may yield students who are more likely to understand and accept biological evolution—without even confronting students' religious beliefs.

Summary and Conclusions

We have tried to articulate a number of aspects that highlight the richness and centrality of the cognition of evolution in people's lives. Although the empirical studies carried out were with U.S. undergraduates, our findings' implications go far beyond both our samples and U.S. borders. Study 1's experiments highlighted human exceptionalism in its finding of a human reticence effect (in contrast to plants) regarding accepting evolutionary explanations. This effect coheres well with the reinforced theistic manifest destiny theory (RTMD) described above (Ranney, in press), which incorporates and extends prior thinking about why the U.S. diverges from peer nations in its relatively diminutive acceptance of evolution as accounting for biological change. Study 1's other findings also relate well. In particular, RTMD resonates with several of Table 7.4's "factors that may influence the acceptance of evolutionary explanations"—especially "consistency with worldview." The other factors are more indirectly related to RTMD, but related nonetheless; for instance, even the perceived adaptiveness of a feature can be a function of whether your theo-political worldview allows you to have a positive view of evolution, such that you have more familiarity with the topic, and such that you will consider the environment to be less of a determinant of the feature.

One of Study 2's findings was that even relatively strong acceptors of evolution, while largely viewing that acceptance as conflicting with creationism, still believed that both evolution and creationism should be taught in schools; indeed 62% of non-theistic evolutionists advocated teaching both perspectives. The data suggest a culture that continues to be dominated by the traditional U.S. principles of fairness and freedom of choice (which infuse both the received view's and RTMD's explanations of the U.S.'s modest acceptance of evolution). These principles are laudable in many aspects of society (although the U.S. has not cornered the market on them), but they cause problems when the drive for equity allows dramatically less scientific (or evidence-infused) explanations such as creationism to encroach on science instruction; we have good reasons to no longer present astrological, phrenological, geocentric, and flat-Earth theories alongside more normative scientific ones, and those reasons apply to creationism. (See Griffith & Brem, 2004, Sinatra, Brem, & Evans, 2008, and Thagard & Findlay, 2010, etc., for some perspectives on the many issues relating to teaching evolutionary biology.)

As noted above, RTMD is a historical account, even as it involves a good deal of cognitive and social theorizing. Some of the conjecture's implications need more development—for instance, that the U.S. reluctance to more aggressively combat anthropogenic climate changes (Leiserowitz, 2007) may have causal roots similar to those that yield the U.S.'s reluctance to fully embrace evolution. In essence, RTMD theory seeks to further extend theorizing about the development of evolutionary understanding beyond individuals—to cultures, to all nations, and to international groups. Of course, as is the way of virtually all theories, it may be subsumed by other ideas, rejected due to some failing(s), or substantially modified due to more data and considerations; hopefully, the theory will prove productive for now.

Since science educators are among this volume's intended readers, let us revisit this piece's focus on the acceptance (e.g., across organisms) and teaching of evolution. In many arenas, acceptance is tantamount to performing reasonably: If one truly doesn't accept chemistry, one is more likely to ingest poison; denying the physics of friction means one's car may quit for want of oil; rejecting supply-and-demand economics may lead to opening yet another café in downtown Seattle; denying physiology might lead to putting off life-saving treatments. However, farmers and ranchers who explicitly reject evolution can still raise produce and livestock effectively. So, if evolution were "just history," why should educators care if students accept it, or if it were only accepted for a subset of species? We believe there are two main reasons for such caring, which need not be seen as of equal weight. First, evolution is the future as well as the past. *Our* future seems to bring nontrivial global climate change, which holds many evolutionary entailments about extinctions and lifestyle, as well as both intra- and interspecies change. So, we must not shrink from frank explications of evolution, regardless of where they lead us. The second reason is that people should accept evolution, for now, if it is the theory that accounts for the greatest breadth of data with the most coherent, parsimonious, etc., explanations. By our lights, it is *clearly* that theory.

Acknowledgments

We thank many members of the Reasoning Group at the University of California, Berkeley, both past and present, including (but by no means limited to) Jennifer Schindel, Sarah Brem, David Kaufman, Janek Nelson, Ed

Munnich, Patricia Schank, Christine Diehl, Andrew Galpern, Luke Miratrix, Mirian Song, Luke Rinne, Min Su Chung, Caslyn Cole, Lauren Barth-Cohen, Naoko Kuriyama, Calinda Martinez, and Lee Nevo. We also thank, among others, Tania Lombrozo, Roger Taylor, Michel Ferrari, Ryan Tweney, Michelle Million, Frank Sulloway, Tom Griffin, Paul Thagard, and Kaiping Peng for conversations and feedback related to this chapter. Finally, we further thank the National Science Foundation and the Committee on Research (and other auspices) of the University of California, Berkeley, for funding parts of this research.

Notes

1. Although the category "animal" technically encompasses humans, they will be herein treated as non-overlapping categories, because they are often viewed as such—and to avoid the cumbersome phrase "non-human animal." This approach is consistent with that taken by many attitudinal studies of evolution, which inquire about human evolution explicitly and don't assume that accepting evolution in some situations implies acceptance of human evolution.

2. In addition, each Likert survey included an item probing evolution's ability to explain traits of *all* living things. The study design was balanced such that six different survey versions were examined, with three different positions for the general item (before the first section, after the first section, and after the last section) and two section orderings (plant → animal → human or human→animal→plant). The section ordering mattered, as participants who saw the low-rated human evolution items first gave relatively high average ratings compared to those who saw the plant evolution items first (Thanukos, 2002); without checking for order effects, one might have mistakenly concluded human evolution to be as (or more) acceptable than plant evolution to the students.

3. Mean responses within survey version and section were not consistently normally distributed, exhibiting left skewness (*skewness/SES* < –2) and significant kurtosis (*kurtosis/SEK* > 2), likely due to a ceiling effect. To allow the use of analyses of variance (ANOVAs), the data were transformed (by $[x+4]^{2.5}$) to more closely approximate normal distributions, eliminating significant skewness and kurtosis, reducing the spread, and yielding distributions with similar standard deviations. The ratio of the largest standard deviation to the smallest standard deviation of the transformed scores was less than two, supporting the use of ANOVAs (Moore & McCabe, 1993). Nonparametric tests were also performed and yielded similar patterns of significance to those obtained using parametric statistics on transformed data; back-transforming the transformed data also yielded appropriate results (Thanukos, 2002).

4. Participants also responded to the item probing evolution's ability to explain characteristics of all living things.

5. When appropriate—as here—all *p*-values are Bonferroni adjusted.

6. Brem et al. (2003) did not compare human evolution with evolution in other organisms, but these associations would seem stronger if accepting evolution entails accepting human evolution and less strong if it does not.

7. Analysis 2 also revealed, as expected, a main effect regarding attitude [$F(2,73) = 11.64$, $p < 0.001$]: those negative toward evolution gave lower ratings than those neutral and positive [$p < 0.01$ for each contrast] (see Table 7.2, part II).

8. Analysis 3 also revealed a main effect of framework type ($F[1,75] = 8.53$, $p < 0.01$),

with similarity items rated higher than adaptation items [$t(227) = 3.60$, mean diff $= 10.09 \pm 5.52$, $p < 0.001$].
9. Note that the relevant three-way interaction involving attitude toward evolution is non-significant, possibly due to power limitations relating to a relatively low number of negative attitude participants.
10. Within-section contrasts suggest that those positive or neutral toward evolution rate human similarity items above human adaptation items ($p < 0.01$; see Table 7.3, part I), but rate plant and animal items similarly.

References

Almquist, A. J., & Cronin, J. E. (1988). Fact, fancy and myth on human evolution. *Current Anthropology, 29*, 520–522.

Bishop, B. A., & Anderson, C. W. (1990). Student conceptions of natural selection and its role in evolution. *Journal of Research in Science Teaching, 27*, 415–427.

Bizzo, N. M. V. (1994). From Down House landlord to Brazilian high school students: What has happened to evolutionary knowledge on the way? *Journal of Research in Science Teaching, 31*, 527–556.

Brem, S. K., Ranney, M., & Schindel, J. (2003). Perceived consequences of evolution: College students perceive negative personal and social impact in evolutionary theory. *Science Education, 87*, 181–206.

Demastes, S. S., Settlage, J., & Good, R. G. (1995). Students' conceptions of natural selection and its role in evolution: Cases of replication and comparison. *Journal of Research in Science Teaching, 32*, 535–550.

DiSpezio, M., Linner-Luebe, M., Lisowski, M., Skoog, G., & Sparks, B. (1994). *Science insights: Exploring living things.* Menlo Park, CA: Addison-Wesley Publishing Company.

Ericsson, K. A., & Simon, H. A. (1993). *Protocol analysis: Verbal reports as data.* Cambridge, MA: MIT Press.

Evans, E. M. (2000). Beyond scopes: Why creationism is here to stay. In K. S. Rosengren, C. N. Johnson, et al. (Eds.), *Imagining the impossible: Magical, scientific, and religious thinking in children* (pp. 305–333). New York: Cambridge University Press.

Evans, E. M., Stewart, S. F., & Poling, D. A. (1997, April). *Humans have a privileged status: Parental explanations for the origins of human and non-human species.* Paper presented at the biennial meeting of the Society for Research in Child Development, Toledo, OH.

Ferrari, M., & Chi, M. T. H. (1998). The nature of naïve explanations of natural selection. *International Journal of Science Education, 20*, 1231–1256.

Fischer, H., Klarman, K., & Oboroceanu, M-J. (2007). *American war and military operations casualties: Lists and statistics* (CRS Report for Congress: order code RL32492). [Online]. Available: www.fas.org/sgp/crs/natsec/RL32492.pdf}

Gallup Organization. (2001, March 5). [Online]. Available: www.gallup.com/poll/releases/pr010305.asp [2001, September 19].

Goldberg, R. F., & Thompson-Schill, S. L. (2009). Developmental "roots" in mature biological knowledge. *Psychological Science, 20*, 485–487.

Griffin, T. D. (2007). Individual differences in epistemic goals and the acceptance of evolution. In D. S. McNamara & J. G. Trafton (Eds.), *Proceedings of the Twenty-*

ninth Annual Conference of the Cognitive Science Society (p. 1765). Mahwah, NJ: Erlbaum.

Griffith, J. A., & Brem, S. K. (2004). Teaching evolutionary biology: Pressures, stress, and coping. *Journal of Research in Science Teaching, 41,* 791–809.

Intergovernmental Panel on Climate Change. (2007). *Fourth Assessment Report Climate Change 2007: Synthesis Report.* Cambridge, UK: Cambridge University Press.

Jenson, M., Settlage, J., & Odem, L. (1996, April). *Investigating the Disney effect: Are students reluctant to apply natural selection principles to life forms with which they identify?* Paper presented at the meeting of the National Association of Research in Science Teaching, St Louis, MO.

Kashti, O., & Rinat, Z. (2010, February 21). Scientists irate after top education official questions evolution. *Haaretz.* [Online]. Available: www.haaretz.com/hasen/spages/1151223.html [2010, February 21].

Kaufman, D., Ranney, M., Lewis, E., Thanukos, A., & Brem, S. (2000). Was *Apatosaurus* a vegan? Dinosaur knowledge rocks when learning about evolution. *Proceedings of the Twenty-second Annual Conference of the Cognitive Science Society* (pp. 741–746). Mahwah, NJ: Erlbaum.

Kaufman, D., Thanukos, A., Ranney, M., Brem, S., & Kwong, C. (1999, April). *Exploring the relationship between conceptual understanding and evolutionary reasoning.* Paper presented at the annual meeting of the American Educational Research Association, Montreal.

Kutschera, U. (2008). Creationism in Germany and its possible cause. *Evolution: Education and Outreach, 1,* 84–86.

Leiserowitz, A. (2007). International public opinion, perception, and understanding of global climate change (Human Development Report 2007/2008): *Fighting climate change: Human solidarity in a divided world,* UNDP. [Online]. Available: http://hdr.undp.org/en/reports/global/hdr2007–2008/papers/leiserowitz_anthony6.pdf [2009, August 30].

Lombrozo, T., Shtulman, A., & Weisberg, M. (2006). The intelligent design controversy: Lessons from psychology and education. *Trends in Cognitive Sciences, 10,* 56–57.

Lovallo, D., & Kahneman, D. (2003). Delusions of success: How optimism undermines executives' decisions. *Harvard Business Review, 81*(July), 56–63.

Mead, L. S., & Mates, A. (2009). Why science standards are important to a strong science curriculum and how states measure up. *Evolution: Education and Outreach, 2,* 359–371.

Miller, J. D., Scott, E. C., & Okamoto, S. (2006). Public acceptance of evolution. *Science, 313,* 765–766.

Moore, D. S., & McCabe, G. P. (1993). *Introduction to the practice of statistics.* New York: W. H. Freeman and Company.

Norris, P., & Inglehart, R. (2004). *Sacred and secular: Religion and politics worldwide.* Cambridge, UK: Cambridge University Press.

Paul, G. (2005). Cross-national correlations and quantifiable societal health with popular religiosity and secularism in the prosperous democracies: A first look. *Journal of Religion & Society, 7,* 1–17.

People For the American Way Foundation. (2000, March). *Evolution and creationism in public education: An in-depth reading of public opinion.* DYG, Inc.

Poling, D. A., & Evans, E. M. (2004). Are dinosaurs the rule or the exception? Developing concepts of death and extinction. *Cognitive Development, 19,* 363–383.

Preston, J., & Epley, N. (2009). Science and God: An automatic opposition between ultimate explanations. *Journal of Experimental Social Psychology, 45,* 238–241.

Ranney, M. (1998, August). *Who are you to play God? Puzzles from an interloping "red-erminist" (reductive determinist).* [In the symposium: Multidisciplinary Perspectives on Evolutionary Reasoning.] Paper presented at the annual meeting of the Cognitive Science Society, Madison, WI.

Ranney, M. A. (in press). Why don't Americans accept evolution as much as people in peer nations do? A theory (Reinforced Theistic Manifest Destiny) and some pertinent evidence. In K. Rosengren, M. Evans, G. Sinatra, & S. Brem (Eds.), *Evolution challenges.* Oxford: Oxford University Press.

Ranney, M., & Schank, P. (1998). Toward an integration of the social and the scientific: Observing, modeling, and promoting the explanatory coherence of reasoning. In S. J. Read & L. C. Miller (Eds.), *Connectionist models of social reasoning and social behavior* (pp. 245–274). Mahwah, NJ: Lawrence Erlbaum Associates.

Ruse, M. (2005). *The evolution–creation struggle.* Cambridge, MA: Harvard University Press.

Schindel, J. E., & Ranney, M. A. (2001, April). *Undergraduate views related to teaching evolution and creation.* Paper presented at the annual meeting of the American Educational Research Association, Seattle, WA.

Scott, E. C. (2000, December 7). *The creationism/evolution continuum.* [Online]. Available: www.ncseweb.org/resources/articles/9213_the_creationevolution_continu_12_7_2000.asp [2008, January 28].

Scott, E. C. (2004). *Evolution vs. creationism: An introduction.* Westport, CT: Greenwood Press.

Scott, E. C. (2006). Creationism and evolution: It's the American Way. *Cell, 124,* 449–451.

Scott, E. C., & Matzke, N. J. (2007). Biological design in science classrooms. *Proceedings of the National Academy of Sciences, 104*(suppl. 1), 8669–8676.

Shtulman, A., & Calabi, P. (2008). Learning, understanding, and acceptance: The case of evolution. In B. C. Love, K. McRae, & V. M. Sloutsky (Eds.), *Proceedings of the 30th Annual Conference of the Cognitive Science Society* (pp. 235–240). Austin, TX: Cognitive Science Society.

Sinatra, G. M., Brem, S. K., & Evans, E. M. (2008). Changing minds? Implications of conceptual change for teaching and learning about biological evolution. *Evolution: Education and Outreach, 1,* 189–195.

Thagard, P., & Findlay, S. (2010). Getting to Darwin: Obstacles to accepting evolution by natural selection. *Science & Education, 19,* 625–636.

Thanukos, A. (2002). *Acceptance of evolutionary explanations as they are applied to plants, animals, and humans.* Unpublished doctoral dissertation, University of California, Berkeley.

ThinkQuest. (1999). *Creation vs. Evolution II: Gallup Poll.* [Online]. Available: http://library.thinkquest.org/29178/gallup.htm [2000, August].

Vince, G. (2009, January 24). One last chance to save mankind [Interview with James Lovelock]. *New Scientist, 2692,* 30–31.

Wake, D., & Vredenburg, V. (2008). Are we in the midst of the sixth mass extinction? A view from the world of amphibians. *Proceedings of the National Academy of Sciences, 105,* 11466–11473.

Wright, J., Coble, C. R., Hopkins, J., Johnson, S., & Lahart, D. (1993). *Life science.* Englewood Cliffs, NJ: Prentice Hall.

Chapter 8

Science and Religion
Ontologically Different Epistemologies?

Gale M. Sinatra and Louis Nadelson

Introduction

According to a 2007 Gallup poll, less than 20% of U.S. adults accept without doubt the scientific explanation of human origins based in evolutionary biology (Newport, 2008). A much larger percentage of Americans (78%) accept that non-human animals have undergone biological change over time, if the word "evolution" is not included in the question (Miller, Scott, & Okamoto, 2006). These numbers have remained relatively stable for decades despite considerable progress in scientists' understanding of evolution (Miller et al., 2006). It is important to acknowledge that the numbers do shift depending on how the question is phrased, but the general trend is remarkably consistent. When Gallup put this question to the American public in May, 2007, "Do you, personally, believe in evolution, or not?" it was a statistic dead heat, with 49% responding yes, 48% responding no, and 2% reporting no opinion (Newport, 2008).

Many factors contribute to the low rates of acceptance of scientific explanations of biological change in the United States. Biological evolution is a very complex scientific theory. Comprehending the scientific explanation for the history of life on Earth requires developing understandings of concepts from disciplines as diverse as archeology, genetics, heredity, ecology, geology, and probability theory in mathematics. Evolution rests on fundamental, complex ideas that are known to be conceptually challenging for many learners, such as deep time (Dodick & Orion, 2003) and emergent systems theory (Ferrari & Chi, 1998). Developmental psychologists suggest that students may have cognitive constraints or biases such as a strong tendency to think of events as purposeful and caused by intentional agents, such as a supernatural being (Evans, 2000, 2001), that make learning about the content of evolutionary theory particularly challenging. Once these biases are developed they are very difficult to change (Sinatra, Brem, & Evans, 2008; Sinatra & Pintrich, 2003).

These conceptual challenges are further complicated by how evolution is typically taught in U.S. public schools, with instruction focusing almost exclusively on micro-evolutionary processes, leaving students with little understanding of macro-evolutionary processes (Catley, 2006). Making matters more difficult, evolution is viewed as controversial in the United States and therefore curriculum designers, textbook publishers, school administrators, and teachers are under tremendous pressure to de-emphasize the theory and minimize the instructional time spent on the topic (e.g., see Miller, 2008 for the story of one high profile example, the 2006 trial in Dover, PA). Given the limited amount of instructional time devoted to this complex topic in K-12 settings, it is likely that many classroom teachers have had very little exposure to evolutionary theory in their educational experiences. Therefore, it is reasonable to suggest that many teachers are underprepared to develop or implement effective instruction to teach biological evolution concepts and some evidence suggests that this is indeed the case (Nadelson, 2009; Nadelson & Nadelson, 2010).

Each of the obstacles hindering the effective learning and teaching of evolution presents significant challenges to science education, and each deserve considerable research attention. Fortunately, some excellent research has advanced our understanding of these challenges and provides a context for promoting possible solutions (see the other contributions to this volume for many examples). In this chapter we address a different, arguably even more vexing, issue for teaching and learning about biological evolution. We argue that, in the United States in particular, the epistemological boundaries between two ways of understanding and explaining the human experience—science and religion—are frequently conflated. In the same Gallup poll cited above, when Americans were asked why they do not "believe" in evolution, four of the top five responses were religious in nature. This suggests that many Americans perceive there to be a conflict between their personal or religious epistemologies and the epistemology of science.

Indeed, in his new book *Only a Theory: Evolution and the Battle for America's Soul* (Miller, 2008) Kenneth Miller claims that we are at a crossroads. He argues that the leadership in the sciences that Americans have enjoyed for more than a century is at risk of slipping away. He claims that the current debate over evolution "reveals a deep and profound split in the American psyche, an unease that threatens the way we think of ourselves as a people..." (p. 16). The risk of blurring the lines between science and religion is that both realms of human experience would be done appreciable harm.

The perceived conflict between science and religion has impacted the acceptance of scientific perspectives since the time of Darwin, if not before (e.g., Galileo's controversy with the church over the movement of the Earth). The conflict has grown more combative at certain times in U.S. history. And, with the emergence of the concept of intelligent design (ID), it appears we are currently in one of those times as Miller asserts (Miller, 2008). Beliefs are compelling systems of thought and they have been found to "trump" knowledge in decision making in many domains, not just science. In a recent book about the effects of lack of knowledge on voter behavior, Shenkman (2008) laments that "in the absence of knowledge, irrational biases often dictate the policies voters support" (p. 45). Evidence from the psychological literature is replete with examples of biased decision making and reasoning, particularly in the absence of knowledge (see, for example, Tversky & Kahneman, 1982).

Later, we will describe findings from our research which demonstrate that students' beliefs are often more predictive of their acceptance of scientific theories than their knowledge of those theories (Sinatra & Southerland, under review; Sinatra, Southerland, McConaughy, & Demastes, 2003). This research, along with a growing body of other evidence, suggests that beliefs play a significant role in the acceptance of scientific constructs such as evolution (Rutledge & Warden, 1999).

Given this state of affairs, we propose that the epistemologies of science and religion should be philosophically differentiated to the extent possible to provide learners with a conceptual "place to stand" (Southerland, Sinatra, & Mathews, 2001), particularly for individuals who perceive a conflict between their beliefs and scientific explanations. We posit that there is justification for conceptualizing science and religion as occupying opposite ends of a number of core epistemological continua. We argue that religion and science should not be viewed as conflicting epistemologies; rather they should be viewed as epistemologies that have different roles and explain different aspects of the human condition.

The National Academy of Sciences' most recent publication on science and evolution supports the notion of moving beyond the epistemic divide and states that evolution acceptance can be compatible with religious perspectives (National Academy of Sciences, 2008). The epistemologies of science and religion do differ in important ways—ways which allow both to productively coexist—but these epistemic assumptions are not currently being addressed in most science curricula. If the epistemic assumptions of science and religion are understood, there is no doubt that ID falls outside the bounds of science. We begin this chapter with a discussion of the epistemic continua along which we feel science and religion may be distinguished. We conclude with curricular suggestions for minimizing the perceived "conflict" by explicitly addressing the epistemological commitments and limitations of science.

Differentiating Epistemologies

Epistemology is the study of the nature of knowledge and knowing and is concerned with such aspects of knowledge as its source, justification, certainty, and structure (see, for example, Hofer & Pintrich, 1997; Greene, Azevedo, & Torney-Purta, 2008). Religion and science are often claimed to be different ways of knowing (Gould, 2002; Miller, 1999; National Academy of Sciences, 1999; Scharmann, Smith, James, & Jensen, 2005; Verhey, 2005) or worldviews (Irzik & Nola, 2007). The question we pose is: exactly how do religion and science differ? As we consider this question, we should acknowledge there is not one universally accepted definition of science, nor is there one universally accepted definition of religion. Much work has been done to characterize and define science for science educators elsewhere (see, for example, Chalmers, 1999 or Cobern & Loving, 2001) and we will not take time to provide an overview of different definitions here. When we refer to *science* we use the definition provided by the National Academy of Sciences (NAS), "The use of evidence to construct testable explanations and predictions of natural phenomena, as well as the knowledge generated through this process" (2008, p. 10). When we refer to *religion* we mean a set of commonly held beliefs and practices often codified through specific religious doctrine or religious law. Although some may argue that religious faiths and belief systems are too diverse to be discussed in such global terms, the generic term "religion" is sufficiently and effectively used in public educational policy and practice as guided by the establishment clause of the First Amendment. Therefore, we feel it is appropriate to use the term "religion" in a global manner as it is used in discussions of education policy.

There are many possibilities that have been suggested for differentiating science and religion. However, many, if not most, philosophers argue that it is impossible to find even one distinction that clearly and definitively demarcates religious views of knowledge from scientific views of knowledge. Rather than attempting to draw strict boundaries in perspectives of evolution, we feel it is more useful to consider how science, ID, and religion differ along a number of epistemic continua. It is our view that while not purely distinct epistemologies, the assumptions of religion and science rest at opposite ends of a number of epistemic continua. To consider these distinctions, we examine both ways of knowing and consider where they lie on the epistemic continua of knowledge source, justification, certainty, and structure. We also consider where ID may rest on these four dimensions of knowledge.

Source as a Continuum of Distinction

One of the most important epistemological distinctions which may help to distinguish science from religion and ID is source of knowledge. Source of knowledge refers to where knowledge originates and where it resides (Hofer & Pintrich, 1997). Science focuses on nature as the source of knowledge, and using experimental and observational means to gather evidence. According to the NAS, science is "based on evidence drawn from examining the natural world" (NAS, 2008, p. 12).

The nature of science (NOS) perspective helps distinguish the epistemic assumptions of science from those of other worldviews. Nature of science is used to describe the processes and procedures that guide the practice of science (Kuhn, 1970; McComas, 1996; McComas, Clough, & Almazroa, 1998; NAS, 1998, 2008). The NOS approach mandates that scientific hypotheses and theories are grounded by reference to natural law. Often called methodological naturalism, scientists generally adopt the notion that "explanations within science should appeal only to acceptable naturalistic entities. This excludes all explanatory appeals to supernatural entities" (Irzik & Nola, 2007, p. 5). Further, it requires that scientific explanations be publicly observable, testable, tentative, and falsifiable, and that information that does not meet these criteria not be considered as scientific evidence.

Whereas the scientific approach of methodological naturalism rejects explanatory appeals to the supernatural, religious epistemologies either view both nature and the supernatural as sources of knowledge or see knowledge as emerging only from revelation and faith (Irzik & Nola, 2007). When both natural and supernatural are considered sources of religious knowledge, some religious epistemologies view the supernatural as a more valid source of knowledge. To be clear, science as a discipline makes no judgment on whether or not supernatural forces or agents exist, and individual scientists differ dramatically in their personal opinions as to this matter. The supernatural could be and has been the subject of scientific investigation, but adhering to methodological naturalism, researchers must gather evidence from the natural world and such evidence must be measurable, testable, and have predictable and replicable outcomes (Shermer, 1997). On the issue of source of knowledge, ID clearly allows for supernatural explanations to be evoked. Thus it is more closely aligned to the religious end of the epistemic continuum than the scientific.

Figure 8.1 depicts each of the continua of distinctions that we intend to discuss. As shown in Figure 8.1, the sources continuum is meant to depict what forms of evidence are considered acceptable sources of knowledge. Scientific epistemology (labeled SE in the figure) rests on the side of naturalism because, as described by methodological naturalism, natural sources of evidence are paramount. Religious epistemology (RE in the figure) is not constrained to natural sources, so it rests on the opposite end of the continuum, where supernatural sources are also allowed. Since ID uses both natural and supernatural sources of evidence we place it toward the mid-point of the source continuum.

Justification as a Continuum of Distinction

Justification of knowledge, or how one knows, is a central question in philosophical epistemology and has recently been receiving more attention in the psychological study of personal epistemology (see, for example, Hofer, 2004; Greene et al., 2008). There are many ways to conceive of justification, but Pollock and Cruz (1999) explain it this way: "In asking how a person knows something we are typically asking for her grounds for believing it. We want to know what justifies her in holding her belief. Thus, epistemology has traditionally focused on epistemic justification more than on knowledge" (Pollock & Cruz, 1999, p. 11, as cited in Greene et al., 2008).

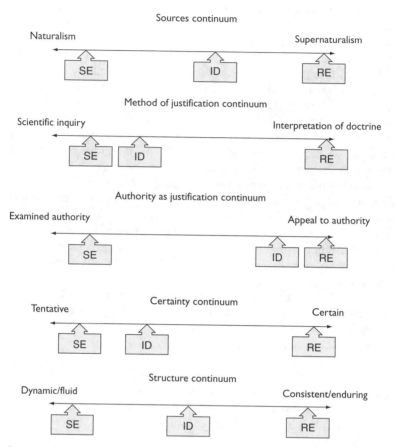

Figure 8.1 Core epistemic continua.

In science, how does knowledge come to be justified? What kinds of claims come to be justifiably called "scientific"? The multiple ways of gaining scientific knowledge include reasoning and logic. For example, scientists reasoned there must be black holes before there was good evidence that they did in fact exist (Thorne, 1994). We focus on two important modes of knowledge justification in science, particularly because we see them as distinct from other ways of knowing—method and authority. Next, we discuss both in turn.

Method as Justification

Methodological naturalism specifies the source and form of knowledge, the scientific methods, procedures, and techniques for gathering, testing, and verifying evidence often referred to in science education as inquiry (McComas,

1998; National Academy of Sciences, 1998; National Research Council, 1996). The method itself provides one form of justification of scientific knowledge. Scientific research embraces an inquiry model of investigation as researchers seek evidence for hypotheses and confirm predictions. Although there is not one specific scientific method for conducting inquiry (McComas, 1996), there are standards by which scientific research is evaluated. For example, the ability to reproduce an experiment or observation is critical to scientific inquiry. Although individual variations in the inquiry process abound, the general form of the processes are consistent enough to provide those within the scientific community an opportunity to "check each other's work."

Inquiry provides a mechanism for providing justifications for scientific knowledge. The aim of scientific inquiry is the collection and interpretation of evidence in the context of nature, moving toward the development of explanations. A critical aspect of inquiry is the verification of hypotheses. In the inquiry process, predictions of results are made based on the hypothesis, and after data have been collected, there is a comparison of the predicted and actual outcomes. Hypotheses are often discarded, adjusted, or restructured to accommodate contradicting evidence (National Research Council, 2000). The ultimate goal of inquiry is to develop and refine models that can explain phenomena and accurately predict future outcomes. In sum, inquiry provides reliable methods for justifying knowledge.

Scientific inquiry can be placed in sharp relief against the methods of knowledge justification in religion. In religious epistemology, justification is not based on testable, verifiable, empirical evidence gained through a scientific method of critical inquiry. Instead, justification for what is known is determined through interpretation of doctrine, scripture, sacred texts, or other sources of inspiration such as personal revelation.

So, in comparing ways of knowing we envision a continuum representing justification for knowing through method. Specifically, we envision critical interpretation of data through scientific inquiry on one end of this continuum and interpretation of doctrine at the other. We place science on the side of justification through scientific inquiry (refer again to Figure 8.1). We place religious epistemic justification at the other end, representing not uncritical analysis necessarily, but interpretation of doctrine and confirmation of beliefs. In examining the assumptions of ID, this view does take into account scientific findings gained through the scientific method of inquiry; thus, we place ID closer to scientific epistemology on the continuum of method of justification.

Authority as Justification

Next consider the epistemological perspectives for the appeal to authority as a justification for knowledge. Appeal to authority is not, in and of itself, an epistemological distinction. For religious epistemology, authority can be a strong source or a justification for knowledge claims; moreover, authority is generally not to be challenged. Scientists also defer to authority. For example, most scientists, who are not themselves astronomers, believe there is a defensible explanation for black holes, but defer to astronomers' authority, expertise, interpretation of evidence, and knowledge on this matter. The difference on the issue of appealing to authority as justification for knowing is important. In scientific epistemology, there are evidential means by which to judge the credibility of the claims made by scientific authorities. That is, even when scientists of great stature make claims, they can be challenged or even refuted by others in the field through the methods of justification described above. Second, in science there is always the possibility that claims by our most respected scientific authorities could be challenged and refuted by anyone who makes the next great discovery and uncovers new evidence or develops a better explanation, for science is a self-correcting process. In addition, authoritative knowledge in science is, at least in principle, publicly accessible and testable by anyone who takes the time to master the tools to do so. Therefore, authority alone is insufficient to establish or maintain scientific knowledge. New scientific ideas must stand up to the scrutiny of the scientific community as a whole and survive rigors of empirical tests over time. At times, the weight of empirical evidence tested against the natural world can and does confront and trump authority in science.

It is important to note that this scenario is much more likely for some scientific claims than for others. Notions about the existence of gravity are not likely to be overturned any time soon, despite the fact that there is still much debate over what actually causes gravity. Science is constantly changing, but most change occurs on the fringes, in new areas of research and development and on the frontiers of new discoveries or technologies. After several centuries of development, changes to the core ideas and theories of science are rare (Bryson, 2003).

So, in placing scientific epistemology on the continuum of authority as justification, we envision a continuum representing appeals to authority. We place science on one end, representing justification based on examined authority (refer again to Figure 8.1). We place religious epistemic justification alternatively at the other end, representing a less critical appeal to authority.

In examining the assumptions of ID, it is clear that it rests on the same side as religion in regards to the epistemic views on knowledge from authority. That is, when some phenomenon appears too complex for our current understanding, or irreducibly complex, as claimed by Behe (1996), proponents of ID appeal to the ultimate authority, an intelligent designer. The assumption that appeal to authority in and of itself constitutes an explanation is outside the epistemology of science. Beyond the epistemic difficulties created by ID's acceptance of a designer as explanation, there is a pragmatic problem as well. Accepting design as an explanation stifles scientific inquiry. Scientists seek scientific explanations for natural phenomena when one is yet to be found.

Foreclosing debates by evoking a designer removes the scientist's motivation to resolve enigmas through the scientific enterprise.

Certainty of Knowledge as a Continuum of Distinction

The distinctions between the epistemic assumptions of certainty of scientific knowledge compared to religious knowledge again place science and religion at opposite ends of this epistemic continuum (refer again to Figure 8.1). The less certain nature of knowledge in science places it on the tentative side of the certainty continuum, while the greater relative stability of knowledge in religion positions it on the side of more certain. It is important to acknowledge that religious epistemologies are not necessarily dogmatic in their certitude, and change in religious doctrine is certainly possible. However, there are usually examples of absolutes in most religious epistemologies that are usually not subject to change, placing religion more toward the certain side of this epistemic dimension.

The distinction we wish to emphasize is that knowledge change is a core epistemic assumption of science. In fact, some might argue that change itself is the only certainty in science, again evidence of its self-correcting nature. This assumption of change as a core epistemic value does not imply that all scientific knowledge is unstable and should be cast in doubt. Rather, it asserts that the tentativeness of knowledge is a fundamental epistemic assumption of the discipline. Science is always poised to consider change and the plausibility of new hypotheses and conjectures, in light of contradicting evidence. Even theories that are considered to be knowledge with the highest degrees of certainty—at least in principle—could change tomorrow, although, as noted earlier, changes to these core ideas are rare.

Religious epistemology does change as well, but religious knowledge is generally not assumed to be in the same degree of flux as scientific knowledge, thus we place it toward the more rather than less certain end of this continuum. Since ID does take into account scientific findings to some extent, it has some degree of tentativeness, although the degree to which this perspective is open to change is not yet clear. Giving this perspective the benefit of the doubt, we place ID toward the tentative side of the certainty continuum, but less tentative than scientific epistemology.

Structure of Knowledge as Continuum of Distinction

The structure of scientific knowledge is fluid and ever changing, leading to new spheres of inquiry and the convergence of areas of investigation. For example, evolution has changed significantly from the Darwinian perspective, to a synthesis which includes genetics, geology, paleontology, and ecology which has completely altered the structure of knowledge in this discipline. Furthermore, advances toward understanding in science do not necessarily progress in a linear march toward a predetermined goal. Scientific discoveries can emerge out of spontaneous insight, serendipity, or even human error, producing knowledge just as generative as a deliberate and carefully crafted approach to experimentation or observation. Discoveries are often made in science while searching for the answer to an unrelated or parallel problem. For example, as the German physicist Wilhelm Conrad Röntgen was studying the effects of cathode ray tubes, he observed glowing that was uncharacteristic of the light produced by the devices. After further investigation, Röntgen determined that these waves could penetrate many substances including the human body. He had accidentally stumbled onto X-rays as he was researching the properties of light, and his discovery revolutionized the practice of modern medicine (Balchin, 2003). It is the generative nature of science which makes it so productive and useful to us as a society. In regards to the structure of knowledge, it could be argued that the epistemic stance of science is by definition dynamic, fluid, ever changing, and even unpredictable. The ever-evolving nature of science motivates us to place scientific epistemology on the dynamic/fluid end of the structure continuum (refer again to Figure 8.1).

In contrast, we posit that the structure of religious knowledge can be placed again on the other side of the epistemic continuum from that of science. Religious knowledge does change, but the structure of religious knowledge is not considered by assumption fluid and dynamic, and unpredictability is not necessarily valued. Religious epistemologies tend to promote a search for singular answers of ultimate truth; in contrast, scientific epistemology promotes the search for the best explanation based upon observable evidence and is always subject to challenge.

Intelligent design is clearly aligned more closely with religion than science in regards to epistemic assumptions about the structure of knowledge. One might speculate that proponents of ID are uncomfortable with the vagaries and the yet unsolved mysteries of science since they appear to resort to the ultimate single answer—a designer did it—rather than accept the epistemic uncertainty that comes with a scientific perspective.

Intelligent Design and the Epistemological Continuum

Even as we argue that science may be placed at opposite ends of these epistemic continua from religion and ID, a distinct and rigid demarcation between the epistemologies remains elusive and imprudent. Intelligent design resembles science in some regards.

As shown in Figure 8.1, we believe ID uses some of the same methods of justification as science in that it does use the scientific method of inquiry, and the conclusions drawn are somewhat tentative. It is also more dynamic in structure than religious epistemology. However, as can be seen in Figure 8.1, intelligent design crisscrosses the epistemological landscape in a way that is incoherent. This makes ID an epistemological grab bag of ideas which makes it difficult to adjudicate knowledge claims.

Moving toward Pragmatism

Philosophers may argue that distinctions between epistemologies are philosophically messy at best and logically impossible at worst. We acknowledge these critiques, respect the goal of philosophical coherence, and encourage future developments. However, we argue that holding out for a philosophically workable and definitive conceptualization of the epistemologies of science and religion before we take action in education has a practically damaging effect. The philosophical issues at stake have been under debate for literally thousands of years and a resolution is not likely to appear soon on the intellectual horizon.

While we hope for a grand synthesis between the philosophies of religion and science, the United States is increasingly falling behind other countries in accepting scientific explanations of biological change (Miller, 2008). Miller et al. (2006) note that our decline below that of other industrialized nations is associated with a rise in fundamentalist beliefs, noting that "the acceptance of evolution is lower in the United States than in Japan or Europe, largely because of widespread fundamentalism and the politicization of science in the United States" (p. 765). When compared to citizens in 33 other countries asked to judge whether the following statement was true or false, "Human beings as we know them, developed from earlier species of animals," the United States ranked 30th just above Turkey, and below Croatia, Bulgaria, Latvia, and Cyprus (Miller et al., 2006, p. 765).

The alarm caused by this trend of moving away from using science to adjudicate knowledge claims about the natural world is disconcerting to many (Miller, 2008). Evolution is the central framework for understanding the biological world (American Association for the Advancement of Science, 1993; Dobzhansky, 1973; National Research Council, 1996), and the implications of this theory affect our everyday lives. From understanding the effects of antibiotic-resistant bacteria, to genetically modified food, to the implications of climate change for species survival, evolution contributes to our choices in how to resolve many current societal, economic, environmental, and global problems. Informed choices and awareness of the associated consequences for our society regarding these issues requires understanding the basic tenets of evolution. Further, the current doubts about the utility of science portray the discipline in a negative light, which could deter future generations from choosing careers in science, resulting in delays in solving critical social, medical, and environmental dilemmas.

We believe the radical "solution" proposed for improving public understanding of evolution through promoting the rejection of religious beliefs (Dawkins, 2006) is profoundly misguided. More importantly, a rejection of religion is not necessary to resolve the perceived conflict. The United States is overwhelmingly a religious country, with 92% of the U.S. population expressing a belief in God (Newport, 2008). Many religious groups have accepted evolution as compatible with their own faith, as exemplified by the Roman Catholic faith. In his popular book on the topic, *Finding Darwin's God*, Miller (1999) explains how he, as a Catholic and a cell biologist, resolves these two worldviews for himself: "As a scientist, I know very well that the earth is billions of years old and that the appearance of living organisms was not sudden, but gradual. As a Christian, I believe that Genesis is a true account of the way in which God's relationship with the world was formed. And as a human being, I find value in both descriptions" (Miller, 1999, p. 257).

This indicates that alternative approaches need to be considered in the teaching of evolution to move beyond the challenges posed by the blurred boundaries of scientific and religious epistemologies. Bringing intelligent design into the classroom would move in the opposite direction, we suggest, by confusing rather than clarifying scientific and religious epistemic assumptions as illustrated in Figure 8.1.

Strong Beliefs Trump Weak Knowledge

The current combination in the United States of strong religious beliefs and weak knowledge of science is not necessarily a successful combination for promoting acceptance of scientific ideas. In a series of studies, Sinatra and her colleagues have demonstrated that beliefs about the nature of knowledge and knowing (epistemic beliefs) and dispositions toward knowledge and belief change are stronger predictors of acceptance of scientific theories than is limited knowledge of those theories (Sinatra et al., 2003, Sinatra & Southerland, under review).

In three studies, we asked college students their views about the nature of knowledge, assessed their openness toward knowledge and belief change, and assessed their knowledge of two scientific theories, photosynthesis and biological evolution. We then asked them to read three brief texts, each describing a theory that is controversial in the areas of photosynthesis, animal evolution, and human evolution. The photosynthesis text described a theory about the diminishing rain forest, the animal evolution text described a theory about the evolution of bird flight, and the human evolution text described a theory about the relationship between meat eating and the development of brain size. Students were asked whether they accepted the controversial ideas presented in the three texts, and whether they accepted the more general theories behind these ideas (photosynthesis, biological evolution of non-human animals, and biological evolution of humans).

In the first study (Sinatra et al., 2003) using primarily college education majors, prior knowledge of the topic was not predictive of acceptance of human or animal evolution. Whereas knowledge was not related to evolution acceptance, epistemic beliefs and dispositions were both significant predictors of whether students reported they accepted the scientific theory of human evolution. More specifically, students who reported a view of knowledge as changing and professed a degree of openness toward knowledge and belief change were more likely to report they accepted the scientific explanation of human evolution.

Since we were concerned that the education majors in our sample might not have had sufficient knowledge of biology to "tip the scales" and reveal a relationship between knowledge and acceptance, we conducted two follow-up studies (Sinatra & Southerland, under review) using college students from a variety of majors, including several in the biological sciences, as participants. The results we found were mostly consistent with Sinatra et al. (2003) with one exception. For students with a substantial degree of biological knowledge (specifically, those who had taken on average over six college level biology courses and showed high performance on the evolution knowledge assessment), knowledge did predict acceptance of human evolution.

We take the implications of this research to indicate that students' personal beliefs about the nature of knowledge and their degree of openness to change play a role in their judgment of biological evolution. Beliefs about knowledge are strongly related to religiosity and belief commitment, with more religious respondents reporting a stronger commitment to their religious beliefs and also reporting a view of knowledge as more fixed, certain, and unchanging than their less religious counterparts (Moosa & Karabenick, 2005; Sinatra & Southerland, under review). Most important, beliefs and dispositions exerted their greatest influence when individuals were novices in the domain. These results are consistent with national polls showing there is a positive correlation between acceptance of evolution and level of education. In the Gallup polls cited earlier, level of education was positively related to "belief" (as the question was phrased) in biological evolution. The percentage answering yes to the belief question for those with a high school education or less was 41%, for those with some college education 50%, for college graduates 48%, and for those with postgraduate education it jumped to 74% (Newport, 2008).

These data suggest that knowledge about biological evolution does relate to acceptance, but building knowledge is not at all a guarantee that acceptance will follow. Objections to a scientific view of biological evolution are so strongly related to religious beliefs in the United States that beliefs can "trump" knowledge. For example, the Gallup poll showed that "belief" in evolution is strongly and inversely related to church attendance in that those who attend more frequently are less likely to report acceptance of evolution. Taken together, we believe these data suggest that both building knowledge and helping learners find that epistemic place to stand by addressing the epistemic assumptions of science are important endeavors for evolution education.

Recommendations for Teaching Epistemology and the Nature of Science within Evolution Education

We conjecture that the most effective evolutionary biology curriculum expands beyond evolutionary science topics, to include content exploring the nature of science and the nature of knowing (epistemology). We posit that these three topics are inextricably related and therefore comprise essential content in an evolutionary biology curriculum. Understanding the nature of science and epistemology may provide students with a "place to stand" (Southerland et al., 2001) in regards to understanding and accepting the idea that science and religion do not necessarily have to be in conflict. Moving beyond the notion of conflict would remove a significant barrier in teaching and learning about biological evolution.

Lack of understanding about evolution is often a result of misconceptions, lack of knowledge, or a combination of both, which poses an interesting instructional challenge. To most effectively approach this complex instructional situation we recommend adopting a conceptual change pedagogical approach to promote knowledge restructuring (for detailed examples of conceptual change pedagogical approaches see, for example, Duit, Treagust, & Widodo, 2008; Jonassen, 2008, and Linn, 2008). Conceptual change pedagogy is designed to help students overcome misconceptions. By adopting a conceptual change pedagogical approach to teaching about the nature of science and epistemology in the context of evolution, students would have the opportunity to overcome misconceptions about the nature of scientific knowledge that may present barriers to their understanding of evolution and other scientific concepts.

To implement a conceptual change instructional approach, we recommend pre-assessing students' conceptions to identity misconceptions and develop targeted interventions. Next, effective conceptual change pedagogy provides students with opportunities to compare their conceptions with the scientific conceptions (Dole & Sinatra, 1998). A critical aspect of a conceptual change curriculum entails encouraging students to engage deeply with conflicting information through discussion, debate, argumentation, experimentation, or other highly engaging instructional activities. The fact that science is a process of weighing and evaluating evidence to construct the most plausible explanation of events should be the model for activities where students engage in argumentation around critical issues and topics in evolution.

Consider, for example, the notion that humans descended from modern day apes, which is a widely held misconception. Before introducing a conceptual change pedagogical approach to confront this misconception, we recommend that students are afforded the opportunity to explore how scientists resolve controversies and determine the validity, significance, and value of scientific evidence. In other words the curriculum should directly address the epistemic assumptions that guide the development of scientific knowledge, specifically knowledge sources, justification, and the relative uncertainty and tentative structure of knowledge in science.

The development of the theory of plate tectonics may be a useful example to illustrate the epistemological roles of authority, justification, and the tentative nature and fluid structure of science in practice. The advantage of this topic is that historically it was a very controversial one so it well illustrates important points about adjudicating knowledge claims in science, but students are unlikely to hold deeply committed beliefs about plate tectonics. Removing strongly emotional beliefs from the discussion will allow students to see how controversies are resolved through justification methods before their own deeply committed beliefs are brought to the fore by the topic of evolution. Thus, plate tectonics, or any other significant, historical scientific debate, can be used to introduce the critical epistemological issues represented on our continua (source of knowledge, method of justification, authority, certainty, and structure) without evoking the strong resistance associated with controversies in evolution.

This lesson could begin by discussing how in the early development of the theory of plate tectonics, groups of geologists supported a variety of alternative perspectives. One group of geologists hypothesized that land masses simply floated about. These scientists were known as "mobilists," reflecting their view that land masses were mobile. Another group of geologists hypothesized that land masses were always in the same location but had subtle motion that was simply the result of expansion and contraction caused by heating and cooling. Known as the "anti-mobilists," these scientists posited that land masses were relatively stationary. This illustrates that science is tentative, fluid, and dynamic, and commonly in a state of flux. It also demonstrates the epistemic role of authority because respected geologists in positions of authority could not maintain their hypotheses in light of overwhelming evidence supporting the mobilists' hypothesis. As has happened many times in science, aspects of the initial hypotheses proposed by the mobilists and anti-mobilists were adopted in the formation of the theory of plate tectonics, even as the hypotheses of the two competing perspectives were overturned (Oreskes, 2002), providing a valuable lesson in the dynamic and evolving structure of scientific knowledge.

Although it took decades of research and development to gain a foothold of acceptance in the scientific community, plate tectonics is now accepted by geologists as the explanation for the movement of land masses (Condie, 1997). Scientists who adopted the plate tectonic view about the planet's continent and land mass formation may have had to change some specific assumptions guiding their research programs, but they did not have to leave the geological scientific community and adopt a new epistemology of science to continue their work. Further, as geologies worked to confirm the hypothesis of plate tectonics, they refined and contributed to the theory, participating fully in the process. This can serve to illustrate how authority and evidence play out as epistemic constructs in science.

Now returning to the misconception about humans evolving from apes, students who have gained some insights into the nature of science and scientific epistemology would now have some tools with which to examine this misconception. Once students have a greater appreciation of how scientific controversies are adjudicated, they can gather evidence for and against this view of human ancestry. Students could develop alternative clades (diagrams reflecting the ancestry among a group such as primates), one reflecting the scientific point of view, and one reflecting the ape as ancestor point of view. As students debate the relative merits of these clades, teachers could introduce the anomalous data that apes and humans evolved separately from a common ancestor millions of years ago. Students would be confronted with the challenge of reconstructing their ape as ancestor clades to accurately represent this data. An accurate explanation of the clade and the recognition of the split in the development of apes and humans would hopefully set the stage for conceptual change and the acceptance of a new idea that apes and humans share a common ancestor. By drawing on the plate tectonics controversy, and the methods scientists used to resolve this controversy, students would be more prepared to understand how theories of ancestry and evolution are evaluated and ultimately accepted or rejected by the scientific community.

McComas (2006) and Scott (2007) also recommend beginning the study of evolution with a discussion about the nature of science. The history of plate tectonics provides an ideal context for introducing the role that the nature of science plays in the study of evolution, as well as the core epistemic constructs of source, justification, certainty, and structure. By having students examine the evidence for different explanations for the continents, one establishes a context for discussing what science is and what it is not. This helps to clarify how the epistemology of science differs from non-science epistemology and may help to promote students' understanding of the distinctions discussed above. If this practice is to be utilized, it needs to be revised and reinforced many times during a course, because as a onetime activity it is unlikely to be comprehended or retained by learners. By continuing to revisit the tenets of science, students' misconceptions of the nature of science can be resolved and they can gain a greater understanding of evolution, while maintaining the curricular focus on scientific concepts.

Teach the Controversies within Science

The tenuous link between acceptance and understanding of evolution among the general public suggests that much work needs to be done in the area of promoting understanding of the nature of controversies within science. Therefore, we support a curriculum that attends to Scott's (2007) suggestion that evolution education should embrace discussion of current controversies among scientists in the field of evolutionary science. These controversies are not about whether evolution happened, but of the details guiding the process. Beginning instruction with the introduction of scientific controversies such as plate tectonics sets the stage for students to understand controversy as part of the nature of science. Scientific controversies commonly occur in situations in which the amassed evidence may be interpreted in multiple ways resulting in divergent explanations as to the *details* of evolutionary theory. By focusing the instruction and content of the curriculum on explorations and debates of the details of evolutionary biology, students are exposed to an authentic application of the nature of science and the epistemology of science in the scientific contexts previously discussed. Further, this approach naturally lends itself to the use of a conceptual change pedagogy that utilizes argumentation to stimulate critical thinking.

Conceptual change learning activities that require students to argue both for and against a position allow them to examine both sides of an issue and create a situation in which learners may challenge their own preconceptions. For example, evolutionary biologists and paleontologists agree that several mass extinctions have happened in the history of life on Earth, but there is still much argument and debate of the details of the causes of mass extinctions. Suggested causes of mass extinction include: meteor impacts, volcanic eruptions, cosmic rays, epidemics, massive floods, and global climate changes. Mass extinctions are significant events in evolutionary history because they are followed by explosions in species diversity, another topic of controversy within the evolutionary biology community. There is a range of hypotheses and supporting evidence for different explanations of the process of mass extinction and explosions of species diversity. This is an ideal topic with which to employ a conceptual change pedagogical approach because it combines elements of evolution, the nature of science, and the epistemology of science. The benefit comes from focusing on the science of evolution and the nature of science by placing learners in the role of scientists arguing for a perspective.

Having students argue for a position on a topic of controversy *within* the field of biological evolution would allow students to develop an understanding of the nature of the controversies in science as well as the epistemic assumptions of science. Argumentation interventions have been shown to produce gains in conceptual understanding of evolution (Asterhan & Schwarz, 2007) as well as greater engagement in learning about science topics (Nussbaum & Sinatra, 2003). Thus, arguing about the controversies within evolution provides the context for integrating the three key domains, while providing a conceptual change learning environment for acquiring new knowledge and resolving misconceptions.

We agree with the recommendation of those who suggest that evolution education adhere to teaching the controversies within science, not those between science and other worldviews. The movements promoting the teaching of different perspectives of the origin of species, both scientific (evolution) and non-scientific (creationism, ID), are fraught with difficulties (Alters & Alters, 2001; Scott, 2004). The complexity of posing alternative explanations and points of view could confuse students rather than bring clarity and may distract from the goal of learning evolution content. Our recommendations are consistent with Scott (2007) who maintains that teaching evolution from a scientific as well as religious or ID perspective could create a condition in which individuals develop a sense of equality of the different explanations, rather than insight into the differences of these two worldviews. Further, teaching evolution from a scientific as well as religious perspective promotes the development of perceptions that evolutionary theory as a whole is uncertain and not well understood or agreed upon by scientists.

The depth of the discussion possible regarding different worldviews may be limited depending on where it is taking place. Post secondary education has more latitude in the exploration of such topics, which provides more leeway to explore, compare, and discuss in depth the philosophical similarities and differences between the epistemologies of science and religion. In K-12 education, there are typically greater limitations on discussions which broach religious territory. However, the utilization of conceptual change pedagogy can be effective if the focus remains on the scientific approaches to explaining evolution.

Mason and Gava (2007) argue that it is essential for learners to engage in situations that promote critical thinking that will impact their personal views of knowledge. This is even more critical when teaching controversial and complex topics such as biological evolution. Through engagement in the process of argumentation, students are more likely to gain a greater understanding of the evidence and perspectives that lead to the development and resolution of controversies. The combination of conceptual change pedagogy with curricular content of evolution, the nature of science, and the nature of epistemology could provide a powerful integrated approach toward a successful evolution curriculum. An evolutionary biology curriculum with an integrated content from all three domains, implemented with a conceptual change pedagogical approach, may be the best chance of success for teaching and learning about this wonderfully complex scientific topic.

References

Alters, B. J., & Alters, S. M. (2001). *Defending evolution: A guide to the creation/evolution controversy.* Sudbury, MA: Jones & Bartlett.

American Association for the Advancement of Science. (1993). *Benchmarks for science literacy.* New York: Oxford University Press.

Asterhan, C. S. C., & Schwarz, B. B. (2007). The effects of monological and dialogical argumentation on concept learning in evolutionary theory. *Journal of Educational Psychology, 99,* 626–639.

Balchin, J. (2003). *Science: 100 scientists who changed the world.* New York: Enchanted Lion Books.

Behe, M. (1996). *Darwin's black box: The biochemical challenge to evolution*. New York: Simon & Schuster.

Bryson, B. (2003). *A short history of nearly everything*. New York: Broadway Books.

Catley, K. M. (2006). Darwin's missing link—a novel paradigm for evolution education. *Science Education, 90*(5), 767–783.

Chalmers, A. F. (1999). *What is this thing called science?* Indianapolis, IN: Hackett Publishing.

Cobern, W., & Loving, C. C. (2001). Defining "science" in a multicultural world: Implications for science education. *Science Education, 85*, 50–67.

Condie, K. C. (1997). *Plate tectonics and crustal evolution*. Oxford: Butterworth-Heinemann.

Dawkins, R. (2006). *The God delusion*. New York: Houghton Mifflin.

Dobzhansky, T. (1973). Nothing in biology makes sense except in the light of evolution. *American Biology Teacher, 35*, 125–129.

Dodick, J., & Orion, N. (2003). Cognitive factors affecting student understanding of geologic time. *Journal of Research in Science Teaching, 40*(4), 429–445.

Dole, J. A., & Sinatra, G. M. (1998). Reconceptualizing change in the cognitive construction of knowledge. *Educational Psychologist, 33*(2/3), 109–128.

Duit, R., Treagust, D., & Widodo, A. (2008). Teaching science for conceptual change: Theory and practice. In S. Vosniadou (Ed.), *International Handbook of Research on Conceptual Change* (pp. 629–646). New York: Routledge.

Evans, E. M. (2000). The emergence of beliefs about the origins of species in school-age children. *Merrill-Palmer Quarterly: A Journal of Developmental Psychology, 46*, 221–254.

Evans, E. M. (2001). Cognitive and contextual factors in the emergence of diverse belief systems: Creation versus evolution. *Cognitive Psychology, 42*, 217–266.

Ferrari, M., & Chi, M. T. H. (1998). The nature of naïve explanations of natural selection. *International Journal of Science Education, 20*, 1231–1256.

Gould, S. J. (2002). *The structure of evolutionary theory*. Cambridge, MA: Harvard University Press.

Greene, J. A., Azevedo, R., & Torney-Purta, J. (2008). Modeling epistemic and ontological cognition: Philosophical perspectives and methodological directions. *Educational Psychologist, 43*(3), 142–160.

Hofer, B. K. (2004). Epistemological understanding as a metacognitive process: Thinking aloud during online searching. *Educational Psychologist, 39*, 43–56.

Hofer, B. K., & Pintrich, P. R. (1997). The development of epistemological theories: Beliefs about knowledge and knowing and their relation to learning. *Review of Educational Research, 67*, 88–140.

Irzik, G., & Nola, R. (2007). Worldviews and their relation to science. *Science & Education*. Retrieved from www.springerlink.com/content/1h7258315r134u60.

Jonassen, D. (2008). Model building for conceptual change. In S. Vosniadou (Ed.), *International Handbook of Research on Conceptual Change* (pp. 676–693). New York: Routledge.

Kuhn, T. S. (1970). *The structure of scientific revolutions* (2nd ed.). Chicago, IL: University of Chicago Press.

Linn, M. C. (2008). Teaching for conceptual change: Distinguish or extinguish ideas. In S. Vosniadou (Ed.), *International Handbook of Research on Conceptual Change* (pp. 694–718). New York: Routledge.

Mason, L., & Gava, M. (2007). Effects of epistemological beliefs and learning text structures on conceptual change. In S. Vosnioadou, A. Baltas, & X. Vamvakoussi (Eds.), *Reframing the conceptual change approach in learning and instruction* (pp. 165–196). Amsterdam: Elsevier.

McComas, W. F. (1996). Ten myths of science: reexamining what we think we know about the nature of science. *School Science and Mathematics, 96*(1), 10–16.

McComas, W. F. (1998). *The nature of science in science education rationales and strategies.* Boston, MA: Kluwer Academic Publishers.

McComas, W. F. (2006). *Investigating evolutionary biology in the laboratory: A complete guide for enhancing laboratory instruction.* Kendall Hunt: Dubuque, IA.

McComas, W. F., Clough, M. P., & Almazroa, H. (1998). The role and character of the nature of science. In W. F. McComas (Ed.), *The nature of science in science education rationales and strategies* (pp. 3–40). Boston, MA: Kluwer Academic Publishers.

Miller, J. D., Scott, E. C., & Okamoto, S. (2006). Public acceptance of evolution. *Science, 313,* 765–766.

Miller, K. R. (1999). *Finding Darwin's God: A scientist's search for common ground between God and evolution.* New York: Cliff Street Books, HarperCollins.

Miller, K. R. (2008). *Only a theory: Evolution and the battle for America's soul.* New York: Viking Penguin Group.

Moosa, S., & Karabenick, S. A. (2005). Culture and personal epistemology: U.S. and middle eastern students' beliefs about scientific knowledge and knowing. *Social Psychology of Education, 8* (4), 375–393.

Nadelson, L. S. (2009). Preservice teacher understanding and vision of how to teach biological evolution. *Evolution: Education and Outreach, 2*(3), 490–504.

Nadelson, L. S., & Nadelson, S. G. (2010). K-8 educators' perceptions and preparedness for teaching evolution topics. *Journal of Science Teacher Education.* On-line First.

National Academy of Sciences. (1998). *Teaching about evolution and the nature of science.* Washington, DC: National Academy Press.

National Academy of Sciences. (1999). *Science and creationism: A view from the National Academy of Sciences.* Washington, DC: National Academy Press.

National Academy of Sciences. (2008). *Science, evolution, and creationism.* Washington, DC: National Academy Press.

National Research Council. (1996). *National science education standards.* Washington, DC: National Academy Press.

National Research Council. (2000). *Inquiry and the national science education standards: A guide for teaching and learning.* Washington, DC: National Academy Press.

Newport, F. (2008). Republicans, democrats differ on creationism. Retrieved July 14, 2008, from www.gallup.com/poll/108226/Republicans-Democrats-Differ-Creationism.aspx.

Nussbaum, E. M., & Sinatra, G. M. (2003). Argument and conceptual engagement. *Contemporary Educational Psychology, 28,* 384–395.

Oreskes, N. (2002). *Plate tectonics: An insider's history of the modern theory of the earth.* Boulder, CO: Westview Press.

Rutledge, M. L., & Warden, M. A. (1999). The development and validation of the measure of acceptance of the theory of evolution instrument. *School Science and Mathematics, 99*(1), 13–18.

Scharmann, L. C., Smith, M. U., James, M. C., & Jensen, M. (2005). Explicit reflective nature of science instruction: Evolution, intelligent design, and umbrellaology. *Journal of Science Teacher Education, 16*(1), 27–41.

Scott, E. C. (2004). *Evolution vs. creationism: An introduction.* Berkeley, CA: University of California Press.

Scott, E. C. (2007). What's wrong with the "Teach the controversy" slogan? *McGill Journal of Education, 42*(2), 307–315.

Shenkman, R. (2008). *Just how stupid are we? Facing the truth about the American voter.* Philadelphia, PA: Basic Books.

Shermer, M. (1997). *Why people believe weird things: pseudoscience, superstition, and other confusions of our time.* New York: W.H. Freeman & Company.

Sinatra, G. M., Brem, S. K., & Evans, E. M. (2008). Changing minds? Implications of conceptual change for teaching and learning about biological evolution. *Evolution: Education and Outreach, 2,* 189–195.

Sinatra, G. M., & Pintrich, P. R. (Eds.). (2003). *Intentional conceptual change.* Mahwah, NJ: Erlbaum.

Sinatra, G. M., & Southerland, S. A. (under review). A little knowledge is a dangerous thing: Using beliefs and dispositions to make judgments about the validity of scientific theories. *Research in Science Education.*

Sinatra, G. M., Southerland, S. A., McConaughy, F., & Demastes, J. (2003). Intentions and beliefs in students' understanding and acceptance of biological evolution. *Journal of Research in Science Teaching, 40*(5), 510–528.

Southerland, S., Sinatra, G. M., & Mathews, M. (2001). Beliefs, knowledge, and science education. *Educational Psychology Review, 13*(4), 325–351.

Thorne, K. S. (1994). *Black holes and time warps: Einstein's outrageous legacy.* New York: Norton.

Tversky, A., & Kahneman, D. (1982). Judgment under uncertainty: Heuristics and biases. In D. Kahneman, P. Slovic, & A. Tversky (Eds.), *Judgment under uncertainty: Heuristics and biases* (pp. 3–20). Cambridge, UK: Cambridge University Press. (Originally in *Science,* 1974, *185,* 1124–1131.)

Verhey, S. D. (2005). The effect of engaging prior learning on student attitudes toward creationism and evolution. *BioScience, 55*(11), 996–1003.

Part III

Teaching Science

Chapter 9

Toward a Cognitive Understanding of Science and Religion

Ryan D. Tweney

Introduction

Most people regard science and religion as distinct categories, the terms as denoting two "natural kinds" that differ in important respects. Indeed, discussions of the evolution vs. creationism issue in teaching have often taken for granted that the two categories are distinct and non-overlapping. In recent years, intelligent design advocates have muddied the waters somewhat, asserting that their approach is also scientific and should receive adequate recognition within the context of science courses (Ruse, 2005). The claim has met with resistance from most scientists and from teachers as well. Intelligent design is not "real" science, they argue, but instead represents a back door by which theological concepts can enter the science classroom (Kitcher, 1982).

What then *is* science? What *is* religion? The present essay will not result in a definitional solution to this issue. Instead, I hope to characterize the kind of thinking that is manifest in each domain. My strategy here is similar to that used by Charles Darwin. In the second chapter of his epochal *Origin of Species* (1859), Darwin sorted through multiple definitions of the term "species," concluding that in fact there was no need for a definition, but only a need to roughly characterize the differences between varieties and species. What was essential, he argued, was recognition of a fundamental fact—that there was variation among individuals within a species (however defined), and a continuum of variation, from individuals within a variety, to varieties within a species, and from species to species. Whether to set terminological limits drawing a boundary between species and varieties, say, was thus an arbitrary move. Instead, the task was to develop a theory that explained how variation arose and how it acted under the pressures of natural selection. Similarly, I approach the topic of the difference between science and religion as a task in which what counts is showing the similarities and differences, not defining each in some fixed, and ultimately arbitrary, fashion.

My goal is to contribute toward an explanation of the ways in which science and religion work on a cognitive level, that is, to characterize the kind of thinking that underlies each, and to locate that thinking within our knowledge of cognition generally. In thus naturalizing the issue, I hope to contribute to an understanding of the most effective ways to educate young people in science. There is general recognition that differing epistemologies are at play in the difficulty (e.g., Sinatra & Nadelson, this volume), and while there have been many discussions of what students need to know by way of scientific method, there is less discussion of how to overcome the gaps, or why it is so difficult to do so. Understanding the differences between science and religion may contribute to the goal, especially when religious beliefs of students are under challenge by theories such as evolution.

The discussion should also highlight the reasons why teaching evolutionary theory is difficult, particularly when competing religious beliefs are directly evoked by fundamental questions about the nature and origin of life and the nature of the human species that are central to an understanding of evolution. Shtulman (2006) has noted how many misinterpretations and misunderstandings of evolution can be found even among students who have long studied it. In part, the difficulties associated with learning about evolution are not different from those associated with learning other sciences. It requires, for example, an understanding of the nature of statistical distributions, a difficult topic in its own right. Learning physics must overcome some aspects of folk physics (a point made by the "misconceptions" literature, e.g., Clement, 1982; Rohrer, 2002); so also much of what has to be learned about evolution contradicts folk biology as well. For example, as Shtulman notes, evolutionary theory abandons the intuitive belief in an "essence" that defines a given species. Unlearning such ontological presuppositions is difficult, especially when the new material requires shifts in epistemological conceptions as well as ontological conceptions (Chi, 1992; Chinn & Malhotra, 2001; Dole & Sinatra, 1998).

When the concepts of science conflict with concepts derived from religious belief, the problem is likely to be especially difficult, given the different ways in which belief in the two domains is maintained. A "young earth" creationist, for example, will necessarily need to abandon his or her conception of the age of the Earth in order to understand one of the fundamental claims grounding evolutionary theory, namely, that the Earth is very old and that processes of random variation and change have had many millions of years to work. Since the young Earth claim is maintained by the mechanisms of deferential authority and is deeply embedded within closely held ontological presuppositions, it is not surprising that the task is difficult, nor that acceptance of evolution presupposes changes in an entire system of epistemological concerns (Hofer & Pintrich, 1997).

My primary example in this chapter is based on a historical figure, Michael Faraday. Historical episodes have a unique contribution to issues of epistemological change because they allow us to see deeply into the epistemological presuppositions of the scientists and to their reflective (and hence more observable) aspects (Tweney, 2001). By contrast with studies of current science, we do not always need to struggle to understand those presuppositions, nor are we as likely to overlook important aspects. Further, it is easier to understand the content of the science itself. Perhaps most importantly, it is easier to see the cultural and social aspects of historical science, given the advantages of hindsight, and their long-term consequences (for similar views on the pedagogical uses of history of science, see Nersessian, 1995; Matthews, Gauld, & Stinner, 2004; Tweney, 2008).

Faraday's Candle

Try the following experiment. You will need an ordinary candle and a match (or lighter). Light the candle. While holding the lit match nearby, blow the candle out and quickly move the lit match an inch or two above the extinguished wick. If you are in a draft-free room, you should see the flame apparently jump from the match to the candle wick. Sometimes, if you are very quiet, you can even hear a very faint "whoosh" as the wick reignites.

Michael Faraday used this simple demonstration before an audience of young people during a series of lectures first given in 1848 (Faraday, 1861/2002). He explained that the purpose was to show how the burning matter in a candle flame was not the wick, but instead invisible particles of hot wax. Faraday explained to his audience that melted wax travels up the wick and is vaporized by the heat of the flame, igniting as it mixes with the oxygen of the air. The flame "jumps" in the demonstration because the still-hot vapor reignites at the match head, above the wick, then ignites downwards, until the flame is reestablished in its normal position. Through a series of experiments, Faraday proved to his audience that the explanation was correct, showing, for example, that the dark area in the center of the flame was flammable hot gas. He did this by drawing the gas out of the dark part of the flame with a thin glass tube, and igniting it at the end of the tube. When the tube is held in the bright part of the flame, the "gas" at the other end of the tube is not flammable. Later in the lecture, he showed that the "gas" in the bright part is actually particulate carbon, which glows as it burns.

Faraday's Explanation, and His Demonstrations, Count as Science

A few years later, Faraday attended a séance in London to observe and examine "table turning" (Faraday, 1853/1859). Often attributed to supernatural agents, the phenomenon is in fact real enough. A group of people sit around a table, their hands flat upon it, their eyes closed. After a time, the table begins to rotate. The movements are explained as the result of an invisible "supernatural force," the means by which the spirit world is connected to this world.

Faraday disproved this explanation by conducting experiments, for example, by placing sheets of cardboard on the table, with a pointer to indicate whether the table was causing the cardboard to move, or whether instead the cardboard was moving because of muscular forces imposed by the sitters' hands. In every case, it was muscular movements, and not the table itself, causing the movement.

The Supernatural Force Explanation Doesn't Count as Science

Faraday believed in the invisible particles of hot wax, but he did not believe in the invisible supernatural force nor in a spirit world spelling out messages in séances. Why not? What's the difference? What can we use to distinguish between science and non-science? Such questions cut to the heart of many of today's issues, especially that of creationism vs. evolution.

There is something fundamentally easy about belief in the supernatural, and there is something fundamentally hard about science. Thus, every culture has some version of belief in the supernatural, but only a few ever developed science. In a seminal essay, the philosopher of science Robert McCauley (2000) pointed out that religion is "natural" and science is "unnatural." What he meant follows from the obvious fact that whereas all cultures have developed some form of religious belief, only a few have ever developed science, and then only recently in historical time. A similar point has been made about mathematics by Tomasello (1999). While most cultures have some form of numerosity, only a few (and only recently) developed anything like a symbolic mathematics. In both cases, mathematics and science, there seem to be cultural prerequisites for the development of the approach, and these are hard to attain. By contrast, there is something "natural" about religion; something about it seems inherently easy and therefore must rest upon fundamental, perhaps innate, characteristics of human cognition. Religion is easy, but science is hard.

Why Science Is Hard

What then does science require that is so hard? Part of the answer is that science requires a certain kind of skepticism, and this is hard to come by. Faraday's epistemological presuppositions led him to distrust the supernatural force explanation of table turning, because such a force, previously unknown to science, possessed properties unlike those of any other force known. Thus, it required for its appearance a particular state of mind among the participants, and it showed no tendency toward attraction or repulsion nor any tendency toward a tangential movement, other than what could be explained by muscular motion. Faraday's approach to the issue was not to rest on his presuppositions, but to carry out experiments that ultimately disproved the presence of any forces acting in the phenomenon, other than the muscular forces.

His presuppositions, and his skepticism, were thus supported by the outcomes of the experiments.

Complete skepticism is too strong for science—the hot vaporized wax in Faraday's candle is invisible, and to accept it as a reality requires an affirmation, not just the rejection or denial of hypotheses. Still, at a certain level, science requires distrust—a measured skepticism—of all hypotheses. We must actively seek to disconfirm each and every one. If left with some that fail to be disconfirmed, these "residue" hypotheses are candidates for scientific belief. If such a hypothesis also fits within a network of larger confirmed statements, so much the better. And if it reflects a pattern of events similar to patterns seen in other, perhaps more observable, cases, then its strength is even further increased. Faraday could not directly see the hot gases in the candle flame, but if they ignite like other invisible gases, conform to the known laws of gaseous behavior, and can be produced artificially by heating paraffin wax, then the strength of the explanation of the particular phenomena of the candle is assured. Each step of the way, Faraday showed his young audience that potential other hypotheses could be ruled out, that the hot gas hypothesis was consistent with other phenomena, and that the idea fit within a larger context of scientific ideas. Faraday showed his listeners that they had to be skeptical, but he also showed how the skepticism leads to increasingly certain knowledge about the candle—and a good deal of chemistry and science besides. The skepticism was measured and under the control of experiment and observation.

The presence of measured skepticism in this sense is helpful in discriminating between real science and non-science or pseudoscience. Science admits only those hypotheses that can potentially be disconfirmed, and it is most certain when the hypothesis fits a larger framework of ideas. By contrast, creationism can always invent yet one more divine intervention to account for any observation, and so it is not science: There is no possibility of disconfirmation.

Measured skepticism is hard on us all-too-human beings. Much psychological evidence shows that we are prone to a "will to believe." Believing is such sweet solace, after all. We really want to believe it is dear departed Aunt Gladys moving the forces of the universe as the table moves in the séance! Yet doing science requires that we not give in to such wishes. It is evidence, not desire, that counts in science.

Even measured skepticism is useless without hypotheses to be skeptical about. Thus, science also requires imagination to generate all those potentially disconfirmable hypotheses, but it is imagination of a special sort: Any new idea in science has to be consistent with everything else known prior to the new idea; science involves pattern-finding. The invisible vaporized wax in Faraday's candle demonstration has to fit all that is known about gases, chemistry, temperature, and so on. It has to fit both prior theory and the evidence. Thus, Faraday was careful not to rest with this one demonstration, but developed others, all of great simplicity, showing that any other hypothesis (it's really not hot gas but the wick burning, flames can travel across empty space, and so on) was untenable—given the evidence!

Prior theories are not eternal, of course; they too can be overturned, but when that happens the demands on our habits of mind are even greater. Darwin asked, not just for a new way to see our place in time and in the biosphere, but for an entire new way to see life and its manifestations. And his idea succeeded because he made potentially disconfirmable claims, showed how his theory was consistent with a huge range of known facts, and because his observations themselves could be trusted. Surviving the measured skepticism of nearly all scientists, his theory became one of the foundations of our current knowledge of ourselves and the universe.

Faraday asks that we believe in invisible particles of hot gaseous wax that cannot be seen. We believe the particles are there, but not because we trust that when Faraday says so it must be true. Instead, we trust that if we redid his candle demonstration, we would see exactly what he says we would see. The evidence could be in front of us. All science rests on such trust—trust that the reported results can (or could) be seen for oneself. It is not blind faith, but trust, and it is always subject to the refined skepticism and constrained imagination that are central in science. Faraday doesn't just *tell* about candles, he *shows*.

It is easy, the physicist Richard Feynman noted (Feynman, Leighton, & Sands, 1964), to imagine invisible angels; just imagine visible angels, and then make them fade to transparency, and you'll eventually get invisible angels. But a scientific concept requires far more. You can't simply imagine invisible particles of hot wax the way you imagine invisible angels. Instead, the invisible particles have to be consistent with what's known, or can be shown, about wax, temperature, flame, and so on. Thomas Ward conducted an interesting series of experiments in which students were asked to draw imagined alien creatures (Ward, 1994; Ward, Patterson, & Sifonis, 2004). In nearly every case, the imaginative figures drawn were constrained by ontological folk presuppositions about creatures. Such "structured imagination" is thus common, but the extent of the structuring, as Feynman noted, is much greater in science.

Faraday was fierce in opposing the pseudoscience of the table turners. He rejected the hypothesis of the supernatural force because it relied upon supernatural agency, and because it failed to rule out potential natural explanations. So he did what good scientists do. He visited a séance, with tests and apparatus to determine the source of table motion. No electric or magnetic fields were detectable, ruling out some possible explanations. The hands of the sitters always moved first, and the table always followed. Even when the table was still, a measurable force was exerted to the side by the hands of the participants. People, not spirits, were the agents. The phenomenon is natural and the claim for supernatural forces collapses.

Faraday's strategies in doing science are, however, special and difficult, in the sense that their manifestation is recent in history and still rare among people, even within the most scientifically advanced cultures. There are two classes of explanations for this difficulty. First, and perhaps most obviously, as science progresses, the sheer amount of material upon which a particular belief needs to be grounded increases enormously. Faraday's candle lectures brought his audience to an appreciation of many of the then-current laws of chemistry and physics—how much more is involved in getting a student to appreciate, much less believe, quantum theory! The prerequisites for science are hard because there is so much content potentially involved.

Some of what makes science hard, however, rests on a different set of constraints. If we think of science as the pursuit of representations of natural phenomena, then it is clear that representation, as such, is not the problem. Everyone "represents" in some sense, and the basis for our ability to form mental representations is found in cognitive characteristics that are pervasive and fundamental. Thus, one of the key findings of the early years of cognitive science was George Miller's (1956) recognition that the capacity of short term memory was not a fixed amount of information, but a fixed number of "chunks," groups of elements united by a previously learned organizational principle. Thus, the sequence of 12 digits 800267712941 is hard to retain after one presentation because it exceeds the span of 7 ± 2 chunks, but the same digits presented in reverse order, 149217762008, are easy to hold in short term memory, provided the sequence is recognized as a sequence of commonly known years; it then becomes only three chunks in short term memory. People do this kind of thing constantly and easily; incoming information is rapidly coded against prior knowledge and used to construct a representation on the spot.

The representations that are important in science are built on the same capacity, of course. Once we follow the prerequisites, we represent a candle flame as consisting in part of hot gas, even though no such thing is visible. But the representation as hot gas is not immediate; to build it calls upon very slow processes of deliberate model construction. Indeed, these processes are slow enough that they can sometimes be tracked in great detail. Thus, Qin and Simon (1995) studied the way college students built representations of relativity theory while reading Einstein's original paper on this topic. Clement (1988) studied physicists constructing models of spring dynamics while solving a difficult physics problem. Nersessian (1999) developed computer simulations of these processes and compared them to the model construction activities of James Clerk Maxwell as he developed his model of the electromagnetic field. She showed that in both cases, model building rests heavily upon the creative generation of known analogies and their subsequent modification. Similar approaches have been applied to Faraday as well; Gooding (1990) developed models of how Faraday's representations of electric and magnetic phenomena were developed, based upon Faraday's extensive diary notes. Ippolito and Tweney (1995) showed that Faraday's model building implies a recursive process; he relied heavily upon perceptual rehearsal, but he also used "inceptual" rehearsal, a kind of mental reworking of perceived events that stripped away varying sets of potentially unessential elements until the resulting "working model" could be formalized.

Beyond the construction of representations and models, science demands the testing of such models. This too is hard for people, but for very different reasons. Thus, a large literature has been devoted to "confirmation bias," the tendency to hold on to a hypothesis, once formed. Much of this work derives from the classic studies by Peter Wason (Wason & Johnson-Laird, 1972). Klayman and Ha (1987) made a classic reformulation of this approach, showing that presuppositions about the problem to be solved, which can lead to a confirmation "bias" in a laboratory task, can be highly adaptive in real environments. In more recent years, attempts have been made to rest such biases upon evolutionarily derived "cheater detection" modules, thus tying reasoning to processes of social interaction shaped in hunter-gatherer societies (Cosmides, 1989). The issue remains controversial, however, because the phenomena in question can equally be explained by "relevance" processes, that is, by the usual way in which aspects of a statement are seen as relevant to discourse in communicative situations (Sperber & Wilson, 1995).

While studies have shown that disconfirmation can be exceedingly difficult, especially in complex tasks (Tweney, Doherty, & Mynatt, 1981), its use has to be tempered with appropriate reliance on confirmatory evidence. There is no point trying to disconfirm the hot gas hypothesis of candle flames until you first know that the idea can in fact explain the phenomena and has at least some evidence in its favor. Faraday in fact showed such sensitivity in his researches; while early in the stages of testing a new hypothesis, he often ignored findings that seemed to disconfirm the hypothesis, but he always then returned to active attempts to disconfirm it, a "confirm early, disconfirm late" strategy (Tweney, 1985). Such heuristic shifts imply a good deal of cognitive control over one's own inferential processes, and it is not hard to see why they are rare.

Science is not all a "hard grind," however, as teachers well know. It is a commonplace to say that scientists are like children at play, and the "fun factor" is often mentioned by scientists, Faraday himself being a prime example! Especially in the realm of exploratory experiment, when new phenomena are being tracked down, the try-and-try-again aspect of the research can be striking. The educational psychologist Elizabeth Cavicchi has worked extensively on this problem, showing that the play-like processes by which Faraday worked on electricity are reflected in the discovery activities engaged in by science students (Cavicchi, 1997, 2003). She has carried out many replications of electrical experiments done by Faraday and by others, and the sense in which her own play with materials and apparatus informs and enlightens her knowledge comes through very strongly in her papers.

An important contributor to the fun factor in science, one especially relevant to pedagogical concerns, resides in the emphasis on "eye–hand–mind" processes (Gooding, 1990). In Faraday's case, such dynamics are especially prominent, as his lectures on the candle suggest. Faraday's extensive laboratory diaries support the point that he spent a huge amount of time in the laboratory, and that his "hands-on" experiences were an integral part of his theorizing, as well as the source of new understandings of phenomena. One cannot understand his science without close attention to his manipulations, whether playful and exploratory or more carefully planned and formal (Tweney, 1985, 1989, 2004, 2006). The understanding of such dynamics has led many historians to the use of replications to unpack the nonverbal, nonpropositional, aspects of science, and these mesh especially well with studies of imagery, analogy, metaphor, and other complex activities in science (e.g., Cavicchi, 2006; Gooding, 2006; Heering, 1994). I will suggest in the final section of this chapter the connections this approach has to educational concerns.

Why Religion Is Easy

Religious beliefs differ from scientific beliefs in many ways, of course, but it is not just the content of the ideas that distinguishes scientific thinking from religious cognition. Instead, each domain calls upon different ways of thinking about reality, and each draws upon vastly different epistemological presuppositions.

Religious beliefs range from straightforward ontological claims, for example "God exists," to claims about necessary ritual, for example "If I go to Confession, God will absolve my sins." To simplify the discussion, I will focus on the ontological beliefs only, since these are most at issue in the comparison to science. Obviously, science also makes ontological claims, but such claims are always subject to measured skepticism, and they must pass certain kinds of tests to be acceptable as objects of belief. One could argue that something similar is true about religious beliefs, with only the nature of the tests and the kind of skepticism brought to bear being different. St. Augustine of Hippo, in his *Confessions* (397–398/1961), outlines both his early skepticism about Christianity and the "tests" that convinced him to accept it. For example, the faith of his mother, Monica, was an important example to Augustine, one that he regarded as an influence on his conversion. Still, the nature of the tests that warrant religious belief differ, as they must, given the nature of the beliefs.

Of the religious beliefs themselves, certain distinctions have to be made, even leaving aside the ritual side of religious belief (for which, see, for example, Boyer & Lienard, 2006; Lawson & McCauley, 1990; Whitehouse, 2004). Thus, while some claims are purely ontological (God exists), others are derivative from these and contain symbolic aspects that are difficult to interpret as purely ontological. For example, the claim that the Communion host in Catholic ritual is the "body of Christ" is rooted in a long series of interpretive practices and disputes about its meaning. Whitehouse (2004) notes that there are two kinds of religiosity, an imagistic and a doctrinal mode, the former centered on rare but emotionally involving rituals (coming of age ceremonies, marriages, funerals, etc.), the latter being repetitive, frequent, and much less "hot" emotionally. Both maintain beliefs, but use very different cognitive strategies to do so. Franks (2003) has recently argued that many religious claims deliberately preserve an air of mystery, and that the mystery is maintained among believers by virtue of the fact that such beliefs are deferential to authority. Complex theological concepts (e.g., the Triune, or "Three Person in One," God), in particular, may require the maintenance of "mystery" by authority.

The sorts of religious belief characteristic of folk religions and the kind of "theologically incorrect" beliefs that most contemporary church-goers manifest even today (Slone, 2004) do not always rest upon such mystery but instead draw upon a kind of near-plausibility. These include animistic ideas (a "bear god," say), many aspects of polytheistic religion (Zeus hurtling thunderbolts), and some popular conceptions (guardian angels, God as an old man in the sky, and so on). Such ideas manifest an interesting property which has been the subject of much recent research: they are *counterintuitive*, although in a characteristic fashion. Boyer (1994, 2001) noted that religious ideas in folk religion often are only *minimally* counterintuitive, and that in a very specific fashion. Thus, to use Boyer's example (2001, pp. 80–81), a black giraffe with six legs would be unusual, but none of the ontological presuppositions about animals would be violated. However, a giraffe that gives birth to an aardvark is really counterintuitive in a deep sense, because it violates the presupposition that animals give birth only to their own kind. Similarly, the counterintuitive concepts that matter for religion violate the ontological presuppositions by which we enrich ordinary concepts (trees become talking trees, say, or a saintly person rises from the dead). Further, as Atran (2002) notes, the violations of intuition in religious beliefs tend to be restrained in the sense that usually no more than one ontological presupposition is violated. While a talking snake is a conceivable religious entity, a talking snake that flies through the air is far less likely, since a talking flying snake violates ontological presuppositions of both folk psychology and folk biology.

Counterintuitive concepts have been the subject of much recent research. It turns out that minimally counterintuitive concepts (but not the more outrageous counterintuitive concepts that violate too many presuppositions) enjoy a number of cognitive advantages; in particular, they are easy to remember and hence easy to transmit to another individual. In part this derives from their distinctiveness, but it also rests upon the tendency to infer agency as an explanation for events in the natural world (Bering & Johnson, 2005). Both aspects of counterintuitiveness, ease of processing and a supportive role in agency detection, have been the subject of recent research by cognitive psychologists, and the circumstances under which they are manifest are beginning to be understood.

The ease of recall and the ease of social transmissibility of counterintuitive concepts, as compared to intuitive concepts, even those with bizarre extensions (like the six-legged giraffe), have been confirmed using both lists of concepts and concepts embedded within stories (Barrett & Nyhof, 2001; Boyer & Ramble, 2001). This has been shown using both recall tasks and serial transmission tasks. The effects are context dependent. By providing appropriate explanatory context, a counterintuitive concept can be made intuitive (and less memorable), whereas an intuitive concept can be made counterintuitive (Gonce, Upal, Slone, & Tweney, 2006; Upal, Gonce, Tweney, & Slone, 2007). Thus, a flying cow, counterintuitive in a story about a roundup, is perfectly intuitive in a context in which a tornado lifts an animal off the ground. The flying cow is relatively memorable (and transmissible) in the first case, but not especially so in the second case.

Atran (2002) notes that there is a difference between the counterintuitive concepts that matter in religious belief and those that occur in fantasy or imaginative fiction; Disney portrays a talking mouse but nobody worships him! In religion, however, the ordinary pragmatic constraints that govern belief and communication are suspended, and the counterintuitive concepts that constitute the web of religious beliefs thereby become immune to disconfirmation. Ontological presuppositions can be violated and the violations tolerated because they are, literally, taken on faith and not subject to the tests that normally are implicit in belief. If I tell you that I saw a six-legged giraffe, you will want to see it for yourself, but once an act of faith is made, then claims about an invisible divinity become accepted without challenge. As long as the source is seen as trustworthy, the claim is taken on authority, as it were. In the extreme, and often in modern religions, such claims are justified as mysteries—believed but not understood and not tested; "I believe because it is impossible," said Tertullian.

Conclusions: The Differences and Their Consequences

We can now see what the relevant similarities and differences are between science and religion. Both domains construct representations of reality, but the status of those constructions differs enormously and the means used to construct and maintain them differ as well. Like religion, science uses counterintuitive representations; wave–particle duality is even less intuitive than flying cows, giraffes that birth aardvarks, and omnipotent and omniscient gods. Many scientific concepts exceed wildly the counterintuitiveness common to religious concepts, and some, like relativity, even ask us to suspend nearly every intuition we have about space and time.

Counterintuitive ideas survive in science because they are developed using a highly constraining imaginative process that requires consistency with massive amounts of other information, even as they violate folk ontologies. Such concepts are tested using inferential processes that undercut the common heuristics that maintain them, heuristics like confirmation bias. Measured skepticism is a hard way to approach one's own beliefs, especially when fundamental ontological presuppositions are involved. But the results, concepts that survive the deadly disconfirmatory attempts, bring a huge body of consequences in their wake, and the accumulated knowledge does grow, in step with the growing sophistication of the epistemological foundations.

Counterintuitive ideas survive in religion for different reasons. They survive because a cultural evolutionary process winnows out those that are too counterintuitive, and the survivors then become insulated from change by a variety of methods, none of which emphasize attempts to disconfirm, and none of which attempt to render the ideas consistent with everything else we know (Whitehouse, 2004). Religions are thereby able to meet other needs— for explanations of the world, emotional needs of belonging, comfort, and fear reduction, needs for standards of conduct, and so on. Rituals affirm these beliefs, and it is obvious, if rarely noted, that religious gatherings are primarily confirmatory, with doubt being a private matter. By contrast, scientists gather in the spirit of changing ideas—adding, subtracting, revising the ideas of science. Science, like religion, also meets emotional needs. Unfortunately, it is harder for an individual "consumer" to reach this level in science, and it is entirely easy in religion. A five-year-old can learn the basics of any religion, but learning evolutionary theory can take decades.

Epilogue

Cognitive scientists and educators have long sought ways to enhance student understanding of scientific methods and concepts, and have pointed out many aspects of why this is difficult (see the comprehensive reviews by Klahr & Simon, 1999, and by Zimmerman, 2000). The recent emphasis on differing epistemological underpinnings for science and for everyday thinking is a promising development, but much more needs to be understood about the way epistemologies change and about how real-world concepts change, embedded as they are within masses of intuitively plausible assumptions and experiences.

That the task can be achieved is suggested by the success of Faraday's *Chemical history of a candle*. I noted in the Introduction that this work, actually a transcription of a series of lectures, was given to a "juvenile audience." In 1848, when his first "candle" lecture was given, it was unusual for an eminent scientist to present such material to young people, and Faraday is often credited for his important role in the historical development of the lecture-demonstration generally, and for his innovative extension of this method to young audiences (Taylor, 1988). As for the transcribed lectures, they have remained continuously in print ever since.

Faraday's lectures remain readable and interesting, and it is especially valuable to note his sensitivity to the epistemological needs of his audience. I strongly recommend a reading of the book to any and all science educators, because of this. It is a short book, readable in an hour or two—except that some of the experiments used are so compelling that the reader might find it hard to resist closing the book and going off to play with matches! Between times, however, pay close attention to the frequent incorporation of children's games as exemplars, and to the language which, at the remove of a century and a half, still appears remarkably "cognitive." Faraday's audience is enjoined to "see," to "try," to "apply," and even, in a Victorian anachronism, to "philosophize." He is speaking to children, but he does not treat them as empty vessels to be filled with facts, but rather as active participants, sharing his curiosity about commonplace and not so commonplace things. Most to the point of the present paper, Faraday knew, as we should, that scientific thinking is hard—hard, but attainable, and fun to boot. And part of the fun is exactly that it must force changes upon one's presuppositions, while opening one's mind to new epistemologies. We educators must do the same, we must adopt a childlike stance, and follow Faraday himself: "I claim the privilege of speaking to juveniles as a juvenile myself" (Faraday, 1861/2002, p. 10).

References

Atran, S. (2002). *In gods we trust: The evolutionary landscape of religion.* New York: Oxford University Press.

Barrett, J. L., & Nyhof, M. A. (2001). Spreading non-natural concepts: The role of intuitive conceptual structures in memory and transmission of cultural materials. *Journal of Cognition and Culture, 1,* 69–100.

Bering, J. M., & Johnson, D. D. P. (2005). "O lord … You perceive my thoughts from afar": Recursiveness and the evolution of supernatural agency. *Journal of Cognition and Culture, 3*(1–2), 118–142.

Boyer, P. (1994). *The naturalness of religious ideas: A cognitive theory of religion.* Berkeley, CA: University of California Press.

Boyer, P. (2001). *Religion explained: The evolutionary origins of religious thought.* New York: Basic Books.

Boyer, P., & Lienard, P. (2006). Why ritualized behavior? Precaution systems and action parsing in developmental, pathological and cultural rituals. *Behavioral and Brain Sciences, 29*(6), 595–613.

Boyer, P., & Ramble, C. (2001). Cognitive templates for religious concepts: Cross-cultural evidence for recall of counterintuitive representations. *Cognitive Science, 25,* 535–564.

Cavicchi, E. (1997). Experimenting with magnetism: Ways of learning of Joann and Faraday. *American Journal of Physics, 65,* 867–882.

Cavicchi, E. (2003). Experiences with the magnetism of conducting loops: Historical instruments, experimental replications, and productive confusions. *American Journal of Physics, 71*(2), 156–167.

Cavicchi, E. (2006). Faraday and Piaget: Experimenting in relation with the world. *Perspectives on Science, 14*(1), 66–96.

Chi, M. T. H. (1992). Conceptual change within and across ontological categories: Examples from learning and discovery in science. In R. N. Giere (Ed.), *Cognitive models of science* (pp. 129–186). Minneapolis, MN: University of Minnesota Press.

Chinn, C. A., & Malhotra, B. A. (2001). Epistemologically authentic scientific reasoning. In K. Crowley, C. D. Schunn, & T. Okada (Eds.), *Designing for science: Implications from everyday, classroom, and professional settings* (pp. 351–392). Mahwah, NJ: Lawrence Erlbaum Associates.

Clement, J. (1982). Students' preconceptions in introductory mechanics. *American Journal of Physics, 50*, 66–71.

Clement, J. (1988). Observed methods for generating analogies in scientific problem solving. *Cognitive Science, 12*, 563–586.

Cosmides, L. (1989). The logic of social exchange: Has natural selection shaped how humans reason? Studies with the Wason selection task. *Cognition, 31*, 187–276.

Darwin, C. (1859). *On the origin of species by means of natural selection, Or the preservation of favoured races in the struggle for life.* London: John Murray.

Dole, J. A., & Sinatra, G. M. (1998). Reconceptualizing change in the cognitive construction of knowledge. *Educational Psychologist, 33*(2–3), 109–128.

Faraday, M. (1853/1859). On table-turning. In M. Faraday (Ed.), *Experimental researches in chemistry and physics* (pp. 382–391). London: Richard Taylor & William Francis. (First published in *The Times*, June 30, 1853.)

Faraday, M. (1861/2002). *The chemical history of a candle: A course of six lectures delivered before a juvenile auditory at the Royal Institution of Great Britain.* New York: Dover Publications. (First published 1861.)

Feynman, R. P., Leighton, R. B., & Sands, M. (1964). *The Feynman lectures on physics, Vol. 2: Mainly electromagnetism and matter.* Reading, MA: Addison-Wesley.

Franks, B. (2003). The nature of unnaturalness in religious representations: Negation and concept combination. *Journal of Cognition and Culture, 3*(1), 41–68.

Gonce, L. O., Upal, M. A., Slone, D. J., & Tweney, R. D. (2006). The role of context in the recall of counterintuitive concepts. *Journal of Cognition and Culture, 6*(3–4), 521–547.

Gooding, D. C. (1990). *Experiment and the making of meaning: Human agency in scientific observation and experiment.* Dordrecht: Kluwer Academic Publishers.

Gooding, D. C. (2006). From phenomenology to field theory: Faraday's visual reasoning. *Perspectives on Science, 14*(1), 40–65.

Heering, P. (1994). The replication of the torsion balance experiment: The inverse square law and its refutation by early 19th-century German physicists. In C. Blondel & M. Dörries (Eds.), *Restaging Coulomb: Usages, controverses et réplications autour de la balance de torsion* (pp. 47–66). Firenze: Leo S. Olschki.

Hofer, B. K., & Pintrich, P. R. (1997). The development of epistemological theories: Beliefs about knowledge and knowing and their relations to learning. *Review of Educational Research, 67*(1), 88–140.

Ippolito, M. F., & Tweney, R. D. (1995). The inception of insight. In R. J. Sternberg & J. E. Davidson (Eds.), *The nature of insight* (pp. 433–462). Cambridge, MA: MIT Press.

Kitcher, P. (1982). *Abusing science: The case against creationism.* Cambridge, MA: MIT Press.

Klahr, D., & Simon, H. A. (1999). Studies of scientific discovery: Complementary approaches and convergent findings. *Psychological Bulletin, 125,* 524–543.

Klayman, J., & Ha, Y.-W. (1987). Confirmation, disconfirmation and information in hypothesis testing. *Psychological Review, 94,* 211–228.

Lawson, E. T., & McCauley, R. N. (1990). *Rethinking religion: Connecting cognition and culture.* Cambridge, UK: Cambridge University Press.

Matthews, M. R., Gauld, C., & Stinner, A. (2004). The pendulum: Its place in science, culture and pedagogy. *Science & Education, 13,* 261–277.

McCauley, R. N. (2000). The naturalness of religion and the unnaturalness of science. In F. C. Keil & R. A. Wilson (Eds.), *Explanation and cognition* (pp. 61–86). Cambridge, MA: MIT Press.

Miller, G. A. (1956). The magical number seven, plus or minus two: Some limits on our capacity for processing information. *Psychological Review, 101,* 343–352.

Nersessian, N. J. (1995). Should physicists preach what they practice? Constructive modeling in doing and learning physics. *Science & Education, 4*(3), 203–226.

Nersessian, N. J. (1999). Model based reasoning in conceptual change. In L. Magnani, N. J. Nersessian, & P. Thagard (Eds.), *Model-based reasoning in scientific discovery* (pp. 5–22). New York: Kluwer/Plenum.

Qin, Y., & Simon, H. A. (1995). Imagery and mental models in problem solving. In J. Glasgow, B. Chandrasekaran, & N. H. Narayanan (Eds.), *Diagrammatic reasoning: Cognitive and computational perspectives* (pp. 403–434). Menlo Park, CA: AAAI Press/MIT Press.

Rohrer, D. (2002). Misconceptions about incline speed for nonlinear slopes. *Journal of Experimental Psychology: Human Perception and Performance, 28*(4), 963–973.

Ruse, M. (2005). *The evolution–creation struggle.* Cambridge, MA: Harvard University Press.

Shtulman, A. (2006). Qualitative differences between naïve and scientific theories of evolution. *Cognitive Psychology, 52*(2), 170–194.

Slone, D. J. (2004). *Theological incorrectness: Why religious people believe what they shouldn't.* New York: Oxford University Press.

Sperber, D., & Wilson, D. (1995). *Relevance: Communication and cognition* (2nd ed.). Oxford: Blackwell.

St. Augustine of Hippo (397–398/1961). *The Confessions of St. Augustine.* Trans. by R. S. Pine-Coffin. New York: Penguin Books.

Taylor, C. (1988). *The art and science of lecture demonstration.* Bristol: Institute of Physics Publishing.

Tomasello, M. (1999). *The cultural origins of human cognition.* Cambridge, MA: Harvard University Press.

Tweney, R. D. (1985). Faraday's discovery of induction: A cognitive approach. In D. Gooding & F. A. J. L. James (Eds.), *Faraday rediscovered: Essays on the life and work of Michael Faraday, 1791–1867* (pp. 189–210). New York: Stockton Press/London: Macmillan.

Tweney, R. D. (1989). A framework for the cognitive psychology of science. In B. Gholson, A. Houts, R. M. Neimeyer, & W. Shadish (Eds.), *Psychology of science and metascience* (pp. 342–366). Cambridge, UK: Cambridge University Press.

Tweney, R. D. (2001). Scientific thinking: A cognitive-historical approach. In K. Crowley, C. D. Schunn, & T. Okada (Eds.), *Designing for science: Implications from everyday, classroom, and professional settings* (pp. 141–173). Mahwah, NJ: Lawrence Erlbaum Associates.

Tweney, R. D. (2004). Replication and the experimental ethnography of science. *Journal of Cognition and Culture, 4,* 731–758.

Tweney, R. D. (2006). Discovering discovery: How Faraday found the first metallic colloid. *Perspectives on Science, 14*(1), 97–121.

Tweney, R. D. (2008). Replication and pedagogy in the history of psychology: I. Introduction. *Science & Education, 17(5),* 467–475.

Tweney, R. D., Doherty, M. E., & Mynatt, C. R. (Eds.). (1981). *On scientific thinking.* New York: Columbia University Press.

Upal, M. A., Gonce, L. O., Tweney, R. D., & Slone, D. J. (2007). Contextualizing counterintuitiveness: How context affects comprehension and memorability of counterintuitive concepts. *Cognitive Science, 31*(3), 415–439.

Ward, T. B. (1994). Structured imagination: The role of conceptual structure in exemplar generation. *Cognitive Psychology, 27,* 1–40.

Ward, T. B., Patterson, M. J., & Sifonis, C. M. (2004). The role of specificity and abstraction in creative idea generation. *Creativity Research Journal, 16*(1), 1–9.

Wason, P. C., & Johnson-Laird, P. N. (1972). *Psychology of reasoning: Structure and content.* Cambridge, MA: Harvard University Press.

Whitehouse, H. (2004). *Modes of religiosity: A cognitive theory of religious transmission.* Walnut Creek, CA: Altamira Press.

Zimmerman, C. (2000). The development of scientific reasoning skills. *Developmental Review, 20,* 99–149.

Chapter 10

Teaching and Learning Evolution as an Emergent Process

The BEAGLE Project

Uri Wilensky and Michael Novak

Introduction

Evolution, and how to teach it, is perhaps the most controversial topic in American schools today. Biologists attest to the ubiquity of evolution, and assert that evolutionary explanations undergird their entire science and are of fundamental import. Yet, according to recent surveys (Gallup, 2008), 44% of Americans say they do not accept evolution in any form, and a shockingly small number, only 14%, say they believe in naturalistic evolution. A century and a half after the publication of *The Origin of Species*, there remains considerable cultural resistance to teaching this "controversial" subject in schools. Many explanations have been proffered for this disconnect between scientific consensus and citizen acceptance. Prominent among these explanations is that conflict with religious belief is the principal cause of objections to evolution (Numbers, 1992; Scott & Branch, 2003; Witham, 2002; Evans, 2001). While acknowledging the importance of religious objections, this chapter proceeds from the assumption that another major cause of rejection of evolution is the cognitive difficulty of understanding the evolutionary process. In this regard, we place evolution in a class of processes known as *emergent processes* that are notoriously difficult for people to understand (Centola, Wilensky, & McKenzie, 2000; Penner, 2000; Resnick & Wilensky, 1993; Wilensky, 2001; Wilensky & Centola, 2007; Wilensky & Resnick, 1999; Centola, McKenzie, & Wilensky, 2000).

Indeed the history of science is replete with scientific knowledge claims that came into sharp conflict with religious beliefs. To take one example, the claim that the Earth is not flat but spherical, which was put forth by the Greeks and Indians before the advent of Christianity, was met with Christian religious objections in the Middle Ages as it conflicted with biblical verses about "the four corners of the earth." As late as the 19th century, even scientists such as William Carpenter (1871) and Samuel Rowbotham (1865) published proofs of a flat Earth. Yet these objections eventually subsided. Now, except for a few fringe "flat earthers," religious and non-religious alike accept the spherical Earth and are not bothered by the "four corners." How did this change in beliefs come about? Major factors in fostering this change of attitude were new technologies that enabled us to view the Earth from afar and other celestial bodies from up-close. For those of us old enough to have been conscious in 1969, how can we forget the first color photographs of the Earth from space taken by Apollo astronauts and published in *Life* magazine (Figure 10.1)?

The new technologies made vivid to our eyes the roundness of the Earth. Is it possible to develop a technology that would make equally visible and vivid the process of evolution? In this chapter we present a sample collection of computer models from a larger "curriculum" of computer-based activities called BEAGLE (Biological Experiments in Adaptation, Genetics, Learning and Evolution), in which we attempt to do just that—to use the computational technology to enable us to "see" evolution in action. Technologies such as telescopes and spaceships are able to compress space, enabling us to

Figure 10.1 Photograph of the Earth from space (*Life* magazine, December 7, 1972).

encompass large distances and faraway objects in a single view. Similarly, computational technologies enable us to compress time, so that large stretches of evolutionary time can be seen in a single viewing. Computer-based models of evolutionary processes provide a "sandbox" for students to experiment with mechanisms and analyze the outcomes that lead to population change over many generations. Our unfamiliarity with "deep time" (Gee, 2000) is one important component of what makes evolution difficult to comprehend. Ever since the late 1700s when Scottish geologist James Hutton described the seemingly infinite stretches of geologic time (see Taylor, 2006), there has been widespread incomprehension of this vastness. In 1805, Hutton's colleague John Playfair said: "the mind seemed to grow giddy by looking so far into the abyss of time." Deep time is certainly one important barrier to comprehension of evolution. But there is another important factor that we believe is an even greater impediment. Evolution is a process that works on populations. Gene frequencies in a population change as a result of the variation in competitive advantage of individual traits. Processes where changes occur at one level, but subsequently lead to aggregate outcomes and changes at a higher level (e.g., phenotype results from interaction of genes, population levels result from interactions of individual organisms, and speciation results from interaction of populations), are known as emergent phenomena (Penner, 2000; Wilensky, 2001; Wilensky & Resnick, 1999). In previous work (Resnick & Wilensky, 1993; Wilensky, 1997b, 1999b; Wilensky & Resnick, 1999) we have shown that emergent phenomena are particularly hard for people to reason about. Commonly people "slip between levels" (Levy & Wilensky, 2008; Sengupta & Wilensky, 2009; Wilensky, 2001; Wilensky & Resnick, 1999), attributing properties of the individual to the population and vice versa. For example, if a colony of ants exhibits intelligent foraging behavior, we commonly attribute that intelligence to the individual ants. But this is a misattribution—science has shown that in fact while ant colonies are efficient at gathering food, individual ants are not. It's through the accumulation of the actions and interactions of many ants, each with simple behavior, that we get the emergent intelligence of the colony (Holldobler & Wilson, 1991; Robson & Traniello, 1995; Sudd, 1957; Wilson, 1971). This slippage between the level of the ant colony and the level of the individual ant is a prototypical example of how people so easily slip between different levels of an emergent phenomenon or complex system. Evolution, itself an emergent process, engenders these same cognitive difficulties. Like other emergent phenomena we have studied, we would expect students of evolution to encounter the same cognitive difficulties reported with these other emergent phenomena. Indeed, we have seen the levels slippage described above when students reason about emergent phenomena. For example, if students are told that a population of dinosaurs evolves into a population of birds, by the levels slippage, they envision that this means that an individual dinosaur must morph into a bird. But such a morphing is clearly absurd. By this implicit reductio ad absurdum, they conclude that evolution of species cannot be true.

Understanding Emergent Phenomena

In the early 1990s, Wilensky and Resnick conducted interviews about emergent phenomena. They asked individuals to explain classic emergent phenomena such as the food gathering of ants, flocking of birds, traffic jams, and so on. Each of these phenomena exhibits characteristic patterns (e.g., V-shape of a goose flock) that emerge from the interactions of individuals (e.g., goose). They found a surprising regularity in the explanations people gave: they tended to explain the phenomena as orchestrated by a leader as opposed to the distributed control organizing these phenomena and they described the phenomena as deterministic with no role for randomness in their explanations. Randomness was seen as destructive of the order perceived in the patterns whereas, in fact, the random perturbations help to stabilize and maintain the patterns. Resnick and Wilensky attributed these explanations to a prevalent habit of mind, which they called the "deterministic-centralized mindset" (DC mindset) (Resnick, 1994; Resnick & Wilensky, 1993; Wilensky & Resnick, 1995, 1999). All emergent phenomena can be perceived at two core levels: the level of the individual element (micro) and the level of the aggregate pattern (macro). A key feature of the DC mindset is the tendency to "slip between levels" (Wilensky & Resnick, 1999), that is, to misattribute properties of the aggregate to the individual (as in attributing intelligence to the ant) and to misattribute properties of the individual to the aggregate (as in misattributing forward motion to a traffic jam because the individual cars are moving forward).

Subsequent work has established that this levels slippage presents a significant barrier to people's understanding of many scientific phenomena. For example, Sengupta and Wilensky (2005, 2008a, 2009) have demonstrated that a primary obstacle for students in understanding electricity arises from their slippage between the levels of individual electrons in a wire and the aggregate current in that wire. The curricular design described in this chapter was based on an identification of levels slippage as a crucial difficulty in understanding evolution; it is easy to slip between properties of individual organisms and those of populations or species.

In previous work we have shown that using computer-based models and simulations, specifically agent-based models, can help people overcome the DC mindset and levels slippage and come to understand emergent phenomena. This has been demonstrated in a wide variety of scientific domains including chemistry (Stieff & Wilensky, 2002, 2003; Levy & Wilensky, 2009a, 2009b), population biology (Wilensky, Hazzard, & Longenecker, 2000; Wilensky & Reisman, 2006; Klopfer, 2003), electricity (Sengupta & Wilensky, 2005, 2008b, 2009), materials science (Blikstein & Wilensky, 2004, 2006, 2007,

2009), and probability and statistics (Wilensky, 1997b; Abrahamson & Wilensky, 2004, 2005). In these studies, it was shown that encoding domain knowledge using agent-based models greatly enhances students' comprehension of the science, enabling the students to connect the micro and macro levels and comprehend how mechanisms operating at the micro level can generate observed regularities at the macro level.

Agent-Based Modeling

The last two decades have seen the creation of the new computer-based methodologies of agent-based modeling. By the term "agent" we refer to a computer-based object or entity that has properties and behavior. For example, we could create "car agents" that look like little cars. Each car agent has properties such as location and speed, and associated behaviors such as moving and accelerating. Once we set the car agents in motion according to their behavioral rules, a characteristic traffic pattern, such as a traffic jam, will emerge. The key idea of agent-based modeling is that much of the regularity and complexity in the world can be explained by choosing agents and behaviors that through their interaction generate the observed macro patterns and regularities. Agent-based modeling has enjoyed a rapid increase as a method of conducting scientific research (Gilbert & Troitzsch, 2005; Railsback, Lytinen, & Jackson, 2006; Wilensky & Rand, in press). It has also become increasingly employed as a vehicle for teaching and learning science.

Learning materials that employ agent-based models can address conceptual barriers caused by levels slippage that make understanding evolution difficult for students. Levels slippage is particularly problematic when teaching evolution because evolutionary mechanisms, properties, and outcomes operate at multiple interacting levels. For example, mutations act on genes, predators act on individuals, and trait variation is a property of a population. And while competition between species appears to be a population-level interaction, it often emerges from competition between individuals or genes. Agent-based models can support student explorations that focus on purposeful inspection of individuals while concurrently comparing the changes and outcomes that are occurring at other levels. Our work suggests that using agent-based models enables students to focus on two levels at a time and to move between them, and that that is a key component of learning and teaching about evolution.

NetLogo is one of the most widely used agent-based languages and modeling environments (Wilensky, 1999a). It was designed to be "low threshold and high ceiling" (Papert, 1980; Tisue & Wilensky, 2004)—that is, easily accessible to novices in computer programming or modeling yet powerful enough to be a central tool for professional research. NetLogo is indeed in widespread use by both researchers and educators. It comes with an extensive models library of sample models (more than 300 models) that can be used in educational settings. This library also includes a section of curricular models. A large body of educational materials and curricular units has been designed using the NetLogo environment, including most of the BEAGLE evolution materials described herein. These materials are all "glass-box," that is, the underlying NetLogo code can be viewed and modified by any user. This ability to easily inspect and modify the code has resulted in educators spawning thousands of variations of curricular materials adapted for their own particular contexts.

Besides its use as a single-user application for demonstrating, modifying, and creating agent-based models, NetLogo also has another multi-user mode. Through a module called HubNet (Wilensky & Stroup, 1999a), multiple users can join a NetLogo simulation once it is started, thereby turning it into a "participatory simulation" (Wilensky & Stroup, 1999b, 2000). Users connect to the computer running the NetLogo simulation through their own computer or handheld device such as a calculator. In this mode, an entire classroom can participate in a simulation, each, for example, playing the role of predator or prey in a shared ecosystem. All of these features and considerations are ideally suited for creating powerful and engaging models and simulations of evolution. As such we decided to create the BEAGLE evolution curriculum using NetLogo as a platform.

The BEAGLE Project

In the project described herein, we have employed agent-based models and representations to teach evolution. The BEAGLE (Biological Experiments in Adaptation, Genetics, Learning and Evolution)[1] project is based on a suite of NetLogo models and supporting materials designed to facilitate inquiry, teaching, and learning of concepts and phenomena related to evolution, adaptation, and natural selection. We have piloted BEAGLE models and materials in several settings, from middle school science to undergraduate biology classes.

The development of BEAGLE models was guided by multiple sources including national learning goals for science literacy, popular science materials, traditional biology topics, reform-based science curriculum units, and the current state of the art evolutionary research. Each BEAGLE model was developed using design principles distilled from our previous work in designing and researching instructional materials that use agent-based computer models. We particularly relied on interface guidelines learned from the Connected Chemistry curriculum project (Levy, Novak, & Wilensky, 2006; Levy & Wilensky, 2009a). Such instructional materials have been shown to be vibrant, compelling, and accessible for adolescents (Stieff & Wilensky, 2003; Levy & Wilensky, 2009b). All models were checked for correctness of code and accessibility of information by a team of students and researchers at the

Center for Connected Learning and Computer-Based Modeling (CCL) and were then reviewed for scientific accuracy and importance by university biologists. The curricular materials developed to accompany each model include conceptual scaffolding for students to interact with and explore models, to run experiments, and to use analysis tools to test model outputs and model assumptions.

There are more than a dozen models used in our BEAGLE materials on evolution, each one addressing different emergent phenomena related to competition, selective breeding, patterns of inheritance, genetic drift, natural selection, mutation, coevolution, speciation, and adaptive radiation. Each BEAGLE model comes with an information tab[2] that includes instructions for students and teachers on how to use the model. The instructions include a section on what the model is trying to show or explain, how the model works, how to use the model, patterns of behaviors for the user to notice while running the model, some suggestions for activities to try with the model, as well as suggestions for possible changes or additions to the model. These embedded model instructions support open exploration and "playing" with the model in a variety of learning settings.

As part of the BEAGLE project we developed a three-week instructional unit on evolution titled "BEAGLE: Mechanisms of Evolution." The unit can be used in a variety of learning settings ranging from middle school through undergraduate biology classes as well as informal settings or online. The unit includes a set of sequenced instructional activities, discussions, outside the classroom readings and homework assignments, related to each computer model. The unit is structured into three learning sets. The first learning set investigates ecosystems, predator/prey/producer relationships, and competition. The second learning set investigates the mechanisms of evolution (natural selection, genetic drift, mutation) as well as selective breeding. The third learning set investigates outcomes that result from interactions between multiple mechanisms of evolution. Such emergent outcomes include extinction, speciation, coevolution, and adaptive radiation.

Below, we present four case studies from the "BEAGLE: Mechanisms of Evolution" unit. These cases are developed from middle school students' experiences with pilot implementations of the BEAGLE models and instructional materials. While we have not yet conducted rigorous classroom research on BEAGLE, we have conducted extensive classroom research and iterative redesign based on classroom use. The cases illustrate the affordances of the models to engage students in thinking about evolution as an emergent process. They provide a sample of some of the ways in which students use agent-based models to explore and understand emergent phenomena and emergent processes in evolution. Each case centers around one focal BEAGLE model and describes (1) how the model works, (2) the emergent phenomenon that the model is designed to teach, and (3) student activities and understanding while engaged in interactions with the model.

The Case Studies

Model 1: Wolf–Sheep Predation

The BEAGLE curriculum is based on a set of models and activities. These models and activities can be used in many different ways and need not be run in a fixed sequence. Typically, however, we begin student explorations with ecological models without evolution. A focus on ecology gets students to reason about the interactions between individuals and the subsequent changes in populations, and this is an important prerequisite step in understanding evolution. A typical first model that addresses this is the Wolf–Sheep Predation model (Wilensky, 1997a) from the NetLogo models library.

The model consists of a simple ecosystem that includes a primary producer (grass) that re-grows throughout the ecosystem over time; grass provides energy for sheep (which eat grass as they move about the ecosystem). Sheep, in turn, provide energy for wolves (which eat sheep as they move about the ecosystem). As wolves and sheep move about they lose energy. When sheep or wolves have enough energy they give birth to new offspring and when they run out of energy they die.

This model enables students to explore the interactions between individuals and populations in a predator–prey ecosystem. Such a system is called unstable if it tends to result in extinction for one or more species involved. In contrast, a system is stable if it tends to maintain itself over time, despite fluctuations in population sizes. The model exhibits a variety of emergent phenomena that can be analyzed and explored to better understand the interactions between the agents in the system. Through various activities with this model, students develop important ideas related to (1) interactions between organisms and the environment, (2) individuals and populations, (3) direct and indirect evolutionary pressures, (4) stability and change over time, and (5) competition.

Model 1: Emergent Phenomenon—Competition

Most students have prior knowledge of some basic interactions between organisms and their environment. The topic of ecosystems is commonly revisited in many contexts in primary school science. If asked, "What can cause a population to change?" we have seen that middle school students will readily identify specific food, predators, and habitat as important factors that cause a change in the size of a population. And these same students are able to predict the immediate or short-term effects that these survival factors would have on a population (e.g., more habitat can support a larger population). But the interrelationships between individual organisms and the population and between individual organisms and their environment are typically described only in very simple or very direct terms, where a single proximate cause is solely responsible for a single immediate effect.

When asked to consider a simple ecosystem containing only three types of organisms, where grass is the primary producer, sheep are the primary consumer, and wolves are the secondary consumer, it is difficult for students to reason about the indirect effects on the populations and individuals within each population for a variety of scenarios. For example, we have seen that students have difficulty connecting how a change in the wolf population would indirectly affect the amount of grass in the ecosystem. To understand this indirect effect, students need to connect at least two relationships: (1) the effect of the number of sheep on the amount of grass and (2) the effect of the number of sheep on the number of wolves. So in order to account for the indirect effect of wolves on grass, they would need to reason out how the change in the grass would affect the scarcity of food for each individual sheep, which in time has an aggregate effect on the population of sheep, which in turn affects the scarcity of food for each individual wolf, which in time has an aggregate effect on the population of wolves.

We have also noted that it is frequently difficult for students to connect limitations on resources to their effect on individuals in an ecosystem. While it is easier to understand that there is an upper limit to the number of individuals that can be sustained in a given environment, it is more difficult to reason about how that upper limit would subsequently result in a form of competition between those individuals of the same population for those resources.

Competition is an emergent process. Maximum sustainable population levels (or carrying capacities) arise as an indirect result of competition between similar agents for similar limited resources. Whenever there is variation in the number and distribution of both types of agents and when there are not enough resources to meet the needs of every individual in a population, the interactions between the agents will result in (and are a result of) a continually changing landscape of resource distribution over time. Relative scarcity of these resources will have both a temporal and a spatial component. In order to observe the interactions that result in (and are affected by) this distribution, the interactions amongst many different individuals need to be observed many times and under many conditions, in compressed time and space.

Repeated examination of when and where such interactions are occurring helps students recognize that survival of individuals is influenced not only by the immediate conditions of the environment surrounding an individual, but also by recent conditions in the past, and upcoming conditions in the future. When individual survival patterns are examined in the context of the changes in species' population (where births and deaths are occurring at different rates through time), students begin to connect individual survival to cycles in population size. Being able to distinguish between effects at the micro level and at the macro level enables students to develop a chain of causal links necessary to explain how individuals of the same species end up indirectly and directly competing against each other. Competition as an emergent process is difficult to understand without this dynamic view of resource distribution in the ecosystem. Many effects that lead to competition between individuals in a population are the result of a delayed sequence of interactions and consequences. For example, rainfall in one year may not immediately affect the number of birds that survive. But it would eventually have an effect, after first affecting the growth of plants which in turn would affect the number of flowers produced, which in turn affects the number of seeds produced, which would affect the amount of food available for birds later this year and the next. Without understanding such indirect and dynamic interactions how can one account for why one individual might thrive while the population simultaneously declines? Or why an individual, in its attempts to survive, is concurrently but unintentionally decreasing the chances of survival for the remaining individuals in the population by decreasing the overall supply of resources available for other individuals?

Model 1: Student Experiences

These ideas are addressed in the BEAGLE Wolf–Sheep Predation activities. Figure 10.2 is a screen capture from the Wolf–Sheep Predation simulation in progress. Notice the window on the right (the "World" or the "View" in NetLogo parlance) displays where different individual wolves and sheep are in space and where the resources necessary for survival are located. Some sheep are very close to large amounts of grass, while others are in regions where there is less grass nearby. Likewise, some wolves are close to sheep (which they need to eat in order to survive), while others are further away from sheep. As time progresses, grass grows and sheep and wolves move about the ecosystem, interacting with each other. Students can track the survival of individual sheep and wolves, study their motion, energy levels, and reproduction, while concurrently comparing what is happening to the population. Tracking and analyzing the changes that occur over time in the population is supported by the realtime graph and monitor updates (shown in graphs and monitors on the bottom left side of the screen capture). It is important for students to have access to both the view and the plots in order to analyze and reason through different conditions to account for differences between what is occurring for an individual and what is occurring for the population. For example, a single individual may be thriving (surviving and reproducing) while the overall population is struggling (the total number of individuals is declining).

The interface in all BEAGLE models supports similar types of analysis (between patterns of change in both populations and individuals). Students can change various parameters in the model using sliders and switches (shown in the top left of Figure 10.2) to design experiments and test various scenarios. Students can use the model to investigate questions such as "What

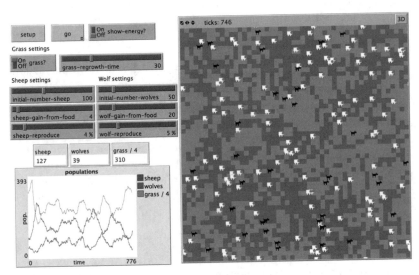

Figure 10.2 NetLogo Wolf–Sheep Predation model.

would happen if I started with more wolves?," or "How would a faster rate of grass growth affect the stability of the sheep population?," or "Why does random placement of individuals have little effect on the overall trend in the cycles in the population?," or "What is the carrying capacity of wolves in this ecosystem?"

One student, Gabrielle, who was engaged with the model, was curious whether the nature of predator–prey oscillations might depend on the parameters of the model. She wondered what would happen if she started the simulation with a very large number of sheep. She guessed that the sheep would then dominate the ecosystem.

When Gabrielle ran the program, she was in for a surprise—all of the sheep died. At first she was perplexed: she had started out with more sheep and ended up with less. We have seen many students become emotionally involved with the fate of the "creatures" in the models. Often, when they see the creatures endangered by the trough of an oscillation in the population size, they attempt to add more of the endangered creatures to ensure its survival. But, in this case, Gabrielle's attempt to help the sheep had exactly the opposite effect.

Gabrielle's initial response is an indication of a typical type of *micro–macro confusion*—between trying to achieve a group-level result by focusing only on the individuals but without considering the interaction among them. It is as if Gabrielle assumed that each sheep had a particular chance of survival, and then added more sheep to increase the chances of a large group surviving. In this way of thinking, their chances of survival just add up. But in fact, there is a feedback mechanism in the system, so that increased numbers of sheep results in increased competition for limited grass which results in reduced chances of survival for all sheep (that outweigh the compensation for the increase in numbers of sheep).

The model enables students to gain powerful insights into how interactions between the individuals within the same population indirectly affect the overall populations (of the same species and of different species). These population effects can be more clearly understood through observing and inspecting what is happening to individuals as these effects emerge within the ecosystem over time. Populations of predators, for example, undergo cyclical fluctuations that are an indirect result of their own behaviors. (The more sheep there are, the more likely it is for each individual wolf to get enough food to survive and reproduce; this in turn leads to more wolves, which eat more prey, which reduces the amount of prey available for the wolves now which allows for more grass to grow back. With the sheep population now low, less grass will be eaten and it is less likely for each wolf to find enough food to survive, which results in fewer wolves. Both of these changes benefit the sheep that survive and reproduce more frequently—and the cycle repeats.)

Reasoning about these types of indirect forces that affect survival in the model serves as an entry point to developing forms of reasoning that can connect indirect and direct competition effects to a variety of emergent outcomes in populations. Competition for limited resources itself is an important mechanism of evolution. But fluency with reasoning about indirect pressures and effects is also necessary to understand even more complex mechanisms of evolution.

Model 2: Bug Hunt Drift

Other sets of introductory models and activities in the BEAGLE curriculum help build familiarity with important mechanisms related to evolution. For example, selective breeding models introduce students to mechanisms that include selection, variation, inheritance, and time. The interaction of these mechanisms in the context of selective breeding helps provide students a basic model of selection that can be expanded on to account for changes that emerge from other forms of selection such as genetic drift.

Genetic drift is a powerful form of selection and, though not well known to the public, it is one of the primary mechanisms of evolution. The phenomenon of genetic drift is the result of purely random selection events or interactions over time. Random interactions (either random breeding or random predation) are events that result in the removal or duplication of a trait (or set of traits) within a population. Within a population where such random events are continually occurring, some traits are carried into future generations while others, over time, disappear.

To explore this emergent outcome, each student uses the Bug Hunt Drift model (Novak & Wilensky, 2008). In this model, a student adopts the role of a "selective agent" and then transitions to the role of a "random agent" and eventually to the role of an observer of "random agents." Students initially use their mouse to select bugs from a multi-colored population of bugs that are moving randomly around the screen. Students can select bugs they wish to die or bugs they wish to reproduce (create an identical offspring). They can be given a variety of scenarios or goals, such as "How long does it take you to generate a population with only one variation of the color trait?" If a bug dies, a new offspring bug is automatically created that is an exact duplicate in color to a randomly selected bug (of the remaining bugs in the population). Likewise, if a student adds a bug (by selecting a bug to have an offspring), another randomly selected bug is removed from the population.

Alternatively, students can also employ progressively more random selection mechanisms for which bug they are selecting, thereby removing themselves from the selection process. One such scenario gives students a "color blind" view of the population of bugs, but keeps them in control of which bug to select for reproduction or removal. Another scenario available to students is automated random removal or reproduction of individuals. Both of these "blind" mechanisms (for randomly selecting bugs to remove or reproduce) result in genetic drift. One mechanism keeps students in a more participatory role, and the other moves the students to more of an observer role in the simulation.

Model 2: Emergent Phenomenon—Genetic Drift

Accounting for how intentional selection (e.g., selective breeding) can lead to changes in frequencies of trait variations in populations is a more straightforward form of reasoning than trying to account for how random selection in a population can lead to the same outcome. Becoming familiar with random interactions and how they lead to similar emergent outcomes is critical to understanding genetic drift. Many types of random interactions (such as random reproduction or random predation) always lead to a similar outcome in populations—loss of genetic diversity and eventually the emergence of only a single variant of a trait in a population over time. Different initial conditions (e.g., size of the population) and different sequences of interactions result in different pathways or histories of events that lead to this outcome (sometimes genetic drift takes longer to observe than other times, due to its basis in random events). Different trait variants disappear from the population in different amounts of time, in part due to the accumulated effect of the random interactions: some cause relative trait frequencies to increase, while other interactions cause them to decrease. And these differences in initial conditions and sequence of interactions will also yield an unpredictable end state for each model run (the resulting population may be one color at the end of a model run one time, e.g., green, and a different color the next time the same experiment is performed, e.g., blue).

Initially, it is difficult for students to understand the similarities and differences in outcome across model runs, without conducting multiple experiments and carefully monitoring their experience with the vast number of interactions that occur within the population. For example, a similar outcome in every model run is that there is a loss of diversity. However, there is a difference in outcome for each run—the final bug color (or colors) is different for different runs and is unpredictable. The length of time for each model run to result in a single-colored bug population also varies from run to run. For example, in a relatively small population of 60 bugs, on average, it takes more than 1,000 clicks to remove all but one type of variation, but sometimes it takes more and sometimes less.

Model 2: Student Experiences

Students are led through three scenarios, each employing different selection mechanisms. In the first scenario, students are asked to start with a multi-colored bug population and try to produce a single-colored bug population by selecting individual bugs for either reproduction or death. Students observe that selecting a bug for reproduction always results in a bug with exactly the same trait produced (a clone) from the parent selected. At the same time a random bug is removed from the population. The student knows the color of the new bug since they are intentionally selecting for it. And so with each single selection, the student can observe the resulting shift in the distribution of traits in the population and also observe how changes in the population accumulate over time (Figure 10.3).

Repeating this selection over time, the target color for the student becomes more prevalent in the population, but the progress toward a completely uniform color in the population does not move at a steady rate. Sometimes the colors that are almost gone from a population rebound in frequency, and sometimes they disappear quickly. The non-linear route toward eliminating other colors from the population helps students recognize how random selection converges on a different end state each time, through a different path, but with the same general pattern of result.

After repeating this selection process as a predator, the user then studies how his or her own actions (when blinded to their effect) would again lead to the same genetic drift outcome. Shifting their predator abilities so that they may still select individuals to reproduce or remove from the population, but now using "color blind" eyesight, leads to the same end result, although the path to the result is different. Random variations in trait frequencies are slow to accumulate (since there is no preferred selection being performed by the student), but even minor changes in frequencies tend to cascade into increases in probabilities of further genetic drift. For example, a doubling of the number

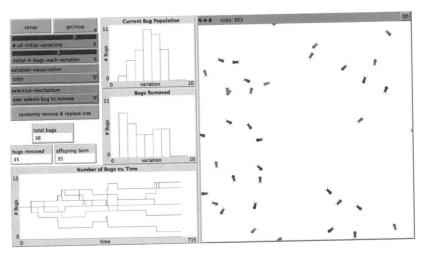

Figure 10.3 NetLogo Bug Hunt Drift.

of red individuals in the populations, and a halving of the number of blue individuals, makes the odds of selecting a red bug for removal far greater than that of selecting a blue bug. So while in this scenario the time to achieve the outcome is greater, requiring many more interactions than with intentional selection, the outcome is similar—a diverse population with many traits becomes a population with only one trait over many "generations."

From here, students explore a third variant scenario using "automated rules" for random (e.g., blind) removal of individuals. By automating the computer to perform selection on individual bugs (e.g., one a second), the student shifts to an observer of the ecosystem, watching the population as a whole as it changes over many generations. These shifts in perspective of how the selection is done (selection as an intentional first person mechanism, unintentional first person mechanism, or unintentional third person mechanism) and comparison of the results of each scenario helps students to appreciate the power of genetic drift and understand that it can arise from a variety of different mechanisms.

One student, Nicholas, exploring this automated selection scenario, initially predicted that random selection would cause trait variations to disappear. This prediction is correct, but his reasoning was connected to the idea of migration events in the real world and an intuition about small populations having less diversity, instead of the role of random selection and changing proportions of trait variations.

When he first explored the model in the first scenario, he directly engaged in the selection process. He made a noticeable effort to intentionally select different-colored bugs with each mouse click. Then when he switched to "color blind" mode, he changed his predicted outcome. At this point, three of the six initial color variations were no longer in the population, but these three variations had been relatively stable for some time during the exploration. "I think it [number of bugs] will just go down to a few bugs for each [color] and then go up and down [fluctuate]." He then switched to automated computer selection and noticed that one of the colors of bugs did disappear and decided to run the model again to see if this would happen again, then stated: "Ok … so not as many bugs have that [color] disappear. One trait would disappear because less bugs had the trait … cause they keep getting selected and then it's down to one and then none and now there is only the others [colors]. It's the one that's not most likely for the offspring, probably because the parent or grandparent didn't have that trait." Here he was starting to connect the relative proportions of the trait in the population to his predicted outcome, recognizing that the previous history of selection in the population is changing these proportions which further influences the chances of what will happen next.

When asked to predict how changing the population size would affect the population, he initially predicted larger populations would show genetic drift more quickly. But immediately upon restarting the model with a larger population size, he revised his prediction and reasons: "There is more of each [color] population, so it takes longer for each trait to die out." And when, subsequently, asked to make a prediction for a smaller population size he stated: "One trait would disappear quicker because less bugs had the trait." Notice how his reasoning has changed to account for the role of proportions of trait variations in the population. The Project 2061 document *Benchmarks for Science Literacy* (American Association for the Advancement of Science, 1993) argues that in order to understand evolution students need to "shift from thinking in terms of selection of individuals with a trait to changing proportions of a trait in populations." This is what Nicholas has started to do in his exploration of genetic drift with this BEAGLE model.

Model 3: Bug Hunt Camouflage and Bug Hunters Camouflage

In the Bug Hunt Camouflage model (Novak & Wilensky, 2006a), students explore how the interplay of predator actions and environmental conditions can lead to natural selection. The emergent phenomenon in this model is that natural selection develops camouflaging for the bugs—that a population hunted by a predator can develop camouflage to increase their chances of survival. For example, in a forest rife with green leaves, green bugs emerge as the predominant bug color.

Using this model, students are placed in the role of a predator to experience how their predatory actions can lead to the emergent outcome of a "more fit" population of prey over time. As a student "bug hunts" (by clicking on bugs in the environment as fast as they can) they play the part of a predator. Students are simply trying to find and eat bugs as fast as they can (so they do not starve from lack of food), without consciously choosing a particular set of traits in one bug over another.

Each bug in the model has an individual genotype that determines the relative proportion of red, green, and blue pigments it produces. This genotype results in a single phenotype (its visible color as produced on the screen). When a bug is eaten, a new one replaces it. This new bug is reproduced asexually from a parent in the remaining population. The new bug has a near duplicate genotype to its parent but with a slight mutation in the proportions of red, green, and blue pigments that it produces.

Since the student naturally uses color and shape to identify the location of prey in an environment, color grants a level of survival fitness for the bugs in a given environment. Environments are real-world photographs of natural settings that are displayed in the background of the model view. If some prey tends to blend into the background photo better, it is more likely to evade detection and survive longer and reproduce more often. If this continues over many generations, the distribution of colors in a population will tend to shift to become better camouflaged in the surrounding environment. The resulting color may give the bugs a competitive advantage for blending into the surrounding environment, but may or may not give them such an advantage in another environment. The environment can be changed, selecting from a large number of different photorealistic backgrounds.

Model 3: Emergent Phenomenon—Natural Selection

To understand natural selection, students need to connect their understanding of how variation of heritable characteristics exists within every species, to the idea that some of these characteristics give individuals an advantage over others in surviving and reproducing in certain environments. The advantaged offspring then, in turn, are more likely than others to survive and reproduce. And, as the proportion of individuals that have advantageous characteristics increases, the competitive advantage of the population also increases. In this manner the characteristics of the bug population do not drift randomly, but move in a general direction that makes them more fit for their environment than the previous generation (most of the time).

When a predator uses color and shape to identify the location of prey in an environment, then the colors and patterns in the environment provide additional selective pressure on the prey. If some prey tend to blend into the background better, they tend to survive longer and reproduce more often. If this continues over many generations, the distribution of colors in a population may shift to become better camouflaged in the surrounding environment. The contribution of mutation can further speed this process, since it can introduce variations that may not have been present in the original population or that were removed because they were not well suited for the previous environment, or it can reintroduce variations that were in the original population, but were removed through the effects of genetic drift.

From previous model explorations in BEAGLE, students will have become increasingly proficient at shifting their reasoning back and forth between individuals (micro reasoning) and populations (macro reasoning). Furthermore, the role of random interactions will have been explored in previous models and can be extended at this point to account for the effect of mutations. They will also have reasoned about how competition is an emergent phenomenon within any population that shares needs for the same resources. What they need to explore further are two new ideas: (1) that certain traits can grant a "competitive advantage" to the survival of individuals in particular environments, making it more likely that organisms with those traits will be more likely than others to survive and have offspring, and (2) that mutations result in new variations of traits within the population, some of which are more advantageous, some of which are less advantageous, and some of which grant little or no competitive advantage.

Model 3: Student Experiences

In one variation of this model, called Bug Hunters Camouflage (Novak & Wilensky, 2006b), students use HubNet to connect their individual computers to participate and interact with each other in a single NetLogo host model. To do this, a single user (teacher or student) launches the host model that other client computers will connect to. A screenshot of this model is shown in Figure 10.4a.

The person who launches the host model then accepts clients who join the model from across a network. Each client who joins (one per student) receives a HubNet Client Window to use to interact with the model. This Client Window looks similar to the host model, but has fewer interface elements for controlling the setup and start of the simulation. A screen shot of the client window is shown in Figure 10.4b.

Each student who receives a Client Window is given control of a single agent in the model. In Bug Hunters Camouflage, each student controls a predator. All the students simultaneously compete for finding prey in the same ecosystem by clicking on the same population of bugs that appear on their screen. When one student finds a bug and clicks on it, it is removed from the screen of all the clients. This classroom-wide competition for the same resources (bugs) is the mechanism that drives the emergence of camouflaging in the bugs. The students' own actions are responsible for generating natural selection. And the harder they compete against each other, the quicker the effects of natural selection emerge.

We observed the use of this model in a seventh and an eighth grade classroom. The students' joy of participating in a risk-free form of competition and

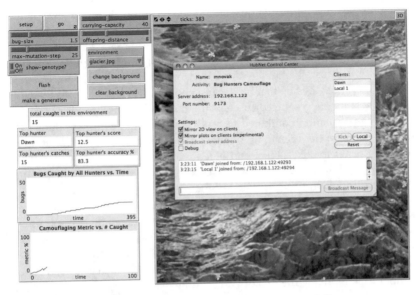

Figure 10.4a NetLogo Bug Hunters Camouflage (host model).

Figure 10.4b NetLogo Bug Hunters Camouflage (HubNet Client Window).

their sense of play generated high levels of engagement. For five minutes, their verbal interactions mimicked the sound and feel of a playground, even while each student was focused closely on their own client interface and the dynamics of the simulation. One student asked the whole class "Who is winning?," while another student responded that the lead (winning) hunter (or "top predator") had just changed. A third student complained that someone just ate "his bug" (i.e., the bug that he was just about to eat).

As the students competed to consume bugs, asexual reproduction of the remaining population continued to replace those eaten with near duplicates of individuals in the remaining population (with random slight variation of offspring genes for red, green, and blue pigmentation). This led to an unexpected result. Since the students tended to eat the easier to see bugs more often, the population that remained became more and more difficult to see over time. Soon some students were claiming they couldn't find any more bugs or that the bugs had simply disappeared (even though there is a constant number of bugs in the environment). The second author, who was the instructor in an eighth grade class, paused the model for a moment and pressed a button in the interface that highlighted where the "hidden" bugs were (by temporarily removing their color and creating brief flashes of white and black at their location). The students' responses were a mix of surprise and puzzlement as they now had been cued into where to look for the bugs. "They blended in," said some students in unison. The teacher then changed the environmental background from a picture of a beach (with pastel-colored shells) to a poppy flower field (with a bright green and red palette dominating the composition of the photo). The same population of bugs was now much more visible against this background. He asked the students to predict what would happen to the population of bugs over time if they hunted them again. There was a debate about what would result. The teacher then asked students to make a specific claim about what would happen the next time and to gather evidence to support or reject their claim. After issuing this challenge and conducting the supporting student activity sheet, where students carefully analyzed and recorded the changes that occurred and discussed (with a partner) possible mechanisms for such change, the teacher led a discussion identifying the new scientific principles that were emerging from the model, drawing on experiences of the whole class. These principles were (1) the variability of traits in offspring increases due to mutation; (2) selection by predators within a particular environment results in removal of easy to hunt variations of the trait over time; and (3) the continued removal of easy to hunt variations and birth of individuals with hard to hunt variations of the trait results in a preferential shift in the distribution of traits in the population so that all subsequent generations of individuals become progressively harder to find over time. Students in the class were then prompted to suggest some ways to test these principles with the model. Some asked to run the model again from the start to see if the exact same outcome would result—and were surprised when a similar, but not exactly identical, result emerged most of the time (camouflaging, but of distributions of different hue, saturation, or brightness). Another student suggested a class-wide coordinated attempt to force the emergent result of the model in a different direction by having everyone try to hunt the ones that blend in and leave the easy to find colored ones behind to see if they can intentionally drive the selection process in the opposite direction compared to when they were unintentionally causing camouflaging to emerge.

Model 4: Bug Hunt Coevolution

The Bug Hunt Coevolution model (Novak & Wilensky, 2007) returns to the study of a simple ecosystem. In this model, the ecosystem consists of two populations—a population of prey (bugs) and a population of predators (birds). It is a model that supports multiple roles for the student. In one role the student can assume the role of a single predator in the ecosystem, directly responsible for generating different types of selective pressures on a population through her own actions as the predator. In another role, the student can assume the role of an outside observer of predators and prey (similar to the Wolf–Sheep Predation model), watching individuals interact, compete, and eventually evolve over time.

When students assume the role of a sole predator, they again attempt to hunt bugs in the world, using their mice to click on bugs. In this scenario, bugs have genetic information for a trait that represents their speed of movement. When the student hunts bugs by chasing after them, they unwittingly select for faster moving bugs (which are harder to catch) and select against slower moving bugs (which are easier to catch). When the student changes the hunting strategy they use to catch bugs by waiting for bugs to come to them (placing the mouse down at a fixed location and clicking on all bugs that arrive where they are positioned), the student unwittingly is now selecting for slower moving bugs (which arrive less often at their location) and selecting against faster moving bugs (which run into the student's mouse cursor more often).

After exploring the opposing selective pressures that the student can generate by simply changing their predation strategies, the student shifts to the role of an observer, watching what happens when both prey and predators (bugs and birds) are allowed to evolve in tandem without intervention by a person playing the part of the predator. Automated bugs and birds (similar to the wolf and sheep in the first model) move about the screen. Unlike the first model, there is variation in the traits for how fast the organisms move and the "depth of vision" of each organism. And further variation for these traits can arise from random mutations in offspring of individuals in the population (for example a fast moving bug may have an offspring that is either the same speed, slightly slower, or slightly faster). Likewise, the depth of vision trait which determines how far away a bug or bird can see a potential target within a cone of vision (if they are a predator it is the distance at which they can see prey, and if they are a prey it is the distance at which they can see a predator) also has a variety of values in both the predator and prey population. Predators (birds) use this trait to help them follow prey (bugs) they can see, and prey (bugs) use this trait to help detect when to turn away from predators (birds) they can see.

The model yields a variety of rich coevolutionary outcomes, depending on the environment (the size of the world) and the rates of mutation of the genes for the traits (settable by the student). For example, both the predator and prey coevolve increasingly faster rates of movement in the model. However, under the same model settings, the prey will evolve an optimal vision value that is between the minimum and maximum possible values. Vision that is too nearsighted does not permit the prey to see predators in time to avoid them, but alternatively vision that is too farsighted causes the prey to overreact to predators that aren't near enough to catch them, forcing them to turn into the path of predators that are chasing them. There is selective pressure for reacting to prey quickly as well as an opposing selective pressure to not overreact.

Model 4: Emergent Phenomenon—Coevolution

The bug and bird coevolution model returns students to a familiar context, predator and prey interactions. By returning to a variation of the original model they explored with wolves and sheep, students' experiences are scaffolded to help connect their initial ideas about individuals, populations, and competition to the mechanisms of selection they discovered in the other models (genetic drift and natural selection). The coevolutionary "arms race" that emerges through interactions of simple automated predators and prey can be explained through careful reasoning about strings of indirect effects between individuals and populations and connecting these to previously learned mechanisms of natural selection (Dawkins, 1998; Hillis, 1991; Ottino-Loffler, Rand, & Wilensky, 2007; Ridley, 1993). For example, an increase in speed, due to random variation, of the offspring of a few bugs results in a slightly different selective pressure on birds; if a bird with a variation of a trait that gives it a competitive disadvantage does not catch enough bugs it will eventually die. The competition between birds for this population of bugs results in selective pressure for faster birds and birds with optimal eyesight. Each interaction of bird with bug reinforces this dynamic, causing a selective pressure on the predators, which results in a population with greater competitive advantage in its trait variations over time, which causes increased selective pressure on the prey, which results in a greater competitive advantage in the trait variations in this population. And so the cycle of interactions continually repeats, reinforcing and speeding up the effects of natural selection through positive feedback.

Model 4: Student Experiences

Students can change and experiment with each of the elements in this model. They can control how fast prey reproduce by taking the role of the predator. They can adjust the rate of mutation for individual genes in the prey and predator. They can adjust the strategies that the predators and prey use to react to each other when they see each other. And they can adjust the size of the environment and the carrying capacity of the ecosystem. Each of these adjustments often leads to different coevolutionary outcomes.

Figure 10.5a is a screen shot of the model for one setting a student was using. Notice the graphs in the bottom left of the model interface. They show that the populations of predators and prey have already undergone substantial evolution. Figure 10.5b shows a zoomed in graph of the average speed vs.

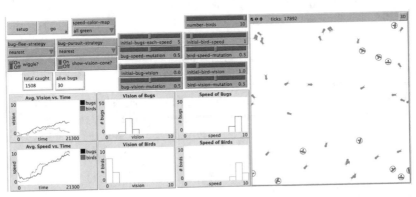

Figure 10.5a The NetLogo Bug Hunt Coevolution model.

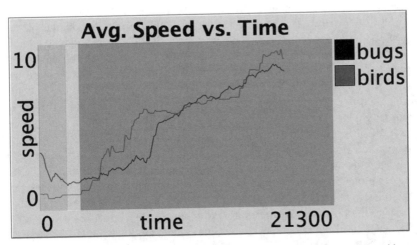

Figure 10.5b A zoomed view of a graph at the bottom left of the Bug Hunt Coevolution model.

time for both the birds and bugs. Notice that in the first shaded interval on the graph, bird speed is evolving to become slower. Fast bird speeds are disadvantageous at this point in the model run. This is due in part to the fact that birds have poor vision during this portion of the model run. As bird vision evolves to become better, eventually a point is reached where bird speed is no longer decreasing. This occurs during the next shaded interval on the graph. Here bug speed is increasing some, but bird speed is not. Then in the last shaded interval on the graph both bug and bird speed increase over time at nearly the same rate. Both populations are coevolving to become faster and faster, since it is disadvantageous for either prey or predator to have a slower speed than the other. Studying the histograms of each population, students can see the relative proportion of different traits and also watch this change in real time as the model continues to run.

Students are asked to account for various evolutionary outcomes in this model using the scientific principles they have developed in the previous activities and models. They account for, explain, and support their explanations with evidence from the model for various questions, such as: "What causes bugs to become faster over time?"; "Why do bugs evolve different speeds of movement, depending on whether they can see or not?"; "Birds and bugs are both changing over time, what is causing each of them to change?"

When using a simpler variation of this model (Bug Hunt Speeds; Novak & Wilensky, 2005) that included only speed variation but not vision, students in a class of eighth graders investigated the question, "What causes bugs to become faster over time?" In a whole class discussion at the end of the student explorations, one student suggested that maybe the bugs were trying to get away from the birds. Many other students immediately challenged that claim, arguing that the bugs could not see the predators and that their actions were completely random. When intentionally pressed by the second author, to try to get students and the class as a whole to use (misuse) a Lamarckian explanation for changes they perceived (e.g., that since the bugs were trying to go fast, their offspring would be faster), the students in class agreed by consensus that they had no evidence for this since everything they observed suggested the change in speed of the offspring bugs was wholly random. Other students suggested that the effect of a faster moving population over time was quite simple, explaining that if you remove the easy to catch individuals and duplicate the faster individuals, eventually the only thing you will have left in the population would be fast moving individuals. When the teacher pressed these students on the choice of the word "eventually," typical responses included explanations that took account both of the inevitability (and obviousness) of the outcome and of the uniqueness in the possible series of interactions that leads to the outcome. Furthermore, other students explained that the reason the outcome could take longer sometimes would be due to whether you were particularly unlucky/lucky as to which speeds (individuals with a particular trait) were reproducing when you were hunting.

This ability to reason about changes in individuals and populations over larger spans of time, to connect how selective pressure, variation, and inheritance results in populations more fit to survive, is not an intuitive form of reasoning for most of us. But the reasoning and discussion of students who have explored BEAGLE models and activities suggests an increased level of literacy regarding the mechanisms of evolution that would have been difficult to develop without the use of agent-based models.

Concluding Remarks

In this chapter we have described the design rationale of BEAGLE and presented four cases of its use in a classroom context. Each case centered on a single BEAGLE model and was designed to present the target evolutionary concepts as emergent phenomena. To review, we started with the Wolf–Sheep Predation model which targets population fluctuations. We followed with Bug Hunt Drift which targets the fixation of a trait in a population without selection. Bug Hunt Camouflage and its participatory simulation activity places students in the role of direct "natural" selecters, targeting natural selection as an emergent process. Finally, we presented Bug Hunt Coevolution, targeting positive feedback mechanisms that lead to evolutionary arms races. These four vignettes demonstrate how agent-based modeling can be used for learning and teaching about evolution. The BEAGLE curriculum contributes two principal innovations: (1) conceptualizing evolutionary phenomena, mechanisms, and processes as emergent, and (2) employing agent-based models both to represent individuals in a population and as microworld environments in which students can explore and experiment with evolutionary scenarios.

Our observations of students engaged with the BEAGLE materials lead us to believe that these two innovations can be highly effective—both in getting students deeply engaged with and excited by evolution and in developing in them a sophisticated understanding of how evolution works. Students learn to think about evolution emergently, to look for the individual-level mechanisms that might account for an evolutionary change, and to test if those mechanisms can plausibly account for the results. In this way the students are not just learning historical evolutionary accounts but are engaged as young scientists, as evolutionary theorists.

The BEAGLE project is ongoing and further models are in development. We continue to engage in a cycle of designing, testing, and refining the BEAGLE materials. The research reported on herein is preliminary yet highly suggestive. We are now engaged in more formal research, including the development of interview protocols and rubrics, in-depth interviews of students before, during, and after using BEAGLE models, and systematic classroom implementations of BEAGLE at several levels of instruction. We are investigating many questions such as what level of scaffolding to give the students, how to deliver the supporting materials, what is the right mix of individual models and participatory simulations, and can the same models be used at multiple levels of instruction? We are hopeful that widespread access to an emergent agent-based approach to learning about evolution will enable students to overcome the significant cognitive obstacles to understanding evolutionary processes and mechanisms and, leading to increasing widespread sophistication in understanding of and appreciation of the importance of evolution.

Acknowledgments

The work reported on herein was supported by National Science Foundation grants (REC-0126227, HCC-0713619) as well as a National Academy of Education Spencer Post-doctoral Fellowship.

We gratefully acknowledge the help and advice of Bill Rand, Seth Tisue, Forrest Stonedahl, Michelle Wilkerson, and Aditi Wagh on the development of the BEAGLE curriculum. Gregory McGlynn and Nathan Nichols contributed additional work on model development. LouEllen Finn, Garth Fowler, and Pratim Sengupta gave valuable feedback on BEAGLE materials. We are also grateful to Keetra Tipton for piloting the curriculum materials in her classroom, to the editors of this volume for their valuable suggestions, and to Joseph Wanka for extensive editorial help with the manuscript.

Notes

1. Many of the BEAGLE models can be downloaded from http://ccl.northwestern.edu/simevolution/beagle.shtml. Some instructions for using the models are embedded in the information tab of the models. Much more extensive materials and a BEAGLE curriculum for middle and high school have been piloted in secondary school and university classes and are expected to be published in the near future. If you wish to pilot the materials, please contact us at oas@ccl.northwestern.edu.
2. All models in the NetLogo model library have information tabs that provide background and guidance to users.

References

Abrahamson, D., & Wilensky, U. (2004). ProbLab: A computer-supported unit in probability and statistics. In M. J. Høines & A. B. Fuglestad (Eds.), *Proceedings of the 28th annual meeting of the International Group for the Psychology of Mathematics Education* (Vol. 1, p. 369). Bergen, Norway: PME.

Abrahamson, D., & Wilensky, U. (2005). ProbLab goes to school: Design, teaching, and learning of probability with multi-agent interactive computer models. In M. Bosch (Ed.), *Proceedings of the Fourth Congress of the European Society for Research in Mathematics Education* (pp. 570–579). Universitat Ramon Llull: FUNDEMI IQS.

American Association for the Advancement of Science. (1993). *Benchmarks for Science Literacy*. New York: Oxford University Press.

Blikstein, P., & Wilensky, U. (2004). MaterialSim: An agent-based simulation toolkit for materials science learning. *Proceedings of the International Conference on Engineering Education*, Gainesville, Florida. Archived at www.succeed.ufl.edu/icee/Papers/402_BliksteinICEEFinalPaper_(3).pdf.

Blikstein, P., & Wilensky, U. (2006). A case study of multi-agent-based simulation in undergraduate materials science education. *Proceedings of the Annual Conference of the American Society for Engineering Education*, Chicago, IL, June 18–21. Archived at www.asee.org/acPapers/code/getPaper.cfm?paperID=10906&pdf=2006Full2496.pdf.

Blikstein, P., & Wilensky, U. (2007, April). *Bifocal modeling: A framework for combining computer modeling, robotics and real-world sensing.* Paper presented at the Annual Meeting of the American Educational Research Association, Chicago, IL.

Blikstein, P., & Wilensky, U. (2009). An atom is known by the company it keeps: A constructionist learning environment for materials science using multi-agent simulation. *International Journal of Computers for Mathematical Learning, 14*(1), 81–119.

Carpenter, W. (1871). *Water not convex, the earth not a globe.* William Carpenter.

Centola, D., McKenzie, E., & Wilensky, U. (2000). Survival of the groupiest: Facilitating students' understanding of the multiple levels of fitness through multi-agent modeling—The EACH project. *Interjournal Complex Systems, 337*.

Centola, D., Wilensky, U., & McKenzie, E. (2000). A hands-on modeling approach to evolution: Learning about the evolution of cooperation and altruism through multi-agent modeling—The EACH project. In B. Fishman & S. O'Connor-Divelbiss (Eds.), *Proceedings of the Fourth International Conference of the Learning Sciences* (pp. 166–173). Mahwah, NJ: Erlbaum.

Dawkins, R. (1998). Universal Darwinism. In D. Hull & M. Ruse (Eds.), *The philosophy of biology* (pp. 15–37). Oxford: Oxford University Press. (First published 1983.)

Evans, E. M. (2001). Cognitive and contextual factors in the emergence of diverse belief systems: Creation versus evolution. *Cognitive Psychology, 42*, 217–266.

Gallup. (2008). As reported in www.pollingreport.com/science.htm.

Gee, H. (2000). *Deep time: Cladistics, the revolution in evolution.* London: Fourth Estate.

Gilbert, N., & Troitzsch, K. G. (2005). *Simulation for the social scientist.* Berkshire, England: Open University Press, McGraw-Hill Education.

Hillis, W. D. (1991). Co-evolving parasites improve simulated evolution as an optimization procedure. In C. Langton, C. Taylor, J. D. Farmer, & S. Rasmussen (Eds.), *Artificial Life II, SFI Studies in the Sciences of Complexity* (pp. 313–324). Boulder, CO: Westview Press.

Holldobler, B., & Wilson, E. O. (1991). *The ants.* Berlin: Springer-Verlag.

Klopfer, E. (2003). Technologies to support the creation of complex systems models—Using StarLogo software with students. *Biosystems, 71*, 111–123.

Levy, S. T., Novak, M., & Wilensky, U. (2006, April). *Students' foraging through the complexities of the particulate world: Scaffolding for independent inquiry in the connected chemistry (MAC) curriculum.* Paper presented at the Annual Meeting of the American Educational Research Association, San Francisco, CA.

Levy, S. T., & Wilensky, U. (2008). Inventing a "mid-level" to make ends meet: Reasoning through the levels of complexity. *Cognition and Instruction, 26*(1), 1–47.

Levy, S. T., & Wilensky, U. (2009a). Crossing levels and representations: The Connected Chemistry (CC1) curriculum. *Journal of Science Education and Technology, 18*(3), 224–242.

Levy, S. T., & Wilensky, U. (2009b). Students' learning with the Connected Chemistry (CC1) curriculum: Navigating the complexities of the particulate world. *Journal of Science Education and Technology, 18*(3), 243–254.

Numbers, R. L. (1992). *The creationists: The evolution of scientific creationism.* Berkeley, CA: University of California Press.

Ottino-Loffler, J., Rand, W., & Wilensky, U. (2007, July). *Co-evolution of predators and prey in a spatial model.* Paper presented at the 2007 Genetic and Evolutionary Computation Conference (GECCO), London, England.

Papert, S. (1980). *Mindstorms: Children, computers, and powerful ideas.* New York: Basic Books.

Penner, D. E. (2000). Explaining systems: Investigating middle school students' understanding of emergent phenomena. *Journal of Research in Science Teaching, 37,* 784–806.

Playfair, J. (1803). *Transactions of the Royal Society of Edinburgh,* Vol. V, Pt. III, 1805, quoted in *Natural History,* June 1999.

Railsback, S. F., Lytinen, S. L., & Jackson, S. K. (2006). Agent-based simulation platforms: Review and development recommendations. *Simulation, 82,* 609–623.

Resnick, M. (1994). Changing the centralized mind. *Technology Review, 97*(5).

Resnick, M., & Wilensky, U. (1993, April). *Beyond the deterministic, centralized mindsets: A new thinking for new science.* Paper presented at the Annual Meeting of the American Educational Research Association, Atlanta, GA.

Ridley, M. (1993). *The red queen: Sex and the evolution of human behavior.* London: Viking.

Robson, J. F. A., & Traniello, S. K. (1995). Trail and territorial communication in social insects. In W. J. Bell & R. Carde (Eds.), *The chemical ecology of insects* (Vol. II, pp. 241–286). New York: Chapman & Hall.

Rowbotham, S. B. (1865). *Zetetic astronomy: Earth not a globe! An experimental inquiry into the true figure of the earth.* Oxford University.

Scott, E., & Branch, G. (2003). Antievolutionism: Changes and continuities. *BioScience, 53*(3), 282–285.

Sengupta, P., & Wilensky, U. (2005). N.I.E.L.S: An emergent multi-agent based modeling environment for learning physics. In F. Dignum et al. (Eds.), *Fourth International Joint Conference on Autonomous Agents and Multiagent Systems* (AAMAS 2005), July 25–29, Utrecht, The Netherlands.

Sengupta, P., & Wilensky, U. (2008a). On learning electricity in 7th grade with multi-agent based computational models (NIELS). In G. Kanselaar, J. van Merriënboer, P. Kirschner, & T. de Jong (Eds.), *Proceedings of the International Conference for the Learning Sciences, ICLS 2008* (Vol. 3, pp. 123–125). Utrecht, The Netherlands: ISLS.

Sengupta, P., & Wilensky, U. (2008b). On the learnability of electricity as a complex system. In G. Kanselaar, J. van Merriënboer, P. Kirschner, & T. de Jong (Eds.), *Proceedings of the International Conference for the Learning Sciences, ICLS 2008* (Vol. 3, pp. 258–264). Utrecht, The Netherlands: ISLS.

Sengupta, P., & Wilensky, U. (2009). Learning electricity with NIELS: Thinking with electrons and thinking in levels. *International Journal of Computers for Mathematical Learning, 14*(1), 21–50.

Stieff, M., & Wilensky, U. (2002). ChemLogo: An emergent modeling environment for teaching and learning chemistry. *Proceedings of the fifth biannual International Conference of the Learning Sciences (ICLS),* October 2002 (pp. 451–458). Seattle, WA.

Stieff, M., & Wilensky, U. (2003). Connected Chemistry—Incorporating interactive simulations into the chemistry classroom. *Journal of Science Education and Technology, 12*(3), 285–302.

Sudd, J. H. (1957). Communication and recruitment in *Monomorium pharaonis. Animal Behaviour, 5,* 104–109.

Taylor, B. (2006). The single largest oceanic plateau: Ontong Java–Manihiki–Hikurangi. *Earth and Planetary Science Letters, 241*(3–4), 372–380.

Tisue, S., & Wilensky, U. (2004, October). *NetLogo:* Design and implementation of a multi-agent modeling environment. *Proceedings of Agent 2004.* Chicago, IL.

Wilensky, U. (1997b). What is normal anyway? Therapy for epistemological anxiety. *Educational Studies in Mathematics, 2*(33), 171–202.

Wilensky, U. (1999a). *NetLogo* [computer software]. Evanston, IL: Center for Connected Learning and Computer-Based Modeling, Northwestern University.

Wilensky, U. (1999b). GasLab: An extensible modeling toolkit for exploring micro-and-macro-views of gases. In N. Roberts, W. Feurzeig, & B. Hunter (Eds.), *Computer modeling and simulation in science education* (pp. 151–178). Berlin: Springer-erlag.

Wilensky, U. (2001). *Modeling nature's emergent patterns with multi-agent languages.* Paper presented at the Eurologo 2001 Conference, Linz, Austria.

Wilensky, U., & Centola, D. (2007, November). *Simulated evolution: Facilitating students' understanding of the multiple levels of fitness through multi-agent modeling.* Paper presented at the Evolution Challenges Conference, Phoenix, AZ.

Wilensky, U., Hazzard, E., & Longenecker, S. (2000, October). *A bale of turtles: A case study of a middle school science class studying complexity using StarLogoT.* Paper presented at the meeting of the Spencer Foundation, New York.

Wilensky, U., & Rand, W. (in press). *An introduction to agent-based modeling: Modeling natural, social and engineered complex systems with NetLogo.* Cambridge, MA: MIT Press.

Wilensky, U., & Reisman, K. (2006). Thinking like a wolf, a sheep or a firefly: Learning biology through constructing and testing computational theories. *Cognition and Instruction, 24*(2), 171–209.

Wilensky, U., & Resnick, M. (1995, April). *New thinking for new sciences: Constructionist approaches for exploring complexity.* Paper presented at the Annual Conference of the American Educational Research Association, San Francisco, CA.

Wilensky, U., & Resnick, M. (1999). Thinking in levels: A dynamic systems approach to making sense of the world. *Journal of Science Education and Technology, 8*(1), 3–19.

Wilensky, U., & Stroup, W. (1999a). *HubNet* [computer software]. Evanston, IL: Center for Connected Learning and Computer-Based Modeling, Northwestern University. http://ccl.northwestern.edu/netlogo/hubnet.html.

Wilensky, U., & Stroup, W. (1999b). Learning through participatory simulations: Network-based design for systems learning in classrooms. In C. M. Hoadley & J. Roschelle (Eds.), *Proceedings of the 1999 Conference on Computer Support For Collaborative Learning, CSCL '99* (p. 80). Palo Alto, CA: ISLS.

Wilensky, U., & Stroup, W. (2000). Networked gridlock: Students enacting complex dynamic phenomena with the HubNet architecture. In B. Fishman & S. O'Connor-Divelbiss (Eds.), *Fourth Annual International Conference for the Learning Sciences* (pp. 282–289). Mahwah, NJ: Erlbaum.

Wilson, E. O. (1971). *The insect societies.* Cambridge, MA: Harvard University Press.

Witham, L. (2002). *Where Darwin meets the Bible: Creationists and evolutionists in America.* New York: Oxford University Press.

Netlogo Model References

Blikstein, P., & Wilensky, U. (2004). *MaterialSim Curriculum* (Materials Science). Evanston, IL: Center for Connected Learning and Computer-Based Modeling, Northwestern University. http://ccl.northwestern.edu/curriculum/materialsim.

Novak, M., & Wilensky, U. (2005). *NetLogo Bug Hunt Speeds model.* Evanston, IL: Center for Connected Learning and Computer-Based Modeling, Northwestern University. http://ccl.northwestern.edu/netlogo/models/BugHuntSpeeds.

Novak, M., & Wilensky, U. (2006a). *NetLogo Bug Hunt Camouflage model.* Evanston, IL: Center for Connected Learning and Computer-based Modeling, Northwestern University. http://ccl.northwestern.edu/netlogo/models/BugHuntCamouflage.

Novak, M., & Wilensky, U. (2006b). *NetLogo HubNet Bug Hunters Camouflage model.* Evanston, IL: Center for Connected Learning and Computer-Based Modeling, Northwestern University. http://ccl.northwestern.edu/netlogo/models/HubNetBug-HuntersCamouflage.

Novak, M., & Wilensky, U. (2007). *NetLogo Bug Hunt Coevolution model.* Evanston, IL: Center for Connected Learning and Computer-based Modeling, Northwestern University. http://ccl.northwestern.edu/netlogo/models/BugHuntCoevolution.

Novak, M., & Wilensky, U. (2008). *NetLogo Bug Hunt Drift model.* Evanston, IL: Center for Connected Learning and Computer-Based Modeling, Northwestern University. http://ccl.northwestern.edu/netlogo/models/BugHuntDrift.

Wilensky, U. (1997a). *NetLogo Wolf–Sheep Predation model.* Evanston, IL: Center for Connected Learning and Computer-Based Modeling, Northwestern University. http://ccl.northwestern.edu/netlogo/models/WolfSheepPredation.

Chapter 11

Teaching Evolution in a Historical Context

From the Wisdom of the Ancient Greeks to Genetic Algorithms

Michel Ferrari, Peter Lee, and Roger S. Taylor

Introduction

There is reason to be concerned about science education in America when most of the adult population does not believe in Darwin's theory of evolution by natural selection. A Gallup poll held in honor of Charles Darwin's 200th birthday (February 6–7, 2009) found that only 39% of Americans say they "believe in the theory of evolution," while 25% say they do not; 36% have no opinion either way. These attitudes are strongly related to level of education and even more so to religiousness. The problem is particularly acute at the high school level: 74% of those with a postgraduate degree believe in the theory and so do 53% of college graduates, but only 21% of those whose highest level of education is high school or less believe in evolution through natural selection.[1]

This is of concern for a variety of reasons. First, the theory of evolution is one of the most compelling and powerful explanatory models in the history of science. An understanding and appreciation of this major intellectual accomplishment is essential for scientific literacy. It also has important implications for personal health and wellbeing, such as helping to explain why vaccines work, as well as why patients should be careful to completely finish prescribed treatments of antibiotics, even if they feel better after only a few doses.

Schools are generally successful at teaching basic literacy and numeracy: Why such trouble with science education, and in particular with this theory? At the very least we would hope that those who leave high school with a basic knowledge of science should understand the overwhelming evidence in support of natural selection. In addition, we would hope students would come to understand that this theory need not undermine deep religious beliefs about the origins of the universe as created by God that many also hold to be true.

Science Education and the Nature of Science

One potential source of difficulty in learning any science is that the methods of natural science are not necessarily the way most people naturally explore complex issues. In fact, scientific inquiry is said to have a unique character that has been developed in Western culture over centuries. According to Crombie (1994, pp. 4–5), when we discuss science today, we mean a particular vision of knowledge of the natural world—one controlled by evidence and argument, rather than by custom, law, authority, revelation, or any other principle or practice. This sort of approach can be traced back to the ancient Greeks, who introduced a notion of science as a rational system in which formal reasoning coordinates with natural causes to explain how natural events necessarily follow from scientific principles, just as logical and mathematical conclusions necessarily follow from their premises. We still find this view of science today, as seen in the National Academy of Sciences definition of science as, "the use of evidence to construct testable explanations and predictions of natural phenomena, as well as the knowledge generated through this process" (National Academy of Sciences, 2008, p. 10).

Styles of Science

Crombie (1994) and Hacking (2002) propose that different styles of science have developed over time, characterized by different styles of argument and evidence, as natural philosophers and scientists pursued different kinds of questions in their efforts to explain nature as well as scientific success and failure in different domains. Crombie identifies six styles. Three investigate individual regularities:

1. The simple method of postulation (Hacking prefers the term "proof") exemplified by Greek mathematical sciences.
2. Experimentation to control population and to explore by observation and measurement.
3. Construction of hypothetical analogical models.

Three other styles investigate regularities of populations ordered in time and space:

1. Ordering varieties by comparison and taxonomy.
2. Calculus of probabilities and statistical analysis of regularities in a population.
3. Historical derivation of genetic or evolutionary development.

Notice that these styles focus on *methods* and they do not line up with particular fields of knowledge. Nor is this list meant to be exhaustive or mutually exclusive.[2]

Hacking goes further and makes the provocative claim that these different methods of investigating don't uncover objective truths about nature, but rather provide a template for what it means for something to be objectively true:

> Every style of reasoning introduces a great many novelties including new types of objects, evidence, sentences, new ways of being candidates for truth or falsehood, laws, or at any rate modalities, [and] possibilities. One will also notice on occasion, new types of classification and new types of explanations.
>
> (Hacking, 2002, p. 189)

Styles become standards of objectivity because they "get at the truth" but only in the context of the style itself, so they are "self-authenticating"; in other words, styles can evolve or be abandoned, but not refuted. They emerge over the long term, and the knowledge they produce is relatively stable, because each style has its own self-stabilization techniques that allow it to persist and endure.

Because evolution by natural selection explains how current biological forms developed from earlier simpler forms, it is a powerful example of the historical or genetic style of science—a style very different from the laboratory style of science typically taught in science classes as exemplifying "the scientific method." However, it is worth noting that intelligent design also claims to involve a genetic style of science. The essential difference is how natural selection and intelligent design combine with other styles of science. Darwinian evolution explains the historical derivation of contemporary biological forms through a statistical science of probabilities, or a modeling of historical changes; intelligent design seeks to limit historical derivation of these forms by postulating a divine origin for some fixed aspects of observed nature (Dembski, 1998, 2006).

The Challenge of Teaching the Science of Evolution

Unlike science topics that lend themselves to classroom laboratory verification, such as chemistry or physics, students can't explore Darwinian principles of historical derivation through an experimental style of science. Nor can they observe evolutionary change directly, either in class or on field trips, because evolution happens so slowly. However, computer simulations are powerful tools that can help in this regard because they allow students to run programs that simulate core evolutionary mechanisms.

Recently, Robert Pennock and his colleagues at Michigan State University have developed a computer program, Avida-ED (http://avida-ed.msu.edu), to allow students to explore evolution directly. The group adapted a research platform called Avida to permit undergraduate students to observe digital organisms called Avideans develop and evolve complex capabilities through natural selection, replication, and mutation (Holden, 2006; Pennock, 2007; Speth, Long, Pennock, & Ebert-May, 2009). Wilensky (Wilensky & Novak, this volume) has also developed software to teach principles of emergence and dynamic systems needed to understand evolution and other phenomena (e.g., electromagnetism) that rely on these concepts.

Genetic Algorithms

Another very basic way to introduce these ideas is to let students use programs such as "Is it Chance?" (Goodnight, 2002) to see genetic algorithms in action. Genetic algorithms are general search and optimization algorithms inspired by Darwinian evolutionary theory. The method was developed in the 1960s and 1970s by John Holland (1975). Because of their wide utility in tackling difficult modeling problems in science and engineering, several practical texts have been written on the subject (e.g., Ashlock, 2006; Eiben & Smith, 2003, Goldberg, 1989; Mitchell, 1998) and students can be encouraged to consult such texts if they wish to undertake a more in-depth study.

A basic genetic algorithm has the following major components:

1. A population of units.
2. A method of calculating the relative fitness of a unit within a population.
3. A method of selecting mating pairs of units based on their fitness levels.
4. A method of mixing component fragments of units, also known as crossover, to form new and possibly better units.
5. A mutation operator to avoid permanent loss of diversity within the population.

Selection applies pressure upon the population of units in ways analogous to natural selection in biological systems. Poorer performing organisms are eliminated and better performing organisms (i.e., those with greater fitness) have a greater than average chance of transmitting their genetic information to the next generation. Crossover permits units to exchange information in a way comparable to that used by a natural organism undergoing sexual reproduction. The simplest method used is called single point crossover, in which a single point is randomly chosen within a selected pair of components and then all the information (digits) to the right of this point is swapped between the two components. Finally, mutation is used to randomly change (flip) the value of single bits within individual units. Mutation is typically used very sparingly. After selection, crossover, and mutation have been applied to a current population, a new population will have been formed and the generation count is incremented by one. This process of selection, crossover, and mutation is repeated until a fixed number of generations have passed.

Genetic algorithms allow students to engage the theory of evolution in a way that permits them to gather empirical evidence in support of it. Students can manipulate the parameters of these genetic algorithms and document the sequence of historical changes, and how they converge on the most adapted response through natural selection with no need of "intelligent design."

Natural Selection as a Central Conceptual Structure in an Integrated Curriculum

Although software packages that use genetic algorithms are highly useful and educational, we believe that also allowing more advanced students to write their own genetic-algorithm-based computer programs adds another important dimension to teaching evolutionary mechanisms. Furthermore, a first-principles approach like this is a viable option for educators seeking to instill a deeper understanding of evolutionary principles as early as in high school. Not only will students learn core evolutionary and computer science concepts, they will also learn about the role of probability in modern science, which is a key element in quantum mechanics and statistical mechanics.

Designing genetic algorithms allows students to build core knowledge and understanding, rather than simply borrowing it from a textbook. The distinction between building and borrowing knowledge was framed by Marc Schwartz and Kurt Fischer (2003) and it seems particularly apt for learning foundational ideas in science and in other subjects—what Robbie Case (1998) called "central conceptual structures." Of course, it is important to build frames that can structure emerging understanding, and that is what instruction in the theory of evolution can do. It is not a matter of letting students try to discover it for themselves, but as Gardner (1999) recommends in *Disciplined Mind*, it is important to give them multiple contexts within which to experience and express their understanding, to make sure that the knowledge they build is robust.

Cao and Wu (1999) propose an application exercise for students learning about genetic algorithms using the mathematical program MATLAB (an alternative is the open source program "Octave") as part of their computer science courses. Indeed, a study by Venables and Tan (2007) shows that having students use genetic algorithms helps them understand some of the mechanisms and dynamics of natural selection, and thus helps them understand the kind of evidence that supports Darwinian natural selection as a mechanism for explaining the historical genesis of species we see today as emerging from earlier biological forms.

The use of central conceptual structures that bridge courses (e.g., biology and computer science) increases the odds that students will more deeply understand the material in both curricula, including the evolutionary mechanisms of natural selection. This approach allows important ideas to be revisited without devoting valuable learning time to re-teaching the exact same material. It also allows a more sophisticated use of technology in the schools; furthermore, ideas about evolutionary mechanisms can be visualized through simulation (making them more concrete). Designing algorithms also makes learning about evolution more active, allowing students to construct their own understanding and to challenge misconceptions. We have included a detailed example of a computer science lesson using genetic algorithms in the appendix.

Christian Fundamentalist Resistance to Darwin's Theory and Meeting the Challenge of Intelligent Design

Upton Sinclair (1935) famously wrote, "It is difficult to get a man to understand something when his salary depends upon his not understanding it." Likewise, it is difficult to get students to understand something when they think that their core beliefs depend on their not understanding it. It is sometimes claimed that Darwin's theory of evolution through natural selection necessarily leads to "godless materialism." If true, that would be a very good reason for Christian students not to believe or understand it—likewise for those who believe in many other religions. Certainly, that is what some of the leading proponents of intelligent design argue; in fact, their concerns go beyond the science of evolution. Phillip E. Johnson, program advisor to the Discovery Institute's Center for Science and Culture, and whom many consider the father of the current intelligent design movement, is quoted in Forrest and Gross (2004) as saying that intelligent design "isn't really, and never has been, a debate about science.... It's about religion and philosophy" (p. 215). Phillip Johnson originated the notorious wedge strategy reflected in the title of one of his books, *The Wedge of Truth: Splitting the Foundations of Naturalism* (Johnson, 2000). The Wedge Strategy document (n.d.), an internal memo issued by the Center for the Renewal of Science and Culture, states: "Debunking the traditional conceptions of both God and man, thinkers such as Charles Darwin, Karl Marx, and Sigmund Freud portrayed humans not as moral and spiritual beings, but as animals or machines who inhabited a universe ruled by purely impersonal forces...." (Center for the Renewal of Science and Culture, n.d.).

Wiker and Dembski (2002) amplify this point and extend its pedigree, arguing that,

> When modernity adopted Epicurean materialism as its scientific foundation ... it simply reinstated the ancient belief in the amorality of nature. The intrinsic purposefulness of nature, which was the foundation of moral claims according to the Christian natural law argument, was given the coup de grâce by Darwin.... Whatever a particular materialist may happen to desire morally, it is simply an incontrovertible fact that, with

the increasing secularization of the West, the repugnance toward abortion, infanticide, eugenics, euthanasia and sexual libertinism, which had its theoretical and historical origin in Christianity (stretching back through Judaism), has given way to acceptance. The cause for this moral reversal is secularization, and as we have seen, the cause of secularization has been the rise of Epicurean materialism as culminating in moral Darwinism.

(Wiker & Dembski, 2002, pp. 296–297)

Some academics agree with the basic argument; Clark, Foster, and York (2007), for example, agree that religious groups have been battling Epicurean materialism since before the emergence of Christianity and that Darwin does advocate this sort of fundamental materialism. But Ruse (2009) contests this view, claiming that Darwin did believe in God. Darwin's own writings support Ruse. For example, in his 1871 *Descent of Man*, Darwin wrote, "The belief in God has often been advanced as not only the greatest, but the most complete of all the distinctions between man and the lower animals" (Darwin, 1871, p. 635). In addition, in both *Origin of Species* and the *Descent of Man* Darwin always respectfully acknowledged critics who believed in intelligent design, while rebutting their claims. In *Origin of Species*, he wrote:

Authors of the highest eminence seem to be fully satisfied with the view that each species has been independently created. To my mind it accords better with what we know of the laws impressed on matter by the Creator, that the production and extinction of past and present inhabitants of the world should have been due to secondary causes, like those determining the birth and death of the individual.

(Darwin, 1859, p. 458)

A little over a decade later in *Descent of Man* (1871), Darwin adds:

I am aware that the conclusions arrived at in this work will be denounced by some as highly irreligious; but he who denounces them is bound to show why it is more irreligious to explain the origin of man as a distinct species by descent from some lower form, through the laws of variation and natural selection, than to explain the birth of the individual through the laws of ordinary reproduction. The birth both of the species and of the individual are equally parts of that grand sequence of events, which our minds refuse to accept as the results of blind chance.

(Darwin, 1871, p. 636)

Certainly, we agree with Wallace (2007), writing today, that while modern science has historically been associated with materialism, there is no necessary link between empirical scientific investigation of the natural world and materialism. By acknowledging this, and Darwin's own views, students can be shown that Darwin's theory does not contradict most forms of Christianity. In fact, the Catholic church under Popes Pius XII, Jean Paul II, and now Benedict XVI, and many mainline Protestant seminaries, believe that once God created the universe, God allowed it to evolve via natural laws—with the exception of the human soul. They have repeatedly affirmed that there is no contradiction between evolution and scripture. In this they are following a very old tradition that claims that God wrote two books: the Bible and the "book of nature." Both are the work of God and cannot contradict each other; any apparent contradiction simply shows a defect or lack in our own understanding. And both must be carefully studied to arrive at the greatest appreciation of God (Tanzella-Nitti, 2004).

Eugenie Scott, Executive Director of the National Center for Science Education and a leading opponent of intelligent design, admits that advocates of intelligent design are divided as to how design operates in nature, whether "front-loading all outcomes at the big bang, episodic intervention of the progressive creationism form, or other, less well-articulated possibilities" (Scott, 2004, p. 128). However, theistic evolution is "ruled out," despite the fact that this view is held by the Catholic church, many mainline Protestant seminaries, and probably by Darwin himself (Ruse, 2009; Scott, 2004). This shows the deeper motivations of the leaders of the intelligent design movement, but there is no reason to think that students will be so close-minded.

Teaching for Contemplative Wisdom

Allow us for a moment to go beyond what is probably possible in U.S. schools that require a strict separation of church and state—although what we say can be followed independently of any specific religious teaching. We believe that students can be more fully engaged if we integrate learning natural science with their concern for the most fundamental issues of personal meaning—in other words, if we teach for wisdom.

Teaching for wisdom does not require adding another subject matter to the curriculum, it simply means that we must guide students to consider the curriculum that is already in the schools as deeply as possible. The Dalai Lama recently proposed a very similar idea at a conference in Washington, DC on "Educating World Citizens for the 21st Century" (2009) focused on contemplative education and compassion. We wholeheartedly endorse this agenda. In fact, we propose that the medieval university curriculum—especially as understood within the 16th century humanist tradition of contemplatives like Lefèvre d'Étaples and Charles de Bovelles—can inspire a modern curriculum for wisdom. Indeed, from the ancient Greek philosophers through the medieval Christian philosophers and even into the Renaissance, science (the Latin *scientia*) and wisdom (*sapientia*) were intimately intertwined, and efforts to teach natural science were integrated into a broader program of teaching philosophy as a pursuit of wisdom. Thus, the origins of contemporary science, and by extension science education, can be traced back to the writings of those ancient philosophers (Dear, 2005; Hadot, 2002).

Science Education among the Ancient Greeks

Not much is known about how natural science (known as natural philosophy) was actually taught by the early Greeks, although we find some indications from Plato's dialogs and texts that have been written about his school (Hadot, 2002). Plato divided the pursuit of wisdom into dialectics, physics, and ethics. *Dialectics* is the science of objective reality—that is, of the Idea (*eidos*), or what we now call metaphysics. *Physics* concerned the physical manifestations of the Idea—that is, the sensed universe. *Ethics* concerned human acts within the sensed universe. Plato's division was soon replaced by Aristotle's more complete division that incorporated Aristotelian logic developed in Aristotle's own school, the Lyceum. Aristotle's scheme of wisdom studies divided science into the theoretical, practical, and poietical, according to whether their scope is purely speculative knowledge (theoria), conduct (praxis), or external production (poiêsis). *Theoretical wisdom* meant something very different than it does today, and included: (a) *physics*, or the study of physical things subject to change—including biology and thus human beings; (b) *mathematics*, or the study of corporeal properties not subject to change, considered by abstraction from matter; and (c) *metaphysics* or the study of unchangeable and incorporeal being (whether naturally or by abstraction). Aristotle gave pride of place to metaphysics, calling it "first philosophy." *Practical wisdom* included ethics, economics, and politics. *Poiêtic wisdom* included artifacts created by human intelligence, including both machines and syllogistic logic (De Wulf, 1911; Zeller, 1931).

Aristotle's classification of the sciences became famous throughout antiquity. Although eclipsed by the Platonic classification during the Alexandrine period, it reappeared in the Middle Ages and is still intuitively used by many today, albeit with changes that reflect our contemporary understanding of physics as involving objects created through evolutionary or other changes (Garber, 2001). This classification has had profound effects on how we understand the pursuit of scientific understanding and science education.

Medieval Teaching for Wisdom through Natural and Theological Science

According to the medieval and Renaissance notion of *sapientia*, inherited from the Greeks, each area of study corresponds to the study of a group of special sciences. In the Aristotelian scheme developed by Charles de Bovelles, for example, natural science (the empirical study of what is observed in nature) prepared the way for the study of mathematics (the science of universals), and ultimately for the study of metaphysics (the study of the most universal first causes). Metaphysics, in turn, prepared an individual for the knowledge of the divine (theology). Note that in this approach man is understood as part of the natural world with both psychology and biology being a subcategory of physics. Ultimately, however, mathematics provided a bridge between the natural world and the immaterial world, and many devout Christian philosophers and theologians of the time, like Bovelles, were also great mathematicians who believed that divine scripture did not contradict God's "book of nature."

This Aristotelian approach to teaching for wisdom fell out of favor with the rise of modern science and its emphasis on empirical investigation and experiment (as opposed to rational postulation and argument) (see Crombie, 1994; Smith, 2009). However, the 17th century scholar Comenius proposed a similar approach more closely aligned with modern public education, designed to educate all children, not just an elite. Comenius aimed to develop a curriculum that promotes what he called "pansophy" or universal wisdom. In his *Pansophiae prodromus* [Introduction to universal wisdom] (1637, 1642), Comenius objected to the then current educational theory as merely a "study of words" without any understanding of the nature of things—what today we might call a lack of deep understanding. Perhaps hoping to revive and deepen the original university mandate to teach for wisdom by integrating new empirical methods for gathering new knowledge, Comenius advocated integrating all verified knowledge into one harmonious and encyclopedic system that would eliminate the atomism characteristic of the fragmentary learning.

Since for Comenius all knowledge is ultimately derived from God, it must be able to be harmonized, and so there can be no fundamental contradiction between religion and science. Any apparent contradiction must be due to our own imperfect understanding of either religion or science and can be resolved by a careful comparison of one to the other (what he called the syncretic method). According to Spinka (1953; see also Piaget, 1957) this system rests on three sources of knowledge: (1) scientific study of nature (of things rather than books), (2) reasoning, or critical thinking, used to classify and interpret evidence from natural science, and (3) divine revelation through scripture. Thus, Comenius wanted a universal schooling to integrate natural science and religion in ways that did not sacrifice intellectual rigor, but did not deny the moral value of religious teachings. Students could learn from both books of nature: observed and scriptural.

Dawkins (1986), in his book *The Blind Watchmaker*, grants that before an understanding of evolution by natural selection only the ignorant would not have been awed by the complexity of biological life. At the time of Comenius, intelligent design was the best explanation available, with the greatest scientists of the day, like Isaac Newton and Rene Descartes, taking intelligent design to be self-evidently true. But today, our understanding of how order can arise from disorder, made tangible through computer simulations and genetic algorithms, shows how things that seemed possible only by design can be achieved by the operation of natural law, pushing back the religious belief requiring "miraculous involvement by God" in those processes to the very beginning of creation. It remains true, however, that ultimate questions of creation are still beyond science to answer.

From this quick historical sketch, we can see a line from the earliest efforts to teach for wisdom, to the present day science education in university and public schools. However, natural science and its associated theories, like the theory of evolution by natural selection, have become separated from other branches associated with a broader pursuit of wisdom (i.e., from other branches of natural science, metaphysics and ethics). This, we believe, is one of the main sources of resistance to Darwinian theories of evolution, and one of the main appeals of intelligent design. Unlike the modern theory of evolution, intelligent design postulates ultimate causes and their links to ethics—but without a careful consideration of the most advanced evidence about the natural world, sometimes even outright denying this evidence.

The essential point we want to make is that students are drawn to systems that claim to teach for wisdom. But to teach for wisdom today in light of what is known about the natural world through modern science (if we follow this medieval model) would begin by mastering the theories and evidence of natural science. Historically, the most advanced understandings of natural science provided a gateway to appreciating the immaterial world through mathematics modeling that informs our understanding of that world, because mathematical understanding is in fact completely abstract and immaterial. That insight, in turn, provided medieval university students a gateway to appreciating that there are mysteries about existence that even mathematics cannot grasp—what many different religions consider the unnamable divine mystery of creation.

Multiculturalism and Public Education in America

Some may object that this approach is Christian-centered and would not be applicable to multicultural schools of North America. True, the medieval universities were Christian, but this approach to teaching for wisdom is congruent with many different faiths. For example, it seems very close to the approach advocated by the Dalai Lama, who has spent decades inquiring into contemporary science—not to verify Buddhist beliefs, but to inform himself about what science has discovered about reality (Dalai Lama, 2009).

This is what we advocate in teaching for wisdom through science education today: students should learn to be intellectually honest and sophisticated in their thinking about the natural world and the human condition, without denying deep existential questions that authentically matter to how they personally live their lives. If so, then perhaps ultimately when even fundamentalist Christians are faced with the powerful evidence in support of the theory of evolution, they could agree with Seneca (*Letters* xvi: 2–5), when he writes to Lucilius:

> [T]here is no reason why you should put confidence in yourself too quickly and readily. Examine yourself; scrutinize and observe yourself in diverse ways; but mark before all else whether it is in love of wisdom or merely in life itself that you have made progress. Love of wisdom ... is a matter not of words, but of facts.... It moulds and constructs the soul [Animum]; ... Without it, no one can live fearlessly or in peace of mind. ... Perhaps someone will say 'How can love of wisdom help me, if Fate exists? Of what avail is love of wisdom, if God rules the universe? Of what avail is it, if Chance governs everything?... Whether the truth, Lucilius, lies in one or in all of these views, we must be lovers of wisdom; .... She will encourage us to obey God cheerfully, but Fortune defiantly; she will teach us to follow God and endure Chance.

What matters for students' education ultimately is not just that they learn current theories about how we came to be as biological beings—ideas now most convincingly expressed in the Neo-Darwinian mechanisms and mathematically modeled by genetic algorithms—but that they consider how as biological beings we can gain insight into what makes our lives meaningful: an embodied personal wisdom (Ferrari, 2006, 2008; Ferrari & Vultic, 2010; Staudinger, Dörner, & Mickler, 2005). By employing educational technologies such as simulations and genetic algorithms, students can see for themselves how one can improve design through the Darwinian principle of natural selection, without an intelligent designer. An integrated curriculum that connects evolution to ecology, ethics, and metaphysics could also show students how evolution matters to their own lives and to important issues in the world today. In this way, science education could teach for wisdom in a way that coordinates theory, ethics, and practice, and still acknowledge that some ultimate mysteries remain beyond science. But no matter what the latest scientific theories about the natural world, it is still critically important to learn to see ourselves as we really are—essential to Buddhist and Christian wisdom (Dalai Lama, 2005, 2007). And that is something that education should strive to encourage every student to pursue as part of their lifelong learning.

Appendix

The Proposed Genetic Algorithm: Main Components

Here, we propose the development of a basic binary genetic algorithm (following closely the genetic algorithm outlined in that it employs the core evolutionary mechanisms of variation, inheritance, and natural selection). We then propose the use of this genetic algorithm in a program that simulates the evolution of a population in two successive environments that favors organisms with certain traits over others.

Organism

The organism is a 16-bit chromosome composed of two 8-bit genes, G_X and G_Y. An example organism is shown in Table 11.1.

The *genes*, G_X and G_Y, are encodings for the organism's traits, X and Y, respectively, which can have the following range of values: $0 \leq X \leq 10, 0 \leq Y \leq 10$.

Fitness Landscape

The values of these traits determine the organism's fitness (i.e., how good or bad the organism is) in the current environment, also known as the fitness landscape. For instance, an organism with trait values $X = 3.02$ and $Y = 8.00$ has a fitness level of $F(3.02, 8.00) = 2.239$ when the equation that defines the fitness landscape is as follows:

$$F(X,Y) = 1.25 + e^{-0.4r} \cos(4r), \quad r = \sqrt{(X-3)^2 + (Y-8)^2}$$

The landscape within which these genes can evolve can be depicted graphically. We choose two genes for purposes of discussion because they can be visually depicted in a 3D graph, which is helpful to show the configuration of the landscape in a much more concrete and aesthetically engaging way. Two views are presented because they allow us to see the peak (optimum) fit at $X = 3$ and $Y = 8$ more easily (see Figure 11.1).

An outline of the program that implements the proposed genetic algorithm is given in Figure 11.2.

Illustrative Run through This Program

Here is an illustrative example of this program.

1. *First, obtain an initial population of organisms.* The population can be randomly generated or preset. For simplicity, a population of five was chosen for this example (see Table 11.2).

2. *Next, find the fitness level of each organism.* To find the fitness level, genes G_X and G_Y must first be decoded to traits X and Y, respectively. (This

Table 11.1 An Example Organism

G_Y	G_X
10110010	01111111

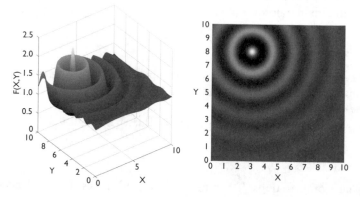

Figure 11.1 Fitness landscape. *Left*: 3D view. *Right*: Top view.

1. Obtain an initial population of organisms (generation 1)
2. Find the fitness of each member (i.e., organism) of the population
3. FOR generation = 2 TO (set number of generations)
    i. Clone the fittest organism and pass it on to a temporary population
    ii. LOOP until temporary population is filled
        Select a pair of mates
        Possibly perform crossover on the pair of offspring
        Pass the offspring pair to the temporary population
    END LOOP
    iii. Mutate the offspring organisms in the temporary population
    (except the fittest organism's clone from before)
    iv. Replace the, now old, population with the, now new, temporary
    population
    v. Find the fitness of each member of the current population
END FOR

Figure 11.2 Outline of the program that implements the proposed genetic algorithm.

Table 11.2 Initial Population of Five Organisms

	G_Y	G_X
Organism 1	10110010	01111111
Organism 2	01100110	10110010
Organism 3	01000000	01001100
Organism 4	01100110	00011001
Organism 5	11001100	01001101

Table 11.3 G_Y and G_X Decoded to Z_Y and Z_X, Respectively

	Z_Y	Z_X
Organism 1	178	127
Organism 2	102	178
Organism 3	64	76
Organism 4	102	25
Organism 5	204	77

involves a multi-step process that will make sense to any student who has completed the Ontario grade 11 or grade 12 introductory computer science courses.) The *first step* in decoding is to convert the binary-encoded genes G_X and G_Y to decimal values Z_X and Z_Y, respectively (see Table 11.3).

The *second step* needed to specify the genetic traits (X and Y) in the example is to use the following two equations to complete the decoding process:

$$X = \frac{Z_X}{2^8 - 1}(X_{max} - X_{min}) + X_{min}, X_{min} \le X \le X_{max}$$

$$Y = \frac{Z_Y}{2^8 - 1}(Y_{max} - Y_{min}) + Y_{min}, Y_{min} \le Y \le Y_{max}$$

Recall that in this example the ranges for traits X and Y are $0 \le X \le 10$ and $0 \le Y \le 10$; given that, we set X_{min}, X_{max}, Y_{min} and Y_{max} to values 0, 10, 0 and 10, respectively. (The complete decoding of the genes is shown in Table 11.4.)

Plugging the trait values X and Y into the fitness function $F(X, Y)$, defined earlier as:

$$F(X,Y) = 1.25 + e^{-0.4r}\cos(4r), \quad r = \sqrt{(X-3)^2 + (Y-8)^2}$$

we get the fitness level of each organism in the population (Table 11.5). Note that organism 5 is the most fit and organism 1 is the least fit within this fitness landscape.

Table 11.4 Z_Y and Z_X Decoded to Y and X, Respectively

	Y	X
Organism 1	6.98	4.98
Organism 2	4.00	6.98
Organism 3	2.51	2.98
Organism 4	4.00	0.98
Organism 5	8.00	3.02

Table 11.5 Fitness of Population

	Fitness
Organism 1	0.893
Organism 2	1.162
Organism 3	1.139
Organism 4	1.350
Organism 5	2.239

3.   *We now enter the FOR loop in the genetic algorithm.* This loop evolves the population, one generation at a time. As indicated in the algorithm outline in Figure 11.2, the next generation population is progressively created and temporarily stored in what we refer to as the "temporary population." Once complete, this temporary population is the offspring of the current population and becomes the parent population of the next generation. Let's consider this process now in detail.

The *first step* in creating the next generation population is to clone the fittest organism in the current population and pass it on to the temporary population.[3] Table 11.6 shows the current population in its original binary form.

The *second step* enters the inner loop, in which we fill in the temporary population. To begin filling the temporary population, we select a pair of mates. Although selection is random, it is proportional to an organism's relative fitness in the population. (In effect, the greater the organism's fitness, the higher its chance of being selected for mating.) The probability of being selected is computed as follows (a procedure also known as roulette wheel selection):

Organism 1

$$P_1 = \frac{0.893}{0.893+1.162+1.139+1.350+2.239} = 0.1317 = 13.17\%$$

Table 11.6 Pass on Clone Offspring of the Fittest Organism

	Current population			Temporary population	
Organism 1	10110010	01111111		????????	????????
Organism 2	01100110	10110010		????????	????????
Organism 3	01000000	01001100		????????	????????
Organism 4	01100110	00011001		????????	????????
Organism 5	11001100	01001101	Clone →	11001100	01001101

Organism 2

$$P_2 = \frac{1.162}{0.893 + 1.162 + 1.139 + 1.350 + 2.239} = 0.1713 = 17.13\%$$

Organism 3

$$P_3 = \frac{1.139}{0.893 + 1.162 + 1.139 + 1.350 + 2.239} = 0.1679 = 16.79\%$$

Organism 4

$$P_4 = \frac{1.350}{0.893 + 1.162 + 1.139 + 1.350 + 2.239} = 0.1990 = 19.90\%$$

Organism 5

$$P_5 = \frac{2.239}{0.893 + 1.162 + 1.139 + 1.350 + 2.239} = 0.3301 = 33.01\%$$

It should be noted that there is a chance of the same organism being chosen twice for the mating pair. This would represent a single organism producing two offspring organisms. For our first pair, let us assume that organisms 3 and 5 are chosen. Let us also assume that crossover occurs at a random single point; in other words, it can occur anywhere along the pair of genes (Table 11.7). The crossover process is responsible for much of the power of genetic algorithms and is analogous to what happens to chromosome pairs in biology.

These offspring (not yet in final form) are then passed on to the temporary population (Table 11.8).

Table 11.7 Single Point Crossover

	Parents		Offspring	
Organism 3	01000 | 000	01001100	01000 | 100	01001101
Organism 5	11001 | 100	01001101	11001 | 000	01001100

Table 11.8 Two Offspring Passed on to the Temporary Population

	Current population		Temporary population	
Organism 1	10110010	01111111	01000100	01001101
Organism 2	01100110	10110010	11001000	01001100
Organism 3	01000000	01001100	????????	????????
Organism 4	01100110	00011001	????????	????????
Organism 5	11001100	00011001	11001100	01001101

We now select another pair of parent organisms, as before, to complete filling the temporary population. Let us assume that organisms 3 and 4 are chosen (note that an organism can mate more than once). In this case, let us assume that crossover does not occur, so that the offspring are identical replicas of their parents (Table 11.9).

These offspring (not yet in final form) are then passed on to the temporary population, thereby completing it (Table 11.10).

Note that errors, called mutations, can occur during replication (i.e., during the production of offspring). This is the *third step* in the FOR loop. Although mutation rates are low, this process is important for diversifying the population. Mutations can be induced by traversing each bit in the temporary population and toggling one on a rare occasion (i.e., a bit 0 is changed to 1 or a bit 1 is changed to 0). After the mutation process is performed, the temporary population represents the actual offspring, in their final form, of the current population (Table 11.11).[4]

In *steps 4 and 5*, the offspring population now becomes the current population (i.e., generation 2). We compute the fitness of each member of this new

Table 11.9 The Production of Clone Offspring

	Parents		Offspring	
Organism 3	01000000	01001100	01000000	01001100
Organism 4	01100110	00011001	01100110	00011001

Table 11.10 Final Two Offspring Passed on to the Temporary Population

	Current population		Temporary population	
Organism 1	10110010	01111111	01000100	01001101
Organism 2	01100110	10110010	11001000	01001100
Organism 3	01000000	01001100	01000000	01001100
Organism 4	01100110	00011001	01100110	00011001
Organism 5	11001100	01001101	11001100	01001101

Table 11.11 The Current Population and its Offspring, in Final Form (Mutated Bits are Underlined and Shown in Bold)

	Current population		Temporary population	
Organism 1	10110010	01111111	01000100	01001101
Organism 2	01100110	10110010	110**1**1000	01001100
Organism 3	01000000	01001100	01000000	01001100
Organism 4	01100110	00011001	01100110	0000**0**1001
Organism 5	11001100	01001101	11001100	01001101

Table 11.12 Fitness of Generation 2 Population

	Current population		Fitness
Organism 1	01000100	01001101	1.156
Organism 2	11011000	01001100	0.995
Organism 3	01000000	01001100	1.139
Organism 4	01100110	00001001	1.389
Organism 5	11001100	01001101	2.239

population as before (Table 11.12) and start the cycle again (i.e., we go back to the beginning of the FOR loop).

Sample Simulation Runs

What does this program look like when it is run as a simulation? We now present the results of two simulation runs utilizing the genetic algorithm described above. The first simulation took a randomly generated initial population and evolved it in the fitness landscape shown in Figure 11.2. The key parameter values used for all three simulations were as follows:

Population size: 41
Probability of crossover: 0.50 or 50%
Mutation rate/probability: 0.01 or 1%
Number of generations: 3,000

Figure 11.3 shows the results of the *first simulation run*. The initial population (left) and evolved population (right) are plotted according to organism traits X and Y. It is evident that the evolved organisms became better suited to

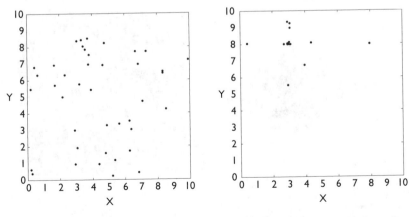

Figure 11.3 Initial population (left) and evolved population (right) from first simulation.

their current environment. In effect, they evolved traits that made them fit in the fitness landscape.

Figure 11.4 shows histogram plots of trait values X and Y for evolved organisms 1 to 41. These plots demonstrate that the population evolved to have the optimum trait values of X = 3 and Y = 8.

For the *second simulation*, we altered the fitness landscape for the evolved population from the first simulation. The main difference in this second

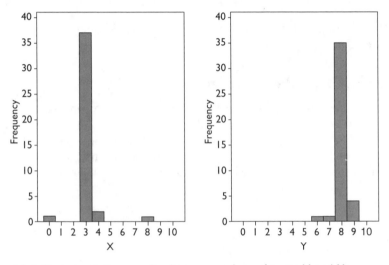

Figure 11.4 First simulation results: histogram plots of traits X and Y.

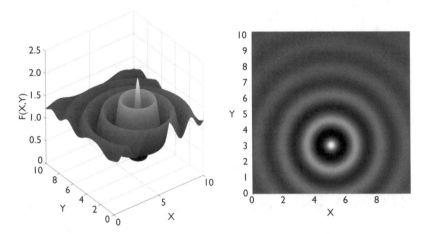

Figure 11.5 Fitness landscape for the second simulation. *Left*: 3D view. *Right*: Top view.

fitness landscape (Figure 11.5) was the set of trait values that rendered an organism fit or unfit. Optimum trait values shifted to X = 5 and Y = 3.

Figure 11.6 shows the results of the *second simulation run*. Again, the initial population (left) and evolved population (right) are plotted according to organism traits X and Y. It is clear that the population was able to evolve traits optimal for the second fitness landscape.

Figure 11.7 shows histogram plots of trait values X and Y for evolved organisms 1 to 41. These plots demonstrate that the population evolved to have the optimum trait values of X = 5 and Y = 3.

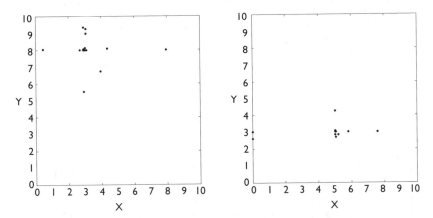

Figure 11.6 Initial population (left) and evolved population (right) from second simulation.

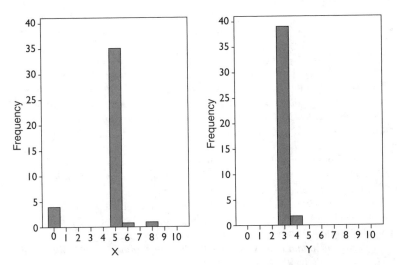

Figure 11.7 Second simulation results: histogram plots of traits X and Y.

It is clear that the population was able to evolve traits optimal for the second fitness landscape.

Notes

1. www.gallup.com/poll/114544/darwin-birthday-believe-evolution.aspx.
2. For example, a hybrid "laboratory style" combines modeling and experimentation, in that scientists build an apparatus or instrument designed to *produce* a phenomenon that will show whether their hypothetical modeling is true or false (using another layer of modeling of how the apparatus or instrument itself works).
3. This first step is optional, but it proves useful when you want to hold on to the fittest organism discovered throughout all generations. Note this step only applies to one organism in any given population. This is not true of Darwinian evolution, and is closer to the way expert knowledge or skill is carried across generations by the greatest disciples of famous teachers—one reason why so many Nobel Prize winners were students of Nobel laureates.
4. Note that we do not allow mutations to occur in the clone of the fittest organism, for obvious reasons.

References

Ashlock, D. (2006). *Evolutionary Computation for Modeling and Optimization*. New York: Springer.

Cao, Y. J., & Wu, Q. H. (1999). Teaching genetic algorithm using MATLAB. *International Journal of Electrical Engineering, 36*, 139–153.

Case, R. (1998). The development of conceptual structures. In W. Damon (Series Ed.) & D. Kuhn & R. S. Siegler (Vol. Eds.), *Handbook of Child Psychology: Vol. 2. Cognition, Perception and Language* (5th ed., pp. 745–800). New York: Wiley.

Center for the Renewal of Science and Culture (n.d.). The Wedge Strategy. Retrieved July 12, 2009 from www.public.asu.edu/ujmlynch/idt/wedge.html.

Clark, B., Foster, J., & York, R. (2007). The critique of intelligent design: Epicurus, Marx, Darwin, and Freud and the materialist defense of science. *Theory and Society, 36*(6), 515–546.

Comenius, J. A. (1637). *Pansophiae prodromus [Introduction to Pansophy]*. London.

Comenius, J. A. (1642). *A reformation of schooles designed in two excellent treatises, the first whereof summarily sheweth, the great necessity of a generall reformation of common learning: what grounds of hope there are for such a reformation: how it may be brought to passe: the second answers certain objections ordinarily made against such undertakings, and describes the severall parts and titles of workes which are shortly to follow/written any years ago in Latine by that reverend, Godly, learned and famous divine Mr. John Amos Comenius one of the seniours of the exiled church of Moravia; and now upon the request of many translated into English and published by Samuel Hartlib for the greater good of this nation.* London: Printed for Michael Sparke senior at the Blew Bible in Greene Arbor, 1642. (Available in Early English Books Online, http://eebo.chadwyck.com.)

Crombie, A. C. (1994). *Styles of Scientific Thinking in the European Tradition: The History of Argument and Explanation especially in the Mathematical and Biomedical Sciences* (3 vols). London: Duckworth.

Dalai Lama (2005). *The Universe in an Atom: The Convergence of Science and Spirituality*. New York: Morgan Road Books.

Dalai Lama (2007). *How to See Yourself as You Really Are* (trans. and ed. by Jeffrey Hopkins). New York: Simon & Schuster.

Dalai Lama (2009). Talk delivered as part of the *Educating World Citizens for the 21st Century* Mind & Life Conference. Washington, DC.

Darwin, C. (1859). *On the Origin of Species by Means of Natural Selection, or the Preservation of Favoured Races in the Struggle for Life* (1st ed.). London: John Murray.

Darwin, C. (1871). *The Descent of Man, and Selection in Relation to Sex* (1st ed.). London: John Murray.

Dawkins, R. (1986). *The Blind Watchmaker*. New York: Norton.

Dear, P. (2005). What is the history of science the history of? Early modern roots of the ideology of modern science. *Isis, 96*, 390–406.

Dembski, W. A. (1998). *The Design Inference*. Cambridge, UK: Cambridge University Press.

Dembski, W. A. (2006). Dealing with the backlash against intelligent design. In W. A. Dembski (Ed.), *Darwin's Nemesis* (pp. 81–104). Downers Grove, IL: InterVarsity Press.

De Wulf, M. (1911). Philosophy. In *The Catholic Encyclopedia*. New York: Robert Appleton Company. Retrieved January 26, 2010 from New Advent: www.newadvent.org/cathen/12025c.htm.

Eiben, A. E., & Smith, J. E. (2003). *Introduction to Evolutionary Computing*. New York: Springer.

Ferrari, M. (2006). Teaching wisdom through deep critical thinking and development of character. In K. Leithwood, P. McAdie, N. Bascia, & A. Rodrigue (Eds.), *Teaching for Deep Understanding: Towards the Ontario Curriculum that We Need* (pp. 94–102). Thousand Oaks, CA: Corwin Press.

Ferrari, M. (2008). Teaching for wisdom from around the world. In M. Ferrari & G. Potworowski (Eds.), *Teaching for Wisdom*. New York: Springer.

Ferrari, M., & Vultic, L. (2010). The intentional personal development of mind and brain through education. In M. Ferrari & L. Vuletic (Eds.), *The Developmental Interplay of Mind, Brain, and Education: Essays in Honor of Robbie Case*. Amsterdam: Springer.

Forrest B., & Gross, P. R. (2004). *Creationism's Trojan Horse: The Wedge of Intelligent Design*. Oxford: Oxford University Press.

Gallup poll (February 6–7, 2009). www.gallup.com/poll/114544/darwin-birthday-believe-evolution.aspx.

Garber, D. (2001). Descartes and the scientific revolution: Some Kuhnian reflections. *Perspectives on Science, 9*, 405–422.

Gardner, H. (1999). *The Disciplined Mind: Beyond Facts and Standardized Tests, The K-12 Education That Every Child Deserves*. New York: Simon and Schuster (and New York: Penguin Putnam).

Goldberg, D. E. (1989). *Genetic Algorithms in Search, Optimization, and Machine Learning*. Menlo Park, CA: Addison-Wesley Professional.

Goodnight, K. F. (2002). *Is it Chance? Software for Population Biology computer program*. Southern Methodist University.

Hacking, I. (2002). *Historical Ontology*. Cambridge, MA and London, England: Harvard University Press.

Hadot, P. (2002). *What is Ancient Philosophy?* (trans. M. Chase). Cambridge, MA: Belknap Press.

Holden, C. (2006). Evolution: Darwin's place on campus is secure—but not supreme. *Science, 311*(5762), 769–771.

Holland, J. H. (1975). *Adaptation in Natural and Artificial Systems.* Ann Arbor, MI: University of Michigan Press.

Johnson, P. E. (2000). *The Wedge of Truth: Splitting the Foundations of Naturalism.* Downers Grove, IL: InterVarsity Press.

Mitchell, M. (1998). *An Introduction to Genetic Algorithms.* Cambridge, MA: MIT Press.

National Academy of Sciences. (2008). *Science, Evolution, and Creationism.* Washington, DC: National Academy Press.

Piaget, J. (1957). L'actualité de Jean Amos Comenius: Préface. Dans: *Jean Amos Comenius, 1592–1670: pages choisies* (pp. 11–33). Paris: UNESCO. (English translation available online, www.ibe.unesco.org/publications/ThinkersPdf/comeniuse. PDF.)

Pennock, R. T. (2007). Learning evolution and the nature of science using evolutionary computing and artificial life. *McGill Journal of Education, 42,* 211–224.

Ruse, M. (2009). The Wiegand Memorial Foundation Lecture 2009—November 23, 2009. *Science and Religion: Why can't Americans be like Canadians?* Toronto, ON.

Schwartz, M. S., & Fischer, K. W. (2003). Building vs. borrowing: The challenge of actively constructing ideas. *Liberal Education, 89*(3), 22–29.

Scott, E. C. (2004). *Evolution vs. Creationism: An Introduction.* Westport, CT: Greenwood Press.

Seneca, *Letters.* [Latin, 1st century ad.] Trans. by E. M. Gummere (Loeb classical library). 3 vols. Cambridge, MA, 1917–25.

Sinclair, U. (1935). *I, Candidate for Governor: And How I Got Licked.* Berkeley, CA: University of California Press.

Smith, P. H. (2009). Science on the move: Recent trends in the history of early modern science. *Renaissance Quarterly, 62,* 345–375.

Speth, E. B., Long, T. M., Pennock, R. T., & Ebert-May, D. (2009). Using Avida-ED for teaching and learning about evolution in undergraduate introductory biology courses. *Evolution Education Outreach, 2,* 415–428.

Spinka, M. (1953). Comenian Pansophic principles. *Church History, 22*(2), 155–165.

Staudinger, U. M., Dörner, J., & Mickler, C. (2005). Wisdom and personality. In R. J. Sternberg & J. Jordan (Eds.), *A Handbook of Wisdom: Psychological Perspectives* (pp. 191–219). New York: Cambridge University Press.

Tanzella-Nitti, G. (2004). The two books prior to the scientific revolution. *Annales Theologici, 18,* 51–83.

Venables, A., & Tan, G. (2007). A 'hands on' strategy for teaching genetic algorithms to undergraduates. *Journal of Information Technology Education, 6,* 249–261.

Wallace, B. A. (2007). *Contemplative Science: Where Buddhism and Neuroscience Converge.* New York: Columbia University Press.

Wiker, B., & Dembski, W. (2002). *Moral Darwinism: How We Become Hedonists*. Downers Grove, IL: InterVarsity Press.

Zeller, E. (1931). *Outlines of the History of Greek Philosophy*, 13th ed., revised by Dr W. Nettle, and trans. by L. R. Palmer, London, Kegan Paul, 1931 (*Grundriss der Geschichte der griechische Philosophie*; originally published in 1907).

Conclusion

Chapter 12

Teach the Demarcation

Suggestions for Science Education

Michel Ferrari and Roger S. Taylor

Introduction

The initial impetus for this collection of chapters was the ongoing controversy and heated discussions about teaching intelligent design in public school science classes. It became clear from the tenor of this debate, both in science classes and in the general media, that beliefs about "science" tend to be relatively impoverished and unsophisticated. This is true of the general public as much as of students in science classrooms, especially at the high school level. Many in the general public view science as essentially a collection of facts and doubt many of those facts on an issue-by-issue basis; they do not have a sophisticated understanding of scientific theories and how these are supported or falsified by evidence. Unfortunately, this is equally true of students who attend science classes. In an in-depth investigation of 9–16-year-olds, Driver, Leach, Millar, and Scott (1996) found that most students at all ages thought good science involved investigations involving sensory perception data, with little understanding of a more sophisticated model-based view of science (Duschl). Likewise, Smith and Wenk (2006) found that most college freshmen understand theories as tested hypotheses, without understanding that theories are the complex explanatory frameworks that guide hypothesis testing (Duschl).

As a case in point, the theory of evolution is one of the most well-established scientific theories we have today, on par with the theory that the Earth is spherical and orbits the sun. And yet, a 2009 Gallup poll showed that less than 40% of the U.S. population accepts evolutionary theory. More surprising, and a little disheartening, Windschitl (2004) found similar results with pre-service science teachers (Duschl).

The fact that people's beliefs about science are so unsophisticated helps explain why intelligent design and creationism remain ideas with a powerful appeal to large segments of the U.S. population. Intelligent design is not merely a view about whether or not God created the world and all living things within it—a view held by all Abrahamic faiths—but about the specific way in which God is claimed to have done so. In denying the facts generated by the scientific study of biological evolution, intelligent design is also an attack on science and the findings generated by science that have implications for many other pressing issues of deep concern to people at large (see Dembski, 1998, 1999). Evolutionary theory is the central framework for understanding the biological world—from genetically modified foods to resistance to antibiotics, both of which are explained by this theory.

For this reason it is worth exploring the controversy between intelligent design and scientific theories of evolution as a way to better understand science and how evolution can be taught more effectively. The chapters in this volume were commissioned for this purpose. Our concluding chapter will not try to repeat them, but to pull out some common themes and conclusions about how best to teach the demarcation between science and pseudoscience or other forms of knowing, such as religious faith.

What Is Science?

Scientific explanation has been a focus of philosophical debate from pre-Socratic times until today. The word "science" comes from the Latin word "scientia." In ancient, medieval, and early modern Europe "scientia" referred to general and necessary truths that were demonstrated through deductive logical derivation. In ancient Greece, several very different conceptions of scientific method were used within this general scheme of demonstrative science. What Crombie (1959, 1994) calls the "postulational method" used by Euclid worked best with highly abstract subjects like pure mathematics, mathematical astronomy, optics, and statics. The same is true for Plato's dialectical method, in which arguments provisionally grant a proposition and then are developed to show self-contradiction or contradiction to something generally accepted as true, or the converse. This gave grounds for rejecting or accepting that argument—the mathematical equivalent of the *reducio ad absurdum* widely used by Greek mathematicians. By contrast, Aristotle's method was essentially empirical. Rather than postulate theoretical entities to explain the observed world, he analyzed observable things into their parts and principles and then rationally reconstructed the observed world from them. Thus, two different traditions of science can be found even in antiquity:

> The dominant Greek mathematicians saw as their goal the reduction of every scientific field to the *axiomatic model* of their most powerful intellectual invention, geometry. At once alternative and complementary to this was the much older medical and technological practice of *exploring and recording by piecemeal observation, measurement, and trial.*
>
> (Crombie, 1996, p. 4)

Medieval and early modern natural philosophers combined both of these traditions. Medieval science of the 13th and 14th centuries developed new ideas about the scientific method that included the use of induction and experimentation, as well as the use of mathematics to explain physical phenomena. These ideas were not fully developed until the 17th century, but they led to a revolution in the conception of science and the kinds of questions it could answer. Ironically, this emerged out of a detailed critique of Aristotelian science by scholastic philosophers themselves (Crombie, 1959; Smith, 2009).

When modern science began its rise around the 17th century, there was still no unified sense of science, as we know it today. In fact, areas of study that we would today call science were typically called either "natural philosophy" (i.e., investigations into the natural causes of things, as in physics or astronomy) or "natural history" (i.e., descriptions of terrestrial content as in botany or zoology) (Godfrey-Smith, 2003). Furthermore, the practices we think of as embodying the scientific revolution were only a subset of all of the theoretical and even empirical approaches to studying nature at that time (Shapin, 1996).

Still, Shapin (1996, p. 13) points to four interrelated aspects of changes in knowledge about the natural world and changes in means of securing that knowledge: first, the increasing use of mechanical metaphors to construe natural processes and phenomena; second, the depersonalization of natural knowledge ... especially as evinced in the distinction between mundane human experience and views of what nature "is really like"; third, the attempted mechanization of knowledge making, that is, the proposed deployment of explicitly formulated rules of method that aimed at disciplining the production of knowledge by managing or eliminating the effects of human passions and interests; and fourth, the aspiration to use the resulting reformed natural knowledge to achieve moral, social, and political ends, the condition of which was agreement that the knowledge in question truly was benign, powerful, and above all *disinterested*.

The contemporary sense of the terms "science" and "scientist" emerged in the 19th century. According to Schaffer (1986), we can trace the first use to "Coleridge's ban on the term 'philosopher'" at the meeting of the British Association in Cambridge in 1833. Coleridge had objected to Davy's "prostituting the name of Philosopher ... to every Fellow who has made a lucky experiment" .... which prompted Whewell to endorse the "new and outlandish term 'scientist' for these 'Fellows'"[1] (both cited in Schaffer, 1986, p. 409). However, we still find traces of the original tension between theoretical explanatory modeling and empirical investigation to support theoretical explanations as hallmarks of science down to the present day. Even so, Daston and Galison (2007) identify a succession of "epistemic virtues" historically associated with science: truth to nature, mechanical objectivity, expert judgment, and model-interpretation that requires building and mastering of technological tools (like computers). Thus, it is important to remain sensitive to the historical specificity of contemporary views of science and scientific methods, even the meaning of scientific objectivity has changed historically.

Scientific Theories vs. Lay Theories Today

The scientific usage of the word "theory" differs from that of the layperson, and is even contested within the field of science. In ordinary conversations, "theory" sometimes refers to unsupported speculation. By contrast, scientific theories must explain evidence, and simple theories with broad explanatory power are preferred.

On the now "classical" view put forward by the logical positivists in the early 20th century,[2] a theory is a set of universal sentences ideally formulated in a formal language like predicate calculus that involves a set of axioms. It is a deductive argument that looks like a formal proof of how the description of a phenomenon to be explained follows from the theory's axioms. Unfortunately, this has not always been possible: for example, no one has successfully done this for some of the most successful sciences like evolutionary biology.

An alternative semantic set or set-theoretic view is that theories are structures that allow one to pick out a specific group of models from a more general set. Scientific theories also sometimes provide explanatory mechanisms that show how phenomena result from the operation of that mechanism—often coordinating different levels of organization (e.g., for emergent phenomena; illness as involving the cellular to the societal level) (Thagard). Scientists sometimes rely on model building based on creative departure from known models (e.g., this is what Faraday did—so did Darwin, drawing on Malthus) and at other times on direct abstract representation of reality (e.g., Mendeleev's periodic table) (Weisberg, 2007).

Scientists use principled means to decide between theories in an unbiased way. Successful theories are considered more probable than their competitors because of their breadth and simplicity, or because they lead to new discoveries. Scientific theories are set within explanatory frameworks (what Kuhn called "paradigms") that include core beliefs that can subsume several theories. Paradigms need not be parsimonious (for example, many methods of speciation might be consistent with core beliefs about evolution).

Kuhn (1962, 1981, 1993) proposed only one paradigm at a time per field, but this seems implausible and, in fact, was immediately answered by theories who proposed several (Lakatos and Laudan); also, Kuhn exaggerated how committed scientists are to their own paradigm. Laudan proposed that something like paradigms co-exist and compete in existing fields of science; he called these "research traditions," and saw theories in these traditions as more loosely grouped than Lakatos, and as less logically sequenced.

New tools and technologies contribute to the scope of a theory and the kind of evidence that can be gathered in support of it. Sometimes theories are associated with successful technologies, but these technologies can often be explained by a succession of competing theories (e.g., how radios work). This is not a problem for constructive empiricists like van Fraassen (2008) for whom scientific representations are necessarily a perspectival look at phenomena within a measurement setup.

How science differs from non-science more generally is a difficult question to answer; but it lies at the heart of the question of whether intelligent design deserves to be taught as science, and therefore is a core issue of many chapters in this volume.

Demarcation or How Science Differs from Non-Science

How science works, even today, has received different answers (Godfrey-Smith, 2003):

1.   Empiricism. On this view the only difference between scientific and everyday knowledge is one of detail and degree—science is construed broadly. Science is successful because it is systematic, organized, and responsive to experience.

2.   Mathematical symbolism. Another belief is that science needs to be written in the mathematics, and thus one must first acquire the prerequisite mathematical tools. This is something that can be combined with empiricist ideas—indeed it is a powerful tool within an empiricist outlook. But science can proceed without mathematics, too, as seen by Darwin's *Origin of Species* and by most of 19th century biology.

3.   Scientific communities. This is a newer idea in which science is something that is only possible within a certain sort of community—science has a unique social structure. This view is often very critical of the empiricist tradition, stressing the balance between cooperation and competition in scientific communities and the transmission of information across generations.

However, beyond these three characteristics, there are other general epistemic features that are said to be characteristic of scientific inquiry. Several chapters set out to contrast scientific knowledge with that of other culturally influential ways of knowing, and in particular with religious ways of knowing (Tweney, Sinatra).

How Science Differs from Religion

Several authors claim that science uses evidence to construct testable explanations and predictions about natural phenomena and the evidence this process generates. By contrast, religion involves a set of commonly held beliefs and practices codified through religious dogma. According to this view, science and religion both construct counterintuitive representations of reality; both also meet emotional needs, but Tweney points out that while some science is more counterintuitive than religious dogma, scientific ideas survive because they consistently explain a lot of information and survive tests that undercut confirmation bias and other common biases that shield beliefs from scrutiny. And along with scientific knowledge come increasingly sophisticated epistemological means for investigating those beliefs, which becomes increasingly difficult as the amount of knowledge in any given area constantly increases.

Religious beliefs that are counterintuitive, on the other hand, survive because cultural selection eliminates those that are too implausible, and protects those that remain from careful scrutiny; furthermore, there is no felt need or special effort undertaken to try to disconfirm them or to align them with other bodies of belief. In other words, religious gatherings and practices are confirmatory, while scientific gatherings and practices are designed to change scientific ideas by adding, subtracting, refining, revising, or adding to the pool of ideas accepted within science.

Tweney and others suggest that this makes science "unnatural" in the sense that science requires a measured skepticism that seeks to disconfirm all hypotheses. Indeed, such skepticism is a key marker differentiating science from pseudoscience. Skepticism is "unnatural" in that our typical habits favor confirming our beliefs. Science also requires precise hypotheses and the need to imagine what might be disconfirmed. In addition, science seeks coherence of all claims on a particular topic (pattern-finding). Science also involves learning to see things (e.g., origin of life) in entirely new ways that may not be popularly accepted.

Religious thinking is not scientific and more natural. Furthermore, religious thinking ranges from ontological claims (e.g., God exists) to epistemic beliefs (e.g., God created the universe), to rituals (e.g., confession will absolve me of my sins). Many religious beliefs aim to heighten and preserve an air of mystery by being nearly plausible (minimally counterintuitive) and violating (usually only one) ontological assumptions about ordinary concepts (e.g., miraculously turning water into wine). Such religious beliefs persist, Tweney argues, because they are easier to remember. Religious tradition also requires that beliefs be accepted on faith or authority, suspending regular rules of disconfirmation. In the extreme such beliefs are justified as mysteries that surpass human understanding.

Of course, these religious beliefs and practices issue from an equally long tradition of interpretative practices and disputes that have intersected with natural science throughout history. Some authors, like Evans and Ferrari, have suggested that some forms of religious belief are perfectly compatible with science. On this view, at least some scientific and religious beliefs can be complementary as well as conflicting (see www.templeton.org). Along these lines, Evans notes that evolution can be understood as compatible with some religious perspectives. Since people use natural–material and supernatural–psychological explanatory frameworks (or hover closer to dogmatism or to skepticism on some issues) and need to coordinate them, it is important to understand how children and adults coordinate natural and supernatural (or material and immaterial) belief systems about biology. Evans notes that this is as true in seeking an understanding of illness and death as it is regarding evolution. However, even this contrast risks setting up a straw man opponent to science and ignores the fact that the most powerful theology invites practitioners to put their faith to an empirical test, and that, historically, religion is as hard to demarcate as science (Dear, 2001, 2005).

Indeed, some make the more radical claim that there is no principled difference between science and other forms of open-minded inquiry, whether religious or otherwise, and that it is better to work from prototypic exemplars of good science (typically taken from physics, chemistry, or biology—the most successful sciences) in seeking to understand the nature of science and science education. An examination of such prototypes shows that sciences like physics and biology are actually very different kinds of endeavors, although they share some very general features that characterize open-minded inquiry of all kinds.

Perhaps at the core we can agree that the question of demarcation is a good one, and involves a strategy for investigating the world, and a scientific way of *handling* ideas, or so Godfrey-Smith (2003) proposes. A scientific way of handling ideas is to try to connect them to other ideas and to embed them in larger conceptual structures that expose them to observation (hence risk)— not just to falsification, but to other ways that allow them to be made manifest and thus adjusted. With this view, ideas like Marxism and psychoanalysis, or religious ideas, will have scientific and unscientific versions; they are not blanketly non-science, pseudoscience, or science. For example, phrenology was based on 18th century neuroscience, but it was conducted in a risk-averse way that turned it into pseudoscience; astrology was a well-respected science in the Middle Ages, but became pseudoscience when understanding of Copernican planetary motion became known; intelligent design was the mainstream view before overwhelming evidence was found in support of Darwin's theory of natural selection. In all cases, we need to be able to tell what difference it makes to theories if they are true or false. Evolution is an idea that has been extensively tested and found to be highly explanatory: could it be falsified? Godfrey-Smith (2003) suggests a "Precambrian rabbit." Even then, that finding would falsify only one part of the theory, because evolutionary theory would still explain changes across generations of fruit flies and bacteria in labs.

Is Intelligent Design (or Is Creationism) Science?

This is a question that comes up in almost every chapter in this book, and it receives different answers. Looking more widely to popular culture gives an even wider range of responses. Advocates claim that intelligent design is science; thus, Dembski claims that intelligent design is the science of how to detect intelligence. But most authors hold that intelligent design is not science, and indeed the Dover, PA judge John Jones III concluded intelligent design is not science and could not be taught as science in the classroom because it is at base non-materialistic and supernatural. Furthermore, intelligent design has no mechanism to explain biological change beyond simply proposing that God has directly intervened to design all living things; and no possibility is given for God to create new living forms, except via miracles.

Some authors nevertheless suggest that intelligent design is a hybrid between religion and science; that in terms of its epistemic criteria; that it operates within a micro-evolutionary framework trying to balance between naturalism and supernaturalism. It does claim to rely on empirical proof rather than interpretation of doctrine, but ultimately appeals to the authority of biblical scripture. However, like science, intelligent design claims to be more tentative than dogmatic religious belief, and finds itself somewhere between the fluid structures of science and the enduring structures of religious dogma.

For all these reasons, it might be more useful to say that, like astrology, which when conducted with an open mind meets the criteria for science but has failed all efforts to prove it true, intelligent design is best thought of as dead or discarded science (cf. Kitcher, 2007). And indeed, intelligent design was discarded by virtually all of the 19th century biologists once they appreciated the explanatory power and evidence in support of Darwin's theory. Even so, it is possible and coherent to endorse a "target-dependent co-existence model" that includes both creationism or intelligent design and the findings of Darwinian macro-evolution, and in fact, this is what the Catholic church and many mainstream forms of Protestantism endorse.

How Can Science Be Taught?

Implications for Students

One idea that is common to all the chapters in this volume is that students have both conceptual and epistemic barriers to learning about evolution and that their conceptual ecologies influence how scientific ideas are received. Students need to understand that their understanding of science is rooted in their own intuitive epistemologies. This is particularly true when students are learning about evolution.

Students have very powerful misconceptions about evolution, including:

• Evolution and religion are not compatible—when actually, they can co-exist under particular understandings of both.
• Species are "immutable" (essential), so macro-evolution is more easily accepted for species that undergo a metamorphosis (i.e., caterpillar to butterfly).
• Human beings are privileged with a psychological or spiritual life that comes with its own essentialism.

- Only non-human species evolve (a position held, incidentally, by Wallace, co-discoverer of the principle of natural selection).
- Evolutionary theory is just a theory about the emergence of life when in actuality it is a theory about how life (or anything) branches and diversifies.

There are many reasons for these misconceptions. Conventional lines of evidence in support of evolution are poorly understood. It is hard to visualize or model macro-evolutionary change (Samarapungavan). Additionally, evolution is one of a class of "emergent" phenomena that are very difficult to teach in science (Wilensky). As if that were not enough, evolution is a controversial topic in U.S. society, with many parents and influential political groups opposed to teaching this topic in school. A possible solution can be found in the "human reticence" effect described by Ranney. Instead of focusing on the more controversial topic of human evolution, teachers could instead focus on the less threatening topic of plant evolution.

Furthermore, abandoning intentional concepts while keeping needs-based ones can be an important transition for students on their way to understanding the current scientific model (Evans).

In her chapter, Hofer makes the important point that students' *personal epistemology* also affects their ability to engage scientific explanations because students see their education and learning through the prism of their current epistemic worldview. According to Hofer, personal epistemology (beliefs about the nature of knowledge and knowing) has been explored in two main ways. The developmental approach proposes a predictable progression from absolutism or dualism, through multiplism, to evaluatism. The epistemic beliefs approach, which assumes people's beliefs are multi-dimensional and somewhat independent, is closely related to philosophical distinctions about epistemology, specifically, the nature of knowledge and the nature of knowing. Still other approaches look at the metacognitive dimensions of knowing and theory coherence, among other important issues.

All of these aspects are important for teachers to bear in mind when teaching students about evolutionary theory, and go beyond the simple content of the theory itself.

Implications for Teachers

Evolutionary theory is a paradigm case for what makes science hard to teach. If there is one theme that emerges from these chapters it can be summed up by the idea that science teachers should "teach the demarcation" between science and other epistemologies. By this we mean, not that teachers should take it upon themselves to teach the difference between science and religion, but rather that they should teach the difference between dogmatism and skepticism. It is recommended that teachers promote students' understanding of the demarcation between a scientific approach to any topic, and one that is not. This involves a balance between those two habitual tendencies of thought, and an epistemology that is essentially evaluative.

A related issue is whether it matters if students merely understand a theory or if they should also believe it to be true. What matters for science education is not that students dogmatically believe the theory of evolution, but that they appreciate the advantage of basing any decision about it on scientifically robust skeptical practices that promote coherent evidentiary support for their views (Samarapungavan). It is this support that makes evolutionary theory stronger than intelligent design.

To achieve this, we believe it is important to *teach science* broadly (and not just "the scientific method"). The National Science Education Standards (National Research Council, 2000) identify five essential features of classroom inquiry: (1) scientifically oriented questions, (2) learning to give priority to evidence needed to evaluate those questions, (3) learning to formulate explanations from evidence, (4) learning to evaluate explanations in light of alternative explanations, and (5) learning to communicate and justify proposed explanations. But missing from much science education is the consideration of theories as complex explanatory frameworks that guide hypothesis testing (Duschl).

On this view, for science education to be most effective, an approach is required that is comprehensive and systematic and that specifically addresses stumbling blocks to conceptual change, both in pre-service teachers and in their students. Unfortunately, most science education today focuses on investigative methods, not on the dialectic between models and methods to investigate them. The "received view" of science as hypothesis verification closely maps onto how most people understand the scientific method (i.e., observe, form hypotheses and deduce consequences from them, test hypotheses with further observations, accept or reject those hypotheses). But scientific inquiry has conceptual, epistemic, and social dimensions. Science is not a matter of rubrics or algorithms for confirming hypotheses, but a dialog over models and theories. Thus, students must be introduced not only to the epistemic frameworks and methods used to develop and evaluate scientific knowledge, but also to the social processes and contexts that influence how such knowledge is discovered, communicated, and received.

Duschl and Grandy propose several tenets for good science education. According to their view, most scientific effort is not theory discovery or acceptance, but theory refinement and improvement, and this is how science should also be taught. Furthermore, unlike the model of the lone scientist that was true in the 17th century, contemporary science increasingly involves research groups and disciplinary communities as the actual units of practice for scientific discourse. That scientific discourse involves a complex set of accepted practices within a disciplinary matrix of shared exemplars that provide appropriate values, instruments, methods, and evidence. Scientific change is produced not only by theory revision or conceptual change, but also of new technology and new methodology for conducting observations and measurement. Indeed, what counts as an observation evolves along with new tools, methods, and theories. Different sciences will have different exemplars and thus different styles of science and even different possibilities for objective scientific truth in that domain (Hacking, 2002).

These tenets can be applied to the science classroom in a variety of ways; for example, by: providing contexts for theory development that mimic the discovery of scientific knowledge; using distributed learning models or investigation, emphasizing the dialectic between theories and evidence; having learners develop criteria for theory evaluation; having students develop and use linguistic, pictorial, and mathematical scientific models; attending to shared exemplars that illustrate theoretical or model-based frameworks that guide scientific inquiry; organizing discussion around big ideas and driving questions, and by focusing meaning making on critical evidence, pivotal cases, and knowledge integration; providing chances to examine alternative explanations and guiding conceptions when explaining phenomena and mechanisms, allowing time to seriously discuss criteria used to judge knowledge claims proposed by scientific theories.

Historical episodes are a powerful way to study epistemological presuppositions and changes, as well as to teach science (Tweney), because we are less immersed in those presuppositions and can see the consequences of holding them. Not only that, the science itself is less complex. As a case in point, intelligent design was plausible before Darwin and in fact most scientists endorsed this view (Chinn). The historical debates Darwin held with creationists of his own day can be persuasive for students who hold similar views today. Also, the history of science shows that science is not all hard work, it is also fun (especially when making exploratory experiments). Faraday incorporated children's games into his lectures for students and lay audiences, inviting his audience to: see, try, apply, philosophize.

Evans goes further to say that the aim in public school classrooms is to provide and promote conceptual ecologies that allow evolutionary ideas and scientific habits of mind to flourish. Thus, science teachers should sequence the introduction of difficult ideas by focusing on non-human and micro-evolution, but also be sure to eventually integrate human macro-evolution from the earliest years. They also need to engage intuitive beliefs, confirming those that science confirms, and challenging those that scientific inquiry has disconfirmed. Synthetic blends might be a good way to do this by providing a bridge between intuition and science knowledge. It is also important to include opportunities to foster intentional conceptual change that makes students aware of their own thinking and reasoning and whether it is likely to improve or distort understanding.

Conceptual Change Pedagogy and Teaching about Evolution

According to Sinatra and many other authors, the most effective biology curriculum will combine a study of the content of biology with a discussion of the nature of science and the nature of knowing (personal epistemology) that together can leverage knowledge by providing an Archimedian "place to stand." In this way, evolutionary biology need not conflict with religion, but complement it—removing a significant barrier to the teaching of evolutionary theory for many teachers. A conceptual change pedagogy for the topic of evolution (Sinatra) and about the nature of science would allow students the chance to overcome misconceptions that impede their learning. Such a pedagogical approach would pre-assess students' conceptions in order to identify misconceptions and provide students with opportunities to compare their conceptions with those of scientists. This approach encourages argumentation, experimentation, or other very engaging instructional activities that allow people to evaluate and weigh evidence from alternative conceptions. Furthermore, it would start with "cold cognition topics" such as plate tectonics (or whether the Earth is round—e.g., replicating Eratosthenes' study and proof without satellites) to give a context for discussing the demarcation between what science is and what it is not. Specific to teaching evolution, it is important to "teach the controversy" but through actual controversies within the science of evolutionary studies (e.g., alternative reasons for historically documented mass extinctions of most life on Earth). Teaching in this way allows students to understand the nature of controversies within science and engages many of the tenets Duschl advocates for good science instruction. According to Sinatra, it is not advisable to teach controversies between science and other worldviews, such as the controversy between evolutionary theory and intelligent design, as this can confuse students and suggest a scientific equality between these different approaches to explaining the biological phenomena of speciation. However, this would probably depend on how intelligent design is introduced into the science curriculum, and whether or not students are open to skepticism about it.

Another problem for science instruction is the sheer amount of material needed to understand the subtleties of different scientific domains, including the science of evolution. One way around this is to teach for deep understanding of a *central core of scientific concepts* (Case, 1998). This central core of scientific notions about the natural world can be made accessible to elementary school students, and then progressively refined and enriched for older students and adults—a "learning progression." Ideally, science instruction would teach science within an integrated curriculum that promotes deep understanding of common central conceptual structures across the curriculum. Unlike Gould and some authors, we do not favor teaching within "nonoverlapping magisteria." Even if we consider the classroom analogous to a hothouse in a hostile environment (in which one does not expose plants to the outside environment) it is still important to foster a unified hothouse environment of school-based inquiry, and not a biodome of separate ecosystems for different classrooms. Historical examples of this sort of unified curriculum are found in the medieval universities, which produced some of the leading natural scientists of the Middle Ages, despite their integration of theology and natural science at the most abstract levels of inquiry.

Technology can help to promote such a unified curriculum. In particular, computer technology can help teach students about the core concepts needed to understand biological evolution by making normally glacial processes of natural selection more visible, for example, through designing and running genetic algorithms that provide a "cold cognitive" example of how natural selection maximizes adaptive fit though a simple process of repeated selection within a population (Ferrari). Likewise, software developed by Wilensky's BEAGLE project allows for fuller appreciation of the difference between observation at differing levels of organization, and how the emergent process of evolution looks very different from the lower level processes that produce it. In general, these technologies allow students to approach the task of understanding evolutionary theory in a variety of ways that engage many different kinds of intelligence, something Gardner (1999) considers important to fostering deep understanding for the largest number of students.

Conclusion

The appeal of creationism and intelligent design will not go away any time soon. In fact, they no doubt appeal to an understanding of human experience, and by extension to the ultimate nature of reality, that is almost universally appealing, at least within Western cultures. But this is no less true of teaching physics, where students also harbor deep misconceptions. What we propose is that science class has, as its most fundamental task, to teach the demarcation between a scientific approach to understanding the natural world—one that hovers between dogmatism and skepticism with an open mind. Beyond that, students interested in particular topics can further pursue the core concepts and subtleties of those particular areas of inquiry. But all should leave high school science classes with a basic understanding of the best theory and evidence that we have been able to acquire about human biology and about the nature of the world around us—if only to more fully appreciate the mystery, perhaps a divine mystery, that stands behind even the most sophisticated theories science has yet devised. The ultimate aim of such an approach to science is to allow students' entire conceptual ecology to flourish in ways that enhance both understanding of natural science (e.g., theory of evolution) and of themselves as agents and knowers: to allow schools to teach for deep understanding of science and to teach for wisdom.

Notes

1. Whewell, W. (1834). On the connexion of the physical sciences. *Quarterly Review*, 51, 59–61.
2. Logical positivism, and its later incarnation of logical empiricism (and related ideas of operationism), were a form of empiricism first developed after World War I in the Vienna Circle (established by Moritz Schlick and Otto Neurath).

References

Case, R. (1998). The development of conceptual structures. In: W. Damon (Series Ed.) & D. Kuhn & R. S. Siegler (Vol. Eds.), *Handbook of Child Psychology: Vol. 2. Cognition, Perception and Language* (5th ed., pp. 745–800). New York: Wiley.

Crombie, A. C. (1959). *Medieval and Early Modern Science* (2 vols). Garden City, NY: Doubleday Anchor Books.

Crombie, A. C. (1994). *Styles of Scientific Thinking in the European Tradition: The History of Argument and Explanation especially in the Mathematical and Biomedical Sciences* (3 vols). London: Duckworth.

Crombie, A. C. (1996). *Science, Art and Nature in Medieval and Modern Thought*. London: Hambledon Press.

Daston, L. & Galison, P. (2007). *Objectivity*. New York: Zone Books.

Dear, P. (2001). *Revolutionizing the Science: European Knowledge and its Ambitions, 1500–1700*. Princeton, NJ: Princeton University Press.

Dear, P. (2005). What is the history of science the history of? Early modern roots of the ideology of modern science. *Isis, 96*, 390–406.

Dembski, W. A. (1998). *The Design Inference: Eliminating chance through small probabilities*. New York: Cambridge University Press.

Dembski, W. A. (1999). *Intelligent Design: The Bridge between Science and Theology*. Downers Grove, IL: InterVarsity Press.

Driver, R., Leach, J., Millar, R., & Scott, P. (1996). *Young People's Images of Science*. Philadelphia, PA: Open University Press.

Gallup. (2009). On Darwin's Birthday, Only 4 in 10 Believe in Evolution, from www.gallup.com/poll/114544/darwin-birthday-believe-evolution.aspx

Gardner, H. (1999). *The Disciplined Mind: Beyond Facts and Standardized Tests, The K-12 Education That Every Child Deserves*. New York: Simon and Schuster (and New York: Penguin Putnam).

Godfrey-Smith, P. (2003). *Theory and Reality: An Introduction to the Philosophy of Science*. Chicago, IL: University of Chicago Press.

Hacking, I. (2002). *Historical Ontology*. Cambridge, MA and London, England: Harvard University Press.

Kitcher, P. (2007). *Living with Darwin: Evolution, Design, and the Future of Faith*. New York: Oxford University Press.

Kuhn, T. (1962). *The Structure of Scientific Revolutions*. Chicago, IL: University of Chicago Press.

Kuhn, T. S. (1981). A function for thought experiments. In: I. Hacking (Ed.), *Scientific Revolutions* (pp. 6–27). New York: Oxford University Press. (Selected by Kuhn for the volume. Originally published in *L'aventure de la science*, Mélanges Alexandre Koyré, vol. 2, pp. 307–334, 1964).

Kuhn, T. (1993). *World Changes*. Cambridge, MA: MIT Press.

National Research Council. (2000). *Inquiry and the National Science Education Standards: A Guide for Teaching and Learning*. Washington, DC: National Academy Press.

Schaffer, S. (1986). Scientific discoveries and the end of natural philosophy. *Social Studies of Science, 16*(3), 387–420.

Shapin, S. (1996). *The Scientific Revolution*. Chicago, IL: University of Chicago Press.

Smith, C., & Wenk, L. (2006). Relations among three aspects of first-year college students' epistemologies of science. *Journal of Research in Science Teaching, 43*(8), 747–785.

Smith, P. H. (2009). Science on the move: Recent trends in the history of early modern science. *Renaissance Quarterly, 62*, 345–375.

van Fraassen, B. C. (2008). *Scientific Representation: Paradoxes of Perspective*. Oxford: Oxford University Press.

Weisberg, M. (2007). Who is a modeler? *British Journal for the Philosophy of Science, 58*, 207–233.

Windschitl, M. (2004). Caught in the cycle of reproducing folk theories of "Inquiry": How pre-service teachers continue the discourse and practices of an atheoretical scientific method. *Journal of Research in Science Teaching, 41*(5), 481–512.

Contributors

Luke A. Buckland is a South African doctoral student at the Rutgers Graduate School of Education, and conducts research focusing on how people learn to reason about science as well as on the epistemological dimensions of cognition. Luke has a background in analytic philosophy and aims to promote more interdisciplinary collaboration between philosophy, education, and educational research.

Clark A. Chinn is an educational psychologist at Rutgers University. His research focuses on epistemic cognition, argumentation, promoting growth in reasoning, conceptual change, and collaborative learning.

Alex DeLisi received his B.A. in Psychology from Middlebury College in 2008, where he conducted his honors thesis research on the change in students' understanding and acceptance of evolution.

Richard A. Duschl (Ph.D. 1983 University of Maryland, College Park) is the Waterbury Chaired Professor of Secondary Education, College of Education, Penn State University. Prior to joining Penn State Richard held the Chair of Science Education at King's College London and served on the faculties of Rutgers, Vanderbilt, and the University of Pittsburgh. He recently served as Chair of the National Research Council research synthesis report *Taking Science to School: Learning and Teaching Science in Grades K-8* (National Academies Press, 2007). With Richard Grandy, he co-edited *Teaching Scientific Inquiry: Implications for Research and Implementation* (SensePublishers, 2008). His research focuses on establishing epistemic learning environments and on the role of students' inquiry and argumentation processes. Richard has twice received the "JRST Award" (1989, 2003) for the outstanding research article published in the *Journal of Research in Science Teaching*. He also served for more than a decade as editor of the research journal *Science Education* and editor for TC Press's "Ways of Knowing in Science and Math" book series.

E. Margaret Evans is a research scientist at the Center for Human Growth and Development at the University of Michigan. She examines knowledge acquisition as a function of the emergence of intuitive causal explanations and the influence of diverse contexts, such as belief system, culture, and learning experience. Currently, she investigates the emergence of developmental learning progressions for evolutionary concepts as children and their parents encounter museum exhibitions on evolution.

Michel Ferrari is an Associate Professor at the Ontario Institute for Studies in Education at the University of Toronto. His research interests include the role of learning technologies and instructional design and the development of personal wisdom. His most recent edited book, with Nic Westrate, is *Personal Wisdom* (in press, Springer). With Chandi Fernando he is editing a *Handbook of Resilience in Children of War* (in press, Springer).

Richard E. Grandy received his B.S. in Mathematics from the University of Pittsburgh and his Ph.D. from the History and Philosophy of Science Program at Princeton University. He is currently the McManis Professor of Philosophy and Cognitive Sciences at Rice University. He has published a number of articles on the implications for science education of philosophy of science and cognitive studies. He is co-editor with Richard Duschl of *Teaching Scientific Inquiry.*

Barbara K. Hofer is a Professor of Psychology at Middlebury College, and a fellow of the American Psychological Association; she received her Ph.D. in Education and Psychology from the University of Michigan and Ed.M. from Harvard University. She is the co-editor (with Paul R. Pintrich) of *Personal Epistemology: The Psychology of Beliefs about Knowledge and Knowing* and the recipient (with Pintrich) of the Review of Research Award from the American Educational Research Association for a review of the literature on epistemology.

Chak Fu Lam received his B.A. in Psychology and Economics from Middlebury College in 2007 and is now a Ph.D. candidate of Management and Organizations at University of Michigan Ross School of Business. His research interests include employees' extra-role, citizenship behaviors, proactive behaviors, and team impression management.

Peter Lee is a doctoral student at the University of Oxford in the area of biophysics. He has a background in electrical and mechanical engineering, developed during his studies at the University of Toronto and M.I.T. During his time in Toronto, he also taught mathematics and science to gifted high school students in after-school programs at the Essel Learning Centre, Inc. His current research interests include the development of optical and robotic technologies to study the electromechanical properties of cardiac tissue, from single cells to the whole heart.

Cristine H. Legare is an Assistant Professor in the Psychology Department at the University of Texas at Austin. Her training and research reflect her interest in interdisciplinary approaches to the study of cognitive development. In her current research she is investigating mechanisms of knowledge acquisition, causal explanatory reasoning, and the development of scientific and religious belief systems.

Louis Nadelson's nearly 20 years of experience as a high school and university science and mathematics teacher provides him with a unique perspective of STEM education, which motivates his research agenda. The range of his research interests include: the influence of professional development on teacher STEM knowledge, teachers' STEM instruction, inquiry for teaching STEM, resolving misconceptions, and learning and teaching in evolution. His current research projects include: informal science education, evolution acceptance, science and math teacher preparation, using evidence to inform systemic change in STEM education, impact of undergraduate research, impact of outreach efforts, teacher change, and misconceptions.

Michael Novak is an instructional materials developer at the Center for Connected Learning and Computer-Based Modeling at Northwestern University. He is the lead author of the BEAGLE (Biological Experiments in Adaptation, Genetics, Learning, and Evolution) curriculum. He is an instructor in the School of Education and Social Policy at Northwestern University and he is an eighth grade science and mathematics teacher at Park View School in Morton Grove, IL.

Michael Andrew Ranney serves on many Berkeley faculties, including education (chairing its Cognition and Development Area), psychology, cognitive/brain sciences, and SESAME (The Graduate Group in Science and Mathematics Education, which he has also chaired). A past Spencer Fellow of the Spencer Foundation and the National Academy of Education, Ranney holds degrees in psychology (e.g., a Ph.D.) and biology, and his publications span many fields. He heads Berkeley's Reasoning Research Group, largely studying conceptual/explanatory coherence and problem solving in formal and informal domains that involve scientific and mathematical thinking.

Karl S. Rosengren is a Professor of Psychology at Northwestern University. He examines cognitive and motor development. In his current research he examines cultural influences in the development of causal reasoning, and how children acquire different types of causal beliefs.

Ala Samarapungavan is a Professor of Educational Psychology at Purdue University. Her research focuses on knowledge acquisition in the sciences and is comprised of three related areas: (a) how changes in the content and structure of students' science concepts develop over time across a variety of disciplines such as observational astronomy, evolutionary biology, and chemistry; (b) the epistemic dimensions of scientific reasoning (how research scientists and science students evaluate and revise scientific knowledge); and (c) the design of learning environments to foster biology learning.

Gale M. Sinatra (Ph.D., Psychology, University of Massachusetts, Amherst) is a Professor of Educational Psychology at the University of Nevada, Las Vegas, editor of the APA Division 15 journal *Educational Psychologist*, a fellow of APA and AERA, and vice-president of AERA's Division C, Learning and Instruction. She is currently co-principal investigator on a National Science Foundation grant exploring the challenges of teaching and learning about biological evolution in the United States, which include emotional and motivational barriers.

Roger S. Taylor is an Assistant Professor in the Psychology Department at the State University of New York, Oswego campus. In addition to his work on epistemological beliefs in science education he focuses on uncovering the relationships between students' learning and their emotional (or affective) states. This line of research includes the goals of refining psychological theory and developing educational applications, such as emotionally adaptive learning environments.

Paul Thagard is a Professor of Philosophy and Director of the Cognitive Science Program at the University of Waterloo, Canada. His books include *The Brain and the Meaning of Life, Mind: Introduction to Cognitive Science*, and *Hot Thought: Mechanisms and Applications of Emotional Cognition*.

Anastasia Thanukos is an editor at the UC Berkeley Museum of Paleontology, where she develops content for the award-winning "Understanding Evolution" (www.understandingevolution.org) and "Understanding Science" (www.understandingscience.org) websites. A former community college biology instructor, she holds a Masters in Integrative Biology and a Ph.D. in Science and Math Education, both from UC Berkeley.

Ryan D. Tweney, Professor Emeritus at Bowling Green State University, is a cognitive psychologist interested in understanding the nature of scientific thinking. He is known for his cognitive-historical studies of the physicist Michael Faraday and for his contributions to the psychology of science. He has edited six books and published over a hundred articles in scientific and scholarly journals and as book chapters. He is currently working on the nature of mathematical representations in physics, as manifested in the works of James Clerk Maxwell.

Uri Wilensky is a Professor of Learning Sciences, Computer Science and Complex Systems at Northwestern University. He is the founder and director of the Center for Connected Learning and Computer-Based Modeling. For the past two decades he has investigated ways of engaging students in doing meaningful science and in understanding an interconnected world of complex systems. His NetLogo agent-based modeling software is in widespread use worldwide in both research and educational settings. Prior to coming to Northwestern, he taught at Tufts University and MIT and was a research scientist at Thinking Machines Corporation. Wilensky received undergraduate and graduate degrees in mathematics, philosophy and computer science and received his Ph.D. from the MIT Media Lab. He is a recipient of the National Science Foundation's Career Award as well as the Spencer Foundation's Post-Doctoral Award. By providing a "low threshold" language for exploring and constructing models, Wilensky hopes to promote modeling literacy—the sharing and critiquing of computational models in the scientific community, in education, and in the public at large.

Index

Page numbers in *italics* denote tables, those in **bold** denote figures. The index does not include all author citations. Readers requiring complete lists of cited authors should refer to the reference lists at the end of each chapter.

absolutism 97, 99
acceptance, of theories 29–30
accretion growth model 17
Ackerman, R. J. 17
afterlife 32,123, 164, 165
Agassiz, Louis 48, 53
agency 206
agent-based modeling 217–18
AIDS, theories of causality 117–20
aims: of inquiry 44–6, 65, 70; of scientific knowledge 42
American Psychological Association 63
Ancient Greece 251, 272
animal evolution 144, 145, 184–5
Answers in Genesis 50, 54
anthropomorphism 130
anti-realism 44
argumentation 99
Aristotle 251, 272
Asterhan, C. S. 90–1
astrology 27
authority, as justification 179–81, 198
Atran, S. 206
Ayer, A. J. 28

barriers, to learning 86–9, 174
Bayesianism 32–3
BEAGLE (Biological Experiments in Adaptation, Genetics, Learning and Evolution): Bug Hunt Camouflage 228–33; Bug Hunt Coevolution 233–7, **235**; Bug Hunt Drift 224–8, **227**; Bug Hunt Speeds 236; Bug Hunters' Camouflage 230–2, **231**; development

218–19; emergent phenomena—coevolution 234–7; emergent phenomena—competition 220–4; emergent phenomena—genetic drift 224–8; emergent phenomena—natural selection 229–33; Mechanisms of Evolution 219; models 219; student experiences 222–4, 226–8, 235–7; summary and conclusions 237–8; Wolf-Sheep Predation 220–4, **223**; *see also* computer simulations; teaching strategies
Behe, Michael 40, 41, 47, 53, 56, 57
belief systems: complementary 112; coordinating 114
beliefs: changing 213–14; coordinating 276–7; counter-intuitive 206, 275–6; cultural and intuitive 126–7; and knowledge 174–5, 184–5; national 163; non-normative 77; religious 205; sources of 112–13; taxonomy of 115
biological knowledge, boundaries 83
Biology's Big Bang 63–4
Bizzo, N. M. V. 145
Blind Watchmaker, The 252–3
boundaries: of biological knowledge 83; blurring 17
Boyer, P. 206
Brem, S. K. 145

Cambrian Explosion, The 63–4
Carey, S. 77
Case, Robbie 247
categorical reasoning 84

Catley, K. M. 89
causal chains 116, 120
causation, as problematic 4
Cavicchi, Elizabeth 204
Center for Science and Culture (CSC) 63, 64
central conceptual structures 247–8
Chapman, M. 17
characteristics, of inquirers 42, 58–61
"cheater detection" modules 204
Chemical History of a Candle 199, 208–9
Chien, Paul 63–4
children: available accounts of speciation 78; concepts of natural world 77–8; ideas about mechanisms of speciation 77–8; naive explanatory frameworks 79–84, 113–14, 126–31; trajectories of conceptual change 84–6; understanding of death 121–3
Chinn, C. 42, 77, 91
Christian fundamentalism 248–50
Churches, attitude to evolutionary theory 250
Clark, B. 249
classroom inquiry, essential features 15–16
Clement, J. 203
climate change 163, 165, 166–7, 168
co-existence models 116, 124–6
coevolution 234–7
cognitive bias 173
cognitive capacities, beliefs about 59–61, 65
cognitive understanding 197–9; differences and consequences 207–8; why religion is easy 205–7; why science is hard 200–1, 203
Collins, Francis 112
Collins, Harry 39
Comenius, J. A. 252
common ancestry 46
compatibility 49–50
competition, as emergent process 220–4
computer simulations 245–6; see also BEAGLE
concepts: 206–7
conceptual change: educational needs 90–1; facilitating 89–91, 186, 189; research method 84–5; trajectories of 84–6
conceptual change pedagogy 186–7, 189, 282–3
conceptual development, factors influencing 77–8

"confirm early, disconfirm late" 204
confirmation bias 204, 208
conflict, science and religion 38–9, 174
Connected Chemistry curriculum project 218
constructive empiricism 35
constructs, of evidence 86–8
"context of justification" 16
Cooperative Institutional Research Program 101
Cosmides, L. 204
counter-intuitive concepts 206–8
court rulings 38
creation: continued appeal 32; evaluation 31–2; scientific status 28, 64–71; truth of 34–5
Creation Research Society 44–5
creationism: defining 41, 124; epistemological debate 39–40; exposing theories to data 52–3; intelligent design creationism 41–2; as intuitive belief 126–31; and multiple epistemologies 111–17; 124–6; repetition of errors 57; as science 277–8; support for teaching 101; versus science, 197; young-Earth creationism 41
creationist frameworks 80
Creationist Research Institute 52, 63
Crombie, A. C. 244, 272, 273
cultural beliefs 115, 116–17, 126–7
cultural models 124
cultural prerequisites 200
curriculum, integrated 254

Darwin, Charles 4–5, 23, 28, 59, 78–9, 197, 202, 249
Darwin's Black Box 47
Darwin's Dangerous Idea 5
Dawkins, Richard 35, 111–12, 116, 183, 252–3
death, multiple epistemologies 120–4
debate, eristic 61
deductive explanations 25
demarcation 275–8; alternative views 28–9; based on practices 14–18; empiricism 275; Laudan's objection to Ruse's criteria 38–9; mathematical symbolism 275; Ruse's criteria 38–9; science and pseudoscience 26–7; science from religion 275; scientific communities 275; theory development and conceptual modification 17

Demastes, S. S. 89
Dembski, W. 24, 41, 49, 50, 54, 57, 248–9, 277–8
Dennett, D. 5
Descent of Man, The 5, 249
deterministic-centralized mindset (DC mindset) 216
dialectical processes, enhanced method 15
dialogic processes: enhanced method 15; importance of 5; in portrayal of science 7; theory development 16
Diamond, J. 126
differentiation of epistemologies 44–69, 175; 198; authority as justification 179–81; certainty of knowledge 181; core epistemic continua **178**; intelligent design 182; justification of knowledge 177–81; method as justification 178–9; nature of science (NOS) 176–7; pragmatism 183–4; research studies 184–5; source of knowledge 176–7; strong beliefs and weak knowledge 184–5; structure of knowledge 181–2; teaching epistemology 186–90
dinosaur essentialist framework 81, 83
disconfirmation 201, 204; immunity from 207; potential of 202
Discovery Institute 45, 52, 63–4
disinterestedness 59, 60–1
divine creation, hypotheses 24–5
Dobzhansky, Theodosius 55
domain specificity 98–9, 113, 116, 124
Dover trial 124, 277–8
Driver, R. 6, 271
dualism 97
Dunbar, K. 61
Duschl, R. 5, 8, 16

Earth, seen from space **214**
education: for conceptual change 90–1; level of 90; multiple epistemologies 133–4; research literature 144–5; tension between science and religion 90
Eflin, J. 3
egocentric subjectivity 96–7
emergent phenomena 215; coevolution 234–7; competition 220–4; genetic drift 224–8; natural selection 229–33; understanding 216–17
empirical evidence 55–8
empiricism 275
enhanced scientific method 13–15, 16

environmental influences 152
epistemic frameworks 5
epistemic practices 40; aims 65, 70; beliefs about cognitive capacities 59–61; characteristics of inquirers 58–61; compatibility with other theories 49–50; constructing explanations 46–52; dimensions of 42–4, *43*; disinterestedness 59; divergence 65; empirical evidence 55–8; evidence 65, 70, 71; explanatory ideals 65; exposing theories to data 52–3; favored explanatory patterns 46–8; human capabilities 65; ignoring evidence 57–8; institutions 62–4, 70; intelligent design creationists (IDCs) 70–1; methodological naturalism 50–1; methods 52–5, 65–6; nineteenth-century scientist-creationists (NCSCs) 70–1; preferred methods 53–5; similarities and differences 66–9; social interactions 61–2; summary and conclusions 64–71
epistemic virtues 273
epistemological boundaries, conflation 174
epistemological development 96–8, 100, 209
epistemological change 198
epistemologies: differentiation *see* differentiation of epistemologies
epistemology: debate 38–40; defining 175; multiple *see* multiple epistemologies *see* personal epistemology recommendations for teaching 186–90
equations 24
eristic debate 61
erotetic view 25
essentialism 126–7, 198
evaluation: alternative views 32–3; evolution and creation 31–2; of theories 29–33
evaluatism 97
Evans, E. M. 80, 87, 114, 116, 125–6, 126–7, 128–9, 130, 145, 152, 153
evidence 42, 65, 70; constructs of 86–8; presenting to laypeople 71
evolution of species, visual representation **24**
evolutionary biology: representation of mechanisms 24; variations in formal instruction 78

evolutionary theory: appeal of 144;
attitude of Churches 250; centrality of
183, 272; challenge of teaching 189,
245–6; changes in 181; cognitive
difficulties 213, 215; compatibility with
other theories 49–50; evaluation 31–2;
evidentiary support 55–6; favored
explanatory patterns 46–8; gaps 23;
mechanisms in 23; religious beliefs as
barrier to 83–4; as representation of
mechanisms 23–5; resistance to
teaching 198, 213; responsiveness to
data 56; scientific status 28; students'
misconceptions 278–9; teachers'
perceptions 90; teaching 91; truth of
34–5; unifying framework 55–6
evolutionists, disinterestedness 59
exemplars, shared 15
experiment-driven science 8
explanations 42, 46–52, 111–39
explanatory breadth 30
explanatory coherence 16–17, 32, 112
explanatory frameworks 78–9; changes in
85; cross-cultural comparison 80,
81–2, 89–90; epistemic status of
questions 82, 83; as intuitive
frameworks 113–14; laypeople 79; as
multiple epistemologies 112; naive
79–84; non-evolutionary 79–80;
ontological and conceptual
assumptions 82; summary and
conclusions 91–2
explanatory gaps 48
explanatory ideals 65
explanatory mechanisms 274
explanatory patterns 46, 51–2
extinction 83
"eye-hand-mind" processes 204–5

faith, as source of knowledge 33–4;
versus trust 202
Fall 60
fairness 161,167
falsification 29; see also disconfirmation
Faraday, Michael: epistemology 200–1;
lectures 208; model construction 204;
science as fun 208–9; séance
explanation 199–200; skepticism 201;
strategies 203
Faraday's candle 199, 208
Feynman, Richard 202
Finding Darwin's God 184
flood geology 56

folk physics 198
folk religion 206
forensic research 54
forensics 47
fossil knowledge 86–7
fossils, knowledge and beliefs about 86–7
Franks, B. 206
friendships 59
Fuller, Steve 39
fun 204–5, 208–9

Gallup polls: multiple epistemologies
111–12; U.S. evolutionary divergence
144, 173, 243, 271
Galton, Francis 53
genetic algorithms 246–7; clone offspring
258–9, 260; decoding 257; example
255–61; example organism 255; first
simulation results 262; fitness
landscape 255, 256, 263; fitness of
generation 2 261; fitness of population
258; initial populations 256; offspring
259; organism 255; populations, initial
and evolved 261, 263; proposal for
254–64; sample simulation runs 261–4;
second simulation results 264; single
point crossover 259
genetic drift 224–8
genetic theory 23, 31
Gill, M. G. 103
Gish, Duane 61–2
global warming 71, 166, 167; see also
climate change
God: as creator 25, 28, 31, 32, 41, 45, 80;
and DNA 125; in evolutionary
framework 87–8; intelligent design
271; nineteenth century views 48, 60
Gooding, D. C. 203, 205
Goodnight, K. F. 246
Gould, S. J. 35, 112, 116
Grandy, R. E. 5, 8
graphs 24
Great Synthesis in Biology 5
Greeks: idea of science 244; science
education 251

Hacking, I. 244–5
Hardy-Weinberg law 24
Harris, P. L. 122
heuristics 204, 208
hierarchical diagrams 24
historical context: Ancient Greece 251,
272; medieval period 251–2, 272;

science education and the nature of
science 244–8; styles of science 244–5;
usefulness 198–9; *see also* nineteenth-
century scientist-creationists
Holland, John 246
HubNet 218
human-centrism 143, 165–7
human evolution 85, 101, 144–7, 152–3,
156, 158, 165, 184–5
human interference 152
human origins acceptance effect 111–12,
114–16, 126–8, 133–4, 154, 156, 157
human reticence effect 147, 152, 279
humans, exempt from evolution 147; *see
also* human origins acceptance effect
Hutton, James 215
Huxley, Thomas 59
hybridization framework 81
hypotheses, avoidance 47
hypothetico-deductive method 8, 14, 32

"ideas about science," in school
curriculum 6–7
illness, multiple epistemologies 117–20
inference to best explanation 29–31
imagination 201; structured 202
inquirers: characteristics 42, 58–61;
interaction 42; social institutions 42
inquiry: aims of 44–6; individual/group
14–15
*Inquiry and the National Standards in
Science Education* 15–16
institutions 62–4, 70
instrumentalism 35
integrated curriculum 254
intelligent design: as attack on science
272; authority as justification 180–1;
epistemological continuum 182–3;
hypotheses 24–5; as science 277–8;
scientific status 28; as supernatural
belief 124; teaching 106; theory of 41–2
intelligent design creationists (IDCs)
41–2; aims 45; beliefs about cognitive
capacities 60; compatibility with other
theories 49; disinterestedness 59, 60;
empirical evidence 56–7, 58; epistemic
practices of science 70–1, 197;
exposing theories to data 52–3; favored
explanatory patterns 47–8; institutions
63–4; methodological naturalism 50,
51; preferred methods 54; social
interactions 62; summary of epistemic
practices 64–71

*Intelligent Design: The Bridge Between
Science and Theology* 41
intentional reasoning 130
interaction, of inquirers 42, 61–2
intuitive beliefs *115*, 116–17, 126–7
intuitive biology 113, 115–16, 121, 126–8
intuitive psychology 113, 115–16, 124,
127–8, 130
intuitive theories 113–14
Ippolito, M. 204
"irreducible complexity" 31, 47, 54, 56

Jenson, M. 144–5
Johnson, Phillip 41, 45, 48, 70, 248
Jones, D.-W. 125
justification, of knowledge 178–81
juxtaposition reasoning 116, 120

Kelemen, D. 77
Kelvin, Lord William Thomson 49–50
Kitzmiller v. Dover Area School District 39
Klayman, J. 204
knowledge: and beliefs 184–5; certainty
of 181; faith as source 33–4;
justification 178–9; structure 181–2;
views of 98
knowledge acquisition research,
constraints on 77
knowledge creation, social interactions
61–2
knowledge systems, dimensions of 42
Kofahl, Robert E. 60
Kuhn, Thomas 8, 97, 274

Lamarckian framework 81–2, 85
language, of theory 15
Laudan, Larry 38–9, 70, 274
laypeople: explanatory frameworks 79;
lack of evidence 71
learners, views on nature of science 5–6
learning: agent-based modeling 217–18;
barriers to 174; conceptual and
epistemic barriers 86–9; and personal
epistemology 99–100
lecture-demonstrations 208
Lederman, N. G. 4
legal rulings 38
Legare, C. H. 119–20
Lerner, L. S. 90
levels slippage 215–16
Levy, S. T. 218
logical positivism 7, 8, 16, 25, 28, 274
Lyell, Charles 45–6, 48, 58

macro-evolutionary change, visualizing and modeling 88–9
macro-evolutionary frameworks 81, 85
magic 116
Malikowski, M. 89, 90
Mason, L. 99
materialism 70
mathematical equations 24
mathematical symbolism 275
mathematics, nature of 200
MATLAB 247
Maxwell, J. C. 203
Mayr, E. 52, 55, 56, 58, 80
Mazur, A. 89–90
McCauley, Robert 200
McComas, W. F. 4
measured skepticism 201–2, 208, 276
mechanisms: levels of organization 22, 22; scientific examples 21; ways of representing 20–1
mechanistic accounts, sources for 22
media, reporting of evolution-creationism debate 111–12
medieval period 251–2, 272
memory 206
metaphysical realism 44
methodological naturalism 50–2, 177, 178–9
methods 42, 52–5, 65–6
Meyer, Stephen 41–2, 63
micro-evolutionary frameworks 80–1, 85
Miller, George 203
Miller, K. 56, 112, 174, 183, 184
misconceptions 198
Mivart, St George 59
model building 203–4, 274
model-theoreticism 44
models, testing 204
modern science 273
modern synthesis 52
molecular biology, effect on understanding 5
Morris, Henry 50
multiculturalism 253–4
multiple epistemologies: applied to biology 114–17; applied to death 120–4; applied to illness 117–20; applied to origin of species 124–31; co-existence models 124–6; coordinating belief systems 114; cultural and intuitive beliefs 126–7; cultural models 124; educational implications 133–4; Gallup polls 111–12; intuitive theories 113–14; overlay models 126–7; research studies 128–30; synthetic blends and intuitive beliefs 127–31; taxonomy of beliefs 115–17, *115*; unanswered questions 131–3
multiplicity 97
multiplism 96, 99

naive explanatory frameworks 79–84
National Academy of Sciences 175, 176, 244
National Association of Science 276
national beliefs 163
National Research Council 15–16
National Science Education Standards 280
natural selection 229–33; in integrated curriculum 247–8
naturalized approach 4
nature of science (NOS) 176–7; and science education 244–8; seven tenets 8, *9–12*, 13; views about 5–7
need-based reasoning 128–9
NetLogo 217–18
Nersessian, N. 203
Newton, Isaac 21
Nguyen, S. 121, 122
nineteenth-century scientist-creationists (NCSCs) 42; aims 45; beliefs about cognitive capacities 60; disinterestedness 59, 60; effect of Darwin's work 45–6; empirical evidence 58; exposing theories to data 53; favored explanatory patterns 48; institutions 63; methodological naturalism 51; preferred methods 54–5; social interactions 62; summary of epistemic practices 64–71
non-evolutionary frameworks, teens 85
non-normative beliefs 77
Novak, M. 225, 230, 233, 236
Novick, L. R. 24

objectivity 7
observation 15
Only a Theory: Evolution and the Battle for America's Soul 174
Origin of Species, The 4–5, 28, 31, 55, 78–9, 197, 249
ontological change 198
ontological claims, religion 205–6
ontological presuppositions 206

organism type and attitude to evolution
153
organism type and framework type 154
origin of species, multiple epistemologies
124–31
Origin of Species 197, 267
Osborne, J. F. 4, 6, 7
overlay models 126–7
Owen, Richard 48, 53, 58, 59

Paley, William 45
paradigms 274
parallel reasoning model 116, 120
Parker, Gary 50
Perry, W. G. 99
personal epistemology 279; certainty
101; conclusions 106–7; developing
95–7; and domain specificity 98–9;
epistemic beliefs 97–8; evolution and
intelligent design 100–1; findings
104–5; future research 107–8; issues
of theory 105–6; and learning
99–100; overview 96–8; religious
beliefs 101; research method 101,
103–4; research participants 103;
research studies 101–6; teaching
intelligent design 106
pessimistic induction 34
philosophy of science: developments 7–8;
epistemological debate 38–9
phlogiston theory 30
physics 198
Piaget, Jean 121
Pickering, A. 17, 39
piety 71
plant evolution 145, 147, 156, 158
plate tectonics 187–8
Plato 251, 272
play, science as 204
Playfair, John 215
Popper, Karl 29
population biology, effect on
understanding 5
population effects 224
postmodernism 33
practical realism 17
pragmatism 183–4
preferred methods 53–5
progress, scientific 15
pseudo-mathematics 54
pseudoscience, and science 26–9, 201–2;
profiles 27
public education 253–4

publication 63–4
pure essentialist frameworks 80, 83
questions, epistemic status *82*, 83
Qin, Y. 203

radical constructivism 39
random interaction 224, 225
randomness 216
Ranney, M. 145, 162–5
rationality 7
recall, counter-intuitive concepts 207
received view 8, 162, 163, 165, 166, 280
reconciliation, science and religion 33
reinforced theistic manifest destiny
(RTMD) view 162–8
"relevance" processes 204
religion: authority in 206; defining 176,
197; functions of 206, 208; as "natural"
200; ontological claims 205–6; role of
mystery 206; types of 206; why religion
is easy 205–7
religiosity 90, 206
religious beliefs: as barrier to accepting
evolution 83–4, 174, 207; and personal
epistemology 101
representations, building 203–4, 207
research traditions 274
resistance, to Darwin's theory 248–50
Resnick, M. 216
Rosengren, K. S. 122–3
Ruse, M. 38–9, 44–5, 46, 48, 58, 59, 60,
63, 112, 249
Ruse's criteria 38–9

Samarapungavan, A. 42, 77, 78, 79, 80,
81, 83–4, 86, 87, 88, 89, 90, 91
Schaffer, S. 273
Schindel, J. E. 159, 160
school curriculum, image of science 6–7
Schwartz, Marc 247
science: defining 176, 197, 272;
demarcating 3–4, 197, 201; as
epistemic practices 40; fun 204–5,
208–9; heuristics of 204; portrayal of 7;
students' understanding of 271;
strategies 203; styles of 244–5; why
science is hard 200–1, 203–5; and
religion, 197, 205, 207–8; as
"unnatural" 200
science, and pseudoscience 26–9; profiles
27
science education, nature of science
(NOS) 244–8

scientific communities 275
scientific controversies, teaching 188–9
scientific inquiry, developments 16
scientific method: enhanced 7–14, 16;
    enhanced dialogic practices view 17;
    enhanced view 13–15; steps 8
scientific progress 15
scientific realism 35
scientists and epistemic practices *see*
    epistemic practices
Scott, Eugenie 250
secularism 70
Seneca 254
Sengupta, P. 216
set-theoretic conception 25–6, 274
seven tenets 8, *9–12*, 13
Shallit, J. 54
Shapin, S. 273
shared exemplars 15
Shenkman, R. 174–5
short term memory, "chunking" in 203
Shtulman, A. 198
simplicity 30, 31
Simpson, George Gaylord 55
Sinatra, G. M. 101, 103, 175, 184–5
Sinclair, Upton 248
skepticism 201–2, 208
Smith, C. 6, 271
Sober, E. 28
social constructivism 33, 35
social institutions, of inquirers 42–3
social interactions 42, 61–2
social processes, in scientific knowledge 5
South Africa, attributions of illness
    117–20
Southerland, S. 175
speciation: children's ideas of 77–8;
    cultural accounts of 78; naive
    explanatory frameworks 79–84
speciation research, scope and method 79
Sperber, D. 204
spontaneous generation frameworks 80
St. Augustine of Hippo 205
Stebbins, G. Ledyard 55
Stieff, M. 218
Structure of Scientific Revolution, The 8
structured imagination 202
students, epistemology 6
Subbotsky, E. V. 116
subjectivity 97
supernatural beliefs 114, 124, 200
supernatural force 199, 202
Suppe, F. 26

synthetic blends 127–31

table turning 199
target-dependent models 116, 121, 124,
    125–6
taxonomy of beliefs 115
"teach the controversy," implications of 8
teachers, perceptions of evolutionary
    theory 90
teaching: basic requirements 283;
    essential features 280; evolutionary
    theory 91, 173–4; in historical context.
    See historical context implications for
    students 278–9; implications for
    teachers 279–81; intelligent design 106;
    recommendations 186–90; scientific
    controversies 188–9
teaching for wisdom 250–1, 253–4
teaching strategies: computer simulations
    245–6; genetic algorithms 246–7;
    natural selection 247–8; *see also*
    BEAGLE
technology 274–5; applications of theory
    34; changing beliefs 214
teenagers, explanatory frameworks 85
teleological framework 85
Thagard, P. 3, 4, 8, 16, 32, 33, 89
theistic evolution 82, 112, 250
"theological incorrectness" 206
theoretical compatibility 49–50
theories: alternative views 25–6; evaluation
    29–33; intuitive 113–14; overturning
    202; rejection of 29; as representations
    of explanatory mechanisms 20–2;
    scientific vs. lay 274–5
theories of speciation 77
theory 15
theory choice, inference to best
    explanation 29–31
theory development 14, 16
theory of mind 97, 113
theory replacement model 89
think-aloud protocols (TAPS) 146–7, 152
Thompson, P. 26
transmissibility, counter-intuitive
    concepts 207
tree diagrams 24; evolution of species **24**
Trott, Richard 61–2
trust 202
truth 33–5; alternative views 35–6;
    approximate 33–4; battle for 112; of
    evolution and creation 34–5; objective
    245; as priority 71

Tweney, Ryan 276
typical features, of science 26–7

U.S. evolutionary divergence 143–4, 213,
271; acceptability of evolution 147–59,
173, 183; contributory factors 173;
descriptive statistics 148–9; effects and
interactions 150–1; interaction
associated with framework across
attitudes 155; organism type and
attitude to evolution 153; organism
type and framework type 154; possible
influencing factors 158; received view
162, 165; reinforced theistic manifest
destiny view 162–7, 167–8; research
literature 144–5; research methods
145–7, 159–60; research questions 158;
research study 1 144–59; research
study 2 159–61; results and discussion
147, 160–1; summary and conclusions
167–8; summary and implications of
research 157–9; surveys 144; think-
aloud protocols (TAPS) 146–7, 152;
topics and framework types 146

van Fraassen, B. 35, 274–5
Venables, A. 247
verification 28–9
vitalism 51

Ward, Thomas 202

Wason, Peter 204
ways of knowing 112
Wedge of Truth: Splitting the Foundations
of Naturalism, The 248
"Wedge Document" 45, 50, 64, 248
Whitehouse, H. 206
Wiers, R. 79, 80, 81, 83–4, 87, 88, 89, 90,
248–9
Wilensky, U. 216, 217–18
"will to believe" 201
Windschitl, M. 6, 271
wisdom 250–4, 283
witchcraft 118–20
Woo, Peter 132
World War II 163
Wright, P. W. G. 39

young Earth creationists (YECs) 41, 198;
aims 44–5; beliefs about cognitive
capacities 60; compatibility with other
theories 49; disinterestedness 59, 60;
empirical evidence 56–8; exposing
theories to data 52–3; favored
explanatory patterns 46–7; flood
geology 56; institutions 63;
methodological naturalism 50;
preferred methods 54; repetition of
errors 57; social interactions 61–2;
summary of epistemic practices 64–71

Zammito, J. H. 17